D0891550

Supreme Court Justices Who
Voted with the Government

ALSO BY JAMES E. LEAHY

Freedom Fighters of the
United States Supreme Court:
Nine Who Championed Individual Liberty
(McFarland, 1996)

Liberty, Justice and Equality:
How These Constitutional Guarantees
Have Been Shaped by United States
Supreme Court Decisions Since 1789
(McFarland, 1992)

The First Amendment, 1791–1991:
Two Hundred Years of Freedom
(McFarland, 1991)

SUPREME COURT JUSTICES WHO VOTED WITH THE GOVERNMENT

Nine Who Favored the State Over Individual Rights

JAMES E. LEAHY

McFarland & Company, Inc., Publishers
Jefferson, North Carolina, and London

British Library Cataloguing-in-Publication data are available

Library of Congress Cataloguing-in-Publication Data

Leahy, James E., 1919–
    Supreme Court justices who voted with the government :
nine who favored the state over individual rights /
James E. Leahy.
        p.   cm.
    Includes index.
    ISBN 0-7864-0547-3 (library binding : 50# alkaline paper) ∞
    1. Civil rights—United States—History. 2. United
States. Supreme Court—History. 3. Judges—United
States—Biography. I. Title.
KF4749.L413   1999
342.73'085'09—dc21   98-37410
                                                                              CIP

Manufactured in the United States of America

*McFarland & Company, Inc., Publishers
    Box 611, Jefferson, North Carolina 28640*

CONTENTS

Contents

PREFACE

At the end of the Supreme Court's term in June 1995, news headlines proclaimed that the Court had made a "right turn." For example, a headline in *U. S. News and World Report* proclaimed a "long anticipated right turn." *Time* reported: "In most of the Supreme Court's important rulings this year, the combination was five right, four left." And *USA Today* identified Chief Justice William H. Rehnquist and Justices Antonin Scalia and Clarence Thomas as "core conservatives." Justices Anthony M. Kennedy and Sandra Day O'Connor were called "swing votes." Justices John Paul Stevens, David H. Souter, Ruth Bader Ginsburg and Stephen Breyer were listed as "moderates."

Abraham Lincoln asked: "What is conservatism? Is it not adherence to the old and tried, against the new and untried?"[1]

"The liberal, emphasizing the civil and property rights of the individual," Wayne L. Morse wrote, "insists that the individual must remain so supreme as to make the state his servant."[2]

Because such definitions do not easily fit Supreme Court justices, I identify those justices who vote most of the time *for* constitutional rights as *Freedom Fighters*.[3] Justices who vote much of the time to uphold governmental infringement on our constitutional rights are *Justices for the Government*.

Freedom Fighters are strong supporters of First Amendment rights, as well as the rights of privacy and equal protection for voters, illegitimate children, aliens, and persons of both genders and all races. *Justices for the Government* vote, much of the time, to uphold government restrictions or limitations on these rights.

This book profiles nine Supreme Court *Justices for the Government*. Their votes and comments on First Amendment freedoms, the right of privacy, equal protection of the law, and the application of the Bill of Rights to the states are recorded. A short personal biography of each justice is also included.

1

Because there are many quotations in the text, I have economized on the documentation in one way, to reduce repetition. All quotations without a numbered note citing the source are taken from the same source as the preceding quotation.

James E. Leahy
March 1998

PROLOGUE

We are under a Constitution, but the Constitution is what the judges say it is, and the judiciary is the safeguard of our liberty and of our property under the Constitution. —Charles Evans Hughes, May 3, 1907.

Long before Governor Charles Evans Hughes assured us that judges would protect our liberty and property, James Madison spoke with similar confidence: "If they [the declaration of rights] are incorporated into the Constitution, independent tribunals of justice will consider themselves in a peculiar manner the guardians of those rights; they will be an impenetrable bulwark against every assumption of power in the Legislature or Executive; they will be naturally led to resist every encroachment upon rights expressly stipulated for in the Constitution by the declaration of rights."[1]

The rights guaranteed by the Constitution are the First Amendment rights to the free exercise of religion, and the freedoms of speech, press, assembly, petition and association. Other constitutional rights include the rights to privacy, travel, and work, which are part of the liberty guaranteed by the Fifth and Fourteenth Amendments' Due Process Clauses. And then there is the right to be treated equally by government, which is protected by the Equal Protection Clause of the Fourteenth Amendment.

These rights, of course, are protected only to the extent that "tribunals of justice ... resist every encroachment upon rights expressly stipulated for in the Constitution by the declaration of rights."

Many of the cases which the Supreme Court hears involve a person who is asserting a constitutional right against some branch of the federal or state government alleged to have violated that right. The Court's decision in a particular case, of course, decides whether the government did infringe upon the constitutional right which the person has asserted. But the decision does much more. The decision becomes the supreme law of the land and determines

3

whether similar actions of government, federal or state, are permissible or unconstitutional.

For example, in declaring segregated public schools to be a violation of the Fourteenth Amendment's Equal Protection Clause, the Court stated: "We conclude that in the field of public education the doctrine of 'separate but equal' has no place. Separate educational facilities are inherently unequal."[2] All school districts in the country, therefore, were told to integrate their school systems "with all deliberate speed."[3]

Neither Madison's prediction that justices would be "guardians" of our rights, nor Hughes' statement that the "judiciary is a safeguard of our liberty," has proven to be accurate. Throughout our history most justices of the United States Supreme Court, for example, have not been guardians of our rights or protectors of our liberty. Some justices, of course, have fulfilled Madison's prediction and have been "an impenetrable bulwark against every assumption of power in the Legislature or Executive."[4]

1

JUSTICE OLIVER WENDELL HOLMES, JR.

PERSONAL LIFE

Growing Up

> The little boy was named for his father and was called "Wendie." He grew quickly and it was soon apparent that except for his striking gray-blue Wendell eyes he would take after his mother's family, the tall and lantern-jawed Jacksons, rather than the little, round-faced Wendells and Holmeses.[1]

The boy referred to was Oliver Wendell Holmes, Jr., born March 8, 1841, to Dr. Oliver Wendell Holmes, Sr., and Amelia Jackson Holmes. Dr. Holmes was an eminent surgeon, lecturer, and writer. The doctor and Amelia had two other children: daughter Amelia Jackson [Holmes] and son Edward Jackson Holmes.

Biographer Liva Baker describes "Wendie's" upbringing: "In anticipation of his assuming his rightful place in society as imagined by Dr. Holmes at his birth, Wendell, as he was called, was pampered like a colt bred to run the Derby. He was groomed, petted, encouraged, tested, carefully surrounded with other boys of his social class, and fed a high-protein intellectual diet."[2]

"The moral upbringing of the children was left to Mrs. Holmes. ... She taught her son to accomplish something each day. She was an abolitionist, and refused to consider such questions complicated. Slavery was an evil, and must be eradicated. The doctor was not an Abolitionist. The Constitution recognized slavery, and required runaway slaves be returned."[3]

Holmes received his education in private schools, first at a local dame school until he was seven and then at a boys' school conducted by Mr. T. Russell Sullivan.

Holmes entered a school operated by Mr. Epse S. Dixwell when he was

JUSTICE OLIVER WENDELL HOLMES, JR. (photo by Harris and Ewing; collection of the Supreme Court of the United States).

12. He studied the classics and "penmanship, drawing, French, algebra, plane geometry, and ancient history."[4] Dixwell's reputation for "turning out well-schooled products preceded him to the Harvard examining board, and his boys ... seemed already to have a little edge when they applied to college."

"The Boston of my youth," Holmes wrote, "was still half-Puritan Boston, with the 'unutterable ennui' of its Sundays ... it was a Boston with no statues, few pictures, little music outside the churches, and no Christmas."[5]

Growing up, Holmes was fortunate to have been exposed to a number of literary men of the time, who were his father's friends. Among them were poets James Russell Lowell, Henry Wadsworth Longfellow, and Ralph Waldo Emerson, whom Holmes called "Uncle Waldo." Of Emerson, biographer Sheldon M. Novick has written: "No one affected Wendell so much or so strongly as this smiling visitor: 'I saw him on the other side of the street and ran over and said to him: 'If I ever do anything, I shall owe a great deal of it to you' which was true. He was one of those who set one on fire.'"

Harvard College

Holmes entered Harvard College at the age of sixteen. "All [students] wore the same clothes—black coats, white waistcoats, and gray trousers—the boys were disciplined if they wore any other costume. Freshmen could not wear hats or smoke pipes; none of the boys was permitted to smoke in public. In the evenings, they stood about the college yard, had snowball fights, broke windows. ... Sophomores 'hazed' the freshmen; throughout his first semester Wendell, like other new students, was threatened with humiliations, was insulted if he ate in a place from which freshmen were barred, wore a forbidden hat, or smoked a pipe. In his first and second years there were bloody football matches between sophomores and freshmen, which became so violent that the faculty stopped them."

Students were required to attend chapel each morning before class. Of this experience, Baker has written: "It is unlikely that this year-long forced feeding of orthodox Christian dogma slipped down Wendell's throat easily, and in the fall of his sophomore year, he joined the recently established Christian Union, a liberal Christian student group that condemned discrimination on the basis of sect and required its member only that they embrace the broadest principles of Christianity."[6]

Holmes found a couple of bookstores whose owners had collections of engravings, and he spent many an evening talking with them about their collection. Women, too, began to interest him, and he began to carry on a flirtation with several. One was Fanny Dixwell, the daughter of his former schoolmaster. "The eldest of the daughters, Fanny, had smooth, dark hair, and resembled her father in many ways. In repose she was a little plain, but her brown eyes were attractive, if closely set, and she was full of energy and sharp wit. She too had artistic inclinations, and talked of studying art. But she was obliged to help care for the younger, prettier daughters, and to share in the management of the house."

"By this time [Holmes's last term at Harvard] Wendell was a 'pretty convinced Abolitionist' and believed in the cause 'devoutly.'"[7]

Civil War Soldier

In April 1861, Holmes enlisted in the Twentieth Regiment of the Massachusetts Volunteer Infantry Regiment, which immediately went into training. In August, he was promoted to 1st Lieutenant. The Twentieth was ordered to the front and eventually into battle where the Lieutenant was wounded in the stomach on October 21 in the battle of Ball's Bluff.

Later Holmes wrote in his diary: "I was hit at 4½ p.m. ...the heavy firing having begun about an hour before, by the watch—I felt as if a horse had kicked me and went over...."[8]

After being released from the hospital, Holmes returned to Boston to recuperate. He rejoined his regiment early in 1862, and was promoted to Captain shortly thereafter. He was wounded a second time, this time in the neck and again sent to a military hospital.

When he recovered he set out to find his regiment, which he did in November 1862. The regiment went into battle again in early December near Fredericksburg. Novick describes the battle: "The Confederate artillery began to fire spherical case-shells filled with shot and fused to explode high over the ground. Wendell, prone with his men, lifted his head and saw the Confederates bring a gun to bear on his regiment. It fired. With the first puff of an exploding shell above them, Wendell saw that the gunners had their range. With the second puff, a ball struck his knapsack supporter, knocking it to pieces. The gun fired again; a white puff overhead; the man in front of him was struck; another puff, and a ball hit the back of Wendell's foot, striking into the bone of his heel."

After hospitalization, Holmes again returned to Boston. When the wound healed, he took a staff position with the Sixth Corps and was assigned as an aide-de-camp to General Horatio W. Wright.

By early 1864, the war had taken its toll on Holmes mentally and physically, and he decided to resign and return to civilian life. "On May 29," author Baker noted, "the last remnant of Holmes's adventurous spirit emerged once again briefly when he was ordered to deliver an important dispatch from General Wright to Major General David A. Russell and instructed 'not to spare [his] horse.' He was attacked on the way by Confederate cavalry and escaped in the best swashbuckling style, 'lying along the neck of my horse Comanche fashion,' while Rebel bullets sought him out. He got through to General Russell, carried his answer back to General Wright, and confessed to a certain feeling of 'triumph' in his services. But still the bitterness could not be suppressed, and he scribbled on the back of the envelope containing his letter: 'It is kill—kill—all the time.'"[9]

Holmes was mustered out of the army July 17, 1864. Later, he expressed regret that he had resigned before the war ended.

Student at Harvard Law School

"Holmes said that he was 'kicked' into the law by his father, and in putting his apathy in such terms gave support to the belief that his own instincts did not impel him to the profession which his great distinctions were to be achieved."[10] He had considered becoming a philosopher, like his friend "Uncle Waldo" Emerson, and even studying medicine, but he entered Harvard Law School in October 1864. There were no requirements to entering law school; the course was two years and there were no examinations. Three professors lectured on legal subjects, and there was a list of readings for the students. "No course was required, no attendance taken at lectures. Courses could be taken in any order; prerequisites were suggested but not required."[11]

There was "moot court" competition, and the students formed law clubs in which they tried cases, acting as judges and lawyers. Holmes lived at home during his early law school days. Among his circle of friends were Fannie Dixwell and William James, with whom he shared many common interests, including philosophy and the need to come to terms with life.

"Fanny was a shy creature," author Baker notes, "but witty and playful once you got to know her. Friends did not forget her quick and vivid perceptions or her originality and charm. The victims of it rarely forgot her tart tongue."

Holmes left law school before the end of the course of study and interned for a while in the law office of his cousin Robert Morse. He was, however, awarded a law degree in June 1866. Holmes then spent several months touring England and the continent.

Philosopher, Lawyer and Lecturer

But although the practice of law absorbed his days—he liked to "think under fire"—his philosophical and scholarly appetite demanded other fare as well. He became one of the group known as the "Metaphysical Club," meeting at each other's homes to hear and discuss papers by one of their number. ... Their common bent was to reduce pretentious philosophic ideas to the more manageable "If ... then" form; indeed the name of the club must have had an ironic turn, save as its members might delight, in Holmes' favorite phrase, to "twist the tail of the cosmos."[12]

Although not yet admitted to the bar, Holmes joined the firm of Chandler, Shattuck and Thayer in the fall of 1866. During this time, he studied for the bar exam, practiced law, and wrote articles for the *American Law Review*. In March 1867, Holmes took an examination before two attorneys and was admitted to the practice of law.

Holmes joined George Shattuck and William Munroe to form the law partnership of Shattuck, Holmes and Munroe. Later, friends circulated a petition supporting his appointment as a federal judge, but to his disappointment he did not get the job.

The prestigious Lowell Institute selected Holmes to present a series of lectures in 1880. He was delighted at being chosen and immediately began to review and rewrite much of the material he had written for the *American Law Review*. He was required to give lectures on Tuesday and Friday evenings for a total of twelve lectures.

Holmes's first sentence was: "The life of the law has not been logic; it has been experience." That has remained one of the memorable statements which the future justice was to make during his lifetime. The lectures were later published in book form under the title *The Common Law*. Although *The Common Law* has since become an important piece of legal work, its reviews were mixed. Of particular gratification to the author, however, was the acceptance of the book by the English legal community. The "London *Spectator* described *The Common Law* as 'the most original work of legal speculation which has appeared in English since the publication of Sir Henry Maine's *Ancient Law.*'"[13]

Holmes had become somewhat disenchanted with the practice of law and therefore accepted a professorship at Harvard Law School in March 1882. He taught Torts, Agency and Carriers, Surety and Mortgages, Jurisprudence, and Admiralty. His career as a law teacher was to be a short one. In December, he was appointed to the Massachusetts Supreme Court.

Love and Marriage

Fanny Dixwell and Oliver Wendell Holmes, Jr., were engaged to be married in March 1872. In discussing their relationship before marriage, author Howe notes: "No letters which they exchanged before their marriage have survived, and the image one forms of her qualities is made largely in one's own imagination. It is clear that Holmes and Fanny Dixwell had been close friends when he went to war. ... There is every reason to suppose, accordingly, that they had been intimate friends when he was an undergraduate and it is not improbable that the roots of their friendship went back to their childhood when her father was Holmes's teacher."[14] Holmes kept a diary, and Fanny's name appears in it frequently.

The couple were married in Old North Church, Boston, in June of that year. They had no children. When Fanny died in 1929, Holmes acknowledged the many condolences by noting: "For sixty years she made life poetry for me and at 88 one must be ready for the end."[15]

Justice of the Massachusetts Supreme Court

Holmes took his seat as a justice of the Massachusetts Supreme Court in January 1883. In July, when the court recessed, Holmes wrote to his friend Sir Frederick Pollock:

Well, I like the work more than I dreamed beforehand—the experience is most varied—very different from what one gets at the bar—and, I am satisfied, most valuable for an all-around view of the law—One sees too a good deal of human nature & I find that I am interested all the time.[16]

Author Baker describes the work of the court "as demanding as anything Holmes had experienced as a practicing lawyer."[17]

As Justice, Holmes wrote opinions denying free-speech claims in two cases. One involved John J. McAuliffe, who had been dismissed as a New Bedford police officer for violating an ordinance which prohibited police personnel from participating in political activities. In upholding the dismissal, Justice Holmes wrote that McAuliffe "may have a constitutional right to talk politics, but he has no constitutional right to be a policeman."[18] In the other case, *Commonwealth v. Davis,*[19] the court upheld the conviction of William F. Davis for speaking in a park without a permit to do so. The United States Supreme Court unanimously affirmed this decision.[20]

Commenting upon these cases, author Baker has written: "Civil liberties questions did not particularly interest Holmes. He didn't believe much in rights. He was much more attentive to the complexities of the tort cases that came to the court in significantly large numbers, and the case for freedom of speech, no burning theme in the 1890s, had made virtually no headway since Holmes, for the court, had upheld the dismissal from the force of the New Bedford policeman in 1892."[21]

Holmes served on the Massachusetts Supreme Court for almost twenty years. He became the court's Chief Justice in August 1899.

A Jurisprudential Philosopher

Others, including Holmes himself, have written extensively about Holmes's legal philosophy.[22] Robert W. Gordon, in the introduction to *The Legacy of Oliver Wendell Holmes, Jr.,* gives this thumbnail sketch of Holmes's jurisprudential thinking:

> In this period (1882–1902) Holmes continued to develop the main themes of his jurisprudence—that law embodies the policy preferences, conscious or unconscious, of the dominant forces in the community; that when enacted in legislation, such preferences should be deferred to by the courts unless plainly unconstitutional; that general conceptions such as "liberty" and "property" could not practically resolve such questions as whether competitors or labor unions might be privileged to injure the business of others in pursuit of their own economic advantage; that on such issues and any others on which lines of precedent and policy conflicted, judges had to make policy choices of their own; that policy decisions, though ideally made "scientifically," were necessarily often arbitrary; that, viewed realistically from the standpoint of the practitioner, law was nothing more than predictions what courts would do—and

expounded them in some notable articles ("Privilege, Malice, and Intent," 1894), and speeches ("The Path of the Law," 1897).[23]

Nomination to the Supreme Court

Theodore Roosevelt became President of the United States upon the assassination of President William McKinley in September 1901. When Justice Horace Gray resigned from the Supreme Court in July 1902, Roosevelt turned to Massachusetts Senator Henry Cabot Lodge for information about Holmes, inquiring particularly whether Holmes was a good Republican. Holmes and Lodge had been close friends for many years. "Lodge called on Holmes," Novick writes, "and verified that he was a good party man. 'I told the President you had always been a Republican,' Lodge said afterward, somewhat amused, 'and never a Mugwump.'"[24]

Roosevelt summoned Holmes to his Oyster Bay home on July 25. After a short visit during which both men came to know and like each other, Roosevelt offered Holmes the appointment and Holmes accepted. Because the Senate was in recess, Holmes's nomination did not come before it until December. He was unanimously confirmed on December 4.

When Holmes joined the Court, Melville Fuller was Chief Justice. Other members of the Court were Justices Edward D. White, Rufus W. Peckham, Henry B. Brown, David J. Brewer, John M. Harlan, Joseph McKenna, and George Shiras. Justice Holmes served as an Associate Justice from December 8, 1902, until his retirement on January 12, 1932.

AS ASSOCIATE JUSTICE (1902–1932)

The Free Exercise of Religion

The questionnaire which applicants must complete when seeking United States citizenship contains the question: "If necessary, are you willing to take up arms in defense of this country?"[25] When Rosika Schwimmer filled out her application for citizenship, she wrote: "I would not take up arms personally." In explaining her answer, Schwimmer said: "I am willing to do everything that an American citizen has to do, except fighting. If American women would be compelled to do that, I would not do that. I am an uncompromising pacifist."

Because Schwimmer was unwilling to take up arms, her citizenship application was denied by the District Court. The Supreme Court upheld that decision. Justice Pierce Butler wrote that the fact that "she is an uncompromising pacifist with no sense of nationalism but only a cosmic sense of belonging to the human family justifies belief that she may be opposed to the use of military force as contemplated by our Constitution and laws. And her testimony clearly suggests that she is disposed to exert her power to influence others to such opposition."[26]

Justice Holmes dissented. He saw Schwimmer as an optimist, and he disagreed with her position "that war will disappear." Nevertheless, he believed that she was entitled to become a citizen: "The notion that the applicant's optimistic anticipations would make her a worse citizen is sufficiently answered by her examination, which seems to me a better argument for her admission than any that I can offer. Some of her answers might excite popular prejudice, but if there is any principle of the Constitution that more imperatively calls for attachment than any other it is the principle of free thought—not free thought for those who agree with us but freedom for the thought that we hate."

Freedom of Speech

Unpopular Speech. Charles T. Schenck and others were charged with "causing and attempting to cause insubordination, &c., in the military and naval forces of the United States, and to obstruct the recruiting and enlistment service of the United States, when the United States was at war with the German Empire."[27] Just prior to World I, Schenck had printed and distributed 15,000 circulars urging men to avoid the draft. The circulars argued that men had a constitutional right not to submit to the draft, and that "If you do not assert and support your rights, you are helping to deny or disparage rights which it is the solemn duty of all citizens and residents of the United States to retain."

Schenck and the others were convicted, and the Supreme Court, with Holmes writing the opinion, upheld the convictions.

In referring to the defendants' rights under the First Amendment, Holmes noted: "We admit that in many places and in ordinary times the defendants in saying all that was said in the circular would have been within their constitutional rights." But he argued, the "most stringent protection of free speech would not protect a man in falsely shouting fire in a theatre and causing a panic." There is a limit to free speech, the Justice argued, and that limit comes when speech creates "a clear and present danger that ... [it] will bring about the substantive evils that Congress has a right to prevent."

Although there was no evidence that the defendants' speech had in fact obstructed the draft, the Court held that their speech had presented a clear and present danger to the war effort, and that the convictions should, therefore, be affirmed.

One week after the Court upheld the convictions of Schenck and his companions, it also affirmed the conviction of Jacob Frohwerk for publishing a newspaper which also urged persons not to subject themselves to the draft.[28]

Holmes again wrote the opinion for a unanimous Court, concluding that the defendant's right to free speech was not being infringed upon here. "We do not lose our right to condemn either measures or men," he noted, "because the Country is at war." Nevertheless, because the record was incomplete, "it is impossible to say that it might not have been found that the circulation of the paper was in quarters where a little breath would be enough to kindle a flame and that the fact was known and relied upon by those who sent the paper out. ... When we consider that we do not know how strong the Government's evidence may have been we find ourselves unable to say that the articles could not furnish a basis for a conviction upon the first count at least."

The fate of Eugene Debs was the same as that of Schenck, Schenck's friends, and Frohwerk for a speech against the draft made in 1918. "The main theme of [Debs'] speech," Holmes noted, "was socialism, its growth, and a prophecy of its ultimate success. With that we have nothing to do, but if a part or the manifest intent of the more general utterances was to encourage those present to obstruct the recruiting service and if in passages such encouragement was directly given, the immunity of the general theme may not be enough to protect the speech."[29] Holmes concluded that Debs had the intent to obstruct recruiting and pointed out that Debs had said "that the master class has always declared war and the subject class has always fought the battles—that the subject class has had nothing to gain and all to lose, including their lives; that the working class, who furnish the corpses, have never yet had a voice in declaring war and have never yet had a voice in declaring peace."

Pamphleteering. "All of the five defendants were born in Russia. They were intelligent, had considerable schooling, and at the time they were arrested they had lived in the United States terms varying from five to ten years, but none of them had applied for naturalization. Four of them testified as witnesses in their own behalf and of these, three frankly avowed that they were 'rebels,' 'revolutionists,' 'anarchists,' that they did not believe in government in any form, and they declared that they had no interest whatever in the Government of the United States."[30] Among the defendants referred to was a man named Abrams.

These defendants were convicted for distributing a leaflet containing "'disloyal, scurrilous and abusive language about the form of Government of the United States;' ... language 'intended to bring the form of Government of the United States into contempt, scorn, contumely and disrepute;' ... language 'intended to incite, provoke and encourage resistance to the United States in said war.'" They were also charged with conspiracy to "unlawfully and willfully, by utterance, writing, printing and publication, to urge, incite and advocate curtailment of production of things and products, to wit, ordnance and ammunition, necessary and essential to the prosecution of the war."

In response to the defendants' argument that their leaflet was protected by the First Amendment, Justice John H. Clarke wrote: "This contention is sufficiently discussed and is definitely negatived in" the cases involving Schenck, Baer, and Frohwerk. Justices Holmes and Louis D. Brandeis dissented.

After discussing the various counts, Holmes concluded that there was no evidence that the defendants intended to curtail or cripple the war effort. With reference to the claim of First Amendment protection, Holmes declared: "I never have seen any reason to doubt that the questions of law that alone were before this Court in the cases of *Schenck*, *Frohwerk* and *Debs* ... were rightly decided." But he thought the present case was very different and wrote some words, often quoted, about the place free expression plays in organized society. "To allow opposition by speech seems to indicate that you think the speech impotent, as when a man says that he has squared the circle.... But when men have realized that time has upset many fighting faiths, they may come to believe even more than they believe the very foundations of their own conduct that the ultimate good desired is better reached by free trade in ideas— that the best test of truth is the power of the thought to get itself accepted in the competition of the market, and that truth is the only ground upon which their wishes safely can be carried out.... That at any rate is the theory of our Constitution. It is an experiment, as all life is an experiment." He then concluded: "Of course I am speaking only of expressions of opinion and exhortations, which were all that were uttered here, but I regret that I cannot put into more impressive words my belief that in their conviction upon this indictment the defendants were deprived of their rights under the Constitution of the United States."

The majority relied upon *Schenck*, *Frohwerk* and *Debs* again to uphold the convictions of defendants Pierce, Creo, and Zeilman.[31] These defendants had distributed a pamphlet entitled "The Price We Pay," which the Court described as "a highly colored and sensational document, issued by the national office of the Socialist Party at Chicago, Illinois, and fairly to be construed as a protest against the further prosecution of the war by the United States."

This time Justice Brandeis wrote a dissenting opinion, which Holmes joined. In order to show that the defendants had not violated the law, Brandeis quoted "The Price We Pay" in its entirety. He could not find "a particle of evidence that these statements were made with intent to interfere with the operation or success of the military and naval forces." He then concluded: "The fundamental right of free men to strive for better conditions through new legislation and new institutions will not be preserved, if efforts to secure it by argument to fellow citizens may be construed as criminal incitement to disobey the existing law—merely, because the argument presented seems to those exercising judicial power to be unfair in its portrayal of existing evils, mistaken in its assumptions, unsound in reasoning or intemperate language. No objections more serious than these can, in my opinion, reasonably be made to the arguments presented in 'The Price We Pay.'"

Another "anarchist" whom Holmes and Brandeis could not save from punishment for his unpopular views was Benjamin Gitlow. Gitlow was charged with, and convicted of, criminal anarchy in violation of a New York statute.

Under the statute, a person committing criminal anarchy is one who "prints, publishes ... any book, paper ... containing or advocating ... [or] teaching the doctrine that organized government should be overthrown by force, violence or any unlawful means."[32] Gitlow had printed a paper titled *The Left Wing Manifesto*, which "advocated, in plain and unequivocal language, the necessity of accomplishing the 'Communist Revolution' by militant and 'revolutionary Socialism', based on 'the class struggle' and mobilizing the 'power of the proletariat in action'...." It was admitted, however, that there "was no evidence of any effect resulting from the publication and circulation of the Manifesto."

Justice Edward T. Sanford, in affirming Gitlow's conviction, cited *Schenck*, *Frohwerk*, *Debs* and other cases for the proposition that the Constitution "does not confer an absolute right to speak or publish, without responsibility, whatever one may choose, or an unrestricted and unbridled license that gives immunity for every possible use of language and prevents the punishment of those who abuse freedom."

Holmes, in writing a dissenting opinion for himself and Justice Brandeis, acknowledged the "clear and present danger test" which he had created in *Schenck*. He pointed out, however, that there was no danger of the overthrow of the government by the defendant and his small band of followers. "It is said," Holmes asserted, "that this manifesto was more than a theory, that it was an incitement. Every idea is an incitement. It offers itself for belief and if believed it is acted on unless some other belief outweighs it or some failure of energy stifles the movement at its birth. The only difference between the expression of an opinion and an incitement in the narrower sense is the speaker's enthusiasm for the result. Eloquence may set fire to reason. But whatever may be thought of the redundant discourse before us it had no chance of starting a present conflagration. If in the long run beliefs expressed in proletarian dictatorship are destined to be accepted by the dominant forces of the community, the only meaning of free speech is that they should be given their chance and have their way."

Freedom of the Press

Contempt of Court for Publication. "The contempt alleged was the publication of certain articles and a cartoon, which, it was charged, reflected upon the motives and conduct of the Supreme Court of Colorado in cases still pending and were intended to embarrass the court in the impartial administration of justice."[33] Thomas M. Patterson, who allegedly published the articles and cartoon, was convicted of contempt of court, and the Supreme Court, with Holmes writing the opinion, upheld the conviction.

The Justice avoided deciding whether the First Amendment governed state as well as federal action. Even if the Amendment was to apply in this case, he argued, it would not protect the defendant because the protection given publications applied "'to prevent all such *previous restraints* upon publications as had been practiced by other governments,' and they do not prevent the subsequent punishment of such as may be deemed contrary to the public welfare." That rule, he notes, applies to criminal libels and to contempt cases.

The Justice points out that publications critical of juries could obstruct justice, and the same is true when the publication is aimed at judges. "No doubt," the Justice writes, "judges naturally would be slower to punish when the contempt carried with it a personally dishonoring charge, but a man cannot expect to secure immunity from punishment by the proper tribunal, by adding to illegal conduct a personal attack. ... We have scrutinized the case, but cannot say that it shows an infraction of rights under the Constitution of the United States...."

Justice John M. Harlan disagreed with Holmes's analysis of freedom of the press, and dissented. He argued: "The public welfare cannot override constitutional privileges, and if the rights of free speech and of a free press are, in their essence, attributes of national citizenship, as I think they are, then neither Congress nor any State since the adoption of the Fourteenth Amendment can, by legislative enactments or by judicial action, impair or abridge them. In my judgment the action of the court below was in violation of the rights of free speech and a free press as guaranteed by the Constitution."

Holmes dissented in *Toledo Newspaper Co. v. United States*,[34] when a majority of the Court upheld the contempt conviction of the *Toledo News-Bee*. Chief Justice Edward D. White wrote for the Court:

> Newspaper publications, concerning injunction proceedings pending in the District Court, and tending in the circumstances to create the impression that a particular decision would evoke public suspicion of the judge's integrity or fairness and bring him into public odium and would be met by public resistance (to his judgment), and tending in the circumstance to provoke such resistance in fact, *held*, contemptuous rendering the company owning the paper and its editor subject to summary conviction and punishment.

In dissent, Holmes argued that there could not have been obstruction of justice in this case. He expressed the opinion that "a judge of the United States is expected to be a man of ordinary firmness of character, and I find it impossible to believe that such a judge could have found anything that was printed even a tendency to prevent his performing his sworn duty."

Denial of Second-class Mail Privileges. The *Milwaukee Leader* was granted a second-class mail privilege by the post office in 1911. That privilege was revoked in September 1917 by Postmaster General Albert S. Burleson shortly after the paper's editor had been found guilty of violating the federal Espionage Law. After a hearing, Burleson concluded that the *Leader* published articles with "a purpose and intent on its part—'to willfully make ... false reports ... with intent to interfere with the operation ... of the military ... forces of the United States, to promote the success of its enemies during the present war, and willfully cause ... insubordination, disloyalty, mutiny, and refusal of duty in the military ... forces ..., and to willfully obstruct the recruiting ... service of the United States,....' "[35]

The publisher of the *Leader* brought an action seeking reinstatement of the privilege which was denied. The Supreme Court, in an opinion by Justice Clarke, upheld that denial. Clarke again cited *Schenck, Frohwerk* and *Debs* for the proposition that the Espionage Law did not violate the Constitution. From that it was easy to conclude that Congress had given the Postmaster General authority to deny or revoke second-class mail permits to those whose publications offended the Espionage Law.

"Freedom of the press," Clarke declared, "may protect criticism and agitation for modification or repeal of laws, but it does not extend to protection of him who counsels and encourages the violation of the law as it exists. The Constitution was adopted to preserve our Government, not to serve as a protecting screen for those who while claiming its privileges seek to destroy it."[36]

Holmes again dissented, because he did not believe that Congress had given the Postmaster General power to censor mail by granting or withholding mailing permits. "The United States," he argued, "may give up the Post Office when it sees fit, but while it carries it on the use of the mails is almost as much a part of free speech as the right to use our tongues, and it would take very strong language to convince me that Congress ever intended to give such a practically despotic power to any one man."

The Pursuit of Liberty

The Right to Work. In 1884, Justice Joseph P. Bradley wrote: "I hold that the liberty of pursuit—the right to follow any of the ordinary callings of life—is one of the privileges of a citizen of the United States."[37]

In *Lochner v. New York,*[38] a majority of the Court struck down a New York law limiting the hours of bakery workers to 60 hours per week or 10 hours per day. Writing for the majority, Justice Rufus W. Peckham declared: "The right to purchase or to sell labor is part of the liberty protected by ... [the Fourteenth] amendment, unless there are circumstances which exclude the right." And, insofar as applying the law to bakers, he continued: "There is no reasonable ground for interfering with the liberty of person or the right of free contract, by determining the hours of labor, in the occupation of a baker. There is no contention that bakers as a class are not equal in intelligence and capacity to men in other trades or manual occupations, or that they are not able to assert their rights and care for themselves without the protecting arms of the State, interfering with their independence of judgment and of action."

Justice Holmes expressed his disagreement with the majority in a short dissent. He believed that the decision was out of step with prevailing opinion in the country with regard to government regulation of the right to work. "The liberty of the citizen to do as he likes so long as he does not interfere with the liberty of others to do the same, which has been a shibboleth for some well-known writers, is interfered with by school laws, by the Post Office, by every state or municipal institution which takes his money for purposes thought desirable, whether he likes it or not." "Men whom I certainly could not pronounce unreasonable," he continued, "would uphold ... [the law] as a first installment of a general regulation of the hours of work."

The Court continued to protect the right to work, and Holmes continued to dissent. That was the situation when William Adair, an agent of the Louisville and Nashville Railroad Company, fired O. B. Coppage because Coppage was a member of a union. Adair was charged with violating a federal law which made it a criminal offense to *"unjustly discriminate against any employe(e) because of his membership in such a labor organization..."*[39]

The Supreme Court reversed Adair's conviction being of the opinion that the law was unconstitutional as a violation of the right to make contracts for work. "It was the right of the defendant [Adair]," Justice John M. Harlan declared, "to prescribe the terms upon which the services of Coppage to become or not, as he chose, an employee of the railroad company upon the terms offered to him."

Furthermore, Harlan wrote: "[T]he right of the employee to quit the service of the employer, for whatever reason, is the same as the right of the employer, for whatever reason to dispense with the services of such employee. It was the legal right of the defendant Adair—however unwise such a course might have been—to discharge Coppage because of his being a member of a labor organization, as it was the legal right of Coppage, if he saw fit to do so—however unwise such a course on his part might have been—to quit the service in which he was engaged, because the defendant employed some persons who were not members of a labor organization."

In dissent, Holmes argued: "So I turn to the general question whether the employment can be regulated at all. I confess that I think that the right to make contracts at will that has been derived from the word liberty in the amendments has been stretched to its extreme by the decisions; but they agree that sometimes the right may be restrained. When there is, or generally is believed to be, an important ground of public policy for restraint the Constitution does not forbid it, whether this court agrees or disagrees with the policy pursued."

For Teachers and Parents. Robert T. Meyer, a teacher at the Zion Parochial School in Hamilton County, Nebraska, was charged and convicted of teaching the German language to Raymond Parpart, a ten-year-old student. The Nebraska statute under which Meyer was convicted prohibited the teaching of "any subject to any person in any language other than the English language."[40]

When the case reached the Supreme Court, Justice James Clark McReynolds wrote that question was "whether the statute ... unreasonably infringes the liberty guaranteed to ... [Meyer] by the Fourteenth Amendment. 'No State shall ... deprive any person of life, liberty, or property, without due process of law.'"

The Due Process Clause, McReynolds pointed out, "denotes not merely freedom from bodily restraint but also the right of the individual to contract, to engage in any of the common occupations of life, to acquire useful knowledge, to marry, establish a home and bring up children, to worship God according to the dictates of his own conscience, and generally enjoy those privileges long recognized at common law as essential to the orderly pursuit of happiness by free men."

Taking note that education has always been regarded "as matters of supreme importance which should be diligently promoted," McReynolds concluded that Meyer's "right to teach and the right of parents to engage him so to instruct their children, ... are within the liberty of that Amendment."

Holmes agreed that a liberty interest of teachers was at issue in the case, but concluded that interest must give way to Nebraska's interest in the education of its children. "The part of the act with which we are concerned deals with the teaching of young children. Youth is the time when familiarity with language is established and if there are sections in the State where a child would hear only Polish or French or German spoken at home I am not prepared to say that it is unreasonable to provide that in his early years he shall hear and speak only English at school. But if it is reasonable it is not an undue restriction of the liberty of either teacher or scholar."

At the same time that the *Meyer* case was heard, the Court had before it similar cases from Iowa and Ohio. The Ohio law specifically prohibited the teaching of German. The Court also held these state laws to be unconstitutional. Holmes again dissented, but did agree that Ohio's law prohibiting the teaching of German was unconstitutional.[41]

For the Mentally Ill.

> Carrie Buck is a feeble minded white woman who was committed to the State Colony (for Epileptics and Feeble Minded).... She is the daughter of a feeble minded mother in the same institution, and the mother of an illegitimate feeble minded child. She was eighteen years old at the time of the trial of her case in the Circuit Court, in the latter part of 1924.[42]

At Carrie Buck's trial, the State sought and received permission to have her sterilized. That decision was upheld by the Supreme Court with the Justice writing the Court's opinion. Holmes noted that it was not the legal procedure with which the decision to sterilize Buck was reached that was at issue. The real question was whether Buck had any substantive right not to be sterilized, and if so did the facts justify an infringement upon that right. The

Justice did not dwell on the question of whether Buck had a liberty interest not to be sterilized. He simply concluded that in "view of the general declarations of the legislature and the specific findings of the Court, obviously we cannot say as a matter of law that the grounds do not exist, and if they exist they justify the result. ... It is better for all the world, if instead of waiting to execute degenerate offspring for crime, or to let them starve for their imbecility, society can prevent those who are manifestly unfit from continuing their kind. ... Three generations of imbeciles are enough." Justice Pierce Butler dissented without opinion.

Equal Protection of the Law

Blacks on Juries. In *Brownfield v. South Carolina*,[43] the Court affirmed the murder conviction of Brownfield, a black, who claimed that he was tried by a jury from which blacks had been excluded. The Court's affirmance rests upon its conclusion that, although Brownfield had alleged such discrimination, he had not introduced evidence to substantiate his claim. "It is suggested," Holmes wrote for the Court, "that the allegations of the motion to quash not having been controverted and having been supported by the affidavit of the defendant, must be taken as true. But a motion, although reduced to writing, is not a pleading, and does not require a written answer. It appears from the grounds on which the judge decided it, apart from anything else, that the allegations were controverted, and under such circumstances it was necessary for the defendant to make an attempt to introduce evidence."

Less than a year later, the Court, with Holmes again writing the opinion, reversed the murder conviction of a Mr. Rogers who alleged discrimination in the selection of the grand jurors who indicted him.[44] Rogers had filed a motion alleging that blacks had been excluded from the grand jury. At the request of the state, the trial judge quashed the motion. Rogers appealed to the Alabama Supreme Court but that court denied relief, relying upon a state law that allowed judges to strike pleadings that were "unnecessarily prolix, irrelevant, or frivolous."

In commenting upon the motion to quash, which took two pages in the record, Holmes declared: "A motion of that length, made for the sole purpose of setting up a constitutional right and distinctly claiming it, cannot be withdrawn for prolixity from the consideration of this court, under the color of local practice, because it contains a statement of matter which perhaps it would have been better to omit but which is relevant to the principal fact averred." Furthermore, Holmes noted: "It is a necessary and well settled rule that the exercise of jurisdiction by this court to protect constitutional rights cannot be declined when it is plain that the fair result of a decision is to deny the rights."

However, in *Martin v. Texas*,[45] Holmes again joined the majority to affirm a murder conviction where no evidence had been offered to prove discrimination in the selection of the grand jury. "The absence of any such proof from the record in this case," Justice Harlan noted, "is fatal to the charge of the accused that his rights under the Fourteenth Amendment were violated."

A somewhat different kind of challenge to jurors arose in the case of Alfred Scott Aldridge, a black man charged with murder for allegedly shooting police officer McDonald, a white man, in Washington, D.C. During examination of prospective jurors, Aldridge's attorney asked the trial judge for permission to inquire whether any of the jury panel held any racial prejudice, in view of the fact that a black man was on trial for allegedly shooting a white man. The judge denied the request. Aldridge was convicted and he appealed to the Court of Appeals, which affirmed. With Chief Justice Charles Evans Hughes writing the opinion, and only Justice McReynolds dissenting, the Supreme Court reversed.[46]

In response to the argument made by the government not to allow such questions to be put to jury panel members, Hughes replied: "We think that it would be far more injurious to permit it to be thought that persons entertaining a disqualifying prejudice were allowed to serve as jurors and that inquiries designed to elicit the fact of disqualification were barred. No surer way could be devised to bring the processes of justice into disrepute." Holmes joined that opinion.

Blacks Have a Right to Vote. "This is a bill in equity brought by a colored man, on behalf of himself 'and on behalf of more than five thousand negroes, citizens of the county of Montgomery, Alabama, similarly situated and circumstanced as himself,' against the board of registrars of that county. The prayer of the bill is in substance that the defendants may be required to enroll upon the voting lists the name of the plaintiff and of all other qualified members of his race who applied for registration before August 1, 1902, and were refused, and certain sections of the constitution of Alabama … may be declared contrary to the Fourteenth and Fifteenth Amendments of the Constitution of the United States, and void."[47] The lower court dismissed the case, and an appeal was taken to the Supreme Court.

The issue before the Court was whether the lower court should have dismissed the case without giving the plaintiff the relief he requested. Writing for the majority, Holmes concluded that the dismissal should be affirmed. The Justice concluded that the lower court simply did not have the power to do what the plaintiff wanted done. It could not declare the Alabama laws unconstitutional and at the same time order the plaintiff to be registered as a voter. Furthermore, the Justice found troublesome the question that if a court were to issue an order in accordance with the plaintiff's demands, against whom should it be issued? "Unless we are prepared to supervise the voting in that State by officers of the court," Holmes asserted, "it seems to us that all that the plaintiff could get from equity would be an empty form."

Justices David Brewer, Henry Brown and John M. Harlan dissented.

After an extensive review of the cases dealing with the jurisdiction of the federal courts, Harlan concluded that "upon the facts alleged in the bill ... the plaintiff is entitled to relief in respect of his right to be registered as a voter. I agree with Mr. Justice Brewer that it is competent for the courts to give relief in such cases as this."

Holmes and the Court gave more consideration to a Mr. Nixon's claim of voter discrimination when he was not permitted to vote in the Texas primary election in 1924 because he was black. The Judges of Elections, in refusing to allow Nixon to vote, were acting in accordance with Texas election laws which provided that "in no event shall a negro be eligible to participate in a Democratic party primary election held in the State of Texas."[48]

The District Court dismissed the case, but the Supreme Court unanimously reversed. In referring to the Texas statutes, Holmes wrote that "it seems to us hard to imagine a more direct and obvious infringement of the Fourteenth [Amendment]. That Amendment, while it applies to all, was passed, as we know, with a special intent to protect the blacks from discrimination against them."

For Aliens. In 1914, the people of Arizona enacted a law that required eighty (80) percent of the employees working for employers with more than five employees, to be "qualified electors or native-born citizens of the United States."[49] At the time, William Truax, Sr., had nine employees in his restaurant in Bisbee, Arizona, seven of whom were aliens. In order to comply with the law, Truax discharged Mike Raich because Raich was a native of Austria. Raich immediately filed an action against Truax seeking to restrain the application of the act, claiming it violated the Equal Protection Clause of the Fourteenth Amendment. The court agreed and the Supreme Court affirmed.

Justice Charles Evans Hughes wrote the Court's opinion, which Holmes joined, and from which only Justice McReynolds dissented. "The discrimination is against aliens as such in competition with citizens in the described range of enterprises and in our opinion it clearly falls under the condemnation of the fundamental law."

Less than a month later, Holmes joined two opinions upholding a New York statute which provided that in construction of public works, "only citizens of the United States shall be employed."[50] The Court made no reference to the *Truax* case.

Holmes also voted to uphold laws of the states of Washington and California that disqualified "aliens who have not in good faith declared intention to become citizens of the United States from taking or holding interests in land in the State."[51]

Writing for the Court in one of those cases, Justice Pierce Butler acknowledged that in the *Truax* case the Court said "that the right to work for a living in the common occupations of the community is a part of the freedom which it was the purpose of the Fourteenth Amendment to secure."[52] He concluded, however, that excluding aliens from owning land was different. "The quality and allegiance of those who own, occupy and use the farm lands within its borders are matters of highest importance and affect the safety and power of the State itself."

Involuntary Servitude. Alonzo Bailey, a black man, signed a contract to work for The Riverside Co. as a farm hand in Montgomery County, Alabama. He was to be paid $10.75 per month and received $15.00 in advance. Bailey worked for a month and a few days and then quit without giving an explanation for his leaving. The County Grand Jury indicted Bailey for entering into the labor contract "with intent to injure or defraud his employer," a crime under Alabama law.[53] The law created a presumption that a laborer who fails to complete a labor contract acts with "intent to injure his employer," and he was thereafter not allowed to testify as to his "motives, purpose or intention."

Bailey was found guilty and sentenced to pay thirty dollars and costs, and if he did not do so he would be sent to prison for "twenty days in lieu of said fine and one hundred and sixteen days on account of said costs." The Supreme Court reversed, with Justice Hughes writing the Court's opinion. After examining the Alabama statute, Hughes concluded that its real purpose was "to expose to conviction for crime those who simply fail or refuse to perform contracts for personal service in liquidation of a debt." That, he concluded, was a violation of the Thirteenth Amendment as well as federal law. "The Thirteenth Amendment," Hughes declared, "prohibits involuntary servitude except as punishment for crime. … The State may impose involuntary servitude as a punishment for crime, but it may not compel one man to labor for another in payment of a debt, punishing him as a criminal if he does not perform the service or pay the debt." Furthermore: "There is no more important concern than to safeguard the freedom of labor upon which alone can enduring prosperity be based. The provisions designed to secure it would soon become a barren form if it were possible to establish a statutory presumption of this sort and to hold over the head of laborers the threat of punishment for crime, under the name of fraud but merely upon evidence of failure to work out their debts."

Holmes dissented. "Peonage," he argued, "is service to a private master at which a man is kept by bodily compulsion against his will. But the creation of the ordinary legal motives for right conduct does not produce it. Breach of a legal contract without excuse is wrong conduct, even if the contract is for labor, and if a State adds to civil liability a criminal liability to fine, it simply intensifies the legal motive for doing right, it does not make the laborer a slave."

The Justice did not believe that the law was merely punishment for breach of a labor contract but rather one to prevent someone from obtaining money by false pretenses. Nor did he believe that there was anything wrong with the presumption that the laborer had acted with intent to defraud. "To sum up," he wrote, "I think that obtaining money by fraud may be made a crime as well as murder or theft; that a false representation, expressed or implied, at the time of making a contract of labor that one intends to perform it and thereby obtaining an advance, may be declared a case of fraudulently obtaining money as well as any other; that if made a crime it may be punished like any other crime, and that an unjustified departure from the promised service without repayment may be declared a sufficient case to go to the jury for judgment; all without in any way infringing the Thirteenth Amendment or the statutes of the United States."

Justice Holmes continued to believe that there was "nothing in the Thirteenth Amendment ... that prevents a State from making a breach of contract, as well a reasonable contract for labor as for other matters, a crime and punishing it as such."[54]

He did, however, agree with the majority that J. J. Reynolds and G. W. Broughton could be prosecuted under a federal law making it a crime to hold a person in peonage. The case before the Court grew out of the following facts: Ed Rivers was convicted of petty larceny and fined $15 and costs of $43.75. J. J. Reynolds offered to be surety for Rivers and paid the fine and costs. Reynolds then had Rivers enter into a contract whereby Rivers agreed to work as a farm hand for $6 per month until the amount of the fine and costs were paid. Rivers worked for about a month and then quit. He was arrested for violating his contract with Reynolds, fined one cent and costs of $87.05. This time, G. W. Broughton became surety for Rivers who was then forced to enter into a contract to perform farm labor for him.

Reynolds and Broughton were both arrested for violating the federal law. Their defense was that they had acted pursuant to the laws of Alabama, which permitted the procedure whereby one convicted of a crime could be forced to work for his surety until the surety had been reimbursed for the amount paid. District Judge Harry T. Toulmin dismissed the charges, being of the opinion that the Alabama procedure did not violate either the federal anti-peonage law or the Thirteen Amendment's prohibition against involuntary servitude. The Supreme Court reversed, concluding that the Alabama "system is in violation of rights intended to be secured by the Thirteenth Amendment, as well as in violation of the statutes to which we have referred, which the Congress has enacted for the purpose of making that amendment effective."

Justice William R. Day pointed out that when "the convict goes to work under ... [his] agreement, he is under the direction and control of the surety, and is in fact working for him. If he keeps his agreement with the surety, he is discharged from its obligations without any further action by the State. This labor is performed under the constant coercion and threat of another possible arrest and prosecution in case he violates the labor contract which he has made with the surety, and this form of coercion is as potent as it would have

been had the law provided for the seizure and compulsory service of the convict."

Holmes concurred, being of the opinion that "successive contracts, each
for a longer term than the last ... [were] the inevitable outcome of the Alabama
laws. On this ground ... I am inclined to agree that the [Alabama] statutes
in question disclose the attempt to maintain service that the ... [federal]
Statutes forbid."

The Deprivation of a Patentee's Rights

"The complainant [International Postal Supply Co.] as the owner of letters
patent of the United States for new and useful improvements in stamp canceling and postmarking machines, brought a bill in equity against the defendant [Bruce], who is the postmaster of the United States post office at
Syracuse, New York, complaining of the use in said post office of two machines,
which infringe the complainant's letters patent, praying for an injunction
against further use of said machines...." "The machines so used were hired by
the United States Post Office Department for a term, which is as yet unexpired from the manufacturer and owner of said machines...."[55]

The Court of Appeals certified to the Supreme Court the question
whether it had the power to grant an injunction against Postmaster Bruce
prohibiting the further use of the postal machines. Holmes, for the majority,
answered the question in the negative. The suit, the Court held, was actually
against the United States and suits against the United States are not permitted. The complainant's request, therefore, must be denied.

Justices John M. Harlan and Rufus W. Peckham dissented. "Such arbitrary destruction of the property rights of the citizen," Harlan declared, "might
be expected to occur under a despotic government, but it ought not to be tolerated under a government whose fundamental law forbids all deprivation of
property without due process of law, or the taking of private property for public use without compensation." Furthermore, he argued: "In my judgment it
is not possible to conceive of any case, arising under our system of constitutional government, in which the courts may not, in some effective mode, and
properly, protect the rights of the citizen against illegal aggression, and to
that end, if need be, stay the hands of the aggressor, even if he be a public
officer, who acts in the interest, or by the direction of the Government."

The Right to Sue

Elizabeth M. Chambers and her husband, Henry, were citizens of Pennsylvania. Henry Chambers, a locomotive engineer, was killed while on duty in
Pennsylvania for the Baltimore & Ohio R.R. Company. Under Pennsylvania
law, Elizabeth Chambers had a cause of action for the wrongful death of her

husband. She chose, however, to sue the railroad in Ohio where she received judgment in the amount of three thousand dollars. The railroad appealed, contending that it was not subject to suit in Ohio, because Ohio law permitted wrongful death actions only for citizens of Ohio. The Supreme Court of Ohio agreed and reversed, and the United State Supreme Court affirmed.

Mrs. Chambers argued that the Ohio law violated Article IV of the United States Constitution, which provides that "*citizens of each State shall be entitled to all privileges and immunities of citizens of the several States.*" Justice William H. Moody and a court majority did not believe that there was any disparity of treatment by the Ohio law. "The [Ohio] courts were open in such cases to plaintiffs who were citizens of other States if the deceased was a citizen of Ohio; they were closed to plaintiffs who were citizens of Ohio if the deceased was a citizen of another State. So far as the parties to the litigation are concerned, the State by its laws made no discrimination based on citizenship, and offered precisely the same privileges to citizens of other States which it allowed to its own."[56] Holmes concurred. He was of the opinion that if the state law was not valid, then no one could maintain an action in Ohio for wrongful death.

Justice Harlan saw the matter differently. He wrote: "In that view, if two persons, one a citizen of Ohio and the other a citizen of Pennsylvania, traveling together on a railroad in Pennsylvania, should both be killed at the same moment and under precisely the same circumstances, in consequence of the negligence or default of the railroad company, the courts of Ohio are closed, by its statute against any suit for damages brought by the widow or the estate of the citizen of Pennsylvania against the railroad company, but will be open in suit by the widow or the estate of the deceased citizen of Ohio, although by the laws of the State where the death occurred the widow or estate of each decedent would have in the latter a valid cause of action."

After reviewing prior cases dealing with the Privileges and Immunities Clause, Harlan concluded: "I submit that no State can authorize its courts to deny or disregard the constitutional guaranty that the citizens of each State shall be entitled to all the privileges and immunities of citizens in the several States."

The Bill of Rights and the States

Prior to 1815, Craig and Barron owned "an extensive and highly productive wharf, in the eastern section of Baltimore, enjoying, at the period of their purchase of it, the deepest water in the harbor."[57] When the city graded and paved the streets near the harbor, the natural water flow was diverted in such a way that heavy rains washed dirt and sand into the bay around the wharf, eventually making it unusable. Barron brought suit against the city, claiming that its action violated the Fifth Amendment to the Constitution, "which declares

that 'private property shall not be taken for public use, without just compensation....' " In dismissing the case, Chief Justice John Marshall wrote for all
members of the Supreme Court: "We are of the opinion that the provision in
the fifth amendment to the constitution, declaring that private property shall
not be taken for public use, without just compensation, is intended solely as
a limitation on the exercise of power by the government of the United States,
and is not applicable to the legislation of the states."

Barron's case settled the question of the application of the Bill of Rights
to actions by state government until the adoption of the Fourteenth Amendment in 1868. Thereafter, lawyers began to argue that it was the intention of
those who proposed the Fourteenth Amendment that it make at least the first
eight amendments to the Constitution applicable to states. The first Justice
John M. Harlan believed that to be true and dissented when the Court upheld
the conviction of Joseph Hurtado for murder in California, even though he
had not been indicted by a grand jury.[58] If Hurtado had been charged with a
crime against the United States, the Fifth Amendment would have required
the federal government to present the case to a grand jury for an indictment
prior to trial. Harlan criticized the majority for not giving Hurtado the same
"immunity or right, recognized at the common law to be essential to personal
security, jealously guarded by our national Constitution against violation by
any tribunal or body exercising authority under the general [federal] government."

When Albert C. Twining and David C. Cornell, president and treasurer,
respectively, of the Monmouth [New Jersey] Trust and Safe Deposit Company were indicted and convicted for knowingly exhibiting a false paper to a
bank examiner, neither man testified at his trial. Under New Jersey law, the
jury was permitted to "draw an unfavorable inference against [a defendant]
... from the failure to testify ... in denial of evidence which tended to incrim-
inate him."[59]

Acting in accordance with the law, the trial judge instructed the jury that
the defendants were not required to prove their innocence nor were they
required to testify in their own behalf. He pointed out, however, that not taking the stand "is sometimes a matter of significance." The judge also commented upon defendant Cornell remaining silent when the bank examiner
testified. Cornell "was not called upon to go upon the stand and deny it, but
he did not go upon the stand and deny it, and it is for you to take that into
consideration."

When the case reached the Supreme Court, Justice William H. Moody
stated that the defendants had to prove "first, that the exemption from compulsory self-incrimination is guaranteed by the Federal Constitution against
impairment by the States; and, second, if it be so guaranteed, that the exemption was in fact impaired in the case at bar."

After an extensive review of prior cases, Moody concluded "that the exemption from compulsory self-incrimination in the courts of the States is not secured by any part of the Federal Constitution." Holmes agreed.

The only dissenter was, again, Justice Harlan. He, too, made an extensive review of history and of prior cases, and wrote: "I am of the opinion that as immunity from self-incrimination was recognized in the Fifth Amendment of the Constitution and placed beyond violation by any Federal agency, it should be deemed one of the immunities of citizens of the United States which the Fourteenth Amendment in express terms forbids any State from abridging—as much so, for instance, as the right of free speech ... or the exemption from cruel and unusual punishments ... or the exemption from being put twice in jeopardy of life or limb for the same offense ..., or the exemption from unreasonable seizures of one's person, house, papers or effect...."

Holmes continued to vote against applying the provisions of the Bill of Rights to the states, except that he agreed that the Fourteenth Amendment required states to follow the commands of the speech and press provisions of the First Amendment. Even then, however, he was willing to give states "a somewhat larger latitude of interpretation than is allowed to Congress by the sweeping language that governs or ought to govern the laws of the United States."[60]

Does the Constitution Follow the Flag?

In 1901, when the Court held that the Constitution does not apply to territories controlled by the United States, Justice Harlan vigorously dissented. He wrote: "The Constitution speaks not simply to the States in their organized capacities, but to all peoples, whether of States or territories, who are subject to the authority of the United States."[61]

When confronted with the question again in *Hawaii v. Mankichi*,[62] the Court, following its prior decision, came to the same conclusion with Justice Holmes joining the majority.

Although the Hawaiian Islands were a territory of the United States in 1899, Osaki Mankichi, who was not indicted by a grand jury, was found guilty of manslaughter by a vote of only nine of twelve jurors, all in accordance with the laws of Hawaii. In affirming Mankichi's conviction, the majority concluded "that the two rights [not being indicted and being found guilty by less than a unanimous jury] alleged to be violated in this case are not fundamental in their nature, but concern merely a method of procedure which sixty years of practice had shown to be suited to the conditions of the islands, and well calculated to conserve the rights of their citizens to their lives, their property and their well-being."

This decision disturbed Justice Harlan, and he again dissented. "In my opinion," he declared, "the Constitution of the United States became the supreme law of Hawaii immediately upon the acquisition by the United States of complete sovereignty over the Hawaiian Islands, and without any act of Congress formally extending the Constitution to those Islands. ... From the moment when the Government of Hawaii accepted the ... formal transfer of its sovereignty to the United States—when the flag of Hawaii was taken down ... and in its place was raised that of the United States—every human being in Hawaii, charged with the commission of crime there, could have rightly insisted that neither his life nor his liberty could be taken, as punishment for crime, by any process ... that was inconsistent with the Constitution of the United States."

The Civil Rights Acts

Being of the opinion that the Fourteenth Amendment's guarantee of due process and equal protection protected persons only from *state* governmental action, the Court, in the *Civil Rights Cases*,[63] struck down the Civil Rights Acts of 1875. Congress, in enacting the Civil Rights Acts, intended to give *individuals* a cause of action against other *individuals* who violate their right "to the full and equal enjoyment of the accommodations, ... privileges of inns, [and] public conveyances...." Holmes was not on the Court at this time.

In *Hodges v. United States*,[64] the Court reached a similar conclusion when it held that the Thirteenth Amendment did not give Congress authority to protect individuals from interference by other individuals with the right to contract for their labor. Holmes voted with the majority, but Harlan again dissented. "I cannot assent" he asserted, "to an interpretation of the Constitution which denies National protection to vast numbers of our people in respect of rights derived by them from the Nation. The interpretation now placed on the Thirteenth Amendment is, I think, entirely too narrow and is hostile to the freedom established by the supreme law of the land." The Supreme Court overruled the *Hodges* case in 1968.[65]

AS A JUSTICE FOR THE GOVERNMENT

In the *Schwimmer* case, the Justice made what is now a widely quoted statement: "[I]f there is any principle of the Constitution that more imperatively calls for attachment than any other it is the principle of free thought— not free thought for those who agree with us but freedom for the thought that we hate."[66]

While Holmes was willing to give protection to free religious thought, he was not so quick to extend the same protection to free speech if he thought that there was a "clear and present danger" that the speech might cause some evil which the government had the right to punish. That was his message in *Schenck*, *Frohwerk* and *Debs*. That message came back to haunt him, however, because it was cited with approval, in spite of his dissents, in *Abrams* and *Pierce*, whose convictions the Court upheld for allegedly violating the Espionage Act; and *Gitlow*, whose conviction for criminal anarchy was also upheld. And the "clear and present danger" test allowed the Court to affirm convictions long after Holmes retired.[67]

Holmes's opinion in *Patterson* indicates he also held a rather narrow view of freedom of the press, i.e., that the constitutional provision of freedom of the press was "'to prevent all such *previous restraints* upon publications as had been practiced by other governments,' and they do not prevent the subsequent punishment of such as may be deemed contrary to the public welfare."[68] And although he dissented when the Court upheld the contempt conviction of the *Toledo News-Bee*, his focus was not on freedom of the press as much as it was upon his belief that there was "no need for immediate action." And because of that, "contempts are like any other breach of law and should be dealt with as the law deals with other illegal acts."[69]

Holmes recognized that the word "liberty" in the Due Process Clause protected the right to work. However, he consistently voted to uphold government infringement upon that right when he believed the infringement was necessary to implement "important government policies."[70]

Although the constitutional right of privacy had not been established in Holmes's day, he participated in several cases which formed the framework of that right as we now know it.[71] For example, he dissented when the Court upheld the right of teacher Robert T. Meyer to teach German to student Raymond Parpart. The majority had held that Meyer's "right thus to teach and the right of parents to engage him so to instruct their children, we think, are within the liberty of the [Fourteenth] Amendment."[72] Even though he did not deny that there was an issue concerning the liberty of Meyer and of Parpart's parents, he was of the opinion that interest could be overridden by action of the state so long as it was reasonable.

Before the Justice upheld the authority of the state to sterilize Carrie Buck because she was mentally ill, he had joined the majority in approving compulsory vaccination for smallpox.[73] The primary concern of the Court in that case was that vaccination was a necessary health measure to prevent the spread of the disease. The necessity for the sterilization of the mentally ill, however, was justified upon the vague assumption that it would prevent crime by imbeciles and possibly keep them from starvation.[74]

Holmes was not a strong supporter of the rights of minorities. He voted to uphold: a Kentucky statute prohibiting corporations from conducting an institution of learning for both white and black students;[75] the laws of Oklahoma and Kentucky requiring railroads to provide separate but equal facilities on trains;[76] and the assignment of Martha Lum, an Oriental, to an all-black school in Mississippi.[77]

The Justice wrote the opinion in one, and voted with the majority in two other cases, denying a claim of discrimination in the selection of a trial jury.[78] In each of these cases, the defendant raised the question of discrimination in selection of the jury panel before trial, and the jury that tried him was composed entirely of white persons. In affirming the convictions, however, Holmes and the majority were of the opinion that, standing alone, the makeup of the jury did not prove discrimination, and therefore the defendant, in each case, had the burden of producing other evidence of discrimination.

Aliens fared no better than minorities insofar as the Justice's votes were concerned. He voted with the majority to uphold the right of aliens to work in Arizona, but voted against their working on government projects or owning land in California.[79]

When confronted with labor contracts, Holmes could see no constitutional violation in laws making it a crime not to perform a labor contract even though the majority struck down such laws on the grounds that sending a laborer to jail for such a breach was involuntary servitude. "The State may impose involuntary servitude as a punishment for crime," Justice Hughes declared, "but it may not compel one man to labor for another in payment of a debt, by punishing him as a criminal if he does not perform the service or pay the debt."[80]

For most of his tenure on the Court, the Justice voted against applying the Bill of Rights to the states. This was also the position taken by most of the justices who served with him. Justice Harlan, however, who served with Holmes from 1902 until 1911, disagreed with this position. Harlan argued: "But, if I do not wholly misapprehend the scope and legal effect [of the Court's decisions] ... the Constitution of the United States does not stand in the way of any State striking down guarantees of life and liberty that English-speaking people have for centuries regarded as vital to personal security, and which men of the Revolutionary period universally claimed as the birthright of freemen."[81]

Holmes did, however, support requiring states to follow the command of the First Amendment in cases involving freedom of speech and of the press.

Four other areas where Justice Holmes voted against individual freedom are the extension of the protection of the Bill of Rights to territories under the control of the United States; Congress's attempt to eliminate discrimination by the enactment of Civil Rights Acts; disregarding the patentee's rights in a postal canceling machine; and denying Elizabeth Chambers the right to sue for the death of her husband. In each of these situations, Holmes generally voted for the government and against the individual involved.[82]

It is clear from the foregoing that Justice Holmes was not a strong protector of individual freedom. More often than not, he voted to uphold government infringement upon constitutional rights and was reluctant to extend the protection of the Bill of Rights to people living in the territories and the states. He is therefore included here as a *Justice for the Government*.

2

JUSTICE FELIX FRANKFURTER

PERSONAL LIFE

Growing Up

Short of stature—he was less than five feet, five inches—he needed eloquence and intellectual power to keep the world of taller men from overlooking him. He succeeded, graduating from City College [New York City] at nineteen, third highest in his class.[1]

In a series of interviews with Justice Frankfurter, Dr. Harlan B. Phillips asked the Justice about his relationship with his parents. Frankfurter responded: "If you were to ask me what I think as I sit here, … the picture in my mind of me and my family is that my father and mother somehow or other saw that they didn't have to bother about this kid, that he was doing all right, and why bother him. I was a sociable creature. I didn't give them any trouble, but please don't infer that I was goody-goody. I've said … that the greatest debt I owe my parents is that they left me alone almost completely."[2]

Frankfurter was born in Vienna, Austria, on November 15, 1882, but his family came to the United States when he was twelve years old, settling in New York's Lower East Side. "Felix sold newspapers after school," Michael E. Parrish has written, "which permitted him to explore the wide boulevards as well as the back alleys of Manhattan. He sampled the mansions of the very rich and the hovels of the poor; factories and department stores; flop houses and museums; ferry boats and push carts. They formed a brilliant kaleidoscope of pleasures to be tasted and misfortunes to be avoided."[3]

After making a trip to the United States in 1893, Leopold Frankfurter decided to move his family there. The Justice's mother, Emma, reluctantly accepted the move. At that time, there were six Frankfurter children: Fred, Otto, Felix, Paul, Ella and Estelle.

JUSTICE FELIX FRANKFURTER (photo by Harris and Ewing; collection of the Supreme Court of the United States).

A strict, disciplined homemaker, with an extensive repertoire of homilies about work, duty, and responsibility, Emma believed that her children would conquer their new environment through education. It was she who drilled into them the necessity for intellectual achievement in a brutally competitive society.

Emma Frankfurter put Felix and another son, Paul, in Public School 25. Frankfurter spoke about his early schooling: "I was pitched into a class. I was in a daze. I don't know where they put me originally, but finally I ended up in the first class. Even that was intellectually much below my knowledge content, but English, of course, was a great barrier. We had a teacher, a middle-aged Irish woman, named Miss Hogan. I suppose she was one of my greatest benefactors in life because she was a lady of the old school. ... She evidently saw this ardent kid who by that time had picked up some English—I'm not a linguist and haven't got a good ear for languages—but she told the boys that if anybody was caught speaking German with me, she would punish him. ... It was wonderful for me that speaking English was enforced upon my environment in school, all thanks to Miss Hogan."[4]

Frankfurter became an avid reader, especially of newspapers. "I also read a good deal of history. I read a lot, a terrible lot. At college I discovered what was the Lenox Library which is now the Frick. ... The reading room there was quite unfrequented. ... I would just look at everything on the open shelves, commentaries on Shakespeare, and so on. I was a browser, and there you could browse."

Upon graduating from PS 25, Frankfurter entered City College where he chose the classical schedule. He grew up without knowing a great deal of science. He was, however, an excellent debater. Nathaniel Phillips described Frankfurter's debating style: "'I shall never forget his stunning performance,' Phillips recalled. 'He looked so boyish, his neatness was striking. He spoke such sense. It was as though no opposition could have any significance. He was extremely courteous in manner but he pierced the arguments of his opponents with a deftness and finality that was devastating.' A dashing orator, Phillips noted, Frankfurter always impressed you with his sincerity, his gaiety, and his charm."[5]

Frankfurter tutored high school students to earn a little extra money. He comments about one of the students he tutored: "I had to tutor a very stupid boy who was living with a very old maiden aunt. I had to teach this kid, who was preparing for college, Latin and geometry in the presence of his maiden aunt—a stupid boy and a fluttering aunt, a wonderful combination!"[6]

Student at Harvard Law School

Frankfurter entered Harvard Law School in 1902. About his decision to study law, Frankfurter told Dr. Phillips: "I do not remember the time when I did not know I was going to be a lawyer. Now why that should be so I do not know, because that is the first appearance of any lawyer in my family—the first and last appearance."

At this time, Sam Rosensohn, a second year law student at Harvard, invited Frankfurter to room with him.

> The first day I went to my classrooms I had one of the most intense frights of my life. I looked about me. Everybody was taller. I wasn't as tall as I am now. That is a joke. I was a little fellow. I was much thinner. There were a lot of big fellows, tall fellows, robust fellows, self-confident creatures around.

Despite misgivings about his size, Frankfurter excelled in law school. Author Parrish wrote: "Apart from his legal studies, Frankfurter found time for concerts, museums, and even a course in German literature to the point where Rosensohn worried he would disgrace himself and City College at examination time. But despite a pace of extralegal activities that would have swamped others, Frankfurter led his class academically for three years, earned a coveted position on the *Harvard Law Review*, and became a research assistant to [Professor] John Gray." [7]

It was a discussion with another Harvard student that made him realize what anti-Semitism was all about. Frankfurter gives this account of that discussion:

> There was another fellow from Maine, Colby College, Julius Fogg. He was a red-headed, a down easter and all that, and we became good friends. We used to go walking. One day he said to me, "I think I ought to tell you something. Do you realize—you probably don't—that you're the first Jew I ever met in my life who wasn't a village peddler in my little village up in Maine. It was through him that I had notions about Jews—unclean," and so on. This grand fellow gave me as good a glimpse as I would get from those big-worded, sociological, jargonized books on some aspects of anti-Semitism. There you had it all in a roll. All he knew about a Jew was that he was a fellow who, if he could beat him out of a nickel, would because he needed a few nickels to sleep that night and was not dandily dressed. He was telling me what it meant to meet a Jew—he said so in so many words—who was clean, who was a nice lad and who was respected by the students at Harvard Law School. He said that was a terrific experience for him. [8]

Assistant United States Attorney

After graduation, Frankfurter interviewed at the firm of Hornblower, Bryne, Miller & Potter because it had never employed a Jew. During the interview the hiring partner suggested, "This is a good time to change your name. Frankfurter—you know, there's nothing the matter with it, but it's odd, funmaking." Even though he did not change his name, he was hired at a salary of $1,000 a year. He worked only a short time when the United States Attorney for New York, Henry L. Stimson, offered him a position as an assistant. Before accepting the position, Frankfurter did some intense soul-searching. He was concerned about leaving the Hornblower firm after being there for only a short time. Furthermore, the position as assistant United States Attorney paid only $750 a year. Later in life, however, he commented: "I knew at once I wanted to do that, because that solved my problem. I could practice law without having a client. There it was. Perfect. But I was in torture because I had said to Horn-blower, Bryne, Miller & Potter that I'd be their slave."

From 1906 until 1911, Frankfurter was Stimson's personal assistant and involved in much of the litigation handled by the office. This began a relationship that was to last until Stimson's death in 1950.

Concerning the time spent as Assistant United States Attorney, Frankfurter said: "Sure it was exciting—my years in the United States Attorney's Office. In the first place, having the government as a client you never have to defend a case that you don't believe in because in cases that had no merit, you'd say, 'No, Uncle Sam doesn't do this.' You don't indict people who oughtn't to be indicted when the United States Attorney was as scrupulous as Mr. Stimson was! I don't see how a young fellow coming to the bar could possibly have had a more desirable, more deepening, and altogether more precious influence during his formative years than to be junior to Henry L. Stimson."

Stimson was later appointed Secretary of War by President William H. Taft. "Stimson quickly offered Frankfurter the position of legal adviser in the department's Bureau of Insular Affairs," author Parrish writes, "with formal jurisdiction over legal issues that touched the nation's overseas possessions and territories, but with an informal understanding that he would also become the secretary's roving assistant and chief trouble shooter on all issues."[9]

Assistant to the Secretary of War

Frankfurter's duties included representing the Bureau in cases before the Supreme Court. He commented on those cases: "They came up from the Supreme Court of Puerto Rico and from the Supreme Court of the Philippines. I don't know how many cases I argued—six to eight—and of course that was very exciting for a youngster. That's how I came to know the Justices."[10]

The election of Woodrow Wilson to the presidency created a problem for Frankfurter as to his future. He did not know whether he should—or even could—remain in the War Department under a democratic president, or whether he should return to the practice of law, which he really did not want to do.

President Wilson appointed Lindley M. Garrison as his Secretary of War, and Frankfurter stayed in the Department for about a year.

Professor of Law at Harvard Law School

When consulted about Frankfurter being added to the Harvard faculty, Professor Edward H. Warren responded: "To a man, we want Frankfurter,"[11] but pointed out that the school did not have money to support adding a new faculty member. Subsequently a drive was commenced to raise funds for the new position.

Stimson, and other friends of Frankfurter, were less than enthusiastic about his becoming a professor. And former President Theodore Roosevelt "cautioned him that as a professor, 'You'll have to adjust your wants. You'll have to have a wife who'll be content with a simple life. Your salary will substantially remain the same for the rest of your life.' Holmes warned him against the academic life and the 'irresponsibility,' as Frankfurter paraphrased his advice, 'of running the universe on paper.' Brandeis, [however] ... urged him to do it...."[12]

Because of the advice suggesting that he not accept the professorship, Frankfurter wrote a memorandum to himself setting forth the pros and cons of the appointment. He finally concluded that "the problem at its lowest terms is not an irrevocable choice of public as against private life."[13]

Frankfurter began his career at Harvard during the summer of 1914, spending much time in research preparing for his first classes in the fall. "With respect to his abilities in the classroom," Michael E. Parrish has written, "students confirmed the observations of Brandeis and others: they ranked him below the school's great lecturers, but many of the ablest scrambled for the limited seats in his third-year seminars on administrative law, federal jurisdiction, or public utilities. 'There were no neutrals about Felix,' one recalled. 'You either thought the sun rose and set down his neck; or you despised him. My guess is that the vote would have gone about two-to-one in his favor.'"[14]

Love and Marriage

Frankfurter met Marion Denman before he left Washington for Harvard. Marion was "well bred, genteel, and concerned about social problems. She had graduated with honors from Smith College and briefly attended the New York School of Social Work. With her shimmering auburn hair and hazel eyes, she reminded [Harold] Laske of a portrait by Luini and he and Justice Holmes called her Luina. Sharp-tongued, intelligent, coquettish, and a trifle vain, she easily won Frankfurter's heart."[15]

The couple were married in December 1919. Frankfurter's mother Emma did not attend the ceremony "because she felt offended by the absence of religious sanctions and the fact that Felix had chosen a shicksa for his bride."

Joseph P. Lash provides this insight into the couple's relationship. "She was reserved but not unfriendly. Dr. Henry A. Murray, the Harvard professor of psychiatry who became a close friend of the Frankfurters, would later speak of her 'mysterious inwardness of spirit,' which, he thought, provided a balance to Frankfurter's 'expansive openness.' He was a 'door-hanger,' she would reproach him mildly, when on speeding a parting guest from their Brattle Street home, he was unable to resist adding another paragraph."[16]

But Marion also had her champions. "Many of the young law school men worshipped at Marion Frankfurter's shrine, and she repaid them with quiet, cynical observations, often at the Professor's expense...." Arthritis finally brought her down in the early 1950s, and she became an invalid. Thereafter Frankfurter devoted much of his time to her care and comfort. The Frankfurters had no children.

A Liberal Activist

Frankfurter was an active participant in many liberal causes. "One of the founders of the Civil Liberties Union, a legal advisor to the NAACP, counsel to the National Consumers' League, Frankfurter followed in the tradition of Brandeis, a close friend, as a 'people's counsel.'"[17]

He participated in the creation of *The New Republic*, "a new magazine of social and political criticism, whose purpose was 'to give a more vigorous, consistent, comprehensive, and enlightened expression to the Progressive principle than ... it receives from any existing publication.'"[18] Over the years, Frankfurter contributed many articles to the magazine.

On behalf of the National Consumers' League, Frankfurter argued and prevailed in several cases before the Supreme Court involving limitation of the working hours for men,[19] and minimum wages for women.[20]

Frankfurter supported Robert LaFollette, a third party candidate for president in the 1924 presidential election and signed a statement, "Why I Shall Vote for LaFollette."[21] "The LaFollette candidacy alone 'represents a determined effort to secure adequate attention for the great interests of the workers and of agriculture in those economic and social compromises which, in the last analysis, underlie all national action.'"

It was not LaFollette's specific program that attracted the Professor. "The specific program of LaFollette meant nothing to me," he said, "but the general direction in which he was going meant everything to me."[22]

One event that left an indelible mark upon both Marion and Felix Frankfurter was the execution of Nicola Sacco and Bartolomeo Vanzetti by the Commonwealth of Massachusetts. Sacco and Vanzetti were convicted of murdering a paymaster and guard during a robbery on April 15, 1920. "For the next seven years, the question of their guilt or innocence as well as the fairness of their trials shook the political and legal foundations of the commonwealth."[23]

"Sacco and Vanzetti's supporters," Parrish writes, "had a simple explanation for the guilty verdicts; they had been convicted by a bigoted judge and jury because they were Italians and anarchists at a time when public sentiment ran high against foreigners and radicals." The prosecution, however, had produced witnesses who saw the defendants at the scene of the crime, and one ballistic expert believed that bullets recovered from the bodies came from a gun owned by Sacco.

After reading the record of the trial, Frankfurter wrote an article for the *Atlantic Monthly* and a book entitled *The Sacco-Vanzetti Case*. Frankfurter's writings brought forth condemnation from Dean John H. Wigmore, of the Northwestern University Law School, and some of Harvard's alumni.

When the committee appointed by Governor Fuller concluded that Sacco and Vanzetti had been properly convicted and Fuller refused to intervene, the two men were executed on August 23, 1927.

A Zionist

On the Jewish High Holy Day of Rosh Hashanah in 1917, Frankfurter remarked to Katherine Ludington that he had been to New York City where "we had another ceremony ... I dreaded.... But somehow it came off very fittingly and on the right early Fall day. I'm rather happy that I can go through these symbolic religious events without a sense of discord or disrespect (by my mere presence) to the believers, tho the significance for me is not creedal."

At about the same time, his friend Walter Lippmann asked him: "What is a 'Jew' anyway?" And he responded: "A Jew is a person whom non-Jews regard as a Jew."[24]

Although Frankfurter never denied his Jewish background, the above quotation indicates that he was not a committed participant in Jewish ceremonies. When Louis D. Brandeis became active in the Zionist movement in 1914, he recruited Frankfurter, Federal Judge Julian Mack, Jacob deHaas and other prominent Jews to join him in the movement.

At the end of World War I, the British Government issued a call for a Jewish homeland in Palestine in a document known as the Balfour Declaration. Frankfurter and other members of the Zionist movement went to the Paris Peace Conference to secure the implementation of that Declaration. As events later indicated, there was much opposition to the establishment of a Jewish homeland, not only among Arabs but from local British officials in Palestine.

Lash reports that "Frankfurter's involvement with the Zionist movement at this time was so extensive that he was a major figure at the crucial Cleveland convention of the American Zionist movement in 1921. There the hard-headed Brandeis-Mack leadership was rejected for that of [Chaim] Weizmann, despite a four-hour speech by Frankfurter, the floor leader of the Brandeis-Mack group, that brought the audience to its feet cheering."[25]

Justices Oliver W. Holmes. Jr. and Louis D. Brandeis

In Washington Frankfurter began to develop relationships with two individuals who would be crucial for much of his life and all of his judicial career—Louis D. Brandeis and Oliver Wendell Holmes. Both of these relationships were highly significant emotionally for Frankfurter; both Holmes and Brandeis more or less adopted him. Both represented the power and influence Frankfurter sought for himself.[26]

The friendship of Brandeis and Frankfurter became especially close. "Still," Hirsch notes, "the Frankfurter-Brandeis relationship was not one of complete equals: Brandeis was very much an authority figure in Frankfurter's life. In 1916 Brandeis began sending Frankfurter money to cover his 'expenses in public matters undertaken at my request or following up my suggestion,' an unusual arrangement that lasted for a number of years. Their relationship was extremely close. Brandeis wrote to Frankfurter's mother in 1916: 'Your son has won so large a place in our hearts and brought so much joy and interest in our lives that we feel very near to you who are nearest to him.'"

Although Holmes and Frankfurter also had a very close relationship, Holmes did not approve of Frankfurter's liberalism.

Adviser to the President

Frankfurter was a supporter of both Theodore Roosevelt and Robert LaFollette during their respective political campaigns. But it was for Franklin D. Roosevelt that he became a trusted advisor. The two met at lunch in 1906 and saw each other when both were in Washington, D.C., during the early years of President Woodrow Wilson's administration.

However, it was not until Roosevelt was elected governor of New York in 1928 that Frankfurter began to cultivate a personal relationship with him which lasted until Roosevelt's death in 1945. Of their relationship, Hirsch comments: "The thirties found Felix Frankfurter center stage in New Deal Washington. Both as a personal advisor to FDR and as the man who would supply scores of Harvard men for the growing federal bureaucracy, Frankfurter's behavior had a profound impact upon the shape and substance of national policy. Although it took a bit of time for the Frankfurter-Roosevelt relationship to warm to the point where Frankfurter could play the part of a palace intimate, by the middle of the decade he was perhaps the single most important nonelected official in national government."[27]

Frankfurter's position in the Roosevelt administration was so important that during the summer of 1935 he lived at the White House. Of this experience, he wrote: "F. D. wants me really around—so that I've not dined out of the White House once."

Nomination to the Supreme Court

On July 9, 1938, Supreme Court Justice Benjamin N. Cardozo died suddenly, leaving a vacancy on the Court for Roosevelt to fill.

On the evening of January 4, 1939, according to Frankfurter, he and Marion were to entertain Professor Robert Morse Lovett of the University of Chicago. Morse arrived promptly at 7 o'clock, while Frankfurter was still in his BVDs. Marion admonished him: "Please hurry! You're always late." At that moment the telephone rang. When Frankfurter answered it, "there was the ebullient, the exuberant, resilient warmth-enveloping voice of the President of the United States..." After an exchange of greetings, the following conversation took place:

> PRESIDENT: You know, I told you I don't want to appoint you to the Supreme Court of the United States.
>
> FRANKFURTER: Yes, you told me that.
>
> PRESIDENT: I mean this. I mean this. I don't want to appoint you to the Supreme Court.
>
> FRANKFURTER: Yes, you told me that. You've made that perfectly clear. I understand that.
>
> PRESIDENT: But unless you give me an unsurmountable objection I'm going to send your name in for the Court tomorrow at twelve o'clock.
>
> FRANKFURTER: All I can say is that I wish my mother were alive.

Later, in recalling this conversation, Frankfurter noted that: "You know, he was given to teasing. Some people said that it was an innocently sadistic streak in him. He just had to have an outlet for fun."

In commenting on Frankfurter's nomination, author Parrish paints a somewhat different picture. "Later in life, Frankfurter always maintained that he had been totally surprised by Roosevelt's telephone call on the evening of January 4, when the president finally offered him the nomination. This image of Frankfurter, clad only in undershorts, struck dumb by Roosevelt's change of heart, has a certain romantic appeal—but it is wholly false."[28]

It is false, Parrish points out because immediately after Cardozo's death a number of Frankfurter's friends began a campaign to secure the nomination for him, and the candidate was fully aware of and participated in that effort.

Although there was some opposition to Frankfurter's nomination during the Senate Judiciary Committee hearings, when it reached the Senate floor Frankfurter was unanimously confirmed.

"He wore well-tailored suits and pince-nez, enjoyed fine food, and drank expensive wines," Parrish wrote of Frankfurter. "He never learned to drive an automobile, but he defended Tom Mooney, communist-anarchists during the worst days of the Red Scare, and Sacco and Vanzetti a few years later."[29]

When Frankfurter joined the Court, Charles Evans Hughes was Chief Justice. Other members of the Court were Justices James McReynolds, Louis D. Brandeis, Pierce Butler, Harlan F. Stone, Owen J. Roberts, Hugo L. Black, and Stanley Reed. Frankfurter served as an Associate Justice from January 17, 1939, until his retirement on August 28, 1962.

AS ASSOCIATE JUSTICE (1939–1962)

The Free Exercise of Religion

"A grave responsibility confronts this Court whenever in course of litigation it must reconcile the conflicting claims of liberty and authority. But when the liberty invoked is liberty of conscience, and the authority is authority to safeguard the nation's fellowship, judicial conscience is put to its severest test. Of such a nature is the present controversy."[30]

It was with those words that Justice Frankfurter opened his opinion in *Minersville District v. Gobitis*. That case involved the expulsion from school of Lillian Gobitis, 12, and her brother William, 10, for refusing to salute and to recite the Pledge of Allegiance to the American flag. The Gobitis family, as members of Jehovah's Witnesses, believed that their children's participation in this ceremony violated God's commandment "not to make unto thee any graven image, or any likeness of any thing that is in heaven above, or that is in the earth beneath, or that is in the water under the earth."

Walter Gobitis, father of Lillian and William, brought an action on behalf of his children in the Federal District Court in Pennsylvania seeking a court order requiring the School District to reinstate the children. Judge Albert B. Maris upheld Gobitis's contention that the suspension violated the First Amendment's free exercise of religion clause and ordered the children reinstated. Judge Maris's decision was affirmed by the Circuit Court but reversed by the Supreme Court, with only Justice Harlan F. Stone dissenting.

Frankfurter, for the Court, recognized that "the affirmative pursuit of one's convictions about the ultimate mystery of the universe and man's relation to it is placed beyond the reach of law." But, he noted, "the manifold character of man's relations may bring his conception of religious duty into conflict with the secular interests of his fellow-men." And this led him to the question: "When does the constitutional guarantee compel exemption from doing what society thinks necessary for the promotion of some great common end, or from a penalty for conduct which appears dangerous to the general good?" The answer to that question, according to the Justice, lay in reconciling these two interests keeping in mind that "we are dealing with interests so subtle and so dear, every possible leeway should be given to the claims of religious faith."

The "common end" sought by Pennsylvania in requiring students to participate in the ceremony, Frankfurter concluded, was "national unity." "The ultimate foundation of a free society," the Justice asserted, "is the binding tie of cohesive sentiment. Such a sentiment is fostered by all those agencies of the mind and spirit which may serve to gather up the traditions of a people, transmit them from generation to generation, and thereby create that continuity of a treasured common life which constitutes civilization."

"What the school authorities are really asserting," he continued, "is the right to awaken in the child's mind considerations as to the significance of the flag contrary to those implanted by the parent." Balancing this asserted governmental interest against the religious beliefs of the children leads to only one conclusion, according to the Justice.

> A society which is dedicated to the preservation of ... ultimate values of civilization may in self-protection utilize the educational process for inculcating those almost unconscious feelings which bind men together in a comprehending loyalty, whatever may be their lesser differences and difficulties. That is to say, the process may be utilized so long as men's right to believe as they please, to win others to their way of belief, and their right to assemble in their chosen places of worship for the devotional ceremonies of their faith, are all fully respected.

The *Gobitis* case did not bring an end to the controversy regarding the constitutionality of requiring school children to salute the flag and recite the Pledge of Allegiance. Three years later, the Supreme Court reached the opposite conclusion and overruled *Gobitis* in *Board of Education v. Barnette*.[31]

Walter Barnette, and others, brought an action on behalf of their children to have the salute and pledge requirement of West Virginia declared unconstitutional. Barnette and the others were also members of Jehovah's Witnesses, and they too argued that participation in such a ceremony was a violation of the Second Commandment. In overruling *Gobitis*, three of the justices who were in the majority in that case changed their position and voted to strike down the West Virginia requirement. These justices were Hugo L. Black, William O. Douglas and Frank Murphy. Justice Frankfurter dissented, and opened his opinion as follows:

> One who belongs to the most vilified and persecuted minority in history is not likely to be insensible to the freedom guaranteed by our Constitution. Were my purely personal attitude relevant I should wholeheartedly associate myself with the general libertarian views in the Court's opinion, representing as they do the thought and action of a lifetime. But as judges we are neither Jew nor Gentile, neither Catholic nor agnostic. We owe equal attachment to the Constitution and are equally bound by our judicial obligations whether we derive our citizenship from the earliest or the latest immigrants to these shores. As a member of this Court I am not justified in writing my private notions of policy into the Constitution, no matter how deeply I may cherish them or how mischievous I may deem their disregard.

This led him to conclude: "I cannot bring my mind to believe that the 'liberty' secured by the Due Process Clause gives this Court authority to deny to the State of West Virginia the attainment of that which we all recognize as a legitimate legislative end, namely, the promotion of good citizenship, by employment of the means here chosen."

Frankfurter then returned to the theme set forth in his *Gobitis* opinion. "An act compelling profession of allegiance to a religion," he noted, "no matter how subtly or tenuously promoted, is bad. But, an act of promoting good citizenship and national allegiance is within the domain of governmental authority and is therefore to be judged by the same considerations of power and of constitutionality as those involved in the many claims of immunity from civil obedience because of religious scruples."

Frankfurter then discusses his belief that it is not the function of judges to make decisions based on their personal views. "The uncontrollable power wielded by this Court," he declared, "brings it very close to the most sensitive areas of public affairs. As appeal from legislation to adjudication becomes more frequent, and its consequences more far-reaching, judicial self-restraint becomes more and not less important, lest we unwarrantably enter social and political domains wholly outside our concern. I think I appreciate fully the objections to the law before us. But to deny that it presents a question upon which men might reasonably differ appears to me to be intolerance. And since men may so reasonably differ, I deem it beyond my constitutional power to assert my view of the wisdom of this law against the view of the State of West Virginia."

The Jehovah's Witnesses won three more cases on May 3, 1943, when the Court struck down the convictions of Witnesses for violating city ordinances that restricted door-to-door solicitation.[32] In two of the cases, the solicitor was required to secure a license and pay a fee before going door-to-door. The third case involved an ordinance that prohibited all such solicitation. In discussing door-to-door solicitation, Justice Black, writing for the majority, pointed out: "The hand distribution of religious tracts is an age-old form of missionary evangelism—as old as the history of printing presses. It has been a potent force in various religious movements down through the years. This form of evangelism is utilized today on a large scale by various religious sects whose colporteurs carry the Gospel to thousands upon thousands of homes and seek through personal visitations to win adherents to their faith. ... This form of religious activity occupies the same high estate under the First Amendment as do worship in the churches and preaching from pulpits. It has the same claim to protection as the more orthodox and conventional exercises of religion."[33]

This led the majority to conclude that an ordinance which requires a license and the payment of a fee for the right to solicit was "a flat tax imposed on the exercise of a privilege granted by the Bill of Rights," and that a "state may not impose a charge for enjoyment of a right granted by the Federal Constitution."

Justice Frankfurter dissented in all three cases. He did not agree with the majority "that the [Jehovah's Witnesses] ... [were] constitutionally exempt from taxation merely because they may be engaged in religious activities or because such activities may constitute an exercise of a constitutional right."[34] He argued that the petitioners were no different than clergymen, [or even judges], who must pay taxes. "It is only fair that he also who preaches the word of God should share in the costs of the benefits provided by government to him as well as to the other members of the community."

The Justice sums up his position with regard to the tax issue as follows:

> All members of the Court are equally familiar with the history that led to the adoption of the Bill of Rights and are equally zealous to enforce the constitutional protection of the free play of the human spirit. ... The real issue here is not whether a city may charge for the dissemination of ideas but whether the states have power to require those who need additional facilities to help bear the cost of furnishing such facilities. Street hawkers make demands upon municipalities that involve the expenditure of dollars and cents, whether they hawk printed matter or other things. As the facts in these cases show, the cost of maintaining the peace, the additional demands upon governmental facilities for assuring security, involve outlays which have to be met.

It was orthodox Jews who sought help from the Court rather than Jehovah's Witnesses in *McGowan v. Maryland*,[35] and *Braunfeld v. Brown*.[36] In these cases, the "Orthodox Jewish retailers and their Orthodox Jewish customers ... [contended that] the Massachusetts Lord's day statute and the Pennsylvania Sunday retail sales act violate the Due Process Clause of the Fourteenth Amendment because, in effect, the statutes deter the exercise and observance of their religion."

The Jewish merchants argued that their Orthodox Jewish faith required them to close their businesses from nightfall Friday until nightfall on Saturday, and that compliance with Sunday closing laws would require them to also close on Sundays. The only way to avoid the loss of two days' business would be to open on Saturday in violation of their religious beliefs. Forcing them to make the choice between their faith and economic survival, they asserted, violated their First Amendment right to the free exercise of religion. A majority of the Court, including Justice Frankfurter, disagreed and upheld the laws.

The court majority believed that "the Sunday law simply regulates a secular activity, and ... operates so as to make the practice of their religious beliefs more expensive."

After an extensive discussion of the history of Sunday closing laws, Frankfurter, in a concurring opinion, concluded that there were "substantial nonecclesiastical"[37] purposes for their enactment.

The Justice's response to the issue of whether Sunday closing laws violated the free exercise rights of the Jewish merchants was: "These statutes do not make criminal, do not place under the onus of civil or criminal disability, any act which is itself prescribed by the duties of the Jewish or other religions. They do create an undeniable financial burden upon the observers of one of the fundamental tenets of certain religious creeds, a burden which does not fall equally upon other forms of observance." "But," he continues, "without minimizing the fact of this disadvantage, the legislature may have concluded that its severity might be offset by the industry and commercial initiative of the individual merchant. More is demanded of him, admittedly, whether in the form of additional labor or of material sacrifices, than is demanded of those who do not choose to keep his Sabbath. ... In view of the importance of the community interests which must be weighed in the balance, is the disadvantage wrought by the non-exempting Sunday statues an impermissible imposition upon the Sabbatarian's religious freedom? Every court which has considered the question during a century and a half has concluded that it is not."

Justice Potter Stewart's response, in dissent, was that making "an Orthodox Jew ... choose between his religious faith and his economic survival ... is a cruel choice. It is a choice which I think no State can constitutionally demand."[38]

Freedom of Speech

Picketing and Parading. "Peaceful picketing is the workingman's means of communication."[39] With those words, the Justice recognized that the First Amendment's freedom of speech clause protects the right to peacefully picket. In cases in which he expressed his opinion on the validity of the picketing involved, however, he voted against the picketers when he thought they were participating in violence and when the picketing was contrary to state public policy.

Frankfurter wrote the Court's opinion in *Drivers Union v. Meadowmoor*,[40] upholding an injunction which prohibited a union from engaging in picketing, violent or peaceful. The ban against peaceful picketing, he argued, was justified because the "picketing in this case was set in a background of violence. In such a setting it could justifiably be concluded that the momentum of fear generated by past violence would survive even though future picketing might be wholly peaceful." And he concluded his opinion by pointing out that "freedom of speech and freedom of the press cannot be too often invoked as basic to our scheme of society. But these liberties will not be advanced or even maintained by denying to the states with all their resources, including the instrumentality of their courts, the power to deal with coercion due to extensive violence."

Justice Stanley Reed saw the case differently. Taking note of the fact that there was "no finding that violence was planned or encouraged by the union," he concluded that to "deny ... [the] right of peaceful picketing to thousands because of the violence of a few means the cutting off of one of the constitutionally protected ways in which orderly adjustments of economic disputes are brought about."

When the picketing was peaceful, Frankfurter and the Court gave it First Amendment protection. The Court, therefore, struck down a permanent injunction against picketing a beauty parlor in an attempt to unionize its employees, because the evidence indicated that the picketing was peaceful.[41] Illinois attempted to justify the injunction on the ground that the picketers were not in the employ of the beauty parlor. "A state cannot," Justice Frankfurter declared, "exclude workingmen from peacefully exercising the right of free communication by drawing the circle of economic competition between employers and workers so small as to contain only an employer and those directly employed by him."

If, however, the picketing was in violation of a state public policy, that was enough for the Court and the Justice to affirm an injunction against it. That was what happened in *Carpenters Union v. Ritter's Cafe.*[42] The facts of the case: "Ritter ... [had] made an agreement with a contractor named Plaster for construction of a building at 2810 Broadway, Houston, Texas. The contract gave Plaster the right to make his own arrangements regarding the employment of labor in the construction of the building. He employed non-union carpenters and painters. [Ritter] was also the owner of Ritter's Cafe, a restaurant at 418 Broadway, a mile and a half away. So far as the record discloses, the new building was wholly unconnected with the business of Ritter's Cafe. All of the restaurant employees were members of the Hotel and Restaurant Employees International Alliance, Local 808."

The carpenters' and painters' unions picketed Ritter's Cafe, and the members of Local 808 joined them. The picketing caused members of other unions to refuse to cross the picket lines. Ritter, therefore, sought—and the court issued—an injunction against the picketers, being of the opinion that the picketing in this case was a violation of a Texas law which made it unlawful to engage in restraint of trade. The Supreme Court affirmed, with Frankfurter writing the Court's opinion.

The Justice acknowledged that the "constitutional right to communicate peaceably to the public facts of a legitimate dispute is not lost merely because a labor dispute is involved, ... or because the communication takes the form of picketing, even when the communication does not concern a dispute between an employer and those directly employed by him."

"In the circumstances of the case before us," Justice Frankfurter wrote, "Texas has declared that its general welfare would not be served if, in a controversy between a contractor and building workers' unions, the unions were permitted to bring to bear the full weight of familiar weapons of industrial combat against a restaurant business, which, as a business, has no nexus with the building dispute but which happens to be owned by a person who contracts with the builder."

Although acknowledging that "peaceful picketing may be a phase of the constitutional right of free utterance," the Justice argued that "[r]estriction of picketing to the area of the industry within which a labor dispute arises leaves open to the disputants other traditional modes of communication. To deny to the states the power to draw this line is to write into the Constitution the notion that every instance of peaceful picketing—anywhere and under any circumstances—is necessarily a phase of the controversy which provoked the picketing." "We [therefore] hold," he concluded, "that the Constitution does not forbid Texas to draw the line which has been drawn here. To hold otherwise would be to transmute vital constitutional liberties into doctrinaire dogma."

Justice Reed closed a dissenting opinion by noting that the "decision withdraws federal constitutional protection from the freedom of workers outside an industry to state their side of a labor controversy by picketing. So long as civil government is able to function normally for the protection of its citizens, such a limitation upon free speech is unwarranted."

Frankfurter's deference to state policy to uphold restriction upon peaceful picketing emerged again in *Teamsters Union v. Vogt, Inc.*[43] In this case, the Court upheld a Wisconsin statute that "prohibited picketing in the absence of a 'labor dispute,'" and allowed an injunction against peaceful picketing during which a union sought to induce employees of a gravel pit to join their union. After reviewing a number of prior cases, the Justice concluded: "This series of cases, then, established a broad field in which a State, in enforcing some public policy, whether of its criminal or its civil law, and whether announced by its legislature or its courts, could constitutionally enjoin peaceful picketing aimed at preventing effectuation of that policy."

Justice William O. Douglas thought the decision was a "formal surrender" of the Court's control over labor picketing. He commented in dissent: "State courts and state legislatures are [now] free to decide whether to permit or suppress any particular picket line for any reason other than a blanket policy against all picketing." He preferred the conclusions reached in prior cases that "this form of expression can be regulated or prohibited only to the extent that it forms an essential part of a course of conduct which the State can regulate or prohibit."

Pamphleteering and Soliciting. Illinois charged that Joseph Beauharnais "did unlawfully ... exhibit in public places lithographs, which publications portray depravity, criminality, unchastity or lack of virtue of citizens of Negro race and color and which exposes ... citizens of Illinois of the Negro race and color to contempt, derision, or obloquy...."[44] This was a crime known as criminal libel.

At one of the meetings of the White Circle League, of which Beauharnais was president, he passed out pamphlets calling upon the "'[o]ne million self respecting white people in Chicago to unite' .... with the statement added that 'If persuasion and the need to prevent the white race from becoming mongrelized by the negro will not unite us, then the aggressions ... rapes, robberies, knives, guns and marijuana of the negro, surely will.'"

Beauharnais was convicted and, being unable to secure reversal by the Supreme Court of Illinois, appealed to the U.S. Supreme Court. He was not successful there either, with Justice Frankfurter writing the Court's opinion. "The precise question before us, then," he said, "is whether the protection of 'liberty' in the Due Process Clause of the Fourteenth Amendment prevents a State from punishing such libels—as criminal libel has been defined, limited and constitutionally recognized time out of mind—directed at designated collectivities and flagrantly disseminated."

In reaching the conclusion that Illinois could punish this kind of publication, the Justice relied upon prior cases in which the Court had held that libelous publications were not protected by the First Amendment's guarantee of freedom of the press. That being the case, it logically followed that the Constitution did not prevent Illinois from enacting this law. "But it bears repeating—although it should not—," Frankfurter argued, "that our finding that the law is not constitutionally objectionable carries no implication of approval of the wisdom of the legislation or of its efficacy. These questions may raise doubts in our minds as well as in others. It is not for us, however, to make the legislative judgment. We are not at liberty to erect those doubts into fundamental law."

Justice Douglas thought that the Court's decision "places speech under an expanding legislative control." "Today," he declared, "a white man stands convicted for protesting in unseemly language against our decisions invalidating restrictive covenants. Tomorrow a Negro will be haled before a court for denouncing lynch law in heated terms. Farm laborers in the West who compete with field hands drifting up from Mexico; whites who feel the pressure of orientals; a minority which finds employment going to members of the dominant religious group—all of these are caught in the mesh of today's decision. Debate and argument even in the courtroom are not always calm and dispassionate. Emotions sway speakers and audiences alike. Intemperate speech is a distinctive characteristic of man. Hot-heads blow off and release destructive energy in the process. They shout and rave, exaggerating weaknesses, magnifying error, viewing with alarm. So it has been from the beginning; and so it will be throughout time."

Rose Staub, an employee of the International Ladies' Garment Workers Union, would have received the same consideration as did Beauharnais if Frankfurter had his way. Staub and Mamie Merritt went to Baxley, Georgia, to solicit membership in the union but did not apply for a license to solicit as required by a Baxley law. Staub was arrested and convicted of violating the ordinance and sentenced to jail for 30 days and ordered to pay a $300 fine. Despite Staub's contention that the ordinance was unconstitutional as a violation of the Free Speech Clause of the First Amendment, her conviction was upheld by the Supreme Court of Georgia. In an opinion written by Justice Charles E. Whittaker, the U.S. Supreme Court reversed.[45]

It is settled by a long line of recent decisions of this Court that an ordinance which, like this one, makes the peaceful enjoyment of freedoms which the Constitution guarantees contingent upon the uncontrolled will of an official— as by requiring a permit or license which may be granted or withheld in the discretion of such official—is an unconstitutional censorship or prior restraint upon the enjoyment of those freedoms.

Justice Frankfurter dissented on the ground that the Supreme Court did not have jurisdiction of Staub's appeal because she had not applied for a permit and did not specify which sections of the ordinance she thought were unconstitutional as required by Georgia law. States, he argued, have a "wide discretion ... to formulate their own procedures for bringing issues appropriately to the attention of their local courts..." "Such methods and procedures may," he continued, "when judged by the best standards of judicial administration, appear crude, awkward and even finicky or unnecessarily formal when judged in the light of modern emphasis on informality. But so long as the local procedure does not discriminate against the raising of federal claims and, in the particular case, has not been used to stifle a federal claim to prevent its eventual consideration here, this Court is powerless to deny to a State the right to have the kind of judicial system it chooses and to administer that system in its own way."

Unpopular Speech. "On the evening of March 8, 1949, petitioner Irving Feiner was addressing an open-air meeting at the corner of South McBride and Harrison Streets in the City of Syracuse, [New York]. At approximately 6:30 p.m., the police received a telephone complaint concerning the meeting and two officers were detailed to investigate. ... They found a crowd of about seventy-five or eighty people, both Negro and white, filling the sidewalk and spreading out into the street. [Feiner], standing on a large wooden box on the sidewalk, was addressing the crowd through a loud-speaker system attached to an automobile. Although the purpose of his speech was to urge his listeners to attend a meeting to be held that night in the Syracuse Hotel, in its course he was making derogatory remarks concerning President Truman, the American Legion, the Mayor of Syracuse, and other local political officials. ... Some of the onlookers made remarks to the police about their inability to handle the crowd and at least one threatened violence if the police did not act. There were others who appeared to be favoring ... [Feiner's] arguments. Because of the feeling that existed in the crowd both for and against the speaker, the officers finally 'stepped in to prevent it from resulting in a fight.'"[46]

Feiner was charged with and convicted of breach of the peace, and his conviction was upheld by the appellate courts of New York and the Supreme Court, with Justices Black, Douglas and Sherman Minton dissenting. The disagreement among the Justices focused upon whether the police should have protected Feiner, the speaker, by controlling the crowd. Writing for the majority, Chief Justice Fred Vinson concluded that the "findings of the state courts as to the existing situation and the imminence of greater disorder coupled with petitioner's deliberate defiance of the police officers convince us that we should not reverse this conviction in the name of free speech." Justice Frankfurter agreed. "It is pertinent, therefore, to note," he wrote, "that all members of the New York Court accepted the finding that Feiner was stopped not because the listeners or police disagreed with his views but because these officers were honestly concerned with preventing a breach of the peace." And further, "[i]t is not a constitutional principle that, in acting to preserve order, the police must proceed against the crowd, whatever its size and temper, and not against the speaker."

The top eleven officials of the Communist Party received no greater consideration from the Court than did Feiner. Court of Appeals Judge Learned Hand described the case:

> The case was tried at great length. The defendants challenged the array, [proceedings] and the trial of that issue extended from January 20, 1949, to March 1, 1949; the trial of the issues began the following week and went on continuously until September 23, 1949. The jury brought in a verdict against all the defendants on October 14, 1949, and they were sentenced on October 21, 1949. The trial of the challenge to the array took 23 days; the government's case on the issues took 40 days, and the appellants, 75 days.[47]

The eleven defendants were Jacob Stachel, Carl Winter, Eugene Dennis, Henry Winston, Irving Potash, Benjamin J. Davis, Jr., John Gates, Gilbert Green, John B. Williamson, Gus Hall, and Robert G. Thompson. They were charged with violating a federal law, commonly known as the Smith Act, which made it unlawful "to knowingly or willfully advocate, abet, advise, or teach the duty, necessity, desirability, or propriety of overthrowing or destroying any government in the United States by force or violence..."[48]

Among the issues presented to the Supreme Court on appeal of the convictions were, (1) was the Smith Act unconstitutional under the First Amendment? and (2) did the defendants violate the law by their activities? The Court answered both questions in the affirmative and upheld the jury's verdicts. "We hold that ... [the various sections] of the Smith Act do not inherently, or as construed or applied in the instant case, violate the First Amendment and other provisions of the Bill of Rights.... Petitioners intended to overthrow the Government of the United States as speedily as the circumstances would permit. Their conspiracy to organize the Communist Party and to teach and advocate the overthrow of the Government of the United States by force and violence created a 'clear and present danger' of an attempt to overthrow the Government by force and violence. They were properly and constitutionally convicted for violation of the Smith Act."

Justice Frankfurter concurred in the judgment but did not join the Court's opinion. For him, the case presented only one question: "In enacting a statute which makes it a crime for defendants to conspire to do what they have been found to have conspired to do, did Congress exceed its constitutional power?" In other words, had Congress violated the First Amendment by the enactment of the Smith Act? His response was that it had not. The Justice acknowledged that "[t]he right of a man to think what he pleases, to write what he thinks, and to have his thoughts made available for others to hear or read has an engaging ring of universality." But, he pointed out: "The historic antecedents of the First Amendment preclude the notion that its purpose was to give unqualified immunity to every expression that touched on matters within the range of political interest." While the proper way to solve the clash between free speech and national security is to weigh these competing interests, there remains the question who is the proper authority to do this balancing. Frankfurter argues that "[f]ull responsibility for the choice cannot be given to the courts. Courts are not representative bodies. They are not designed to be a good reflex of a democratic society." Therefore, the "[p]rimary responsibility for adjusting the interests which compete in the situation before us of necessity belongs to the Congress."

"It is not for us," he argues, "to decide how we would adjust the clash of interests which this case presents were the primary responsibility for reconciling it ours. Congress has determined that the danger created by advocacy of overthrow justifies the ensuing restriction on freedom of speech. The determination was made after due deliberation, and the seriousness of the congressional purpose is attested by the volume of legislation passed to effectuate the same ends.

Justice Black saw this decision as a watering down of the values of the First Amendment. "Public opinion being what it now is," he noted in dissent, "few will protest the conviction of these Communist petitioners. There is hope, however, that in calmer times, when present pressures, passions and fears subside, this or some later Court will restore the First Amendment liberties to the high preferred place where they belong in a free society."

Miscellaneous Speech. "Appellant [Samuel Saia] is a minister of the religious sect known as Jehovah's Witnesses. He obtained from the Chief of Police permission to use sound equipment, mounted atop his car, to amplify lectures on religious subjects. ... When this permit expired, he applied for another one but was refused on the ground that complaints had been made. Appellant nevertheless used his equipment as planned on four occasions, but without a permit. He was tried in Police Court for violations of the ordinance. It was undisputed that he used his equipment to amplify speeches in the park and that they were on religious subjects. Some witnesses testified that they were annoyed by the sound, though not by the content of the addresses; others were not disturbed by either. The court upheld the ordinance against the contention that it violated appellant's rights of freedom of speech, assembly, and worship under the Federal Constitution. Fines and jail sentences were imposed. His convictions were affirmed without opinion by the County Court for Niagara County and by the New York Court of Appeals."[49]

Because the ordinance in question gave the Chief of Police the authority to grant permits but contained no standards to guide him in doing so, the Supreme Court reversed. Citing several prior cases,[50] Justice Douglas for the majority pointed out: "The right to be heard is placed in the uncontrolled discretion of the Chief of Police. He stands athwart the channels of communication as an obstruction which can be removed only after criminal trial and conviction and lengthy appeal. A more effective previous restraint is difficult to imagine."

Frankfurter disagreed. He responded to Douglas's contention that the ordinance gave the Chief of Police too much discretion in granting or denying permits by noting that "it is not unconstitutional for a State to vest in a public official the determination of what is in effect a nuisance merely because such authority may be outrageously misused by trying to stifle the expression of some undesired opinion under the meretricious cloak of a nuisance. Judicial remedies are available for such abuse to enforce such remedies."

The case of *Kovacs v. Cooper*,[51] also involving sound trucks, brought forth a discussion whether the First Amendment occupied a "preferred position" in the hierarchy of constitutional values. Kovacs was convicted of violating a Trenton, N.J., ordinance making it unlawful to use sound amplification devices on the city streets which emitted "loud and raucous noises." His conviction was affirmed by the Supreme Court. Three justices were of the opinion that it was "a permissible exercise of legislative discretion to bar sound trucks with broadcasts of public interest, amplified to a loud and raucous volume from the public ways of municipalities."

Frankfurter and Justice Robert H. Jackson concurred, relying principally upon their dissents in the *Saia* case. Frankfurter, however, took the occasion to discuss at length "the preferred position of freedom of speech." The preferred position of freedom of speech, he writes "is a phrase that has uncritically crept into some recent opinions of this Court. I deem it a mischievous phrase, if it carries the thought, which it may subtly imply, that any law touching communication is infected with presumptive invalidity. ... I say the phrase is mischievous because it radiates a constitutional doctrine without avowing it. Clarity and candor in these matters, so as to avoid gliding unwittingly into error, make it appropriate to trace the history of the phrase 'preferred position.'"

After examining the cases in which the Court has used the phrase, he concludes that "the claim that any legislation is presumptively unconstitutional which touches the field of the First Amendment ... has never commended itself to a majority of this Court."

Having said that, the Justice turned to the regulation of sound trucks, and finding them different from natural speech, concluded that it was within the province of legislatures to regulate them.

Frankfurter's discussion of the "preferred position of freedom of speech" brought a comment from Justice Wiley B. Rutledge. "I think my brother Frankfurter demonstrates the conclusion opposite to that which he draws, namely, that the First Amendment guaranties of the freedoms of speech, press, assembly and religion occupy preferred position not only in the Bill of Rights but also in the repeated decisions of this Court."

Freedom of Association

Affidavits and Oaths. "Wrapped up in this problem are two great concerns of our democratic society—the right of association for economic and social betterment and the right of association for political purposes."[52]

With those words, the Justice recognized the existence of a constitutional right to freely associate for the advancement of economic and political purposes. He does not, however, refer to any particular constitutional provision that guarantees this right, but presumably had in mind the First Amendment, which protects the freedoms of speech and assembly.

Having recognized a right of association, Frankfurter nevertheless agreed with the majority that freedom was not infringed upon by a federal requirement that officers of labor unions file with the National Labor Relations Board an affidavit that they were not members of the Communist Party.

"It must suffice for me to say that the judgment of Congress that trade unions which are guided by officers who are committed by ties of membership to the Communist Party must forego the advantages of the Labor Management Relations Act is reasonably related to the accomplishment of the purposes which Congress constitutionally had a right to pursue."

"Congress," Frankfurter argued, "was concerned with what it justifiably deemed to be the disorganizing purposes of Communists who hold positions of official power in labor unions, or, at least, what it might well deem their lack of disinterested devotion to the basic tenets of the American trade union movement because of a higher loyalty to a potentially conflicting cause."

He was of the opinion, however, that the part of the law which required a labor union officer to affirm that he or she "'does not believe in, and is not a member of or supports any organization that believes in ... the overthrow of the United States Government ... by an illegal or unconstitutional methods,'" was an unconstitutional requirement. "It is asking more than rightfully may be asked of ordinary men to take oath that a method is not 'unconstitutional' or 'illegal' when constitutionality or legality is frequently determined by this Court by the chance of a single vote."

While Justice Frankfurter voted to uphold an oath which required denial of membership in the Communist Party,[53] he joined the Court in striking down an oath requirement for all government employees, including teachers, in Oklahoma. Oklahoma's oath required all state employees to affirm that they were "not affiliated directly or indirectly … with any foreign political agency, party, organization or group … which has been officially determined by the United States Attorney General … to be a communist front or subversive organization."[54]

The majority declared the oath to be unconstitutional because it condemned both innocent and knowing membership, a position with which the Justice agreed. "Since the affiliation which must thus be forsworn," he declared, "may well have been for reasons or for purposes as innocent as membership in a club of one of the established political parties, to require such an oath, on pain of a teacher's loss of his position in case of refusal to take the oath, penalizes a teacher for exercising a right of association peculiarly characteristic of our people."

Blacklisting and Punishment for Membership. When Attorney General Tom C. Clark listed the Joint Anti-Fascist Refugee Committee, the National Council of American-Soviet Friendship, Inc., and the International Workers Order, Inc., as communist organizations, each brought legal action to have its name removed from the list. These cases were dismissed by the trial court "for failure to state a claim upon which relief can be granted."[55] The Supreme Court reversed, and ordered the cases to be heard.

In a concurring opinion, Justice Frankfurter pointed out that these organizations "have been designated 'communist' by the Attorney General of the United States. This designation imposes no legal sanction on these organizations other than that it serves as evidence ridding the Government of persons reasonably suspected of disloyalty. It would be blindness, however, not to recognize that in the conditions of our time such designation drastically restricts the organizations, if it does not proscribe them. Potential members, contributors or beneficiaries of listed organizations may well be influenced by use of the designation, for instance, as ground for rejection of applications for commissions in the armed forces or permits for meetings in the auditoriums of public housing projects." Due process, the Justice argued, required that these organizations be given a hearing on their claim that they were not communist. "No better instrument has been devised for arriving at truth than to give a person in jeopardy of serious loss notice of the case against him and opportunity to meet it. Nor has a better way been found for generating the feeling, so important to a popular government, that justice has been done."

The question in *Harisiades v. Shaughnessy*[56] was not the validity of listing an organization as communist, but "whether the United States constitutionally may deport a legally resident alien because of membership in the Communist Party which terminated before the enactment of the Alien Registration Act of 1940."

Peter Harisiades came to the United States in 1916 at the age of thirteen. He joined the Communist Party in 1925 and served in various official capacities until October 1939, when he was dropped from the party because he was not a citizen. Proceedings to deport Harisiades were started in 1930 but not served until 1946. After procedural hearings he was ordered deported, and he appealed. The Supreme Court upheld the deportation order, with Justice Frankfurter concurring. One of the arguments made by Harisiades was that being a member of the Communist Party was protected by the First Amendment, and therefore deportation was unconstitutional. The majority disagreed, being of the opinion that the "Constitution sought to leave no excuse for violent attack on the status quo by providing a legal alternative—attack by ballot. To arm all men for orderly change, the Constitution put in their hands a right to influence the electorate by press, speech and assembly. This means freedom to advocate or promote Communism by means of the ballot box, but it does not include the practice or incitement of violence."

For Justice Frankfurter, the solution to this case was quite simple. "The conditions for entry of every alien, the particular classes of aliens that shall be denied entry altogether, the basis for determining such classification, the right to terminate hospitality to aliens, the grounds on which such determination shall be based, have been recognized as matters solely for the responsibility of the Congress and wholly outside the power of this Court to control."

Frankfurter was forced to address the First Amendment issues in cases involving the Communist Party in the United States in the case of the *Communist Party v. Control Board.*[57] After conducting hearings, the Subversive Activities Control Board ordered the Communist Party to register as a "Communist-action organization." The Party appealed, but the order was upheld by the Court of Appeals and the Supreme Court, with the Justice writing the Supreme Court's opinion.

In discussing the relevance of the First Amendment to this case, the Justice wrote: "Of course, congressional power in this sphere, as in all spheres, is limited by the First Amendment. Individual liberties fundamental to American institutions are not to be destroyed under pretext of preserving those institutions, even from the gravest external dangers. But where the problems of accommodating the exigencies of self-preservation and the values of liberty are as complex and intricate as they are in the situation described in the findings of … the Subversive Activities Control Act—when existing government is menaced by a world-wide integrated movement which employs every combination of possible means, peaceful and violent, domestic and foreign, overt and clandestine, to destroy the government itself—the legislative judgment as to how that threat may best be met consistently with the safeguarding of personal freedom is not to be set aside merely because the judgment of judges would, in the first instance, have chosen other methods."

Justice Black's response was somewhat different. "I would reverse this case," he declared, "and leave the Communists free to advocate their beliefs in proletarian dictatorship publicly and openly among the people of this country with full confidence that the people will remain loyal to any democratic

Government truly dedicated to freedom and justice—the kind of Government which some of us still think of as being 'the last best hope of earth.'"

Associational Privacy. After graduating from the University of New Mexico School of Law, Rudolph Schware applied for admission to the New Mexico bar. The Board of Bar Examiners denied the request after a hearing on the merits, giving as reasons for denial "the use of aliases by the applicant, his former connection with subversive organizations, and his record of arrests."[58]

Schware told the Board that he grew up in a poor family, became interested in socialism and trade-unionism, and had joined the Young Communist League and the Communist Party, from which he resigned in 1940. Because he was a Jew, he used the name Di Caprio to avoid discrimination in getting employment. He had been arrested during a maritime strike on the West Coast, but never prosecuted. He was a paratrooper during World War II and later entered law school, where he had an exemplary record.

When the New Mexico Supreme Court upheld the denial of a license to practice law, Schware appealed to the U.S. Supreme Court, which reversed. "The State contends that even though the use of aliases, the arrests, and the membership in the Communist Party would not justify exclusion of ... [Schware] from the New Mexico bar if each stood alone, when all three are combined his exclusion was not unwarranted. We cannot accept this contention. ... There is no evidence in the record which rationally justifies a finding that Schware was morally unfit to practice law."

Justice Frankfurter concurred. He acknowledged that it was "beyond this Court's function to act as overseer of a particular result of the procedure established by a particular State for admission to its bar." "But," he continued, "judicial action, even in an individual case, may have been based on avowed considerations that are inadmissible in that they violate the requirements of due process. Refusal to allow a man to qualify himself for the profession on a wholly arbitrary standard or on a consideration that offends the dictates of reason offends the Due Process Clause. Such is the case here."

The Justice was particularly concerned over the inferences that had been drawn from Schware's Communist Party membership. "To hold, as the [New Mexico] court did, that Communist affiliation for six to seven years up to 1940, fifteen years prior to the court's assessment of it, in and of itself made the petitioner 'a person of questionable character' is so dogmatic an inference as to be wholly unwarranted."

Frankfurter was also concerned about the First Amendment rights of Paul M. Sweezy. Sweezy had been called to testify twice by New Hampshire Attorney General Wyman, who was conducting an investigation into communist activities in that state. Sweezy testified that he had not been a member of the Communist Party "or that he had ever been part of any program to overthrow the government by force or violence."[59] However, he refused to answer any question with regard to the Progressive Party or about the contents of a lecture he had given to students at the University of New Hampshire. Questions as to these matters, he argued, violated his First Amendment rights. Sweezy was found guilty of contempt, and that finding was upheld by the New Hampshire Supreme Court but reversed by the U.S. Supreme Court.

Justice Frankfurter concurred. He was especially concerned with the intrusion of the state into the intellectual pursuits of universities. "These pages," he declared, "need not be burdened with proof, based on the testimony of a cloud of impressive witnesses, of the dependence of a free society on free universities. This means the exclusion of governmental intervention in the intellectual life of a university. It matters little whether such intervention occurs avowedly or through action that inevitably tends to check the ardor and fearlessness of scholars, qualities at once so fragile and so indispensable for fruitful academic labor."

The Justice was also concerned that Sweezy's associational privacy be protected. "For a citizen to be made to forego even a part of so basic a liberty as his political autonomy, the subordinating interest of the State must be compelling."

Although the Justice was concerned about Sweezy's freedom of association, he did not have the same concern for the rights of Herman A. Beilan, a Philadelphia school teacher. Beilan, who had been a teacher for 22 years, was questioned by the school superintendent about his association with allegedly subversive organizations. When he refused to answer the questions, he was discharged. His discharge was upheld by Pennsylvania courts and the Supreme Court.

Justice John M. Harlan, writing for the Court, pointed out that "[b]y engaging in teaching in the public schools, ... [Beilan] did not give up his right to freedom of belief, speech and association. He did, however, undertake obligations of frankness, candor and cooperation in answering inquiries made of him by his employing Board examining into his fitness to serve it as a public school teacher."[60]

For Frankfurter, who concurred, the issue was simply the power of the Board to determine the qualifications of its employees. "When these two employees,[61] were discharged, they were not labeled 'disloyal.' They were discharged because governmental authorities, like other employers, sought to satisfy themselves of the dependability of employees in relation to their duties. Accordingly, they made inquiries that, it is not contradicted, could in and of themselves be made. These inquiries were balked. The services of the employees were therefore terminated."[62]

Justice Douglas protested. "Our legal system is premised on the theory that every person is innocent until he is proved guilty. In this country we have, however, been moving away from that concept. We have been generating the belief that anyone who remains silent when interrogated about his unpopular beliefs or affiliations is guilty. I would allow no inference of wrongdoing to flow from the invocation of any constitutional right. I would not let that principle bow to popular passions. For all we know we are dealing here with citizens who are wholly innocent of any wrongful action. That must indeed be our premise. When we make the contrary assumption, we part radically with our tradition."

Teacher B. T. Shelton received the same treatment from Justice Frankfurter as teacher Beilan. "Shelton had been employed in the Little Rock [Arkansas] Special School District for twenty-five years. In the spring of 1959 he was notified that, before he could be employed for the 1959-1960 school year, he must file ... [an] affidavit ... listing all his organizational connections over the previous five years. He declined to file the affidavit, and his contract for the ensuing school year was not renewed."[63] Shelton brought an action against the School District seeking to have the requirement of listing one's organizations declared unconstitutional. The court upheld the requirement, but the Supreme Court determined that it was unconstitutional as a violation of associational freedom protected by the First Amendment.

In addressing the issue in this case, Justice Potter Stewart pointed out: "The question to be decided here is not whether the State of Arkansas can ask certain of its teachers about all their organizational relationships. It is not whether the State can ask all of its teachers about certain of their associational ties. It is not whether teachers can be asked how many organizations they belong to, or how much time they spend in organizational activity. The question is whether the State can ask every one of its teachers to disclose every single organization with which he has been associated over a five-year period." Stewart then concluded that the "statute's comprehensive interference with associational freedom goes far beyond what might be justified in the exercise of the State's legitimate inquiry into the fitness and competency of its teachers."

Frankfurter dissented and wrote: "As one who has strong views against crude intrusions by the state into the atmosphere of creative freedom in which alone the spirit and mind of a teacher can fruitfully function, I may find displeasure with the Arkansas legislation now under review. But in maintaining the distinction between private views and constitutional restrictions, I am constrained to find that it does not exceed the permissible range of state action limited by the Fourteenth Amendment." The Justice believed that the state had an interest in the number of organizations to which teachers belonged because belonging to too many might affect the teacher's work and dedication. Furthermore, a "teacher's answers to the questions ... may serve the purpose of making known to school authorities persons who come into contact with the teacher in all of the phases of his activity in the community, and who can be questioned, if need be, concerning the teacher's conduct in matters which this Court can certainly not now say are lacking in any pertinence to professional fitness."

Freedom of the Press

Contempt of Court for Publication. In *Bridges v. California*,[64] the Court considered two cases in which individuals had been found in contempt of court for publishing information which allegedly interfered with the orderly administration of justice. In one case, the *Times-Mirror Company* and its managing editor L. D. Hotchkiss were held in contempt by Judge A. A. Scott for publishing editorials relating to the sentencing of two union members who had been found guilty of assault during a labor dispute. One editorial stated that "Judge A. A. Scott will make a serious mistake if he grants probation to Matthew Shannon and Kennan Holmes." The trial judge, before whom the *Times* and Hotchkiss were being tried, was of the opinion that the editorial had an "inherent tendency"; and the California Supreme Court thought it had a "'reasonable tendency' to interfere with the orderly administration of justice in an action then before a court for consideration."

The other case involved Harry R. Bridges, President of the International Longshoremen's and Warehousemen's Union. Bridges was disturbed by a ruling made by Judge Ruben S. Schmidt in a labor dispute case the judge was handling. In a telegram sent to the Secretary of Labor, Bridges not only called Judge Schmidt's decision "outrageous," but he also stated: "Attempted enforcement of Schmidt decision will tie up port of Los Angeles and involve entire Pacific Coast," and that the Union "does not intend to allow state courts to override the majority vote of members in choosing its officers and representatives...."

Bridges was charged with, and convicted of, contempt of court, and that decision was also affirmed by the California Supreme Court. The U.S. Supreme Court reversed, with Justices Frankfurter, Owen J. Roberts, James F. Byrnes and Chief Justice Harlan F. Stone dissenting.

After reviewing the history of the adoption of the Bill of Rights, Justice Black, for the majority, held that "the only conclusion supported by history is that the unqualified prohibitions laid down by the framers were intended to give to liberty of the press, as to the other liberties, the broadest scope that could be countenanced in an orderly society."

Commenting upon the *Times-Mirror*'s editorial, Black said "this editorial, given the most intimidating construction it will bear, did no more than threaten future adverse criticism which was reasonably to be expected anyway in the event of a lenient disposition of the pending case." And with regard to the Bridges telegram, Black pointed out for the majority, "we find exaggeration in the conclusion that the utterance 'tended' to interfere with justice."

But Frankfurter and the dissenters disagreed. "Our whole history repels the view that it is an exercise of one of the civil liberties secured by the Bill of Rights for a leader of a large following or for a powerful metropolitan newspaper to attempt to overawe a judge in a matter immediately pending before him."

In assessing the application of the First Amendment to cases involving alleged interference with the orderly administration of justice, Frankfurter declared: "Of course freedom of speech and of the press are essential to the enlightenment of a free people and in restraining those who wield power. Particularly should this freedom be employed in comment upon the work of courts, who are without many influences ordinarily making for humor and humility, twin antidotes to the corrosion of power. But the Bill of Rights is not self-destructive. Freedom of expression can hardly carry implications that nullify the guarantees of impartial trials. And since courts are the ultimate resorts for vindicating the Bill of Rights, a state may surely authorize appropriate historic means to assure that the process for such vindication be not wrenched from its rational tracks into the more primitive mêlée of passion and pressure. The need is great that courts be criticized, but just as great that they be allowed to do their duty."

Turning to the particular facts of each case, the Justice was of the opinion that the editorial at issue was indeed coercive and tended to influence the decision of the judge. "A powerful newspaper," he argued, "brought its full coercive power to bear in demanding a particular sentence. If such sentence had been imposed, readers might assume that the court had been influenced in its action; if lesser punishment had been imposed, at least a portion of the community might be stirred to resentment. It cannot be denied that even a judge may be affected by such a quandary. We cannot say that the state court was out of bounds in concluding that such conduct offends the free course of justice."

Frankfurter and the dissenters were of the opinion that Bridges' telegram also contained a threat to the fair administration of justice in the case then before the court. That conclusion was crucial to Frankfurter's determination of whether or not a publisher should be held in contempt. In *Pennekamp v. Florida*,[65] he wrote: "Inaccurate and even false comment on litigation no longer pending may not be dealt with by punishing for contempt as a means of assuring the just exercise of the judicial process." This led him to concur in reversal of the contempt conviction of the *Miami Herald* and John D. Pennekamp, its associate editor, for publishing certain editorials and a cartoon which were critical of the way local courts were handling criminal cases. "Where the power to punish for contempt is asserted, it is not important that the case is technically in court or that further proceedings, such as the possibility of a rehearing, are available. ... The decisive consideration is whether the judge or the jury is, or presently will be, pondering a decision that comment seeks to affect. Forbidden comment is such as will or may throw psychological weight into scales which the court is immediately balancing." The Justice then pointed out that the *Herald's* criticism related to the way the courts had been handling cases rather than to any particular case then pending before the court.

Although Frankfurter acknowledged the right of the press to freely publish, he balanced that right against the need for the administration of justice. "The press," he said, "does have the right, which is its professional function, to criticize and to advocate. The whole gamut of public affairs is the domain for fearless and critical comment, and not the least the administration of justice. But the public function which belongs to the press makes it an obligation of honor to exercise this function only with the fullest sense of responsibility. Without such lively sense of responsibility a free press may readily become a powerful instrument of injustice. It should not and may not attempt to influence judges or juries before they have made up their minds in pending controversies."

Obscenity and Other Vague Laws. *Lady Chatterley's Lover* is a film about adultery. When Kingsley Pictures Corp. sought a license to show the film in New York, the license was denied on the ground that "the whole theme of this motion picture is immoral under ... [the] law, for that theme is the presentation of adultery as a desirable, acceptable and proper pattern of behavior."[66] Under New York law, a license could be denied for the exhibition of a film if it was found to be "immoral." An "immoral" film was considered one "which portrays acts of sexual immorality, perversion, or lewdness, or which expressly or impliedly presents such acts as desirable, acceptable or proper patterns of behavior." The New York Court of Appeals upheld the denial of the license, but the U.S. Supreme Court reversed.

After analyzing the state law and the interpretation given to it by the New York Court of Appeals, the majority concluded that the law was unconstitutional as construed, and as applied to *Lady Chatterley's Lover.* "What New York has done," Justice Stewart declared, "... is to prevent the exhibition of a motion picture because that picture advocates an idea—that adultery under certain circumstances may be proper behavior. Yet the First Amendment's basic guarantee is of freedom to advocate ideas. The State, quite simply, has thus struck at the very heart of constitutionally protected liberty."

Justice Frankfurter concurred, but did not agree that the law was unconstitutional. He concluded that the license should have been issued because the film was not immoral. "Unless I misread the opinion of the Court, it strikes down the New York legislation in order to escape the task of deciding whether a particular picture is entitled to the protection of expression under the Fourteenth Amendment." This, he wrote, "exceeds the appropriate limits for decision." "Ours is the vital but very limited task of scrutinizing the work of the draftsmen in order to determine whether they [the legislature] have kept within the narrow limits of ... censorship.... The legislation must not be so vague, the language so loose, as to leave to those who have to apply it too wide a discretion for sweeping within its condemnation what is permissible expression as well as what society may permissibly prohibit."

Justice Black decided to "add a few words because of concurring opinions by several Justices who rely on their appraisal of the movie Lady Chatterley's

Lover for holding that New York cannot constitutionally bar it. Unlike them, I have not seen the picture. My view is that stated by Mr. Justice Douglas, that prior censorship of moving pictures like prior censorship of newspapers and books violates the First and Fourteenth Amendments. If despite the Constitution, however, this Nation is to embark on the dangerous road of censorship, my belief is that this Court is about the most inappropriate Supreme Board of Censors that could be found. So far as I know, judges possess no special expertise providing exceptional competency to set standards and to supervise the private morals of the Nation."

Justice Frankfurter had previously expressed his views with regard to the Court striking down obscenity legislation in the case of *Winters v. New York*.[67] Murray Winters, a New York bookdealer, was convicted of violating a statute which made it illegal to sell any magazine "'made up of criminal news, police reports, or accounts of criminal deeds, or pictures or stories of deeds of bloodshed, lust or crime...'" In reversing Winter's conviction, Justice Stanley Reed wrote for the Court: "There must be ascertainable standards of guilt. Men of common intelligence cannot be required to guess at the meaning of the enactment. The vagueness may be from uncertainty in regard to persons within the scope of the act, ... or in regard to the applicable tests to ascertain guilt."

In applying that standard to the New York law, Reed concluded: "It does not seem to us that an honest distributor of publications could know when he might be held to have ignored such a prohibition. ... Where a statute is so vague as to make criminal an innocent act, a conviction under it cannot be sustained."

Frankfurter agreed with that statement but thought that the Court was misapplying it, and dissented. "Legislation must put people on notice as to the kind of conduct from which to refrain. Legislation must also avoid so tight a phrasing as to leave the area for evasion ampler than that which is condemned. How to escape, on the one hand, having a law rendered futile because no standard is afforded by which conduct is to be judged, and, on the other, a law so particularized as to defeat itself through the opportunities it affords for evasion, involves an exercise of judgment which is at the heart of the legislative process. It calls for the accommodation of delicate factors. But this accommodation is for the legislature to make and for us to respect, when it concerns a subject so clearly within the scope of the police power as the control of crime. Here we are asked to declare void the law which expresses the balance so struck by the legislature, on the ground that the legislature has not expressed its policy clear enough. That is what it gets down to."

The Pursuit of Liberty

The Right to Travel. The Justice voted to protect the right of an individual to travel in *Edwards v. California*,[68] *Kent v. Dulles*,[69] and *Dayton v. Dulles*.[70]

The Court, however, did not specifically deal in any of these cases with the question of whether there was a constitutional right to travel. In *Edwards*, the Court struck down a California law that made it a misdemeanor to bring an "indigent person" into the state, because the law placed an unconstitutional burden on interstate commerce. In both *Kent* and *Dayton*, the majority held that Congress had not given the Secretary of State the power to withhold passports from people because the Secretary believed that the person was a communist or affiliated with organizations that were communist.

In the case of *New York v. O'Neil*,[71] when the question of the existence of a constitutional right to travel was squarely at issue, the Justice acknowledged that the right did exist, but that the state's interest in this case outweighed it.

Joseph C. O'Neil, who was attending a convention in Miami, Florida, was wanted as a witness before a grand jury in New York. Acting under a law relating to attendance of witnesses, the District Attorney of New York petitioned the Circuit Court of Dade County, Florida, for an order requiring O'Neil to be forcibly transported from Florida to New York. Judge George E. Holt, Jr., held the law to be unconstitutional as a violation of a person's right to travel across state lines. The Florida Supreme Court agreed, and affirmed. The Supreme Court, with Frankfurter writing the Court's opinion, disagreed, and reversed:

> The finding of the Florida Supreme Court that the right to ingress and egress is a privilege of national citizenship protected by the Fourteenth Amendment raises an issue that has more than once been stirred in opinions of this Court. See concurring opinions in *Edwards v. California*,…. However, even if broad scope be given to such a privilege, there is no violation of that privilege by the Florida statute.

For the Justice, whatever interference there was with O'Neil's right to travel, it was "[a]t most … a temporary interference with voluntary travel."

Without further discussion of the right to travel, Justice Frankfurter then turned to the power of the state to enact this legislation. "The Constitution of the United States," he argued, "does not preclude resourcefulness of relationships between States on matters as to which there is no grant of power to Congress and as to which the range of authority restricted within an individual State is inadequate. … A citizen cannot shirk his duty, no matter how inconvenienced thereby, to testify in criminal proceedings and grand jury investigations in a State where he is found. There is no constitutional provision granting him relief from this obligation to testify even though he must travel to another State to do so. Comity among States, an end particularly to be cherished when the object is enforcement of internal criminal laws, is not to be defeated by *a priori* restrictive view of state power."

Justice Douglas, writing for himself and Justice Black, saw the matter differently and dissented. "Whether the right of ingress and egress be bottomed on the Privileges and Immunities Clause of the Fourteenth Amendment, the Commerce Clause, or a basic 'liberty' inherent in national citizenship, I know of no way in which a State may take it from a citizen. To say that there is no interference here because O'Neil will be free to return to Florida later is to trifle with a basic human right."

Equal Protection of the Law

Blacks on Juries. In *Hill v. Texas*,[72] the Court unanimously reversed the conviction of Henry Allen Hill for rape because blacks had been systematically excluded from the grand jury which had indicted him. Frankfurter participated in the case. Following that decision, 21 grand juries were summoned in the county, but only one black person served on each.

Five years after the *Hill* case, when Lee Cassell was indicted for murder in the same county, there were no blacks on the grand jury. Cassell was convicted and on appeal argued that there was discrimination in the selection of grand jurors, a claim which was rejected by the Texas Court of Criminal Appeals.

Cassell had argued that the jury commissioners were purposefully selecting only one black person for each grand jury, and that this violated the Equal Protection Clause of the Fourteenth Amendment. The Supreme Court agreed and reversed. The jury commissioners had testified that they "chose jurymen only from those people with whom they were personally acquainted."[73] Justice Stanley Reed responded: "When the commissioners were appointed as judicial administrative officials, it was their duty to familiarize themselves fairly with the qualifications of the eligible jurors of the county without regard to race and color. They did not do so here, and the result has been racial discrimination."

Justice Frankfurter agreed and filed a concurring opinion: "The prohibition of the Constitution against discrimination because of color," he noted, "does not require in and of itself the presence of a Negro on a jury. But neither is it satisfied by Negro representation arbitrarily limited to one. It is not a question of presence on a grand jury nor absence from it. The basis of selection cannot consciously take color into account. Such is the command of the Constitution."

Integration of Public Schools. The Justice was a member of the Court that unanimously struck down segregated schools in *Brown v. Board of Education*.[74] In that case, the Court held: "We conclude that in the field of public education the doctrine of 'separate but equal' has no place. Separate educational facilities are inherently unequal."

Three days after the *Brown* decision, the Little Rock [Arkansas] District School Board commenced proceedings to integrate their school system as soon as possible.

While the School Board was thus going forward with its preparation for desegregating the Little Rock school system, other state authorities, in contrast, were actively pursuing a program designed to perpetuate in Arkansas the system of racial segregation which this Court had held violated the Fourteenth Amendment. First came, in November 1956, an amendment to the State Constitution flatly commanding the Arkansas General Assembly to oppose "in every Constitutional manner the Un-constitutional desegregation decisions of May 17, 1954 and May 31, 1955 of the United States Supreme Court," ... and through an initiative, a pupil assignment law,.... Pursuant to this state constitutional command, a law relieving school children from compulsory attendance at racially mixed schools, ... and a law establishing a State Sovereignty Commission ... were enacted by the General Assembly in February 1957.[75]

When school was about to commence in Little Rock in September 1957, the Governor of Arkansas sent the National Guard to the high school and "placed the school 'off limits' to colored students." The National Guard stayed at the school until Federal District Judge Ronald N. Davies, Fargo, North Dakota, who had been assigned to the case, granted an injunction against the governor ordering the troops to be withdrawn. Shortly thereafter, President Dwight Eisenhower ordered federal troops to Little Rock to assure the integration of the schools.

Because of the difficulty in integrating the school, the Board sought to postpone its desegregation plan, and Federal District Judge Harry J. Lemley permitted them to do so. Judge Lemley's order, however, was overturned by the Court of Appeals and the Supreme Court affirmed that decision. During these proceedings the governor and the legislature of Arkansas argued that they were not bound by the Court's decision in *Brown*. The Court responded: "It follows that the interpretation of the Fourteenth Amendment enunciated by this Court in the *Brown* case is the supreme law of the land, and Art. VI of the Constitution makes it of binding effect on the States, 'any Thing in the Constitution or Laws of any State to the Contrary notwithstanding.'"

Justice Frankfurter wrote a concurring opinion. In commenting upon the actions taken by the Arkansas Legislature and Governor, he pointed out that "the tragic aspect of this disruptive tactic was that the power of the State was used not to sustain law but as an instrument for thwarting law. The State of Arkansas is thus responsible for disabling one of its subordinate agencies, the Little Rock School Board, from peacefully carrying out the Board's and the State's constitutional duty."

Integration of Public and Private Facilities. Following *Brown v. Board of Education*, the Justice voted with the majority to require integration of a number of public facilities, including city park facilities, public beaches and bathhouses, golf courses, buses, and athletic contests.[76]

Because the Equal Protection Clause prohibits *government* from denying equal protection, whether the government is a participant in any alleged discrimination is a question the Court must resolve before considering whether the discrimination is a violation of the Fourteenth Amendment. That was the issue in *Burton v. Wilmington Pkg. Auth.*[77] The Wilmington Parking Authoity leased part of a public parking garage to the Eagle Coffee Shoppe, Inc. for a restaurant and cocktail lounge. After parking his car in the garage, William H. Burton entered the restaurant but was denied service because he was black.

Burton brought suit against the Parking Authority claiming that it denied him equal protection of the law by allowing the Coffee Shoppe to exclude blacks. The trial court agreed, but the Supreme Court of Delaware concluded that "Eagle was acting in 'a purely private capacity,'" and reversed.

After examining the facts surrounding the ownership of the garage and the lease to Eagle, the United States Supreme Court held "that when a State leases public property in the manner and for the purpose shown to have been the case here, the proscriptions of the Fourteenth Amendment must be complied with by the lessee as certainly as though they were binding covenants written into the agreement itself."

The Justice dissented. He would not have reached the question of the connection between the Parking Authority and Eagle Shoppe. He would have returned the case to the Delaware Supreme Court to determine whether state law required Eagle to operate a segregated restaurant. If the law prohibited Eagle from serving blacks, then the state is clearly involved in the discrimination. If, on the other hand, state law did not require segregation, only then would the Court have to analyze the facts, as the majority had done, to find out how much state involvement there was in the lease arrangements.

Gender Discrimination. Valentine Goesaert and Gertrude Nadroski brought suit to have a Michigan law declared unconstitutional. The law in question provided that only males over the age of 21 were entitled to a bartender's license, "but no female may be so licensed unless she be 'the wife or daughter of the male owner' of a licensed liquor establishment."[78] District Judge Robert R. Nevin held that the law did not violate equal protection and therefore was constitutional. Justice Frankfurter agreed. He wrote for a majority: "We are, to be sure dealing with a historic calling. We meet the alewife, sprightly and ribald, in Shakespeare, but centuries before him she played a role in the social life of England. ... The Fourteenth Amendment did not tear history up by the roots, and the regulation of the liquor traffic is one of the oldest and most untrammeled of legislative powers. Michigan could, beyond question, forbid all women from working behind a bar. This is so despite the vast changes in the social and legal position of women. The fact that women may now have achieved the virtues that men have long claimed as their prerogatives and now indulge in vices that men have long practiced, does not preclude the States from drawing a sharp line between the sexes, certainly in such matters as the regulation of the liquor traffic."

The fact that a woman, whose husband or father owned the bar, could be a bartender did not change Frankfurter's opinion. "Michigan evidently believes," he said, "that the oversight assured through ownership of a bar by a barmaid's husband or father minimizes hazards that may confront a barmaid without such protecting oversight. This Court is certainly not in a position to gainsay such belief by the Michigan legislature."

For Voters.

> The Jaybird Association or Party was organized in 1889. Its membership was then and always has been limited to white people; they are automatically members if their names appear on the official list of county voters. It has been run like other political parties with an executive committee named from the county's voting precincts. Expenses of the party are paid by the assessment of candidates for office in its primaries. Candidates for county offices submit their names to the Jaybird Committee in accordance with the normal practice followed by regular political parties all over the country. Advertisements and posters proclaim that these candidates are running subject to the action of the Jaybird primary. While there is no legal compulsion on successful Jaybird candidates to enter Democratic primaries, they have nearly always done so and with few exceptions since 1889 have run and won without opposition in the Democratic primaries and the general elections that followed. Thus the party has been the dominant political group in the county since organization, having endorsed every county-wide official elected since 1889.[79]

John Terry and several other blacks brought an action against A. J. Adams and others who were the officers of the Jaybird Party, seeking an order of the court permitting them to vote in the Jaybird Primary. District Judge Thomas M. Kennerly held that the Party was subject to the laws of Texas and that therefore Terry and others similarly situated were entitled to vote in the Party's elections. The Court of Appeals reversed, holding that "there was no constitutional or congressional bar to the admitted discriminatory exclusion of Negroes because Jaybird's primaries were not to any extent state controlled." The Supreme Court reversed. Writing for himself and Justices Douglas and Harold H. Burton, Justice Black pointed out that:

> It is significant that precisely the same qualifications as those prescribed by Texas entitling electors to vote at county-operated primaries are adopted as the sole qualifications entitling electors to vote at the county-wide Jaybird primaries with a single proviso—Negroes are excluded. Everyone concedes that such a proviso in the county-operated primaries would be unconstitutional. The Jaybird Party thus brings into being and holds precisely the kind of election that the Fifteenth Amendment seeks to prevent. When it produces the equivalent of the prohibited election, the damage has been done.

Justice Frankfurter concurred: "The State here devised a process for primary elections. The right of all citizens to share in it, and not to be excluded by unconstitutional bars, is emphasized by the fact that in Texas nomination in the Democratic primary is tantamount to election. The exclusion of Negroes from meaningful participation in the only primary scheme set up by the State was not an accidental, unsought consequence of the exercise of civic rights by voters to make their common viewpoint count. It was the design, the very purpose of this arrangement that the Jaybird primary in May exclude Negro participation in July. That it was the action in part of the election officials charged by Texas law with the fair administration of the primaries, brings it within the reach of the law."

When the City of Tuskegee, Alabama, also attempted to disenfranchise its black citizens, the Supreme Court again found it a violation of the Fifteenth Amendment. In July 1957, the Alabama State Legislature passed special legislation giving the City of Tuskegee authority to rearrange its borders. At the time, the boundaries of the city formed a square. Acting pursuant to the law, Tuskegee redefined its borders to resemble a "sea dragon."[80] This action eliminated all but a few blacks from being able to vote in the City.

C. G. Gomillion and others brought suit against city officials, arguing that the law was "but another device in a continuing attempt to disenfranchise Negro citizens ... of their right to vote in municipal elections." District Judge Frank M. Johnson, Jr., dismissed the case, being of the opinion that the District Court had "no control over, no supervision over, and no power to change any boundaries of municipal corporations fixed by a duly convened and elected legislative body, acting for the people in the State of Alabama." The Supreme Court, with Justice Frankfurter writing the Court's opinion, disagreed and reversed:

"A statute which is alleged to have worked unconstitutional deprivations of petitioners' rights," he declared, "is not immune to attack simply because the mechanism employed by the legislature is a redefinition of municipal boundaries. According to the allegations here made, the Alabama Legislature has not merely redrawn the Tuskegee city limits with incidental inconvenience to the petitioners; it is more accurate to say that it has deprived the petitioners of the municipal franchise and consequent rights and to that end has incidentally changed the city's boundaries. While in form this is merely an act redefining metes and bounds, if the allegations are established, the inescapable human effect of this essay in geometry and geography is to despoil colored citizens, and only colored citizens of their theretofore enjoyed voting rights."[81]

In the Criminal Justice System. After Griffin and Crenshaw were convicted for armed robbery, they asked the trial court for a transcript of their trial so that they could file an appeal but said that they did not have money to pay for it. "Under Illinois law in order to get full direct appellate review of alleged errors [occurring at the trial] ... it is necessary for the defendant to furnish the appellate court with a bill of exceptions or report of proceedings at the trial certified by the trial judge. As Illinois concedes, it is sometimes impossible to prepare such bills of exceptions or reports without a stenographic transcript of the trial proceedings. Indigent defendants sentenced to death are provided with a free transcript at the expense of the county where convicted. In all other criminal cases defendants needing a transcript, whether indigent or not, must themselves buy it."[82]

The trial judge refused to order that a transcript be provided Griffin and Crenshaw without cost, and the Supreme Court of Illinois upheld that decision. The U.S. Supreme Court reversed, concluding that the petitioners had been denied equal protection of the law.

"In criminal trials," Justice Black declared, "a State can no more discriminate on account of poverty than on account of religion, race, or color. Plainly the ability to pay costs in advance bears no rational relationship to a defendant's guilt or innocence and could not be used as an excuse to deprive a defendant of a fair trial." "There can be no equal justice," he continued, "where the kind of trial a man gets depends on the amount of money he has. Destitute defendants must be afforded as adequate appellate review as defendants who have money enough to buy transcripts."

In concurring, Justice Frankfurter agreed that "when a State deems it wise and just that convictions be susceptible to review by an appellate court, it cannot by force of its exactions draw a line which precludes convicted indigent persons … from securing such a review merely by disabling them from bringing to the notice of an appellate tribunal errors of the trial court which would upset the conviction were practical opportunity for review not foreclosed."

Convicted burglar Burns had a problem different from that of Griffin and Crenshaw. Burns also wanted to appeal his conviction but did not have the money to pay the $20 filing fee required by the Supreme Court of Ohio. The Clerk of that Court returned Burns's papers informing him that the appeal could not be accepted without the fee. Burns then petitioned the U.S. Supreme Court, which accepted his papers and appointed Attorney Helen G. Washington to represent him in that Court.

In the papers which Burns sent to the Court, he stated that the question to be determined was: "Whether in a prosecution for Burglary, the Due Process Clause, And The Equal Protection Clause, of the Fourteenth (14) Amendment to the United States Constitution are violated by the refusal of the Supreme Court of Ohio, to file the aforementioned legal proceedings, because Petitioner was unable to secure the costs."[83] The Court answered the question in the affirmative. "In Ohio," Chief Justice Earl Warren noted, "a defendant who is not indigent may have the Supreme Court consider on the merits his application for leave to appeal a felony conviction. But as that court has interpreted [the law] … and its rules of practice, an indigent defendant is denied that opportunity. There is no rational basis for assuming that indigents' motions for leave to appeal will be less meritorious than those of other defendants. Indigents must, therefore, have the same opportunities to invoke the discretion of the Supreme Court of Ohio."

Frankfurter dissented without addressing the question raised by Burns. His disagreement with the majority was that he did not believe that the Clerk's letter to Burns was a final order of the Ohio Supreme Court. Not being a final order of that court, he argued, the Supreme Court should not have taken jurisdiction of the case. "The appellate power of this Court," he argued, "to review litigation originating in a state court can come into operation only if the judgment to be reviewed is the final judgment of the highest court of the State." Frankfurter pointed out that if the Court had not accepted Burns's petition, he would not have been left without other means to appeal the decision of the Ohio court. "Adherence to the dictates of the laws which govern our jurisdiction," the Justice declared, "though it may result in postponement of our determination of petitioner's rights, is the best assurance of the vindication of justice under law through the power of the courts. We should dismiss the writ of certiorari inasmuch as there has been no final judgment over which we have appellate power."

The Bill of Rights and the States

Justice Frankfurter was one of the justices who did not believe that the Fourteenth Amendment required the application of the Bill of Rights to states. In 1947, he wrote: "Between the incorporation of the Fourteenth Amendment into the Constitution and the beginning of the present membership of the Court—a period of seventy years—the scope of that Amendment was passed upon by forty-three judges. Of all these judges, only one, who may respectfully be called an eccentric exception, ever indicated the belief that the Fourteenth Amendment was a shorthand summary of the first eight Amendments theretofore limiting only the Federal Government, and that due process incorporated those eight Amendments as restrictions upon the powers of the States."[84] The "eccentric exception" to which the Justice referred was the first Justice John Marshall Harlan.

In response to the suggestion that the Court ought to selectively apply some of the first eight amendments to the states, Frankfurter wondered which ones should be so applied and which should not. "Some are in and some are out, but we are left in the dark as to which are in and which are out. Nor are we given the calculus for determining which go in and which stay out." The only clue which he could find for making the determination of which Amendments were in was a reference to a prior case in which the Court stated "that due process contains within itself certain minimal standards which are 'of the very essence of a scheme of ordered liberty.'"

Rather than be concerned with the application of the Bill of Rights to the state, the Justice was of the opinion that in state criminal cases the Court ought to simply inquire "whether the criminal proceedings which resulted in conviction deprived the accused of the due process of law to which the United States Constitution entitled him." "Judicial review of that guaranty of the Fourteenth Amendment," he argued, "inescapably imposes upon the Court an exercise of judgment upon the whole course of the proceedings in order to ascertain whether they offend those canons of decency and fairness which express the notions of justice of English-speaking peoples even toward those charged with the most heinous offenses."

But the issue wouldn't go away and was before the Court again a few years later in the case of *Wolf v. Colorado.*[85] In that case, Julius A. Wolf, a physician and surgeon, and A. H. Montgomery, a licensed chiropractor, were charged with illegally performing an abortion on Mildred Cairo. In the process of gathering evidence, representatives of the district attorney's office arrested Dr. Wolf at his office without a warrant and took possession of his patient's records. These records were used at the trial in which Dr. Wolf and Montgomery were convicted. Their convictions were upheld by the Supreme Court of Colorado and by the U.S. Supreme Court, with Justice Frankfurter writing the Court's opinion.

The Justice started the opinion with this question: "The precise question for consideration is this: Does a conviction by a State court for a State offense deny the 'due process of law' required by the Fourteenth Amendment, solely because evidence that was admitted at the trial was obtained under circumstances which would have rendered it inadmissible in a prosecution for violation of a federal law in a court of the United States because there deemed to be an infraction of the Fourth Amendment...?" Frankfurter answered by stating that the admission of the illegally seized evidence did not deny the defendants due process of law, and the convictions were therefore affirmed.

With regard to whether the Fourth Amendment's prohibition against unreasonable searches and seizures applied to the states, Frankfurter declared: "The notion that the 'due process of law' guaranteed by the Fourteenth Amendment is shorthand for the first eight amendments of the Constitution and thereby incorporates them has been rejected by this Court again and again, after impressive consideration."

But, he continued:

> The security of one's privacy against arbitrary intrusion by the police—which is at the core of the Fourth Amendment—is basic to a free society. It is therefore implicit in 'the concept of ordered liberty' and as such enforceable against the States through the Due Process Clause. The knock at the door, whether by day or by night, as a prelude to a search, without authority of law but solely on the authority of the police, did not need the commentary of recent history to be condemned as inconsistent with the conception of human rights enshrined in the history and the basic constitutional documents of English-speaking peoples.

> Accordingly, we have no hesitation in saying that were a State affirmatively to sanction such police incursion into privacy it would run counter to the guaranty of the Fourteenth Amendment.

The Justice then turned to the question of whether the application of the Fourth Amendment to this case required that the evidence which was illegally seized should have been excluded from the trial. His answer was "that in a prosecution in a State court for a State crime the Fourteenth Amendment does not forbid the admission of evidence obtained by an unreasonable search." The Justice reached this conclusion even though the Court in 1914 had held that the Fourth Amendment prohibited the use of illegally seized evidence in prosecutions in federal courts.[86]

In several cases involving the free exercise and establishment of religion clauses of the First Amendment, Justice Frankfurter did vote to apply those clauses to the states.[87] In one case, he joined an opinion by Justice Robert H. Jackson wherein Jackson, in referring to the Bill of Rights, declared: "It was intended not only to keep the states' hands out of religion, but to keep religion's hands off the state...."[88]

The Japanese Cases

A little more than two months after the Japanese bombed Pearl Harbor, Hawaii, on December 7, 1941, President Franklin D. Roosevelt signed an Executive Order giving Military Commanders the authority "to prescribe military areas in such places ... as [they] ... may determine, from which any or all persons may be excluded, and with respect to which, the right of any person to enter, remain in, or leave shall be subject to whatever restrictions the ... Military Commander may impose in his discretion."[89] Shortly thereafter, Congress made it a crime to disobey a Military Commander's restrictions. On May 3, 1942, Commanding General J. L. DeWitt issued an order excluding persons of Japanese ancestry from remaining in San Leandro, California. Toyosuburo Korematsu, having been found in San Leandro, was convicted of disobeying General DeWitt's order, and he appealed. The Court of Appeals and the Supreme Court both upheld Korematsu's conviction.[90] Justice Frankfurter concurred. He was of the opinion that, regardless of the hardship placed upon Korematsu and similarly situated Japanese, the order was justifiable under the power of Congress and the President to wage war. He wrote, "[B]eing an exercise of the war power explicitly granted by the Constitution for safeguarding the national life by prosecuting war effectively, I find nothing in the Constitution which denies to Congress the power to enforce such a valid military order by making its violation an offense triable in the civil courts. ... To find that the Constitution does not forbid the military measures now complained of does not carry with it approval of that which Congress and the Executive did. That is their business, not ours."

Justice Owen J. Roberts saw the matter much differently, and dissented. This is a "case," he wrote, "of convicting a citizen as a punishment for not submitting to imprisonment in a concentration camp, based on his ancestry, and solely because of his ancestry, without evidence or inquiry concerning his loyalty and good disposition towards the United States." And Justice Frank Murphy said that the "exclusion [order] goes over 'the very brink of constitutional power' and falls into the ugly abyss of racism."

AS A JUSTICE FOR THE GOVERNMENT

Judicial review, itself a limitation on popular government, is a fundamental part of our constitutional scheme. But to the legislature no less than to courts is committed the guardianship of deeply-cherished liberties. ... Where all the effective means of inducing political changes are left free from interference, education in the abandonment of foolish legislation is itself a training in liberty. To fight out the wise use of legislative authority in the forum of public opinion and before legislative assemblies rather than to transfer such a contest to the judicial arena, serves to vindicate the self-confidence of a free people....[91]

As a member of this Court I am not justified in writing my private notions of policy into the Constitution, no matter how deeply I may cherish them or how mischievous I may deem their disregard. ... The only opinion of our own even looking in that direction that is material is our opinion whether legislators could in reason have enacted such a law.[92]

These two statements reflect Justice Frankfurter's judicial philosophy and account for the many times he voted for government infringement on constitutional rights rather than for protecting the individual freedom guaranteed by those rights.

When the Court struck down, as a violation of the First Amendment, a city ordinance that prohibited all door-to-door solicitation, Frankfurter wrote in dissent: "But it is not our business to require legislatures to extend the area of prohibition or regulation beyond the demands of revealed abuses. And the greatest leeway must be given to the legislative judgment of what those demands are. The right to legislate implies the right to classify. We should not, however unwittingly, slip into the judgment seat of legislatures."[93]

There are two errors in Frankfurter's position. First, as Chief Justice John Marshall pointed out in 1803, the very essence of judicial power includes the authority to declare laws unconstitutional. "So," Marshall wrote, "if a law be in opposition to the constitution; if both the law and the constitution apply to a particular case, so that the court must either decide that case, conformable to the law, disregarding the constitution; or conformable to the constitution, disregarding the law; the court must determine which of these conflicting rules governs the case: this is the very essence of judicial duty. If then, the courts are to regard the constitution, and the constitution is superior to any ordinary act of the legislature, the constitution, and not such ordinary act must govern the case to which they both apply."[94]

Secondly, as a general rule, legislatures are not "committed to the guardianship of deeply-cherished liberties." Just the opposite is true. Courts are continually being called upon to determine the constitutionality of ordinances, laws, and regulations adopted by some legislative body or promulgated by some executive officer. And, despite Frankfurter's reluctance to join in doing so, the Supreme Court has found many such ordinances, laws, regulations and orders unconstitutional.

The Justice, however, at times, wrote eloquently about free speech. For example, you find the following passage in the *Dennis* case:

> On the other hand is the interest in free speech. The right to exert all gov-
> ernmental powers in aid of maintaining our institutions and resisting their
> physical overthrow does not include intolerance of opinions and speech that
> cannot do harm although opposed and perhaps alien to dominant, traditional
> opinion. The treatment of minorities, especially their legal position, is among
> the most searching tests of the level of civilization attained by a society. It is
> better for those who have almost unlimited power of government in their hands
> to err on the side of freedom. We have enjoyed so much freedom for so long
> that we are perhaps in danger of forgetting how much blood it cost to estab-
> lish the Bill of Rights.[95]

Despite those words, Frankfurter voted to convict the eleven members of the Communist Party of conspiracy to organize a group to teach and advocate the overthrow of the government.

In *Kovacs*, Justice Stanley Reed makes reference to the "preferred position of freedom of speech." This disturbed Frankfurter. "I deem it a mischievous phrase," he declared, "if it carries the thought, which it may subtly imply, that any law touching communication is infected with presumptive invalidity."[96] He then examines a number of cases in which the phrase, or one similar, has been used. He concludes that "the claim that any legislation is presumptively unconstitutional which touches the field of the First Amendment and the Fourteenth Amendment, insofar as the latter's concept of 'liberty' contains what is specifically protected by the First has never commended itself to a majority of this Court." While that may have been true at the time Frankfurter wrote it, strong arguments have been made that the First Amendment does indeed occupy a "preferred position" in our hierarchy of values.[97]

In dealing with conflicts between First Amendment rights and government restriction thereof, Frankfurter approached the solution by asking whether the restriction was reasonable. In voting to uphold the Arkansas statute requiring teachers to list all of the organizations to which they had belonged within the previous five years, he wrote: "The issue remains whether, in light of the particular kind of restriction upon individual liberty which a regulation entails, it is reasonable for a legislature to choose that form of regulation rather than others less restrictive."[98]

If one is willing, as Frankfurter was, to defer to legislative judgment, it is then an easy step to the conclusion that the Arkansas restrictions, and other governmental restrictions on associational rights, do not violate the First Amendment. This was in contrast to the position taken by most justices, as Justice Potter Stewart points out: "In a series of decisions this Court has held, even though the governmental purpose be legitimate and substantial, that purpose cannot be pursued by means that broadly stifle fundamental personal liberties when the end can be more narrowly achieved. The breadth of legislative abridgment [of fundamental personal liberties] must be viewed in the light of less drastic means for achieving the same basic purpose."

Frankfurter voted to uphold the associational privacy rights of Schware and Sweezy. He did not do so, however, for Beilan, Lerner, or Shelton and the other Arkansas teachers, nor for many others who came to the Court seeking protection for those rights.[99]

With the exception of the obscenity cases, Frankfurter did not participate in many cases involving freedom of the press. In three cases involving contempt charges for publication of material allegedly interfering with the administration of the judicial system, the Justice voted once for freedom of the press and twice to uphold the contempt charges against those publishing the material.[100]

By joining the majority in *Roth v. United States*,[101] the Justice agreed that those dealing in obscenity were not protected by the First Amendment and could be punished. He was also of the opinion that it was the duty of the justices to examine the material and make their own independent judgments of whether it was or was not obscene. In concurring in *Lady Chatterley's Lover*, he argued that in obscenity cases, the justices have an obligation to view the material allegedly claimed to be obscene to determine whether it was or not. He argued: "We cannot escape such instance-by-instance, case-by-case application of that clause in all the varieties of situations that come before this Court."[102] This, of course, leaves to five of the nine justices of the Supreme Court the final word whether or not a particular book, movie, work of art, or other printed or written material is obscene.

With rare exception, Justice Frankfurter voted to reverse convictions of those who had been indicted by a grand jury from which blacks were excluded. In *Michel v. Louisiana*,[103] however, he voted with the majority to uphold convictions of several persons "who are colored, were indicted, convicted and sentenced to death in a Louisiana state court. The grand jury indicting the petitioners was drawn from the parish of Orleans where 32% of the population are colored. Only once within the memory of people living in that parish had a colored person been selected as a grand juror. That juror, who happened to look like a white man, was selected under the mistaken idea that he was one. The foregoing facts are not disputed here."

Justice Frankfurter consistently voted to force the integration of universities and public schools. He ended his concurring opinion in *Cooper v. Aaron*[104] with the admonition to state governments that compliance with the supreme Law of the Land was essential in order to accomplish the goal of school integration. "Compliance with decisions of this Court, as the constitutional organ of the supreme Law of the Land, has often, throughout our history, depended on active support by state and local authorities. It presupposes such support. To withhold it, and indeed to use political power to try to paralyze the supreme Law, precludes the maintenance of our federal system as we have known and cherished it for one hundred and seventy years."

In *Shelley v. Kraemer*[105] and *Hurd v. Hodge*,[106] the Court held that courts could not enforce private agreements prohibiting the sale of real estate to persons other than Caucasians. Frankfurter concurred. Enforcement of such agreements, he said, "violates the Constitution—and violates it, not for any narrow technical reason, but for considerations that touch rights so basic to our society that, after the Civil War, their protection against invasion by the States was safeguarded by the Constitution." The right he was referring to, in these cases, was the right of blacks not to be discriminated against in the purchase of a home.

Justice Frankfurter adhered to the stereotyping of women when he wrote the opinion upholding the Michigan law prohibiting women from being licensed bartenders.[107]

In a concurring opinion in *Adamson v. California*,[108] the Justice strenuously argued that the Fourteenth Amendment did not "incorporate" the first eight amendments to the Bill of Rights and thereby make them applicable to the states. Throughout his tenure on the Court, he continued to believe that the constitutionality of state criminal proceedings was to be governed by the general concept of due process as guaranteed by the Fourteenth Amendment.[109] Even when he agreed that states were required to follow the commands of the First Amendment, he often voted to allow them great leeway in its application.[110]

During World War II, with the permission of President Franklin D. Roosevelt, the Army issued orders establishing a curfew for, and the evacuation of, Japanese citizens who lived along the West Coast. In three of the four cases that came before it, the Supreme Court held that these orders did not violate any constitutional right of the Japanese.[111] Justice Frankfurter voted with the majority in each case. He argued that these orders were justified under Congress's power to wage war. "To find that the Constitution does not forbid the military measures now complained of," he noted, "does not carry with it approval of that which Congress and the Executive did. That is their business, not ours."[112]

The statement "That is their business, not ours" sums up the Justice's judicial philosophy in dealing with many actions taken by government, federal and state, when those actions are called into question as being unconsti-tutional.[113] With the exception of the equal protection cases involving dis-crimination against blacks, much of the time Frankfurter voted *for* the government and *against* individual freedom. He is, therefore, included as a *Justice for the Government.*

3

JUSTICE ROBERT H. JACKSON

PERSONAL LIFE

Growing Up

He grew up as a farm boy in northwestern Pennsylvania on a farm where his ancestors had lived for three generations. His formal education ended in high school. He was interested in law and he went to work in the local law office of a relative. After a few years he borrowed some money and went to the Albany Law School for one year, not for the full term. ...

He grew up in a community of very ordinary people, but he was different. ... His success as a great lawyer and a great judge came, I think, not only from his unusual ability as a lawyer, but also from the character of his own personality and the great charm which he exercised over everybody with whom he came in contact.[1]

These words were written 15 years after Justice Jackson's untimely death in 1954, by John Lord O'Brian, Esq., a long-time friend of Jackson's.

Robert H. Jackson was born in Spring Creek Township, Pennsylvania, on February 13, 1892, the son of William E. and Angelina Houghwout Jackson. Of Jackson's mother, biographer Eugene C. Gerhart wrote: "She was a teacher as well as mother to her only son. She made a habit of reading the youngster to sleep at night, and from her lips young Robert learned the old hymns and Bible stories. Often the selections were from the McGuffey Readers or other good books, of which the Jacksons had an unusual number. But also, now and then, as a special favor, she would read him some of the adventures of *Peck's Bad Boy*, which appealed to the impish streak in her young son."[2]

His father, William, also had considerable influence upon Jackson's education. "William constantly stressed the importance of independence to his young son. He pointed out to young Bob that a man could just as easily be independent when poor as he could be if he were rich. It was a man's *spirit* of independence that was important. To make his point clear he often put it this

JUSTICE ROBERT H. JACKSON (collection of the Supreme Court of the United States).

way to his growing boy: 'Keep always in the position where you have a right to, and can, tell any man to go to Hell.'"

The Jacksons were not a religious people, but religion played an important part in their lives. "Robert Jackson said in later life, 'I was always taught to respect other people's religion, and never to start a religious argument.'"

"Schooling was adequate but not extraordinary, except for an English teacher, Mary R. Willard, who instilled a love of language that served him throughout his life. 'Her influence would be hard to overestimate.' Public speaking was Jackson's forte from the beginning. On graduation from Jamestown High School, where he took an extra year after graduating from Frewsburg High School, Jackson was the class orator."[3] The family had moved to Frewsburg, New York, when Jackson was five years old.

Practicing Law

Jackson began the study of law right after high school by going into the Jamestown law office of Frank H. Mott, his mother's cousin. Although he enjoyed and profited by working in Mott's office, he borrowed money and entered Albany (New York) Law School in September 1911, where he studied for one year. Upon completion of the course there, Jackson returned to Jamestown and to Mott's office. He applied for admission to the New York bar in September 1913, and after passing the required bar exam was admitted to the practice in November. Before his admission to the bar, however, Jackson, with the permission of the court, defended some workers who were on strike from a traction plant. His friend John O'Brian describes this incident:

> In Jamestown, the workers on the traction line went on strike. To say that it was an unpopular strike would be an understatement, because of the discomfort caused to the patrons of the traction company. The workers were thereupon indicted for a violation of the laws which were generally grouped under the head of syndicalism—which we would say was communism.
>
> Jackson was outraged by this indictment. He had not yet been admitted to the bar, but nobody else appearing, he promptly came forward and volunteered his service to defend those unpopular strikers. With the permission of the court, because he was not yet admitted to the bar, he was permitted to act as their defense counsel and secured their acquittal.

Just before Jackson's admission to practice, Frank Mott took a position as Secretary of the New York Public Service Commission and moved to Albany.

> Later Jackson, to save expense, shared office space with other lawyers. Each lawyer contributed about thirty dollars a month to pay for rent, telephone, heat, light and the one stenographer the office boasted. This young lady was paid eight dollars a week—not a bad salary in the days before World War I. The lawyers were in their offices by 8:30 A.M. and did not leave until 5:30 or later in the evening. On Saturday nights, the night when the farmers came to town, law offices in Jamestown were often open until 8:00 or 9:00 in the evening.[4]

While attending law school in Albany, Jackson met Irene Gerhardt, who at the time was a secretary to New York Excise Commissioner William W.

Farley. The couple carried on a courtship over the next few years and were married early in 1916. Two children were born to the family, William Eldred in 1919, and Mary Margaret in 1921.

Jackson, who referred to himself as a "country lawyer,"[5] gave this description of what it meant to be one:

> He did not specialize, nor did he pick and choose clients. He rarely declined service to worthy ones because of inability to pay. Once enlisted for a client, he took his obligation seriously. He insisted on complete control of the litigation—he was no mere hired hand. But he gave every power and resource to the cause. He identified himself with the client's cause fully, sometimes too fully. He would fight the adverse party and fight his counsel, fight every hostile witness, and fight the court, fight public sentiment, fight any obstacle to his client's success. He never quit. ... He loved his profession, he had a real sense of dedication to the administration of justice, he held his head high as a lawyer, he rendered and exacted courtesy, honor and straightforwardness at the bar.[6]

Jackson was very active in bar association activities during his practice in Jamestown. He was president of the local bar association and helped organize the Federation of Bar Associations of Western New York. The then-governor of New York, Franklin D. Roosevelt, appointed him to the Commission to Investigate the Administration of Justice in New York State.[7]

Political Activities

Jackson was elected to the Democratic State Committee when he was 21 years old. When Woodrow Wilson became president in 1913, one of Jackson's assignments was to dole out patronage, including postmasterships. His contact with the Democratic Party in Washington, D.C., was Assistant Secretary of the Navy, Franklin D. Roosevelt. Of this experience, Jackson later said: "We had no access to anybody in Washington except through Roosevelt. I came to Washington in the years 1913 and 1914 with frequency. ... As a result of ... [a] party squabble for offices I had some acquaintance in the early years with Roosevelt and also gained some political experience. The upshot of it was, however, that when the end of my term as state committeeman arrived, I said, 'Never again!' It was taking my attention away from my law practice. I was getting into fights over these little post office jobs which didn't have any importance to anything that I was interested in a larger way."[8]

His belief in the Democratic Party, however, ran deep. In addressing a rally in late 1932, he expressly aimed his message at the young people in the audience. "You young men are destined to have an interesting experience. You will be razzed editorially if you stand up for the Democracy. You can make any kind of a speech for a Republican candidate and be hailed as a statesman in the local press. Any kind of a Democratic speech will be denounced. But you will find that you will grow in the respect and esteem of people just in proportion to the abuse that is spent on you."[9]

After Roosevelt was elected president in 1932, Jackson carried the New Deal message to the people in and around Jamestown. Jackson toured New York State with Democratic National Chairman Jim Farley in 1933, urging the election of Democrats to the State Legislature. Farley offered him a position in the new administration, but Jackson declined. Later, he was asked to come to Washington to be interviewed for the position as General Counsel of the Bureau of Internal Revenue. When he expressed the opinion that he did not have any tax experience, he was told by Secretary of the Treasury Henry Morganthau that that was one of the reasons he was called.

Some of his friends urged him to go to Washington while others, especially his clients, were hoping that he would not do so. Mrs. Jackson was not enthusiastic over the idea of leaving Jamestown. After giving the matter serious consideration, Jackson declined the offer, telling Secretary Morganthau that he did not want to give up his practice, which at the time was giving the family a comfortable living. Morganthau then asked if he would take a part-time position. Jackson, thinking that he might be able to work during the week in Washington and return to Jamestown to his law practice on weekends, accepted. Shortly after the family moved to Washington, it became clear that the work at the Bureau was taking all of his time, and he turned his law practice over to his partners.

In the Roosevelt Administration

General Counsel of the Bureau of Internal Revenue. Jackson took over as General Counsel on February 1, 1934. His first impression was that the department was "a typical bureaucracy, confusing in its bigness, cold in its attitude and pretty well wound up in red tape." But within a few weeks, he had changed his mind, and at the first meeting of the staff six weeks later, "he said that he had discovered that, with very few exceptions, he had found the men in the General Counsel's office doing hard, conscientious and thorough work."

The new General Counsel played a significant role in President Roosevelt's desire to change the nation's tax system. The President had proposed to Congress several far-reaching changes in the system. Among them were the adoption of laws providing for inheritance and gift taxes, taxes on income of corporations, including a tax on intercorporate dividends. In August 1935, Congress enacted the Revenue Act of 1935 containing many of the President's proposals.

Jackson, accompanied by Mrs. Jackson, made a business trip on behalf of the government to Europe in September of 1935, during which he interviewed our Ambassador to Germany, William E. Dodd, Jr. Following that visit, Dodd wrote in his diary: "Mr. Jackson seems to me to be the ablest and wisest man who has come here from the United States in a long time."

Assistant Attorney General. Jackson served as Assistant Attorney General for the Tax Division and for the Antitrust Division of the Justice Department.

Among the cases which he argued before the Supreme Court while Assistant Attorney General was *Steward Machine Co. v. Davis.*[10] The issue in that case was whether Congress had exceeded its authority when it enacted the Social Security Act, which included taxes for old-age assistance and unemployment compensation. The Court upheld the law, with Justice Benjamin Cardozo writing the majority opinion.

Much of Jackson's time as Assistant Attorney General of the Antitrust Division was spent on political matters for the president. "The period of Jackson's service in the Antitrust Division of the Department of Justice," Gerhart has written, "marked his maximum activity in political and legislative matters. He became involved in things of that kind far deeper than he had ever really wished to be. During 1937 his time was much occupied with several legislative projects. One was the fight over the 'Court-packing plan,' ....."[11]

Jackson was a delegate to the 1936 Democratic national convention and campaigned vigorously for Roosevelt prior to the general election in the fall.

During these early years of the Roosevelt administration, the Supreme Court was striking down as unconstitutional much of the New Deal legislation aimed at solving the economic crisis in the country. Although Jackson was disturbed over the Court's decisions, he was not at the center of the Court-packing plan. Attorney General Homer Cummings became Roosevelt's frontman to push the plan through Congress. The plan would have offered aged justices an opportunity to retire with a pension, and for those who did not retire, the president would have the power to appoint additional justices to the Court.

Despite Jackson's misgivings, he appeared before the Senate Judiciary Committee on March 11, 1937, to promote the plan. And although he was complimented for his fine performance, opposition to the plan was widespread.

Several events combined to kill the Court-packing plan. The Court handed down several decisions upholding Congress's power to enact economic legislation,[12] and Justice Willis Van Devanter, one of the Court's most conservative members, retired in June 1937.

Later, in writing about Roosevelt's attempt to change the makeup of the Court, Jackson wrote: "'Many who had felt obliged to support the plan 'to save the Constitution from the Court and the Court from itself,' had done so with sadness in their hearts. As soon as the Court began to show contrition and do penance for its sins, sentiment grew for forgiveness.' 'The President's enemies,' he wrote, 'defeated the court reform bill—the President achieved court reform.' The President lost the Court battle—and won the New Deal war."[13]

The work at the Justice Department, combined with his involvement in politics, took Jackson away from the thing he wanted to do most—practice law. He therefore decided to resign as of January 1, 1938, and made an appointment to see the President. The President would not hear of it, and said that "Jackson should withhold any action toward resignation for the time being at least," and Jackson agreed to do so.

Solicitor General of the United States. On February 24, during a speech to the Young Democratic Club of New York, Jackson said: "The Solicitor General is the chief advocate for public causes before the Supreme Court of the United States.... The office is probably the only office every lawyer happy in the work of his profession covets." Just a month before, President Roosevelt had nominated him for that position. His nomination, however, was met with sustained opposition from some senators. He was questioned about the content of many of the speeches he had given over the years as well as about his practice of law. The opposition proved fruitless, and he was confirmed by a Senate vote of 62 to 4.

Being Solicitor General was like returning to the practice of law for Jackson. Of that experience he has written: "Coming back to the practice of law, which I did in the Solicitor General's office, was like coming home after being out in a bad storm. I was delighted with the work. I cut off other types of things as fast as I could and settled down to the legal work of the Department of Justice in the Supreme Court and other appellate courts. I entered upon the most enjoyable period of my whole official life."[14]

Of the work of the Solicitor General he wrote: "The Solicitor General has a great deal to do with shaping the position that the government will take on many legal issues. [He] has power to approve or disapprove all government appeals in the lower courts. ... He will exercise his oversight so that cases do not come up through the courts on an inadequate record, or which present a question in such a manner that it is made difficult to sustain."

During these years as Solicitor General, Jackson continued to be an advisor to President Roosevelt. When Justice Benjamin Cardozo died, the President discussed with Jackson the possibility of Jackson being appointed to the Court. Roosevelt thought that it would be better for Jackson to come into the Cabinet before being nominated to the Court. The two discussed the appointment of Felix Frankfurter, and both agreed that he should be the one to take Cardozo's place on the Court. Frankfurter, therefore, was nominated and confirmed.

An opportunity to appoint Jackson to the Cabinet occurred when Homer Cummings resigned as Attorney General in late 1938. But because Roosevelt wanted to find a position in the government for Frank Murphy, recently defeated as governor of Michigan, Jackson was passed over. In explaining this to Jackson, the President said: "Bob, I've got to fill the place of Attorney General. I've told you before that I want you in the Cabinet. Here's the vacancy. But here's my problem. Frank Murphy has been beaten for governor of Michigan. Frank hasn't got one nickel to rub against another. He's got to have a job. ... I can't offer him anything less than a Cabinet position. ... I don't think Frank ought to be Attorney General. It isn't his forte, but temporarily I don't know of anything to do but to appoint him and take care of him." Jackson graciously accepted the President's decision.

Shortly thereafter, another opening occurred on the Court with the retirement of Justice Louis Brandeis. This time Roosevelt chose William O. Douglas, Chairman of the Securities and Exchange Commission.

The opportunity to have Jackson join the Cabinet occurred in late fall 1939 when Justice Pierce Butler died. Roosevelt created an opening in the Cabinet by nominating, and the Senate confirming, Attorney General Frank Murphy to replace Butler on the Supreme Court.

At the end of the Supreme Court's term in June 1939, "*Time* Magazine reported .... 'Lawyers like to say that the brilliance of John Marshall as Chief Justice reflected in no small part the brilliance of Lawyer Daniel Webster, who argued often before him. By such a token, the Supreme Court term was the term of Solicitor General Robert Houghwout Jackson. Working like a nailer, 14 hours a day, he argued 24 cases (in 14 groups)—a prodigious number compared to the ten or a dozen average of his busiest predecessors—and lost but two of them.'"[15]

Justice Louis D. Brandeis said of Jackson's tenure as Solicitor General: "Jackson should be Solicitor General for life."

Attorney General of the United States. The President appointed Jackson to the post of Attorney General in January 1940. As a member of the Cabinet, Jackson's role as advisor to the President continued. However, he saw the role of the Attorney General to also be the legal representative of the government. Philip B. Kurland quotes Jackson as saying: "I think the Attorney General has a dual position. He is the lawyer for the President. He is also, in a sense, laying down the law for the government as a judge might. I don't think he is quite as free to advocate an untenable position because it happens to be his client's position as he would be if he were in private practice. He has a responsibility to others than the President. He is the legal officer of the United States."[16]

In celebrating its 150th anniversary in February 1940, the Supreme Court chose the Attorney General to give the main address. Jackson concluded his address with the statement:

> The judgments and opinions of this Court deeply penetrate the intellectual life of the nation. This Court is more than an arbiter of cases and controversies. It is the custodian of a culture and is the protector of a philosophy of equal rights, of civil liberty, of tolerance, and of trusteeship of political and economic

power, general acceptance of which gives us a basic national unity. Without it our representative system would be impossible.[17]

During his tenure as Attorney General, Jackson ordered an investigation of tactics the FBI was accused of using when investigating cases; was considered as a potential presidential candidate; advocated a third term for Roosevelt; and, when the President was nominated, campaigned for him.

During 1941, as the war in Europe was escalating, Roosevelt relied upon Jackson for advice concerning what actions the United States should take. Among the thorny legal issues was the desire of the President to transfer 50 destroyers to Great Britain in exchange for bases in that country. The Attorney General issued an opinion to the President stating that the acquisition of the bases and the transfer of the destroyers were within the powers of the presidency, but that the transfer of so-called "mosquito boats" which were under construction would be a violation of law.[18]

Nomination to the Supreme Court

Justice James C. McReynolds submitted his resignation to the President effective February 1, 1941. Soon thereafter, Chief Justice Charles Evans Hughes gave the President a note that he would retire on July 1, 1941. Upon receiving notice of Hughes's retirement, the *Philadelphia Record* ran the following headline: "F.D.R. to Pick Jackson as Successor." The *Washington Post* put it this way: "Chief Justice Hughes Retires July 1, Jackson Most Likely Successor."

Shortly after receiving Hughes's note, the President and Jackson met at the White House. The President explained that in their conversation, Hughes suggested that in appointing a new chief justice the president should choose from members of the present Court, and that Justice Harlan F. Stone be that person. Jackson recites the following conversation with the President:

> I said very frankly, "Mr. President, if you feel disposed to appoint Stone, which I think is probably better for the Court and the country than to appoint me, that's perfectly satisfactory. If you were going to appoint a New Dealer to [be Chief]—anyone other than Stone—then I think my claims would be entitled to consideration."
> He said, "So do I, I think they'd be unanswerable" ...
> I said, "In any event, Mr. President, Associate Justice of the Supreme Court is a long way from the farm in Spring Creek. It's all that I'm entitled to."[19]

There was little opposition to Jackson being confirmed as Associate Justice, and the Senate Judiciary Committee voted unanimously to confirm him.

When Jackson joined the Court, Harlan F. Stone was Chief Justice. Other members of the Court were Justices Owen J. Roberts, Hugo L. Black, Stanley Reed, Felix Frankfurter, William O. Douglas, Frank Murphy, and James F. Byrnes.

United States Chief Prosecutor at the Nuremburg Trials

Late in April 1945, after the Justice had been on the Court for about four years, he received a phone call from Judge Samuel Rosenman informing him that President Harry S Truman wanted him to go to Germany and act as a prosecutor at the trials of Germans alleged to have committed war crimes during World War II. Commenting upon the Justice's reaction, author Gerhart has written: "Jackson's zest for advocacy was too compelling, the lure of a world trial too attractive, the stakes too high to let this chance of several lifetimes pass by. He immediately began telephoning and getting people together for his staff. Robert Jackson decided that he would be America's advocate at the first international criminal trial in world history."[20] In assembling his staff, Jackson included his son, Ensign William E. Jackson, USNR.

Jackson left for Europe in May 1945, and returned to the Supreme Court in the fall of 1946. In 1951, Justice Jackson was among nine Americans nominated for the Nobel Peace Prize. He was nominated "because of his brilliant work as chief United States prosecutor at the Nuremburg trials of the top Nazi war criminals...."

Jackson served as an Associate Justice from July 7, 1941, until his death on October 9, 1954.

AS ASSOCIATE JUSTICE (1941–1954)

The Free Exercise of Religion

Justice Jackson joined the dissenters in three cases involving distribution of literature by Jehovah's Witnesses.[21] A majority of the Court had held that laws requiring payment of license taxes for distributing religious literature, and prohibiting persons from going door-to-door to distribute such literature, violated the free exercise rights of the distributors.

Justice Douglas, referring to the license tax, pointed out that it "is a flat license tax levied and collected as a condition to the pursuit of activities whose enjoyment is guaranteed by the First Amendment. Accordingly, it restrains in advance those constitutional liberties of press and religion and inevitably tends to suppress their exercise."[22]

In concluding that the ordinance prohibiting all door-to-door soliciting also violated the First Amendment, Justice Black noted that the "ordinance does not control anything but the distribution of literature, and in that respect it substitutes the judgment of the community for the judgment of the individual householder. It submits the distributor to criminal punishment for annoying the person on whom he calls, even though the recipient of the literature distributed is in fact glad to receive it."[23] Furthermore: "Freedom to distribute information to every citizen wherever he desires to receive it is so clearly vital to the preservation of a free society that, putting aside reasonable police and health regulations of time and manner of distribution, it must be fully preserved."

Justice Jackson took issue with the Court's striking down these laws without considering the impact the distribution was having upon the potential recipients. He discussed at length the campaign of the Jehovah's Witnesses in the communities involved, and acknowledged that his dissent was "induced in no small part by the facts recited."

Justice Douglas referred to the activities of the Jehovah's Witnesses as occupying "the same high estate under the First Amendment as do worship in the churches and preaching from the pulpits." But, Jackson protested: "How ... can the Court today hold it a 'high constitutional privilege' to go to homes, including those of devout Catholics on Palm Sunday morning, and thrust upon them literature calling their church a 'whore' and their faith a 'racket?'"

Jackson was of the opinion that the majority was not giving sufficient consideration to the privacy of the homeowner. "Nor am I convinced that we can have freedom of religion only by denying the American's deep-seated conviction that his home is a refuge from the pulling and hauling of the market place and the street. For a stranger to corner a man in his home, summon him to the door and put him in the position either of arguing his religion or of ordering one of unknown disposition to leave is a questionable use of religious freedom."

School children forced to salute and recite the Pledge of Allegiance to the flag received more consideration from the Justice than did door-to-door solicitors. He wrote the majority opinion striking down the salute and pledge requirement of West Virginia.[24] "To sustain the compulsory flag salute," he wrote, "we are required to say that a Bill of Rights which guards the individual's right to speak his mind, left it open to public authorities to compel him to utter what is not in his mind."

Jackson's opinion contains two widely read and acclaimed passages relating to the part the Bill of Rights plays in our governmental scheme.

> The very purpose of a Bill of Rights was to withdraw certain subjects from the vicissitudes of political controversy, to place them beyond the reach of majorities and officials and to establish them as legal principles to be applied by the courts. One's right to life, liberty, and property, to free speech, a free press, freedom of worship and assembly, and other fundamental rights may not be submitted to vote; they depend on the outcome of no elections.

> * * * * *

> If there is any fixed star in our constitutional constellation, it is that no official, high or petty, can prescribe what shall be orthodox in politics, nationalism, religion, or other matters of opinion or force citizens to confess by word or act their faith therein. If there are any circumstances which permit an exception, they do not now occur to us.

Justice Jackson, however, did not believe that the above applied to Carl Jacob Kunz, a Baptist minister who believed that it was his duty to "go out on the highways and byways and preach the word of God."[25] In order to do so in New York City, however, it was necessary to obtain a permit from the police commissioner, which Reverend Kunz did. The permit, however, was later revoked "on evidence that he [Kunz] had ridiculed and denounced other religious beliefs at his meetings." Kunz continued to preach without the permit, however, and was arrested, convicted and fined ten dollars. His appeal to New York courts was to no avail, but the Supreme Court reversed. In giving the Court's opinion, Chief Justice Fred Vinson declared: "We have here, then, an ordinance which gives an administrative official discretionary power to control in advance the right of citizens to speak on religious matters on the streets of New York. As such, the ordinance is clearly invalid as a prior restraint on the exercise of First Amendment rights."

Vinson, and the majority, relied upon several cases in which the Court had "consistently condemned licensing systems which vest in an administrative official discretion to grant or withhold a permit upon broad criteria unrelated to proper regulation of public places."

Justice Jackson did not find the case so simple. He believed that Kunz had lost his right to speak because of the scurrilous attacks he made on other religions. "At these meetings," Jackson pointed out, "Kunz preached, among many other things of like tenor, that 'The Catholic Church makes merchandise out of souls,' that Catholicism is 'a religion of the devil,' and that the Pope is 'the anti–Christ.' The Jews he denounced as 'Christ-killers,' and he said of them, 'All the garbage that didn't believe in Christ should have been burnt in the incinerators. It's a shame they all weren't.'"

Jackson criticized the majority for not pointing out what standards would be appropriate to guide the administrative official in issuing permits. "If the Court is deciding that the permit system for street meetings is so unreasonable as to deny due process of law, it would seem appropriate to point out respects in which it is unreasonable. This I am unable to learn, from this or any former decision."

Jackson then returned to the question of the effect such scurrilous speech would have upon people on the street. "Every individual in this frightening aggregation [the people of New York] is legally free to live, to labor, to travel, when and where he chooses. In streets and public places, all races and nationalities and all sorts and conditions of men walk, linger and mingle. Is it not reasonable that the City protect the dignity of these persons against fanatics who take possession of its streets to hurl into its crowds defamatory epithets that hurt like rocks?" For him, the answer was clear. "Racial fears and hatreds," he declared, "have been at the root of the most terrible riots that have disgraced American civilization. They are ugly possibilities that overhang every great American city. The 'consecrated hatreds of sect' account for more than a few of the world's bloody disorders. These are the explosives which the Court says Kunz may play with in the public streets, and the community must not only tolerate but aid him. I find no such doctrine in the Constitution."

Freedom of Speech

Picketing, Soliciting and Distributing Literature. Jackson joined Justice Frankfurter's opinion in *Ritter's Cafe* wherein the Court upheld an injunction against union members picketing in front of a cafe whose owner had employed a nonunion contractor to construct a building some distance away. The majority concluded that the picketing violated a state law aimed at preventing restraint of trade. Justice Black objected because he believed that the injunction prevented the public from receiving information about the dispute between the nonunion contractor and the building workers' union. "I can see no reason," Black argued, "why members of the public should be deprived of any opportunity to get information which might enable them to use their influence to tip the scales in favor of the side they think is right."[26]

On the same day that the Court decided *Ritter's Cafe*, however, the justices voted unanimously to strike down an injunction against picketing, with Justice Jackson writing the opinion.[27] The injunction arose out of a dispute between union truck drivers and peddlers who distributed baked goods. The increase in the use of peddlers by the bakeries to distribute their products constituted a threat to the livelihood of union drivers. When efforts to persuade the peddlers to join the union were unsuccessful, the union drivers picketed peddlers Wohl and Platzman. Wohl and Platzman then obtained an injunction against the picketing, which the New York appellate courts upheld.

In holding that the injunction infringed upon the right of the union members to picket, Jackson explored at length the dispute between the parties. "We ourselves," he concluded, "can perceive no substantive evil of such magnitude as to mark a limit to the right of free speech which the ... [union members] sought to exercise. ... A state is not required to tolerate in all places and all circumstances even peaceful picketing by an individual. But so far as we can tell, ... [Wohl's and Platzman's] mobility and their insulation from the public as middlemen made it practically impossible for ... [the union members] to make known their legitimate grievances to the public whose patronage was sustaining the peddler system except by the means employed and contemplated..."

Jackson later voted once to strike down an injunction against picketing and five times to uphold such injunctions.[28]

Joseph Beauharnais's problem was the distribution of a leaflet allegedly portraying the "depravity, criminality, unchastity or lack of virtue of citizens of Negro race and color."[29] Jackson dissented when the Court upheld Beauharnais's conviction. The Justice wanted it understood, however, that "the

Fourteenth Amendment did not 'incorporate' the First, that the powers of Congress and of the States over this subject are not of the same dimensions, and that because Congress probably could not enact this law it does not follow that the States may not." Nevertheless he argued, the state should not be permitted to punish just the printed words without a showing of some specific injury. "Punishment of printed words, based on their *tendency* either to cause breach of the peace or injury to persons or groups, in my opinion, is justifiable only if the prosecution survives the 'clear and present danger' test." Because no proof was offered that any violence or injury occurred from Beauharnais' leaflet, the Justice concluded that the Court in applying the law to this case "lost sight of ... [individual] rights."

Unpopular Speech. The following was the scene at an auditorium in Chicago where Father Arthur W. Terminiello gave a speech in the late 1940s.

> The court below ... heard ... that the crowd reached an estimated number of 1,500. Picket lines obstructed and interfered with access to the building. The crowd constituted 'a surging, howling mob hurling epithets' at those who would enter and 'tried to tear their clothes off.' One young woman's coat was torn off and she had to be assisted into the meeting by policemen. Those inside the hall could hear the loud noises and hear those on the outside yell, 'Fascists,' 'Hitlers' and curse words like 'damn Fascists.' Bricks were thrown through the windowpanes before and during the speaking. About 28 windows were broken. The street was black with people on both sides for at least a block either way; bottles, stink bombs and brickbats were thrown. Police were unable to control the mob, which kept breaking the windows at the meeting hall, drowning out the speaker's voice at times and breaking in through the back door of the auditorium. About 17 of the group outside were arrested by the police.[30]

Father Terminiello was arrested and charged with breach of the peace. At his trial, the judge instructed the jury that "'breach of the peace' consists of any 'misbehavior which violates the public peace and decorum'; and that the 'misbehavior may constitute a breach of the peace if it stirs the public to anger, invites dispute, brings about a condition of unrest, or creates a disturbance, or if it molests the inhabitants in the enjoyment of peace and quiet by arousing alarm.'"

When the case reached the Supreme Court, a majority ignored the actual melee that had occurred during Terminiello's speech, and focused solely on the judge's charge to the jury. Concluding that the charge was erroneous, the majority reversed. They were of the opinion that the First Amendment barred conviction of one whose speech stirred the listeners to anger and invited dispute. "Accordingly," Justice Douglas noted, "a function of free speech under our system of government is to invite dispute. It may indeed best serve its high purpose when it induces a condition of unrest, creates dissatisfaction with conditions as they are, or even stirs people to anger. Speech is often provocative and challenging. It may strike at prejudices and preconceptions and have profound unsettling effects as it presses for acceptance of an idea."

But for Justice Jackson, that was not the real issue. The real issue was the fact that there was mob violence, rioting, and public disorder which the police had an obligation to stop. "In the long run," he argued, "maintenance of free speech will be more endangered if the population can have no protection from the abuses which lead to violence." "The choice is not between order and liberty," he continued. "It is between liberty with order and anarchy without either. There is danger that, if the Court does not temper its doctrinaire logic with a little practical wisdom, it will convert the constitutional Bill of Rights into a suicide pact."

Although Eugene Dennis and the other leaders of the Communist Party, who were charged with violating the Smith Act, did not create the kind of situation that Terminiello had, Jackson nevertheless voted with the majority to affirm their convictions.[31]

For the Justice, the Communist Party was an anathema.

> The Communists have no scruples against sabotage, terrorism, assassination, or mob disorder; but violence is not with them, as with anarchists, an end in itself. The Communist Party advocates force only when prudent and profitable. Their strategy of stealth precludes premature or uncoordinated outbursts of violence, except, of course, when the blame will be placed on shoulders other than their own. They resort to violence as to truth, not as a principle but as an expedient. Force or violence, as they would resort to it, may never be necessary, because infiltration and deception may be enough.

Although the majority had concluded that the activities of these eleven communist leaders presented a "clear and present danger" to the security of the United States, Jackson would not have given them the benefit of that test.

The Justice was of the opinion that all that was necessary in this case was to prove that these defendants had entered into a conspiracy to teach and advocate the overthrow of the government by force or violence. "The law of conspiracy," he argued, "has been the chief means at the Government's disposal to deal with the growing problems created by such organizations. I happen to think it is an awkward and inept remedy, but I find no constitutional authority for taking this weapon from the Government." With that said, Jackson added that he had "little faith in the long-range effectiveness of this conviction to stop the rise of the Communist movement. Communism will not got to jail with these Communists."

Miscellaneous Speech. Reverend Samuel Saia "is a minister of the religious sect known as Jehovah's Witnesses. He obtained from the Chief of Police permission to use sound equipment, mounted atop his car, to amplify lectures on religious subjects. The lectures were given at a fixed place in a public park on designated Sundays. When this permit expired, he applied for another one but was refused on the ground that complaints had been made. [Reverend Saia], nevertheless, continued to use his equipment as planned on four occasions, but without a permit." He was arrested and tried in Police Court for violations of the [permit] ordinance. "It was undisputed that he used his equipment to amplify speeches in the park and that they were on religious subjects. Some of the witnesses testified that they were annoyed by the sound, though not by the content of the addresses; others were not disturbed by either."[32]

Saia's conviction was reversed by the Supreme Court because the ordinance granted complete discretion to the Chief of Police in the granting or withholding permits. "When a city allows an official to ban [loud-speakers] ... in his uncontrolled discretion, it sanctions a device for suppression of free communication of ideas. In this case a permit is denied because some persons were said to have found the sound annoying. In the next one a permit may be denied because some people find the ideas annoying. Annoyance at ideas can be cloaked in annoyance at sound. The power of censorship inherent in this type of ordinance reveals its vice."

"To my mind," Justice Jackson argued in dissent, "this is not a free speech issue. Lockport [New York], has in no way denied or restricted the free use, even in its park, of all of the facilities for speech with which nature has endowed the ... [Reverend Saia]." Municipalities, he asserted, should have the right to keep out of parks "installations of devices which would flood the area with religious appeals obnoxious to many and thereby deprive the public of the enjoyment of the property for the purposes for which it was properly set aside." Furthermore, the Justice did not agree that it was the duty of courts to balance the interests of the community against the right of the individual to exercise a constitutional right. "I disagree entirely with the idea that 'Courts must balance the various community interests in passing on the constitutionality of local regulations of the character involved here.' It is for the local communities to balance their own interests—that is politics—and what courts should keep out of. Our only function is to apply constitutional limitations."

Jackson's dislike for the use of sound equipment caused him to concur when the Court upheld Charles Kovacs's conviction for violating a Trenton, New Jersey, ordinance prohibiting the use of amplification equipment emitting "loud and raucous noises."[33] "Freedom of speech," he declared, "for Kovacs does not, in my view, include freedom to use sound amplifiers to drown out the natural speech of others." There was, however, no evidence that Kovacs's speech was interfering with anyone else's speech. As Justice Black pointed out: "The record reflects not even a shadow of evidence to prove that the noise was either 'loud or raucous,' unless these words of the ordinance refer to any noise coming from an amplifier, whatever its volume or tone."

R. J. Thomas's problem was not sound amplification but rather his solicitation of Pat O'Sullivan to join the Oil Workers Union. Thomas, a vice-president of the Congress of Industrial Organizations, went to Texas to speak and recruit union members. In anticipation of Thomas's speech, the local District Attorney secured a court order preventing Thomas from speaking without securing a labor "organizer's card," as required by law. Thomas, ignoring the order, gave the speech and solicited O'Sullivan to join the Union. He was charged with and convicted of contempt of court, which conviction was upheld by the Texas Supreme Court but reversed by the U.S. Supreme Court.[34] "If the exercise of the rights of free speech and free assembly cannot be made a crime," Justice Wiley Rutledge declared, "we do not think this can be accomplished by the device of requiring previous registration as a condition for exercising them and making such a condition the foundation for restraining in advance their exercise and for imposing a penalty for violating such a restraining order. So long as no more is involved than the exercise of the rights of free speech and free assembly, it is immune to such a restriction."

Jackson agreed. "The very purpose of the First Amendment is to foreclose public authority from assuming a guardianship of the public mind through regulating the press, speech, and religion. In this field every person must be his own watchman for truth, because the forefathers did not trust any government to separate the true from the false for us. ... Very many are the interests which the state may protect against the practice of an occupation, very few are those it may assume to protect against the practice of propagandizing by speech or press. These are thereby left great range of freedom."

Freedom of Association

Affidavits and Oaths.

> If the statute before us required labor union officers to forswear membership in the Republican Party, the Democratic Party or the Socialist Party, I suppose all agree that it would be unconstitutional. But why, if it is valid as to the Communist Party?
>
> The answer, for me, is in the decisive differences between the Communist Party and every other party of any importance in the long experience of the United States with party government.[35]

That was Justice Jackson's response to the question of the constitutionality of a provision of the National Labor Relations Act which required officers of unions to file an affidavit "that he is not a member of the Communist Party or affiliated with such party, and that he does not believe in, and is not a member of or supports any organization that believes in or teaches, the overthrow of the United States Government by force or by any illegal or unconstitutional methods."

In voting to uphold the oath requirement as applied to the Communist Party, Jackson described at length why that Party was not the same as the

Republican, Democratic or Socialist Parties. The Communist Party, he argued, wants to seize power rather than "acquire power through the vote of a free electorate." It "is dominated and controlled by a foreign government;" its methods are "[v]iolent and undemocratic;" the Party wants to gain a "hold on the American population by acquiring control of the labor movement;" and every member "is an agent to execute the Communist program."

The Justice made it clear, however, that, while he believed that government had power to control people's actions, it did not have power to control their beliefs.

"A catalogue of rights was placed in our Constitution, in my view," he concluded, "to protect the individual in his individuality, and neither statutes which put those rights at the mercy of officials nor judicial decisions which put them at the mercy of the mob are consistent with its text or its spirit." In spite of the Justice's comments upon the "catalogue of rights ... placed in our Constitution," he did not believe that these rights protected communists.

Blacklisting and Punishment for Membership. The *Anti-Fascist Committee v. McGrath* case,[36] spawned six opinions. Five of those opinions, including one by the Justice, held that the dismissal of the lawsuits by the District Court denied the plaintiffs their constitutional rights. The plaintiffs—the Joint Anti-Refugee Committee, the National Council of American-Soviet Friendship, Inc., and the International Workers Order, Inc.—had all been listed by Attorney General J. Howard McGrath as Communist organizations and their names given to the Loyalty Review Board of the Civil Service Commission. That Board had authority to refuse government employment to, or to remove from employment, individuals who were members of organizations designated as subversive.

The plaintiffs' action against McGrath had been dismissed by the District Court, and the dismissal was upheld by the Court of Appeals. The Supreme Court, however, reversed.

In concurring, Jackson did not believe that the organizations had any right to complain about being listed as a subversive organization. The injuries which they claim they suffer, he argued, "is that they cannot attract audiences, enlist members, or obtain contributions as readily as before."

The Justice was concerned, however, with the rights of the organizations' individual members. "But the real target of all this procedure," he noted, "is the government employee who is a member of, or sympathetic to, one or more accused organizations. He not only may be discharged, but disqualified from employment, upon no other ground than such membership or sympathetic affiliation. And he cannot attack the correctness of the Attorney General's designation in any loyalty proceeding."

Justice Jackson did not extend his concern for the rights of individual members of an organization if that organization was the Communist Party. For example, he wrote the majority opinion upholding the deportation of Peter

Harisiades, Mr. Mascitti and Mrs. Coleman because they had been a members of the Communist Party.[37]

"Harisiades, a Greek national, accompanied his father to the United States in 1916, when thirteen years of age, and has resided here since. He has taken a wife and sired two children, all citizens. He joined the Communist Party in 1925, when it was known as the Workers Party, and served as an organizer, Branch Executive Committeeman, secretary of its Greek Bureau, and editor of its paper 'Empros.' The party discontinued his membership, along with that of other aliens, in 1939, but he has continued association with members. He was familiar with the principles and philosophy of the Communist Party and says he still believes in them. He disclaims personal belief in use of force and violence and asserts that the party favored their use in defense." Harisiades was ordered deported in 1939, but because the government was unable to locate him, the orders were not served until 1946.

"Mascitti, a citizen of Italy, came to this country in 1920, at the age of sixteen. He married a resident alien and has one American-born child. He was a member of the Young Workers Party, the Workers Party and the Communist Party between 1923 and 1929. His testimony was that he knew the party advocated proletarian dictatorship, to be established by force and violence if the capitalist class resisted. He heard some speakers advocate violence, in which he says he did not personally believe, and he was not clear as to the party policy. He resigned in 1929, apparently because he lost sympathy with or interest in the party. A warrant for his deportation issued and was served in 1946."

"Mrs. Coleman, a native of Russia, was admitted to the United States in 1914, when thirteen years of age. She married an American citizen and has three children, citizens by birth. She admits being a member of the Communist Party for about a year, beginning in 1919, and again from 1928 to 1930, and again from 1936 to 1937 or 1938. She held no office and her activities were not significant. She disavowed much knowledge of party principles and program, claiming she joined each time because of some injustice the party was then fighting. The reasons she gives for leaving the party are her health and the party's discontinuance of alien memberships. She has been ordered deported because after entry she became a member of an organization advocating the overthrow of the Government by force and violence."

In approving the deportation of these individuals, the Justice pointed out that Congress had concluded that the Communist Party was a threat to our national security. "It would be easy," Jackson noted, "for those of us who do not have security responsibility to say that those who do are taking Communism too seriously and overestimating its danger. But we have an Act of one Congress which, for a decade, subsequent Congresses have never repealed but have strengthened and extended. We, in our private opinions, need not concur in Congress' policies to hold its enactments constitutional. Judicially we must tolerate what personally we may regard as a legislative mistake."

Jackson did not think much of the argument of the petitioners that their First Amendment rights to freedom of speech, press and assembly were being violated. "Our Constitution," he declared, "sought to leave no excuse for violent attack on the status quo by providing a legal alternative—attack by ballot. To arm all men for orderly change, the Constitution put in their hands a right to influence the electorate by press, speech and assembly. This means freedom to advocate or promote Communism by means of the ballot box, but it does not include the practice or incitement to violence." There was no evidence, however, that either Harisiades, Mascitti, or Mrs. Coleman had ever practiced or incited violence.

Freedom of the Press

Contempt of Court for Publication. In a case involving the right to possession of a building in Corpus Christi, Texas, Judge Joe D. Browning refused to accept the verdict of the jury, and ordered them to render a different one. After refusing several times to do so, the jury finally gave verdict as Judge Browning directed but noted that it was being coerced to do so. When local newspapers heard about the case, they printed several articles about it. Justice Douglas describes the situation: "Browning, the judge, who is a layman and who holds an elective office, was criticized for taking the case from the jury. That ruling was called 'arbitrary action' and a 'travesty on justice.' It was deplored that a layman, rather than a lawyer, sat as judge. Groups of local citizens were reported as petitioning the judge to grant Mayes [who was the loser in the case] a new trial and it was said that one group had labeled the judge's ruling as a 'gross miscarriage of justice.' It was also said that the judge's behavior had properly brought down 'the wrath of public opinion upon his head,' that the people were aroused because a service man [Mayes] 'seems to be getting a raw deal,' and that there was 'no way of knowing whether justice was done, because the first rule of justice, giving both sides an opportunity to be heard, was repudiated.' And the fact that there could be no appeal from the judge's ruling to a court 'familiar with proper procedure and able to interpret and weigh motions and arguments by opposing counsel' was deplored."[38]

Conway C. Craig, Bob McCracken, and Tom Mulvaney, the publisher, managing editor, and reporter, respectively, of the *Corpus Christi Caller* and *Corpus Christi Times*, were charged and convicted of contempt for the articles which they ran in their newspapers criticizing Judge Browning.

When the case reached the Supreme Court, it reversed in an opinion written by Justice Douglas. "In a case where it is asserted that a person has been deprived by a state court of a fundamental right secured by the Constitution, an independent examination of the facts by this Court is often required to be made." With that understanding, Douglas examined all of the news articles relating to the trial and concluded there "was strong language, intemperate language, and we assume, an unfair criticism." "But," he pointed out, "a judge may not hold in contempt one 'who ventures to publish anything that tends to make him unpopular or to belittle him....'"

In referring to the vehemence of the language in the editorials, he said: "The fires which it kindles must constitute an imminent, not merely a likely, threat to the administration of justice. The danger must not be remote or even probable; it must immediately imperil." And that was not the situation in this case. "In the circumstances of the present case," Douglas declared, "it amounts at the very most to an intimation that come the next election the newspaper in question will not support the incumbent. But it contained no threat to oppose him in the campaign if the decision on the merits was not overruled, nor any implied reward if it was changed."

Jackson thought the Court's decision sent the wrong message to the press and the public, and dissented. "I think this opinion conveys a wrong impression of the responsibilities of a free press for the calm and dispassionate administration of justice and that we should not hesitate to condemn what has been done here." He acknowledged the importance of a free press, but thought the material published had passed the boundaries of that freedom. "The right of the people to have a free press is a vital one, but so is the right to have a calm and fair trial free from outside pressures and influences. ... I think this publisher passed beyond the legitimate use of press freedom and infringed the citizen's right to a calm and impartial trial."

The Pursuit of Liberty

The Right to Travel.

> The facts of this case are simple and are not disputed. Appellant [Edwards] is a citizen of the United States and a resident of California. In December, 1939, he left his home in Marysville, California, for Spur, Texas, with the intention of bringing back to Marysville his wife's brother, Frank Duncan, a citizen of the United States and a resident of Texas. When he arrived in Texas, ... [Edwards] learned that Duncan had last been employed by the Works Progress Administration. [Edwards] ... thus became aware of the fact that Duncan was an indigent person and he continued to be aware of it throughout the period involved in this case. The two men agreed that ... [Edwards] should transport Duncan from Texas to Marysville in ... [Edwards's] automobile.[39]

Shortly after their arrival in Marysville, Edwards was charged with and convicted of "bringing into the State ... [an] indigent person ... knowing him to be an indigent person...."

Edwards's conviction was upheld by a California appellate court but reversed by the U.S. Supreme Court, in an opinion written by Justice James F. Brynes. For the majority, there was only one constitutional issue to be resolved. "We are of the opinion," Brynes concluded, "that ... [the law] is not a valid exercise of the police power of California; that it imposes an unconstitutional burden upon interstate commerce, and that the conviction under it cannot be sustained."

Justice Jackson agreed with the Court's decision but not with its reasoning. He decried the majority's use of the Commerce Clause to adjudicate what he considered human rights. "To hold that the measure of ... [a person's] rights is the commerce clause is likely to result eventually either in distorting the commercial law or in denaturing human rights." For him, Duncan had a right to travel which was protected by the Privileges and Immunities Clause of the Fourteenth Amendment. "This Court should ... hold squarely that it is a privilege of citizenship of the United States, protected from state abridgment, to enter any state of the Union, either for temporary sojourn or for the establishment of permanent residence therein and for gaining resultant citizenship thereof. If national citizenship means less than this, it means nothing."

The Justice then turned to what he saw as the real issue in the case and that was whether California could use indigency as the criterion to determine who could move into the state. And he concluded that it could not. "Any measure which would divide our citizenry on the basis of property into one class free to move from state to state and another class that is poverty-bound to the place where it has suffered misfortune is not only at war with the habit and custom by which our country has expanded, but is also a short-sighted blow at the security of property itself."

Equal Protection of the Law

Blacks on Juries.

> The case before us is that of a Negro convicted of murder by crushing the skull of a sleeping watchman with a piece of iron pipe to carry out a burglary. No question is here as to his guilt. We are asked to order his release from this conviction upon the sole ground that Negroes were purposefully discriminated against in selection of the grand jury that indicted him. It is admitted that Negroes were not excluded from the trial jury by which he was convicted.
>
> In setting aside this conviction, the Court is moved by a desire to enforce equality in that realm where, above all, it must be enforced—in our judicial system. But this conviction is reversed for errors that have nothing to do with the defendant's guilt or innocence, or with a fair trial of that issue. This conflicts with another principle important to our law, *viz.*, that no conviction should be set aside for errors not affecting substantial rights of the accused.[40]

With those words the Justice, the lone dissenter in the reversal of the conviction of Lee Cassell, a black, took issue with the Court's practice of reversing convictions when blacks were excluded from either the grand jury that indicted the defendant or the petit jury that tried him or her.

In reversing Cassell's conviction, the Court pointed out that "an accused is entitled to have charges against him considered by a jury in the selection of which there has been neither inclusion nor exclusion because of race." Justice Reed, writing for himself and three other justices, examined the process by which the grand jury that indicted Cassell was chosen. "The statements of the jury commissioners that they chose only whom they knew," Justice Stanley Reed pointed out, "and that they knew no eligible Negroes in an area where Negroes made up so large a proportion of the population, prove the intentional exclusion that is discrimination in violation of ... [Cassell's] constitutional rights."

In dissenting, Jackson pointed out that it is the right of those blacks excluded from the jury that is involved in these kinds of cases, not the right of the defendant to have blacks on the jury. "The Negro's right to be selected for grand jury service," he argued, "is unquestionable and should be directly and uncompromisingly enforced. But I doubt if any good purpose will be served in the long run by identifying the right of the most worthy Negroes to serve on grand juries with the efforts of the least worthy to defer or escape punishment for crime. ... I would treat this as a case where the irregularity is not shown to have harmed this defendant, and affirm the conviction."

For Aliens. In 1934, and again in 1937, Kajiro Oyama, a Japanese citizen who was not eligible for United States citizenship, purchased land in California taking title in the name of his son Fred, who was a United States citizen by birth. At the time, California's Alien Land Law prohibited Kajiro Oyama from owning land in California because he was an alien.

Because Fred was only six years old in 1934, his father was appointed as his legal guardian and took over the management of the 1934 parcel, and the 1937 parcel when that was purchased.

The Oyamas were evacuated from the Pacific Coast in 1942, when aliens were ordered to do so because of the Japanese attack on Pearl Harbor.

In 1944, while the Oyamas were still forbidden to return home, California petitioned a court to have the land escheat to the state, arguing that in putting the title in his son's name Kajiro Oyama sought to circumvent the law. The court agreed, and that decision was affirmed by the California Supreme Court. Without addressing the question of the constitutionality of California's Alien Land Law, the United States Supreme Court reversed.[41]

The Court pointed out that under California law when a parent purchases land and takes title in the name of a minor, it is presumed that the parent has made a completed gift to the minor. That is not true, however, if land is purchased by an alien and title is taken in the name of the alien's minor child. In such cases, there is no presumption that the parent had made a gift to the minor, and the minor, in this case Fred, is required to prove that there was a completed gift to him. The Court concluded that California's procedure of treating citizens different than aliens, in land transactions such as this one, was a violation of equal protection of the law.

Justice Jackson, in dissent, chided the majority for not deciding the question of the constitutionality of the Land Law but did not address that issue himself. He reasoned that, assuming the law to be constitutional, California had the right to determine the procedure by which it was enforced. "While I think that California has pursued a policy of unnecessary severity by which the Oyamas lose both land and investment, I do not see how this Court, while conceding the State's right to keep the policy on its books, can strip the State of the right to make its Act effective."

Although some of the justices thought Lothar Eisentrager was being treated unequally by the government, Jackson did not. Eisentrager was a civilian employee of the German government working in China when Germany surrendered, ending the war in Europe in May 1945. At the time, the place where Eisentrager worked was under the control of Japanese armed forces. In August 1946, the United States brought charges against Eisentrager for "violating laws of war, by engaging in, permitting or ordering continued military activity against the United States after surrender of Germany and before surrender of Japan."[42] A United States military commission, sitting in China, convicted Eisentrager, and he was taken to Germany to serve his sentence in a prison operated by the United States Army.

Eisentrager sought review of his case by a petition for a writ of habeas corpus served upon Secretary of Defense James A. Forrestal. He argued that his confinement was in violation of the Fifth Amendment to the United States Constitution, and that the military commission was without jurisdiction to try him.

The District Court dismissed the writ, being of the opinion that it did not have jurisdiction of the case. The Court of Appeals reversed. Writing for himself, and Judges Henry Edgerton and James M. Proctor, Judge E. Barrett Prettyman said: "We think that any person who is deprived of his liberty by officials of the United States ... and who can show that his confinement is in violation of a prohibition of the Constitution, has a right to the writ."[43] Justice Jackson and a majority of the Supreme Court disagreed and reversed.

Referring to rights of an alien generally, the Justice explained:

> Mere lawful presence in the country creates an implied assurance of safe conduct and gives him certain rights; they become more extensive and secure when he makes preliminary declaration of intention to become a citizen, and they expand to those of full citizenship upon naturalization. ...
>
> But, in extending constitutional protections beyond the citizenry, the Court has been at pains to point out that it was the alien's presence within its [the United States'] territorial jurisdiction that gave the Judiciary power to act.[44]

Furthermore, he argued: "If this Amendment [the Fifth] invests enemy aliens in unlawful hostile action against us with immunity from military trial, it puts them in a more protected position than our own soldiers. American citizens conscripted into the military service are thereby stripped of their Fifth Amendment rights and as members of the military establishment are subject to its discipline, including military trials for offenses against aliens or Americans." The Justice then concluded: "We hold that the Constitution does not confer a right of personal security or an immunity from military trial and punishment upon an alien enemy engaged in the hostile service of a government at war with the United States."

Justice Black, writing for himself and Justices William O. Douglas and Harold H. Burton, vigorously dissented.

> Our constitutional principles are such that their mandate of equal justice under law should be applied as well when we occupy lands across the sea as when our flag flew only over thirteen colonies. Our nation proclaims a belief in the dignity of human beings as such, no matter what their nationality or where they happen to live. Habeas corpus, as an instrument to protect against illegal imprisonment, is written into the Constitution. ... I would hold that our courts can exercise it whenever any United States official illegally imprisons any person in any land we govern.

In the Criminal Justice System. Joseph S. Fay and James Bove were tried and found guilty of conspiracy to extort and of extortion by a special or so-called "blue ribbon" jury in New York.[45] Under New York's procedure, after the panel of general jurors had been chosen, a special jury could be called from that panel at the request of either the prosecution or the defense. Special jurors were personally interviewed under oath by the county clerk as to their qualifications. No one who had "been convicted of a criminal offense, or found guilty of fraud or misconduct by judgment of any civil court," or who might be prejudiced against the prosecution or the defense, or could not give the defendant a fair trial, could serve as a special juror. Although there were approximately 60,000 persons in the county eligible for service as a general juror, application of the criteria for a "blue ribbon" juror shrunk the panel to about 3,000. The defendants argued that this procedure was a denial of due process and equal protection of the law.

The courts of New York disagreed and upheld the defendants' convictions, as did the Supreme Court. In finding no due process violation, Justice Jackson noted for the majority that one of the benefits of the system was to substantially reduce the time spent in choosing a jury at the beginning of a trial. "Many of the standards of elimination which the clerk is directed to apply in choice of the panel are those the court would have to apply to excuse a juror on challenge for cause."

As to the question of whether the system denied them equal protection of the law, the defendants argued that the selection of the so-called "blue-ribbon" jury resulted in the creation of a "special panel ... so composed as to be more prone to convict than the general panel."

After examining some statistics, Jackson concluded that the defendants had failed to prove that special juries were more prone to convict than those chosen from the general panel.

This did not satisfy Justices Murphy, Black, Douglas and Rutledge. Murphy wrote: "The constitutional vice inherent in the type of 'blue ribbon' jury panel here involved is that it rests upon intentional and systematic exclusion of certain classes of people who are admittedly qualified to serve on the general jury panel. Whatever may be the standards erected by jury officials for distinguishing between those eligible for such a 'blue ribbon' panel and those who are not, the distinction itself is an invalid one. It denies the defendant his constitutional right to be tried by a jury fairly drawn from a cross-section of the community. It forces upon him a jury drawn from a panel chosen in a manner which tends to obliterate the representative basis of the jury."

Less than a year later, two men convicted of murder and sentenced to death raised the "blue ribbon" jury question again but the result was the same—their convictions were upheld by a majority of the Supreme Court. This caused Justice Murphy to dissent again, and write: "Two men must forfeit their lives after having been convicted of murder not by a jury of their peers, not by a jury chosen from a fair cross-section of the community, but by a jury drawn from a special group of individuals singled out in a manner inconsistent with the democratic ideals of the jury system."[46]

The Bill of Rights and the States

In striking down West Virginia's law requiring students to salute the flag and recite the Pledge of Allegiance, Justice Jackson held that such requirement violated the students' First Amendment rights to the free exercise of religion. In order to reach that conclusion, however, it was necessary to acknowledge that the Free Exercise Clause was binding upon states by virtue of the Fourteenth Amendment's Due Process Clause. "In weighing arguments of the parties," he pointed out, "it is important to distinguish between the due process clause of the Fourteenth Amendment as an instrument for transmitting the principles of the First Amendment and those cases in which it is applied for its own sake. The test of legislation which collides with the Fourteenth Amendment, because it also collides with the principles of the First, is much more definite than the test when only the Fourteenth is involved. Much of the vagueness of the due process clause disappears when the specific prohibitions of the First become its standard."[47]

It therefore appears that the Justice, at least insofar as the Free Exercise Clause was concerned, would apply the same standards to both the federal and state governments to judge infringements upon free exercise rights. "We think," he concluded, "the action of the local authorities in compelling the flag salute and pledge transcends constitutional limitations on their power and invades the sphere of intellect and spirit which it is the purpose of the First Amendment to our Constitution to reserve from all official control."

The Justice held the same opinion with regard to the Establishment of Religion Clause. In writing about the Establishment Clause, he declared: "It was intended not only to keep the states' hands out of religion, but to keep religion's hands off the state, and, above all, to keep bitter religious controversy out of public life by denying to every denomination any advantage from getting control of public policy or the public purse."[48]

Jackson's position changed when confronted with the question of the application of the First Amendment's Free Speech Clause to the states. In his dissent in *Beauharnais*, the Justice declared: "The history of criminal libel in America convinces me that the Fourteenth Amendment did not 'incorporate' the First, that the powers of Congress and of the States over this subject are not of the same dimensions, and that because Congress probably could not enact this law it does not follow that the States may not."[49]

On the broader question of the application of all of the Bill of Rights to the states, Jackson accepted Justice Benjamin Cardozo's conclusion in *Palko v. Connecticut*.[50] In *Palko*, a majority of the Court held that states, while not bound by all of the specific restrictions in the Bill of Rights, were limited in legislative power by those provisions of the Bill of Rights "found to be implicit in the concept of ordered liberty, and thus, through the Fourteenth Amendment, become valid as against the states."[51]

The Japanese Cases

"The questions for our decision are whether the particular restriction violated, namely that all persons of Japanese ancestry residing in such an area be within their place of residence daily between the hours of 8:00 p.m. and 6:00 a.m., was adopted by the military commander in the exercise of an unconstitutional delegation by Congress of its legislative power, and whether the restriction unconstitutionally discriminated between citizens of Japanese ancestry and those of other ancestries in violation of the Fifth Amendment."[52]

A unanimous Court concluded that the establishment of the curfew was not an unlawful delegation of Congress's power to a military commander, nor was it an illegal discrimination against American citizens of Japanese descent. The Court, therefore, upheld the conviction of Gordon Kiyoshi Hirabayashi, an American citizen of Japanese descent, for violating the curfew which had been imposed on Japanese living along the West Coast after the bombing of Pearl Harbor in 1941.

In upholding the curfew, Chief Justice Harlan F. Stone conceded: "Distinctions between citizens solely because of their ancestry are by their very nature odious to a free people whose institutions are founded upon the doctrine of equality." Nevertheless, the majority concluded that because the nation had been attacked by Japan, the decision to impose the curfew upon those of Japanese ancestry—even though they were United States citizens—was a reasonable one. Jackson agreed.

In addition to placing a curfew upon Japanese citizens living along the West Coast, the military commander ordered the evacuation of many of them to relocation centers inland. However, Toyosaburo Korematsu, a Japanese-American living in San Leandro, California, had refused to be evacuated and was arrested and convicted of violating the evacuation order. His conviction was upheld by the Supreme Court, but this time Justice Jackson dissented.[53] He explained that the curfew order, sustained in *Hirabayashi*, was a "mild and temporary deprivation of liberty." But in Korematsu's case "the principle of racial discrimination is pushed from support of mild measures to very harsh ones, and from temporary deprivations to indeterminate ones."

The Justice was disturbed as to the effect the Court's decision would have in the future. "Much is said of the danger to liberty from the Army program for deporting and detaining these citizens of Japanese extraction. But a judicial construction of the due process clause that will sustain this order is a far more subtle blow to liberty than the promulgation of the order itself. A military order, however unconstitutional, is not apt to last longer than the military emergency. ... But once a judicial opinion rationalizes such an order to show that it conforms to the Constitution, or rather rationalizes the Constitution to show that the Constitution sanctions such an order, the Court for all time has validated the principle of racial discrimination in criminal procedure and of transplanting American citizens."

AS A JUSTICE FOR THE GOVERNMENT

The Justice's views on rights of religious proselytizers was much narrower than that of the majority, as his dissents in those cases indicate. He could not "accept the holding in the *Murdock* case that the behavior ... [of the Jehovah's Witnesses] 'occupies the same high estate under the First Amendment as do worship in the churches and preaching from the pulpits.'"[54] And when he voted to reverse the conviction of Sarah Prince for allowing her niece to distribute Jehovah's Witnesses literature, he did not do so because he believed that she was protected by the Free Exercise Clause. On the contrary, he believed that he was bound by the decision in *Murdock*, even though he disagreed with it.

The Justice wrote: "My own view may be shortly put: I think the limits [on First Amendment activities] begin to operate whenever activities begin to affect or collide with liberties of others or of the public. Religious activities which concern only members of the faith are and ought to be free—as nearly absolutely free as anything can be. But beyond these, many religious denominations or sects engage in collateral and secular activities intended to obtain means from unbelievers to sustain the worshippers and their leaders."[55] This, of course, ignores the fact that going into the byways and highways to promote their views is part of the religious beliefs of the Jehovah's Witnesses. Furthermore, the Court has said that it would be a violation of their free exercise rights to relegate the Witnesses to some other public place: "But, as we have said, the streets are natural and proper places for the dissemination of information and opinion; and one is not to have the exercise of his liberty of expression in appropriate places abridged on the plea that it may be exercised in some other place."[56]

While a majority of the justices during this period of time believed that the Court had an obligation to balance the rights of the speaker against the rights of the others on the streets or in their home, Jackson disagreed. He believed that the Court had a very narrow function in these cases. "I disagree entirely," he argued in the *Saia* case, "with the idea that 'Courts must balance the various community interests in passing on the constitutionality of local regulations of the character involved here.' It is for the local communities to balance their own interests—that is politics—and what courts should keep out of. Our only function is to apply constitutional limitations."[57]

Local communities, however, are not noted for their concern for people's rights. Just the opposite is true, as the *Saia* case indicates. In commenting upon the power of the Chief of Police, the majority pointed out: "He stands athwart the channels of communication as an obstruction which can be removed only after criminal trial and conviction and lengthy appeal." That was exactly what Reverend Saia was required to do before his First Amendment right to use the sound truck was finally upheld.

Justice Jackson wrote the opinion in *Bakery Drivers Local v. Wohl*, discussed above, to strike down an injunction against peaceful picketing. Nevertheless, he continued to believe that "[a] state is not required to tolerate in all places and all circumstances even peaceful picketing by an individual."[58] That belief permitted him to vote more often to uphold injunctions against picketing than voting to strike them down.[59]

In matters relating to the Communist Party and other allegedly subversive organizations, the Justice consistently deferred to congressional action. For example, in upholding the deportation of Peter Harisiades, Mr. Mascitti and Mrs. Coleman, Jackson argued that people have the "freedom to advocate or promote Communism by means of the ballot box, but it does not include the practice or incitement of violence."[60] There was no proof, however, that any of these individuals were engaged in violence or were inciting others to do so. They were deported solely because, many years before, they had been members of the Communist Party, even though it has never been a crime to belong to that organization.

Jackson did not participate in very many cases involving freedom of the press. He did, however, vote to uphold the conviction of Winters for possessing, with the intent to sell certain magazines "principally made up of criminal news, police reports, or accounts of criminal deeds, or pictures, and stories of deeds of bloodshed, lust or crime."[61] A majority of the Court, however, held the statute unconstitutional as a violation of due process because it was so vague and indefinite that it presented a danger to freedom of the press.

The Justice also voted to uphold the so-called "Green River" ordinance, which prohibited soliciting on private residences without permission of the owner as applied to solicitors of subscription for magazines.[62] The majority did not believe that the cases upholding the right of Jehovah's Witnesses to solicit door-to-door were applicable, and concluded that municipality had reached a proper accommodation between freedom of the press and the privacy of the property owner. In arguing against the validity of the ordinance, the dissenters acknowledged that the "homeowners can if they wish forbid newsboys, reporters or magazine solicitors to ring their doorbells. But when the homeowner himself has not done this ... the First Amendment ... bars laws like the present ordinance which punishes persons who peacefully go from door to door as agents of the press."

In the cases involving racial discrimination, Jackson voted most of the time to strike down such discrimination, declaring it to be a violation of the Equal Protection Clause. The Justice also joined the unanimous opinion in *Brown v. Board of Education* to require states to integrate their public schools.

The one area in which he disagreed with the majority was in those cases where the Court found discrimination in the selection of the grand or petit jury before which the defendant was indicted or tried. He agreed that there should be no discrimination against blacks serving on juries. He did not believe, however, that the conviction of an obviously guilty defendant should be reversed because of the exclusion of minorities from the jury selection process. In *Cassell v. Texas*,[63] the Justice argued: "I do not see how this Court can escape the conclusion that any discrimination in selection of the grand jury in this case, however great the wrong toward qualified Negroes of the community, was harmless to this defendant."

In *Oyama*, the Justice could have supplied the fifth vote to declare the California Alien Land Law unconstitutional as a denial of equal protection. Instead, ignoring that issue, he dissented, concluding that California should have been allowed to apply the law to Oyama. Jackson also voted to uphold another California alien law and deny a coastal fishing license to Torao Takahashi, an alien of Japanese descent.[64]

The Justice's view of the application of the Bill of Rights to the states was also a narrow one, and he joined the majority opinion in which Justice Reed wrote: "Nothing has been called to our attention that either the framers of the Fourteenth Amendment or the states that adopted it intended its due process clause to draw within its scope the earlier amendments to the Constitution. *Palko* held that such provisions of the Bill of Rights as were 'implicit in the concept of ordered liberty' ... became secure from state interference by the clause. But it held nothing more."[65]

Jackson aligned himself with that statement and voted against applying the Self-Incriminating Clause of the Fifth Amendment to the states as part of the Fourteenth Amendment's Due Process Clause. This puts him squarely in the camp of those who did not believe that the Fourteenth Amendment was a shorthand method of applying the Bill of Rights to the states.

Because Justice Jackson was often willing to accept government infringement upon individual rights, he is included as a *Justice for the Government.*

4

JUSTICE JOHN
MARSHALL HARLAN

PERSONAL LIFE

Growing Up

He was a marvelous father when he was around. He very seldom got angry or lost his temper. He was humorous, very witty; he could be quite a tease. Mainly, I'd say our household was a happy one. ... But ... he was a career man and lawyer all the time, and I guess I would have liked to see more of him when I was growing up. He worked all the time, and I think he found family life difficult. He left most of the day-to-day family matters to my mother.[1]

With those words, John Marshall Harlan's daughter Eve described her father.

Harlan (II) was born May 20, 1899, to John Maynard and Elizabeth Palmer Harlan. He was the grandson of Justice John Marshall Harlan (I), who served on the Supreme Court from 1877 to 1911.

John Maynard Harlan, an attorney, served as a Chicago alderman and twice ran unsuccessfully for mayor. He married Elizabeth Palmer Flagg, the daughter of a prominent and wealthy New York family. Although John Maynard Harlan had an established law practice, he spent a great deal of his time and effort involved in Chicago politics. The family was able, however, to spend their summers in Murray Bay, Quebec, on the St. Lawrence River.

In addition to son John Marshall (II), John Maynard and Elizabeth Harlan had three daughters, Elizabeth, Janet and Edith. Biographer Tinsley E. Yarbrough writes: "The family's spacious three-story home was situated on Division Street, a few blocks from Lake Shore Drive, in one of the city's more fashionable residential areas. The Harlans' eldest daughter Elizabeth made her debut in Chicago, and as a young child John attended the exclusive Chicago Latin School, located across the street from the Harlan Home."

JUSTICE JOHN M. HARLAN (photo by Harris and Ewing; collection of the Supreme Court of the United States).

John Marshall (II), at the age of eight, was sent to school in Toronto, Canada, where he remained for four years. His next schooling was at "New York's prestigious Lake Placid School. There he studied and played with young men from some of the nation's leading families. The school's fall and spring terms were held in Lake Placid and the winter term in Coconut Grove, Florida.

Its elite student body totaled about forty-five, with ten to twelve in each class. While there, John played basketball, football, and baseball, and also acted the role of Julius Caesar in a school play."

Upon completing his schooling at Lake Placid School, Harlan entered Princeton University where he was "chairman of the *Daily Princetonian* and president of his class for three of his four years there." While at Princeton, he became friends with Adlai E. Stevenson, who later became governor of Illinois, and was twice the Democratic Party's candidate for president. The two friends joined the Princeton Naval Unit and persuaded the admiral in charge to form a band, although neither could play any musical instrument.

> The band and its conductors practiced assiduously every afternoon, and eventually they mastered two tunes—"I've Been Working on the Railroad" and "Smiles."

While marching in a parade in New York, with the two leaders at the head, the band turned to proceed down Fifth Avenue. When the sound of the band grew weaker, the leaders realized that the band had not made the turn. They rescued the band and continued in the parade.

"In 1920 Harlan received his A. B. degree and proceeded to Balliol College in Oxford, England, as a Rhodes scholar. During his three years at Oxford he was in the top 5 percent of his class and earned B. A. and M. A. degrees in jurisprudence."[2]

The Practice of Law and Law School at Night

Shortly after Harlan graduated from Oxford, his sister Elizabeth's husband Roger A. Derby introduced him to two of the senior partners of the New York law firm of Root, Clark, Bruckner and Howland. The firm agreed to hire him, but because Emory Bruckner did not believe that the Oxford education had prepared Harlan to practice law in New York, he therefore persuaded him to go to New York Law School in the afternoons. After studying at the Law School for two years, Harlan was admitted to the New York bar.

> As he has in other settings, Harlan quickly became a popular addition to the Root, Clark staff. Herbert Brownell, who entered the firm in 1927, and, as President Eisenhower's attorney general, was to play a key role in Harlan's appointment to the federal judiciary, first met Harlan at an annual office party to celebrate the staff's Christmas bonuses. Like the others in the firm, Brownell found him "a delightful companion ... warm-hearted, witty, erudite—a considerate and cultured gentleman."[3]

When Emory Bruckner became United States Attorney for the Southern District of New York, he took Harlan with him as a deputy and made him head of the Prohibition Division. Although both Bruckner and Harlan disliked prohibition, they began to enforce it by closing nightclubs that were serving liquor.

After a couple of years as U.S. Attorney, Bruckner resigned to return to the practice of law, and Harlan did the same. Their time as practitioners was short-lived, however, when Bruckner was appointed by Governor Al Smith to serve as a special assistant attorney general for New York to investigate corruption in the Borough of Queens. Harlan again became Bruckner's assistant. After extensive investigation by Harlan, Borough president Maurice E. Connolly was brought to trial and convicted of accepting bribes. He appealed, but with Harlan again writing a brief in opposition to reversal, Connolly's conviction was upheld.

Harlan was made partner in the Root, Clark law firm in 1931 and became its leading trial lawyer.

Love, Marriage and Family

"My brother's success in life," John Marshall Harlan's sister Edith has written, was "perhaps due in part to [the] total supportive role played by his three adoring sisters, his mother, and his wife, in their view he could do no wrong."[4]

Harlan and Ethel Andrews met at a party given by the law firm. She was the sister of one of the firm's associates. In the months that followed, John and Ethel saw each other often. When Ethel became ill and confined to her apartment, John delivered a tray of food to her, and then, as reported by the Harlans' only child Eve, "sat and talked to her for two hours about trout fishing, in which she had no interest whatever, and then popped the question—to her utter astonishment."

Ethel's immediate acceptance created a problem for Harlan. He now had to break the news to his mother that he was going to marry a divorcée. He waited until his mother had gone to the family's summer home in Murray Bay, Canada, and then wrote her a letter. After telling his mother that he was engaged, he wrote: "The lady is Ethel Andrews, and of course she's the most wonderful girl in all the world. You'll love her as much as I do when you meet her."

The Harlans lived in "increasingly commodious and comfortable Manhattan apartments" during the early years of their marriage and later built a country home in Weston, Connecticut. Ethel, who was a beautiful and charming woman, "was fond of fox hunting, and the couple often hosted hunt breakfasts at their Weston home."

Harlan enjoyed fishing and became a partner in a fishing club with some friends. As a result, the family joined others on fishing trips in Canada.

Military Service

Harlan was in his early forties when the United States became involved in World War II.

> When the United States entered World War II, Harlan became chief of the Operational Analysis Section of the Eighth Air Force. The section's mission was to provide technical advice on bombing operations, and it consisted of selected civilians in the fields of mathematics, physics, electronics, architecture, and law. Harlan served in London until 1945, volunteering in 1943 for a daylight bombing raid in which he sat as a waist gunner. For his military contributions, Harlan won the U.S. Legion of Merit as well as the Croix de Guerre of France and of Belgium.[5]

The Practice of Law and Public Service

When Harlan returned to the practice of law, his clients included many large corporations such as American Telephone and Telegraph, International Telephone and Telegraph, Gillette Safety Razor, and E. I. Du Pont de Nemours & Co. He also successfully defended Pierre S. and Irènée Du Pont in an antitrust suit. Author Yarbrough writes: "Harlan's defense, like Judge LaBuy's decision, naturally pleased the Du Ponts and their employees."[6]

In 1951, Harlan was appointed by New York Governor Thomas Dewey as chief of a commission to investigate organized crime. Harlan assembled a staff and began an extensive investigation.

Of the crime commission's work, author Yarbrough writes: "By early 1953, they had conducted more than six thousand interviews and called over two hundred witnesses before five public hearings." The commission's activities resulted in the creation of the Waterfront Commission of New York Harbor.

The future justice was active in bar association activities serving as vice president of the Association of the Bar of the City of New York and on its Bill of Rights and judiciary committees. He also served as a member of the board of the National Legal Aid and Defender Association. And he participated in several political campaigns on behalf of Republican Party candidates.

"The Justice's sensitivity to the feelings and needs of others extended to subordinates. Whether out of a genuine concern or a sense of *noblesse oblige*, Harlan was unusually solicitous of household servants, often loaning them money, giving them Christmas gifts early when they were financially strapped, intervening in their behalf with the Internal Revenue Service (IRS) and public housing officials. When a creditor complained that Arlene Wardlaw, a faithful Washington servant, had failed to pay a bill, Harlan paid the account, with assurances that 'Arlene had no intention of ignoring her obligation, but with her children growing up she had been hard pressed, and I am sorry I did not learn about the matter before.' When Arlene became ill and unable to continue in the family's employ, Harlan sent her a monthly check. 'Arlene was very dear to both of us,' he wrote her husband following her death, 'and we share your loss of her profoundly.'"

Judge of the Court of Appeals

By 1953, author Yarbrough notes, "Harlan not only enjoyed a reputation as an outstanding corporate attorney whose selection to the federal bench was likely to find favor with Republican loyalists, he had also devoted a respectable share of his time and energy to party, bar, and public service causes. Of greater significance were his ties to Thomas E. Dewey and the governor's political associates."

Early in 1954, President Dwight Eisenhower nominated Harlan for a seat on the Court of Appeals for the Second Circuit. He was confirmed, and took his seat in late March.

Nomination to the Supreme Court

Harlan's tenure on the Court of Appeals, however, was to be short. When Supreme Court Justice Robert H. Jackson died suddenly in October 1954, Harlan was nominated to fill the vacancy.

"The nomination was applauded by the press as non-partisan. Congress, however, delayed hearings because southern senators were angry at the Supreme Court's recent school desegregation decision. Moreover, some senators feared that Harlan's studies at Oxford had made him a 'one-worlder' who would surrender American sovereignty to 'world government.' The president resubmitted the nomination January 10, 1955, and hearings were held the following month. The Senate confirmed the nomination by a 71-11 vote March 16, and Harlan took his seat twelve days later."[7]

When Harlan joined the Court, Earl Warren was Chief Justice. Other members of the Court were Justices Hugo L. Black, Stanley Reed, Felix Frankfurter, William O. Douglas, Tom C. Clark, Sherman Minton and Harold Burton. Harlan served as an Associate Justice from March 16, 1955, until September 23, 1971.

AS ASSOCIATE JUSTICE (1955–1971)

The Free Exercise of Religion

Justice Harlan joined Justice Frankfurter's concurring opinion to uphold Sunday closing laws, in the *Sunday Closing Law* cases.[8] Orthodox Jewish merchants, whose Sabbath began Friday evening and ended at sundown Saturday, argued that requiring them to also close on Sunday violated their right to free exercise of religion. Frankfurter wrote: "The Sunday observer may practice his faith and yet work six days a week, while the observer of the Jewish Sabbath, his competitor, may work only during five days, to the latter's disadvantage. … Sabbatarians feel that the power of the State is employed to coerce their observance of Sunday as a holy day; that the State accords a recognition to Sunday Christian doctrine which is withheld from Sabbatarian creeds." The Jewish merchants, therefore, argued that they should be exempt from the Sunday closing laws.

Frankfurter and Harlan responded: "There are tenable reasons why a legislature might choose not to make such an exception. To whatever extent persons who come within the exception are present in a community, their activity would disturb the atmosphere of general repose and reintroduce into Sunday the business tempos of the week. Administration would be more difficult, with violations less evident and, in effect, two or more days to police instead of one."

Harlan did not give Ardell H. Sherbert's free exercise claim any greater consideration than he did the claim of the Orthodox Jewish merchants. Sherbert "became a member of the Seventh-day Adventist Church in 1957, at a time when her employer, a textile-mill operator, permitted her to work a five-day week. It was not until 1959 that the work week was changed to six days, including Saturday, for all three shifts in the employer's mill."[9]

Because Saturday was the Sabbath for Seventh-Day Adventists, Sherbert refused to work that day and was discharged. She applied for unemployment compensation, but that was denied because she would not take Saturday work. She brought suit against the South Carolina Employment Security Commission, but the South Carolina courts upheld the Commission's decision.

The Supreme Court reversed, with Justice William J. Brennan, Jr. writing the Court's opinion. The Court held that not to pay Sherbert unemployment compensation was an infringement upon her right to the free exercise of religion.

> Here not only is it apparent that … [Sherbert's] declared ineligibility for benefits derives solely from the practice of her religion, but the pressure upon her to forego that practice is unmistakable. The ruling forces her to choose between following the precepts of her religion and forfeiting benefits, on the one hand, and abandoning one of the precepts of her religion in order to accept work, on the other hand. Governmental imposition of such a choice puts the same kind of burden upon the free exercise of religion as would a fine imposed against … [her] for her Saturday worship.

In a dissenting opinion, Justice Harlan argued: "Since virtually all of the mills in the Spartanburg area were operating on a six-day week, … [Sherbert] was 'unavailable for work,' and thus ineligible for benefits, when personal considerations prevented her from accepting employment on a full-time basis in the industry and locality in which she had worked. The fact that these personal considerations sprang from her religious convictions was wholly without relevance to the state court's application of the law. Thus in no proper sense can it be said that the State discriminated against ... [her] on the basis of her religious beliefs or that she was denied benefits *because* she was a Seventh-day Adventist. She was denied benefits just as any other claimant would be denied benefits who was not 'available for work' for personal reasons."

The Selective Service application for those seeking exemption from military service because they are conscientious objectors requires the applicant to affirm that "by reason of ... [my] religious training and belief, [I am] conscientiously opposed to participation in war in any form."[10]

When Elliott Ashton Welsh II applied for conscientious objector status, he struck from the application the words "my religious training," thus leaving the statement to read: "I am, by reason of my ... belief conscientiously opposed to participation in war in any form." Because his objection to war was not premised upon a religious belief, his application was denied. When he refused to submit to induction into the armed forces, he was charged and convicted for failure to be inducted, which conviction was reversed by the Supreme Court. Harlan concurred in the result.

In a very similar case, the Court had previously held that a registrant is entitled to a conscientious objector classification if his "claimed belief occup[ies] the same place in the life of the objector as an orthodox belief in God holds in the life of one clearly qualified for exemption."[11] The Court then applied this to Welsh and concluded: "On the basis of these beliefs and the conclusion of the Court of Appeals that he held them 'with the strength of more traditional religious convictions,' ... we think Welsh was clearly entitled to conscientious objector exemption."[12]

Justice Harlan agreed that Welsh was entitled to the exemption but took a different approach to arrive at that conclusion. He was of the opinion that in creating an exemption for conscientious objectors, Congress had intended that their opposition to war be grounded upon *religious beliefs*. For him, this presented the constitutional question of whether "limiting this draft exemption to those opposed to war in general because of theistic beliefs runs afoul of the religious clauses of the First Amendment." And he concluded that it did. He pointed out that if Congress had eliminated all exemptions for conscientious objectors, it could have done so without violating the Free Exercise Clause of the First Amendment. "However," he argued, "having chosen to exempt, it cannot draw the line between theistic or nontheistic religious beliefs on the one hand and secular beliefs on the other. Any such distinctions are not, in my view, compatible with the Establishment Clause of the First Amendment."

Freedom of Speech

Unpopular Speech. The California Court of Appeal describes the case of Paul Richard Cohen as follows:

> On April 26, 1968, the defendant was observed in the Los Angeles County Courthouse in the corridor outside of division 20 of the municipal court wearing a jacket bearing the words 'Fuck the Draft' which were plainly visible. There were women and children present in the corridor. The defendant was arrested. The defendant testified that he wore the jacket knowing that the words were on the jacket as a means of informing the public of the depth of his feelings against the Vietnam War and the draft.[13]

Although Cohen did not create any disturbance, he was convicted of breach of the peace which conviction was affirmed by an Appellate court. Justice Harlan wrote the Supreme Court's opinion, which reversed. California argued that it acted "as it did in order to protect the sensitive from otherwise unavoidable exposure to appellant's crude form of protest." But, Harlan responded: "The ability of government, consonant with the Constitution, to shut off discourse solely to protect others from hearing it is ... dependent upon a showing that substantial privacy interests are being invaded in an essentially intolerable manner."

Not finding any privacy interest here, Harlan then pointed out that "the issue flushed by this case stands out in bold relief. It is whether California can excise, as 'offensive conduct,' one particular scurrilous epithet from the public discourse, either upon the theory of the court below that its use is inherently likely to cause violent reaction, or upon a more general assertion that the States, acting as guardians of public morality, may properly remove this offensive word from the public vocabulary."

He concluded that the "rationale of the California court is plainly untenable." "The constitutional right of free expression," he declared, "is powerful medicine in a society as diverse and populous as ours. It is designed and intended to remove governmental restraints from the arena of public discussion, putting the decision as to what views shall be voiced largely into the hands of each of us, in hope that use of such freedom will ultimately produce a more capable citizenry and more perfect polity and in the belief that no other approach would comport with the premise of individual dignity and choice upon which our political system rests."

With regard to the particular word Cohen used, the Justice pointed out that "while the particular four-letter word being litigated here is perhaps more distasteful than most of its genre, it is nevertheless often true that one man's vulgarity is another's lyric."

Neither the burning of a draft card in protest of the draft, nor the wearing of black armbands to school in protest of the Vietnam War, received the same consideration from Harlan as did Cohen's use of the four-letter word.

The Justice, therefore, voted to uphold the conviction of David Paul O'Brien who burned his draft card on the steps of the South Boston courthouse before a sizable crowd including several FBI agents.[45] The Court did not accept O'Brien's assertion that the act of burning the draft card was speech protected by the First Amendment. "For ... [the] noncommunicative impact of his conduct," Chief Justice Warren asserted, "and for nothing else, he was convicted."

Students who wanted to wear black armbands to school to show their opposition to the Vietnam War did not receive any more consideration from Harlan than did David Paul O'Brien.

When the principals of several Des Moines, Iowa, schools learned that some students intended to wear black armbands to school, they decreed that if those students who wore the armbands did not remove them when asked to do so, they would be suspended. In spite of this regulation, Mary Beth Tinker, age 13, John F. Tinker, age 15, and Christopher Eckhardt wore black armbands to school and were immediately suspended because they refused to remove them.[15]

The students, through their parents, brought an action against the school district seeking an order of the court preventing the school from disciplining them. District Judge Roy L. Stephenson concluded that the restriction on wearing the armbands infringed only a little upon the students' First Amendment rights and granted judgment for the school district.

Justice Abe Fortas, writing for a majority of the Supreme Court, reversed. "First Amendment rights, applied in light of the special characteristics of the school environment," he noted, "are available to teachers and students. It can hardly be argued that either students or teachers shed their constitutional rights to freedom of speech or expression at the schoolhouse gate. This has been the unmistakable holding of this Court for almost 50 years."

After examining the record and not finding evidence that the armbands caused any disruption at the school, Fortas concluded: "These petitioners merely went about their ordained rounds in school. Their deviation consisted only in wearing on their sleeve a band of black cloth, not more than two inches wide. They wore it to exhibit their disapproval of the Vietnam hostilities and their advocacy of a truce, to make their views known, and, by their example, to influence others to adopt them. They neither interrupted school activities nor sought to intrude in the school affairs or the lives of others. They caused discussion outside of the classrooms, but no interference with work and no disorder. In the circumstances, our Constitution does not permit officials of the State to deny their form of expression."

Justice Harlan dissented. Believing that "school officials should be accorded the widest authority in maintaining discipline and good order in their institutions," he would place "upon those complaining the burden of showing that a particular school measure was motivated by other than legitimate school concerns—for example, a desire to prohibit the expression of an unpopular point of view, while permitting expression of the dominant opinion."

Freedom of Association

Blacklisting and Punishment for Membership. Ephram Nestor "came to this country from Bulgaria in 1913 and lived here continuously for 43 years, until July 1956. He was then deported from this country for having been a Communist from 1933 to 1939. At that time membership in the Communist Party as such was not illegal and was not even a statutory ground for deportation. From December 1936 to January 1955 Nestor and his employers made regular payments to the Government under the Federal Insurance Contributions Act.... These funds went to a special federal old-age and survivors insurance trust fund, ... in return for which Nestor, like millions of others, expected to receive payments when he reached the statutory age. In 1954, 15 years after Nestor had last been a Communist, and 18 years after he began to make payments into the old-age security fund, Congress passed a law providing, among other things, that any person who had been deported from this country because of past Communist membership ... should be wholly cut off from any benefits of the fund to which he had contributed under the law. After the Government deported Nestor in 1956 it notified his wife, who remained in this country, that he was cut off and no further payments would be made to him."[16]

When Nestor's case reached the Supreme Court, it upheld the termination of Nestor's social security benefits because of his past membership in the Communist Party. Justice Harlan wrote the majority opinion, concluding that Nestor was not deprived of his property without due process of law in violation of the Fifth Amendment, nor was Congress's action an *ex post facto* law or a *bill of attainder*.

Harlan acknowledged that "persons gainfully employed, and those who employ them, are taxed to permit the payment of benefits to the retired and disabled, and their dependents, [and] ... the expectation is that many members of the present productive work force will in turn become beneficiaries rather than supporters of the program." "But," he argued, "each worker's benefits, though flowing from the contributions he made to the national economy while actively employed, are not dependent on the degree to which he was called upon to support the system by taxation." Because Nestor's interests in the fund was not the same as an annuity, Harlan concluded that "a person covered by the Act has not such a right in benefit payments as would make every defeasance of 'accrued' interests violative of the Due Process Clause of the Fifth Amendment."

Justice Black wrote in dissent: "The fact that the Court is sustaining this action indicates the extent to which people are willing to go these days to overlook violations of the Constitution perpetrated against anyone who was ever even innocently belonged to the Communist Party."

The 11 leaders of the Communist Party, whose convictions were upheld in *Dennis v. United States*,[17] lost more than Nestor had; they lost their freedom. These individuals were convicted for advocating the overthrow of the government "as speedily as circumstances would permit." Advocating the overthrow of the government, or being a member of an organization that advocated the overthrow of the government was made a crime by a federal law commonly referred to as the Smith Act. Harlan was not on the Court at this time.

In *Scales v. United States*,[18] however, with Harlan writing the opinion, the Court upheld the conviction of Junnius Irving Scales for being a member of the Communist Party which advocated the overthrow of the government. The Justice pointed out that if sending Communist Party members to jail for advocating the overthrow of government does not violate the First Amendment, as was held in *Dennis*, then there should be no violation of the First Amendment to send them to jail for being an active member of the Party.

Justice Douglas protested. "We legalize today," he declared, "guilt by association, sending a man to prison when he committed no unlawful act. Today's break with tradition is a serious one. It borrows from the totalitarian philosophy."

Harlan wrote two other opinions dealing with convictions of individuals for violating the Smith Act. In reversing the convictions of Oleta O'Connor Yates and John Francis Noto, the Justice did not find the Smith Act to be unconstitutional, but held that there was not sufficient evidence that the Yates and Noto had violated either the advocacy or membership part of the law.[19]

Associational Privacy.

> The question presented is whether Alabama, consistently with the Due Process Clause of the Fourteenth Amendment, can compel petitioner [NAACP] to reveal to the State's Attorney General the names and addresses of all its Alabama members and agents, without regard to their positions or functions in the Association.[20]

The Justices unanimously answered that it would be a violation of NAACP's freedom of association to have to disclose the names of its officers and agents.

Justice Harlan wrote the Court's opinion. "It is beyond debate," the Justice declared, "that freedom to engage in association for the advancement of beliefs and ideas is an inseparable aspect of the 'liberty' assured by the Due Process Clause of the Fourteenth Amendment, which embraces freedom of speech. ... Of course, it is immaterial whether the beliefs sought to be advanced by association pertain to political, economic, religious or cultural matters, and state action which may have the effect of curtailing the freedom to associate is subject to the closest scrutiny."

In this case, the Justice noted that the NAACP had "made an uncontroverted showing that on past occasions revelation of the identity of its rank-and-file members has exposed these members to economic reprisal, loss of employment, threat of physical coercion, and other manifestations of public hostility."

"We hold," Harlan asserted, "that the immunity from state scrutiny of membership lists which the Association claims on behalf of its members is here so related to the right of the members to pursue their lawful private interests privately and to associate freely with others in so doing as to come within the protection of the Fourteenth Amendment."

Justice Harlan consistently voted to uphold the right of the NAACP not to disclose their membership lists, with one exception.[21] That exception came in the case of *Gibson v. Florida Legislative Comm.*[22] During an investigation by a Florida Legislative Committee, Theodore R. Gibson, who was president of the Miami Branch of the NAACP, refused to produce any of the Associations records concerning its membership. When asked by the Committee to look at photos of certain persons who had been identified as Communists, Gibson responded that "he could associate none of them with the N. A. A. C. P." However, because he had not produced the records of the Association, he was held in contempt, a conviction which the Supreme Court which reversed.

In an opinion written by Justice Arthur Goldberg, the Court held that Florida had not proven that it had an overriding and compelling reason for needing the information Gibson had refused to give it. "Without any indication of present subversive infiltration in, or influence on, the Miami branch of the N. A. A. C. P.," Goldberg argued, "and without any reasonable, demonstrated factual basis to believe that such infiltration or influence existed in the past, or was actively attempted or sought in the present—in short without any showing of a meaningful relationship between the N. A. A. C. P., Miami branch, and subversives or subversive or other illegal activity—we are asked to find the compelling and subordinating state interest which must exist if essential freedoms are to be curtailed or inhibited. This we cannot do."

Harlan dissented because he could find no "unfairness in the Committee's proceedings," therefore, Gibson's contempt conviction should be upheld. The Justice did not address the effect that such disclosure may have had upon the associational rights of the NAACP and its members.

The Justice also voted to uphold California's denial of a license to practice law to Raphael Konigsberg because of his refusal to answer questions about his association with allegedly subversive organizations.

Raphael Konigsberg, graduated from the Law School of the University of Southern California in 1953 and four months later satisfactorily passed the

California bar examination. Nevertheless, the State Committee of Bar Examiners, after several hearings, refused to certify him to practice law on the grounds he had failed to prove (1) that he was of good moral character and (2) that he did not advocate overthrow of the Government of the United States or California by unconstitutional means.[23]

During the hearings held to determine Konigsberg's qualifications to practice law, 42 individuals "attested to his excellent character." "These testimonials came from persons in every walk of life. Included among them were a Catholic priest, a Jewish rabbi, lawyers, doctors, professors, businessmen and social workers."

Focusing attention, however, upon Konigsberg's refusal to answer questions relating to his beliefs and associations, the Committee denied his application to practice law. The California Supreme Court upheld the Committee's action, but the U.S. Supreme Court reversed.

Writing for the majority, Justice Black pointed out that the only evidence in the record that Konigsberg was not of good moral character were the inferences drawn by the Committee from his refusal to answer the questions. This, Black said, was a denial of equal protection and due process of law.

Konigsberg was, therefore, entitled to a license to practice law, Black concluded, because "there is no evidence in the record which rationally justifies a finding that Konigsberg failed to establish his good moral character or failed to show that he did not advocate forceful overthrow of the Government."

In a lengthy dissent, Justice Harlan argued that in spite of Konigsberg's assertion that under the First Amendment he was not required to answer questions relating to his beliefs and associations, such questions were proper and he was properly barred from admission for not answering them. The Justice acknowledged that Konigsberg had "stated readily enough that he did not advocate overthrow of the government by force, violence, or other unconstitutional means." Nevertheless, he argued "[t]here is no conceivable reason why the Committee should not attempt by cross-examination to ascertain whether the facts square with petitioner's bare assertion that he was qualified for admission." And, he concluded: "The petitioner's refusal to answer questions in order to dispel doubts conscientiously entertained by the Committee as to his qualifications under a valid statutory test can, it seems to me, derive no support from the Fourteenth Amendment."

Subsequently, Konigsberg reapplied for admission to the bar. The Committee then held another round of hearings during which he again refused to answer questions relating to membership in the Communist Party. The Committee again refused to admit him, specifically resting its denial upon Konigsberg's refusal to answer the questions. He then appealed a second time to the Supreme Court.

This time, with Harlan writing the opinion, the Court concluded: "We think it clear that the Fourteenth Amendment's protection against arbitrary state action does not forbid a State from denying admission to a bar applicant so long as he refuses to provide unprivileged answers to questions having a substantial relevance to his qualifications."[24]

Harlan responded to Konigsberg's argument that the state was prohibited from asking questions relating to his beliefs and associations. "As regards questioning of public employees relative to Communist Party membership it has already been held that the interest in not subjecting speech and association to the deterrence of subsequent disclosure is outweighed by the State's interest in ascertaining the fitness of the employee for the post he holds, and hence that such questioning does not infringe constitutional protections." This, he concluded, also applies to admission to the bar.

"The recognition that California has subjected 'speech and association to the deterrence of subsequent disclosure'" Justice Black declared in dissent, "is, under the First Amendment, sufficient in itself to render the action of the State unconstitutional unless one subscribes to the doctrine that permits constitutionally protected rights to be 'balanced' away whenever a majority of this Court thinks that a State might have interest sufficient to justify abridgment of those freedoms. As I have indicated many times, I do not subscribe to that doctrine for I believe that the First Amendment's unequivocal command that there shall be no abridgment of the rights of free speech and assembly shows that the men who drafted our Bill of Rights did all the 'balancing' that was to be done in this field."

On the same day that Court upheld California's denial of Konigsberg's application to practice law, it also upheld the denial of George Anastaplo's application to practice law in Illinois.[25] Anastaplo had also refused to answer questions concerning membership in the Communist Party. Harlan, in writing the Court's opinion in this case also, conceded that the Illinois Committee on Character and Fitness [to practice law] "had before it uncontroverted evidence as to Anastaplo's 'good moral character,' in the form of written statements or affidavits furnished by persons of standing acquainted with him, and the record of rehearing contains nothing which could properly be considered as reflecting adversely upon his character or reputation or on the sincerity of the beliefs he espoused before the Committee."

Nevertheless, the Justice argued, "the State's interest in enforcing such a rule as applied to refusals to answer questions about membership in the Communist Party outweighs any deterrent effect upon freedom of speech and association, and hence that such state action does not offend the Fourteenth Amendment."

This decision disturbed Justice Black. "Too many men," he asserted, "are being driven to become government-fearing and time-serving because the Government is being permitted to strike out at those who are fearless enough to think as they please and say what they think. This trend must be halted if we are to keep faith with the Founders of our Nation and pass on to future generations of Americans the great heritage of freedom which they sacrificed so much to leave to us. The choice is clear to me. If we are to pass on that great heritage of freedom, we must return to the original language of the Bill of Rights. We must not be afraid to be free."

Justice Black's position that government had no business making inquiries into a bar applicant's membership in allegedly subversive organizations ultimately commanded a majority of the justices in the case of Sarah Baird. Baird's application to practice law in Arizona was denied when she refused to "state whether she had ever been a member of the Communist Party or any organization 'that advocates the overthrow of the United States Government by force or violence.'"[26]

Justice Black, writing for himself and three other justices, concluded that "[t]he record is wholly barren of one word, sentence, or paragraph that tends to show this lady is not morally and professionally fit to serve honorably and well as a member of the legal profession."

Harlan wrote in dissent: "Nor do I think that the questioning of candidates as to their beliefs in violent overthrow necessarily runs afoul of true First Amendment concerns. I do not dispute that the First Amendment, as reflected in the Fourteenth, prevents States from denying admission to candidates merely because of theoretical beliefs in the 'right' of revolution, but I do maintain that there is no constitutional barrier to denying admission to those who seek entry to the profession for the very purpose of doing away with the orderly processes of law, and that temperate inquiry into the character of their beliefs in this regard, which is all that is shown here, is a relevant and permissible course to that end."[27] What the Justice thought were permissible questions that states could ask of prospective members of the bar, he thought were also permissible questions to ask of teachers.

When the Court struck down, as a violation of teacher's right of free association, an Arkansas law requiring them to list "all organizations to which he at the time belongs and to which he has belonged during the past five years,"[28] Justice Harlan dissented. He acknowledged that teachers had a right to free speech and association, but concluded "that information about a teacher's associations may be useful to school authorities in determining the moral, professional, and social qualifications of the teacher, as well as in determining the type of service for which he will be best suited in the educational system."

Justice Stewart and the majority, however, believed that the "statute's comprehensive interference with associational freedom goes far beyond what might be justified in the exercise of the State's legitimate inquiry into the fitness and competency of its teachers."

Association for the Advancement of Legal Goals

For many years, the Virginia Conference of the NAACP financed and provided lawyers to handle lawsuits aimed at ending racial segregation in public schools. It maintained its own legal staff and assumed "all expenses of litigation in an assisted case."[29] In order to find individuals who were willing to participate in such lawsuits, "a local NAACP branch ... [would] invite a member of the legal staff to explain to a meeting of parents and children the legal steps necessary to achieve desegregation. The staff member ... [would] bring printed forms to the meeting authorizing him, and other NAACP ... attorneys of his designation, to represent the signers in legal proceedings to achieve desegregation. ... It is usual, after obtaining authorizations, for the staff lawyer to bring into the case the other staff members in the area where suit is to be brought, and sometimes to bring in lawyers from the national organization.... In effect, then, the prospective litigant retains not so much a particular attorney as the 'firm' of NAACP ... lawyers, which has a corporate reputation for expertness in presenting and arguing the difficult questions of law that frequently arise in civil rights litigation."

Although the Virginia statutes regulating the practice of law made it illegal to solicit legal business by the use of runners or cappers, in 1956 the laws were amended to include within "the definition of 'runner' or 'capper', an agent for an individual or organization which retains a lawyer in connection with an action to which it is not a party and in which it has no pecuniary right or liability."

The Virginia Court of Appeals held that the activities of the NAACP fell within this "expanded definition of improper solicitation of legal business," and could therefore be prohibited. The Supreme Court reversed.

In the majority opinion, Justice Brennan pointed out that: "We meet at the outset the contention that 'solicitation' is wholly outside the area of freedoms protected by the First Amendment. To this contention there are two answers. The first is that a State cannot foreclose the exercise of constitutional rights by mere labels. The second is that abstract discussion is not the only species of communication which the Constitution protects; the First Amendment also protects vigorous advocacy, certainly of lawful ends, against governmental intrusion."

Virginia argued that the activities of the NAACP "being 'improper solicitation' ... fall within the traditional purview of state regulation of professional conduct." Brennan did not agree. "Resort to the courts to seek vindication of constitutional rights is a different matter from the oppressive, malicious, or avaricious use of the legal process for purely private gain. Lawsuits attacking racial discrimination, at least in Virginia, are neither very profitable nor very popular. They are not an object of general competition among Virginia lawyers; the problem is rather one of an apparent dearth of lawyers who are willing to undertake such litigation."

"We conclude," Brennan declared, "that although the petitioner [NAACP] has amply shown that its activities fall within the First Amendment's protections, the State has failed to advance any substantial regulatory interest, ... which can justify the broad prohibitions which it has imposed."

After examining the record, Justice Harlan concluded in dissent, that "the litigation program of the NAACP, as shown by this record, falls within an area of activity which a State may constitutionally regulate." He also pointed out, however, that: "(Whether it was wise for Virginia to exercise that power in this instance is not, of course, for us to say.)"

Harlan agreed that First Amendment rights were involved in this case, but argued that when speech and conduct are involved, the state is freer to regulated that speech/conduct. And the activities of the NAACP fall into that category. "But litigation, whether or not associated with the attempt to vindicate constitutional rights, is *conduct;* it is speech *plus.* Although the State surely may not broadly prohibit individuals with a common interest from joining together to petition a court for redress of their grievances, it is equally certain that the State may impose reasonable regulations limiting the permissible form of litigation and the manner of legal representation within its borders."

Following its decision in this case, a majority of the Court upheld similar arrangements whereby national unions provided legal assistance for their members. In *Railroad Trainmen v. Virginia Bar,*[30] the Union maintained a legal department "which recommend[ed] to Brotherhood members and their families the names of lawyers whom the Brotherhood believes to be honest and competent." A majority of the justices held "that the First and Fourteenth Amendments protect the right of the members through their Brotherhood to maintain and carry out their plan for advising workers who are injured to obtain legal advice and for recommending specific lawyers."

Some three years later, the Court had before it the question of the validity of the United Mine Workers of America legal assistance program. In that program, the Union "employed a licensed attorney on a salary basis to represent any of its members who wished his services to prosecute workmen's compensation claims before the Illinois Industrial Commission."[31]

In reversing a state court decree holding that this arrangement constituted unauthorized practice of law, the Supreme Court declared: "The decree [of the Illinois court] at issue here thus substantially impairs the associational rights of the Mine Workers and is not needed to protect the State's interest in high standards of legal ethics."

A third case involving allegedly unauthorized solicitation of clients involved the activities of the United Transportation Union. Its activities on behalf of its members were somewhat more sophisticated than those of either the Railroad Workers or the Mine Workers unions. The Transportation "Union recommended selected attorneys to its members and their families ... [from whom] it [had] secured a commitment ... that the maximum fee charged would not exceed 25% of the recovery...."[32] At the request of the State Bar of Michigan, a court issued an order "enjoining the Union's activities on the ground that they violated the state statute making it a misdemeanor to 'solicit' damage suits against railroads." The Supreme Court reversed. "The common thread running through our decisions in *NAACP v. Button, Trainmen*, and *United Mine Workers*," Justice Black asserted, "is that collective activity undertaken to obtain meaningful access to the courts is a fundamental right within the protection of the First Amendment. However, that right would be a hollow promise if courts could deny associations of workers or others the means of enabling their members to meet the costs of legal representation."

In dissenting in these cases, Harlan recognized that people on the bottom rung of the economic ladder do not have the same opportunity as others to secure adequate legal assistance. "I share my Brothers' concern," he noted, "with the problems of providing meaningful access to competent legal advice for persons in the middle and lower economic strata of our society. This is a matter of public concern deserving our best efforts at resolution, a task that the organized bar may be thought to have been too slow in recognizing." Nevertheless, he did not believe that the arrangements made by the unions to provide such legal assistance was protected by the First Amendment, and therefore those activities could be prohibited by states. "The issue ... [in these cases]," he argued, "is the scope left by the Federal Constitution for state action in the regulation of the practice of law. Despite the First Amendment implications of denial of access to the courts in other situations ... all that is involved here is a combination of purchasers seeking to increase their market power. The relationship to First Amendment interests seems to me remote at best."

Freedom of the Press

Contempt of Court for Publication. During a grand jury investigation of alleged corruption in an election, the judge, in charging the jury pointed out "that there appeared to be 'an inane and inexplicable pattern of Negro bloc voting' in Bibb County, and that 'rumors and accusations' had been made which indicated candidates for public office had paid large sums of money in an effort to gain favor and to obtain the Negro vote. The charge explained that certain Negro leaders, after having met and endorsed a candidate, had switched their support to an opposing candidate who put up a large sum of money, and that this 'create[d] an unhealthy, dangerous, and unlawful situation [which] tend[ed] to corrupt public office holders and some candidates for public office.'"[33]

The next day Sheriff James I. Wood, a candidate for reelection, issued a statement criticizing the judge's charge, and cautioned "the citizenry to take notice when their highest judicial officers threatened political intimidation and persecution of voters in the county under the guise of law enforcement." Wood also wrote a letter to the grand jury in which he implied that the judge's charges were false, and that the real culprit was the Bibb County Democratic Executive Committee, and it was that organization that should be investigated. He also released a statement to the press repeating what he had said to the grand jury.

Wood was cited for contempt of court, tried, convicted and sentenced. And when the appellate courts affirmed his conviction, he appealed to the Supreme Court arguing that the conviction infringed upon his right of free expression. The Supreme Court agreed, and reversed.

Chief Justice Earl Warren, writing for the majority, noted that in order to punish one for contempt "[t]he fires which [the expression] kindles must constitute an imminent, not merely a likely, threat to the administration of justice. The danger must not be remote or even probable; it must immediately imperil." Warren pointed out: "The prosecution called no witnesses to show that the functioning of the jury was in any way disturbed; no showing was made that the members of the grand jury, upon reading ... [Wood's] comments in the newspapers, felt unable or unwilling to complete their assigned tasks because ... [Wood] 'interfered' with its completion."

The Court then concluded that: "Our examination of the content of ... [Wood's] statements and the circumstances under which they were published leads us to conclude that they did not present a danger to the administration of justice that should vitiate his freedom to express his opinions in the manner chosen."

Justice Harlan disagreed with the Court's assessment of the case. He was of the opinion that even if there was no evidence that Wood's statements had any effect upon the jury, they were punishable even if not successful. "Of equal if not greater importance," he argued, "is the fact that ... [Wood's] statements were calculated to influence, not a judge chosen because of his independence, integrity, and courage and trained by experience and the discipline of law to deal only with evidence properly before him, but a grand jury of laymen chosen to serve for a limited term from the general population of Bibb County. It cannot be assumed with grand jurors, as it has been with judges, ... that they are all 'men of fortitude, able to thrive in a hardy climate.'"

Libel.

> The constitutional guarantees require, we think, a federal rule that prohibits a public official from recovering damages for a defamatory falsehood relating to his official conduct unless he proves that the statement was made with "actual malice"—that is, with knowledge that it was false or with reckless disregard of whether it was false or not.

That statement, written by Justice Brennan in *New York Times Co. v. Sullivan*,[34] sets forth the rule governing legal action brought by a public official against a newspaper, in which the official alleges that he or she was defamed.

Such a rule, Brennan points out, is consistent with "a profound national commitment to the principle that debate on public issues should be uninhibited, robust, and wide-open, and that it may well include vehement, caustic, and sometimes unpleasantly sharp attacks on government and public officials."

Justice Harlan voted with the majority in this case to reverse a substantial judgment in favor of L. B. Sullivan, the Montgomery, Alabama, Police Commissioner, against the New York Times Co., publisher of the *New York Times*.

Justices Black and Douglas concurred, but they would have given the press even greater protection than the majority did. "In my opinion," Black declared for himself and Douglas, "the Federal Constitution has dealt with this deadly danger to the press in the only way possible without leaving the free press open to destruction—by granting the press an absolute immunity for criticism of the way public officials do their public duty."

Some years later, in the case of *Curtis Publishing Co. v. Butts*,[35] the Court faced the question whether one who is a "public figure," but not a public official, must also prove that the press acted with "actual malice" in publishing false information about him or her.

The *Butts* case involved an article published in the *Saturday Evening Post* concerning Wally Butts, the athletic director at the University of Georgia, and Paul "Bear" Bryant, the football coach at the University of Alabama. The *Post's* story claimed that "[b]efore the University of Georgia played the University of Alabama [in football] ... Wally Butts... gave [Bryant] ... Georgia's plays, defensive patterns, all the significant secrets Georgia's football team possessed." Butts sued the publishing company for libel and recovered judgment for $60,000 in general damages and $3,000,000 in punitive damages, the latter being reduced by the trial judge to $460,000.

Upon appeal by Curtis Publishing Co., the Supreme Court affirmed, but the justices were unable to agree upon the standard of proof that should apply to Butts, a recognized "public figure."

Harlan, writing for himself, and Justices Tom Clark, Potter Stewart and Abe Fortas, concluded that "a 'public figure' who is not a public official may ... recover damages for a defamatory falsehood whose substance makes substantial danger to reputation apparent, on a showing of highly unreasonable conduct constituting an extreme departure from the standards of investigation and reporting ordinarily adhered to by responsible publishers." While these four justices did not adopt the "actual malice" standard used in cases involving public officials, they agreed that the conduct of Curtis Publishing Co., in this instance, was "highly unreasonable," and they voted to affirm the award to Butts.

Although George Rosenbloom was neither a public official nor a public figure, a majority of the Court held that he could not recover damages for being named in a radio station's newscast concerning a city crackdown on "Smut Merchants."[36]

> While the [Philadelphia] police were making an arrest [for selling obscene material] at ... [a] newsstand, ... [Rosenbloom] arrived to deliver some of his nudist magazines and was immediately arrested along with the newsboy. Three days later, ... the police obtained a warrant to search ... [Rosenbloom's] home and the rented barn he used as a warehouse, and seized the inventory of magazines and books found at these locations.

After this search, Rosenbloom turned himself in to the police where he was arrested again.

The next day, a radio station's news program carried an item relating to Rosenbloom's arrest, the opening line of which was: "City Cracks Down on Smut Merchants." The broadcast stated that the police had "confiscated 3,000 obscene books" at Rosenbloom's barn. Later that same day, although the station continued to broadcast the news item, it changed the wording of the seizure to refer to the books as "allegedly" or "reportedly" obscene.

Rosenbloom, claiming the books were not obscene, sought an injunction against "further police interference with his business as well as further publicity of the earlier arrests." In response, the station broadcast another news item concerning Rosenbloom's lawsuit. Without naming him, the broadcast referred to "girlie-book peddlers [who] say the police crackdown and continued reference to their borderline literature as smut or filth is hurting their business."

In the meantime, Rosenbloom was acquitted when the trial judge instructed the jury that the books in question were not obscene. Rosenbloom then brought a second suit against the radio station alleging that he had been defamed by its newscasts. A jury agreed and awarded him $25,000 in general damages and $725,000 in punitive damages, which the court reduced to $250,000. The Court of Appeals reversed concluding "that the broadcasts concerned matters of public interest and that they involved 'hot news' prepared under deadline pressure." The radio station, therefore, was protected by the First Amendment's guarantee of freedom of the press. Although the Supreme Court affirmed, the Justices were unable to agree on an opinion supporting the decision.

Because Rosenbloom was neither a public official nor a public figure, he argued "that the Constitution should be held to require that the private individual prove only that the publisher failed to exercise 'reasonable care' in publishing defamatory falsehoods..." Chief Justice Warren Burger and Justices Brennan and Blackmun rejected this approach. "We honor the commitment to robust debate on public issues," Brennan declared, "which is embodied in the First Amendment, by extending constitutional protection to all discussion and communication involving matters of public or general concern, without regard to whether the persons involved are famous or anonymous." For them, Rosenbloom's activities were part of the police crack-down on the sale of obscene material which was a matter of public concern, and therefore the radio station was protected by the First Amendment unless he could prove that it acted "with malice, or with reckless disregard of the truth."[37]

Justice Harlan did not believe that the decision adequately balanced the competing interests of the person allegedly defamed versus the freedom of the press rights of the media. "I ... think that, when dealing with private libel, the States should be free to define for themselves the applicable standard of care so long as they do not impose liability without fault; that a showing of actual damage should be a requisite to recovery for libel; and that it is impermissible, given the substantial constitutional values involved, to fail to confine the amount of jury verdicts in such cases within any ascertainable limits." He was of the opinion that requiring a person who claims to have been libeled, to only prove that the press did not exercise "reasonable care" gave adequate protection to the press.

Obscenity. In 1942, Justice Frank Murphy, in discussing the kinds of speech not protected by the First Amendment, wrote: "There are certain well-defined and narrowly limited classes of speech, the prevention and punishment of which have never been thought to raise any Constitutional problem. These include the lewd and obscene, the profane, the libelous, and the insulting or 'fighting' words—those which by their very utterance inflict injury or tend to incite an immediate breach of the peace."[38]

It was not until much later, however, that the Court came to grips with the validity of federal and state laws making it a crime to publish, possess, sell, distribute or mail obscene material. At that time, the Court had before it the cases of *Roth v. United States*, and *Alberts v. California*.[39] *Roth* involved the validity of a federal law that made it a criminal offense to mail an "obscene, lewd, lascivious, or filthy book, [etc.]." The California statute in *Alberts* made it a misdemeanor to publish, sell, distribute, etc. "any obscene or indecent writing, paper or book."

A majority of the Court upheld both laws and affirmed the convictions of the individuals who had been convicted under them. "We hold," Justice Brennan declared, "that obscenity is not within the area of constitutionally protected speech or press." And that the proper standard to be used by courts to identify such material is, "whether to the average person, applying contemporary community standards, the dominant theme of the material taken as a whole appeals to prurient interest."

Justices Black and Douglas dissented in both cases. Writing for both, Douglas argued: "Thus, if the First Amendment guarantee of freedom of speech and press is to mean anything in this field, it must allow protests even against the moral code that the standard of the day sets for the community. In other words, literature should not be suppressed merely because it offends the moral code of the censor."

For Justice Harlan, the solution to the question was not so simple. He was of the opinion that the First Amendment's protection for freedom of speech and the press prohibited the federal government from punishing the distribution of allegedly obscene material but did not prevent the states from doing so. "The Constitution differentiates between those areas of human conduct subject to the regulation of the States and those subject to the powers of the Federal Government. The substantive powers of the two governments, in many instances, are distinct. And in every case where we are called upon to balance the interest in free expression against other interests, it seems to me important that we should keep in the forefront the question of whether those other interests are state or federal." With that caveat, the Justice voted to reverse the conviction of Roth, and affirm the conviction of Alberts.

Insofar as *Roth* was concerned, Harlan found the federal law to be too broad, believing that it should be narrowly construed to cover only "'hardcore' pornography." He therefore concluded, that because the "material here involved [in *Roth*] cannot be said to be hard-core pornography, I would reverse this case with instructions to dismiss the indictment."

But the *Alberts* case was different. Harlan believed that because "the domain of sexual morality is pre-eminently a matter of state concern, this Court should be slow to interfere with state legislation calculated to protect that morality." Furthermore, the state should not be held to the same standard as the federal government, and ought to be able "to prosecute one who sells books whose dominant tendency might be to 'deprave or corrupt' a reader." After examining the material which Alberts allegedly had for sale, Harlan concluded that to suppress them would not "interfere with the communication of 'ideas,'" and therefore Alberts' conviction should be affirmed.

Ten years after *Roth* and *Alberts*, and nearing the end of his term, Harlan continued to argue that the application of the First Amendment to obscenity differed as between the federal and state governments.[40]

The Pursuit of Liberty

The Right to Travel. Vivian Marie Thompson applied to the Connecticut Welfare Department for assistance under the Aid to Families with Dependent Children. "She was a 19-year old unwed mother of one child and pregnant with her second child when she changed her residence in June 1966 from Dorchester, Massachusetts, to Hartford, Connecticut, to live with her mother, a Hartford resident. She moved to her own apartment in Hartford in August 1966, when her mother was no longer able to support her and her infant son. Because of her pregnancy, she was unable to work or enter a work training program. Her application for AFDC assistance, filed in August, was denied in November solely on the ground that ... she had not lived in the State for a year before her application was filed."[41]

Thompson filed suit in the Federal District Court which held that she was denied equal protection of the law because she was not being treated the same as those persons who had lived in the state for more than a year. The Supreme Court agreed, being of the opinion that the law requiring new residents to live in the state for at least one year before being eligible for benefits, would discourage people from traveling from one state to another.

> This Court long ago recognized that the nature of our Federal Union and our constitutional concepts of personal liberty unite to require that all citizens be free to travel throughout the length and breadth of our land uninhibited by statutes, rules, or regulations which unreasonably burden or restrict this movement.

Connecticut, however, offered four reasons for the residency requirement: to prevent people from moving just to collect benefits; to prevent fraud; to assist in predicting the welfare budget; and to restrict funds to persons who had made some contribution to the state's economy. The majority did not believe that any one or all of these were sufficient to override Thompson's right to travel. "In sum," Justice Brennan asserted, "neither deterrence of indigents from migrating to the State nor limitation of welfare benefits to those regarded as contributing to the State is a constitutionally permissible state objective."

Harlan reached the opposite conclusion. For him, the reasons advanced by the state were sufficient to outweigh the right to travel. "I cannot find," he declared, "that the burden imposed by residence requirements upon ability to travel outweighs the governmental interests in" the use of the one-year waiting period. He then takes the majority to task. "Today's decision, it seems to me, reflects to an unusual degree the current notion that this Court possesses a peculiar wisdom all its own whose capacity to lead this Nation out of its present troubles is contained only by the limits of judicial ingenuity in contriving new constitutional principles to meet each problem as it arises. For anyone, who, like myself, believes that it is an essential function of this Court to maintain the constitutional divisions between state and federal authority and among the three branches of the Federal Government, today's decision is a step in the wrong direction."

The Right of Privacy. Although Justice Harlan retired before the Court had developed the *right of privacy* to the extent that it exists today, he had the opportunity to express his views on this subject in *Poe v. Ullman.*[42] In this case a husband and wife sought to contest the validity of Connecticut laws which made it a criminal offense to use contraceptives.

The Supreme Court affirmed a dismissal of the case because a majority did not believe that the facts presented a real live issue for the Court to decide. By dismissing the case, the Court avoided having to decide whether Connecticut's laws violated the Constitution. This brought a lengthy dissent from Justice Harlan. He not only believed that the case should have been heard, but was of the opinion that the laws were unconstitutional. The Justice wrote:

> I consider that this Connecticut legislation, as construed to apply to ... [the Poes] violates the Fourteenth Amendment. I believe that a statute making it a criminal offense for *married couples* to use contraceptives is an intolerable and unjustifiable invasion of privacy in the conduct of the most intimate concerns of an individual's personal life.

After reviewing prior cases which have interpreted the word "liberty" found in the Due Process Clause, the Justice points out: "This 'liberty' is not a series of isolated points pricked out in terms of the taking of property; the freedom of speech, press, and religion; the right to keep and bear arms; the freedom from unreasonable searches and seizures; and so on. It is a rational continuum which, broadly speaking, includes a freedom from all substantial arbitrary impositions and purposeless restraints, ... and which also recognizes, what a reasonable and sensitive judgment must, that certain interests require particularly careful scrutiny of the state needs asserted to justify their abridgment."

The Connecticut anti-contraceptive law was back before the Court again five years later in the case of *Griswold v. Connecticut.*[43] This time, a majority of the justices concluded that the statute was unconstitutional, and Harlan concurred. However, he took issue with the majority that the right of privacy can be found within the "penumbra" of some of the provisions of the Bill of Rights. "In my view," he declared, "the proper constitutional inquiry in this case is whether this Connecticut statute infringes the Due Process Clause of the Fourteenth Amendment because the enactment violates basic values 'implicit in the concept of ordered liberty.' ... For reasons stated at length in my dissenting opinion in *Poe v. Ullman,* ... I believe that it does."

Equal Protection of the Law

Integration of Public Schools. Justice Harlan was not on the Court when it held, in *Brown v. Board of Education,*[44] that states were violating the Equal Protection Clause by maintaining separate schools for black children. He did, however, join a unanimous Court in the second *Brown* case,[45] which told "District Courts to take such proceedings and enter such orders and decrees consistent with this opinion as are necessary and proper to admit [black children] to public schools on a racially nondiscriminatory basis with all deliberate speed."

Integration of Public and Private Facilities. Following the two *Brown* cases, Harlan consistently voted with the majority to integrate public facilities.[46] For cases involving the integration of *private* facilities, the Justice insisted that the action of private individuals be substantially intertwined with government action in order to make the Fourteenth Amendment applicable. In *Peterson v. Greenville,*[47] he wrote: "The ultimate substantive question is whether there has been 'State action of a particular character' ...—whether the character of the State's involvement in an arbitrary discrimination is such that it should be held *responsible* for the discrimination." And he did not believe that a state became involved in discrimination when it enforced trespass laws to assist "private business establishments from which the management, of its own free will, has chosen to exclude persons of the Negro race." On the other hand, he also believed that the existence of a city ordinance or state law requiring private businesses to operate segregated facilities made "out a *prima facie* case of invalid state action." In this context, the reference to "state action" refers, not only to state government, but to all branches of state government such as counties, cities, and towns as well.

In the *Peterson* case, the manager of the S. H. Kress department store called the police to arrest several blacks for trespass because they were sitting-in at the lunch counter. Justice Harlan voted to reverse the convictions because the manager testified that he wanted the blacks removed because of local custom, and because of a city ordinance requiring segregated facilities. "This suffices to establish state action," Harlan concluded.

The Court decided several other cases on the same day it decided the *Peterson* case, each of which also involved blacks sitting in at segregated lunch counters.[48] In one of these cases, *Lombard v. Louisiana,*[49] "three Negro and one white college students ... entered the McCrory Five and Ten Cent Store in New Orleans, Louisiana. They sat down at a refreshment counter at the back of the store and requested service, which was refused. Although no sign so indicated, the management operated the counter on a segregated basis, serving only white patrons. ... Negroes were welcome to shop in other areas of the store. The restaurant manager, believing that the 'unusual circumstance' of Negroes sitting at the counter created an 'emergency,' asked ... [the students] to leave and, when they did not do so, ordered that the counter be closed. The restaurant manager then contacted the store manager and called the police. He frankly testified that the ... [students] did not cause any disturbance, that they were orderly, and that he asked them to leave because they were Negroes. Presumably he asked the white ... [student] to leave because he was in the company of Negroes."

The students were arrested for the crime of "criminal mischief," convicted and sentenced to 60 days in jail and fined $350. The convictions were upheld by the Louisiana Supreme Court but reversed by the U.S. Supreme Court.

The central issue in the case was whether the state, i.e., the city, was involved in any way with the discrimination against these students. The majority held that the state (city) was involved because shortly before the incident the Superintendent of Police and the Mayor had issued statements concerning prior sit-in demonstrations in the city. "[W]e want everyone to fully understand," the Superintendent's statement read, "that the police department and its personnel is ready and able to enforce the laws of the city of New Orleans and the state of Louisiana."

The Mayor wrote: "I have today directed the superintendent of police that no additional sit-in demonstrations ... will be permitted ... regardless of the avowed purpose or intent of the participants...."

In reversing the convictions Chief Justice Earl Warren, for the majority, concluded that: "The official command here was to direct continuance of segregated service in restaurants, and to prohibit any conduct directed toward its discontinuance; it was not restricted solely to preserve the public peace in a nondiscriminatory fashion in a situation where violence was present or imminent by reason of public demonstrations."

Harlan did not agree. In referring to the statements of the Superintendent and the Mayor, he said: "I think they are more properly read as an effort by these two officials to preserve the peace in what they might reasonably have regarded as a highly charged atmosphere. That seems to me the fair tenor of their exhortations. If there were nothing more to this case, I would vote to affirm the convictions for want of a sufficient showing of state action denying equal protection." However, he voted to vacate the judgments and send the cases back for further consideration because he saw "some evidence in the record which might indicate advance collaboration between the police and McCrory with respect to these episodes."

The Justice could find no connection to the City of Macon, Georgia, in the case of *Evans v. Newton*.[50]

> In 1911 United States Senator Augustus O. Bacon executed a will that devised to the Mayor and Council of the City of Macon, Georgia, a tract of land which, after the death of the Senator's wife and daughters, was to be used as "a park and pleasure ground" for white people only, the Senator stating in the will that while he had only the kindest feeling for the Negroes he was of the opinion that "in their social relations the two races (white and negro) should be forever separate."

The park was managed by a Board of Managers, some of whom brought suit seeking to remove the city as trustee, and to have the court appoint new trustees. Several blacks intervened, arguing that operating the park on a segregated basis would be unconstitutional. The trial court ordered the appointment of new trustees, and the blacks brought the case to the Supreme Court, which reversed.

Justice Douglas, for the majority, put the case in perspective. "There are two complementary principles to be reconciled in this case. One is the right of the individual to pick his own associates so as to express his preferences and dislikes, and to fashion his private life by joining such clubs and groups as he chooses. The other is the constitutional ban in the Equal Protection Clause of the Fourteenth Amendment against state-sponsored racial inequality, which of course bars a city from acting as trustee under a private will that serves the racial segregation cause."

In this case, the Court found that, although the title to the park had been transferred from the city to new trustees, "there has been no change in municipal maintenance and concern over this facility." "Under the circumstances of this case," Douglas declared, "we cannot but conclude that the public character of this park requires that it be treated as a public institution subject to the command of the Fourteenth Amendment, regardless who now has title under state law."

Justice Harlan dissented, being of the opinion that there was no state-action here. "From all that now appears, this is a case of 'private discrimination.' Baconsfield had its origin not in any significant governmental action or on any public land but rather in the personal social philosophy of Senator Bacon and on property owned by him. The City of Macon's acceptance and, until recent years, its carrying out of the trusteeship were both entirely legitimate, and indeed in accord with the prevailing *mores* of the times."

Because the Court held that Baconsfield could not be maintained as a segregated park even with private trustees, Senator Bacon's heirs sought to have the trust terminated and the land given to them. The "Supreme Court of Georgia ruled that Senator Bacon's intention to provide a park for whites only had become impossible to fulfill and that accordingly the trust had failed and the parkland and other trust property had reverted by operation of Georgia law to the heirs of the Senator."[51] A majority of the United States Supreme, including Justice Harlan, agreed.

Where Blacks Live. Mr. and Mrs. Lincoln W. Mulkey sought to rent an apartment from Neil Reitman, one of the owners of an apartment building in Orange County, California. Reitman refused to rent the apartment to the Mulkeys because they were black. The Mulkeys then brought an action seeking an order restraining Reitman from discriminating against them. Superior Court Judge Raymond Thompson refused to grant the order and dismissed the case.

At the time, California law provided that all persons in the state were "entitled to full and equal accommodations, advantages, facilities, privileges, or services in all business establishments of every kind whatsoever."[52] However, before the case was concluded, California voters passed a constitutional amendment, known as Proposition 14, which prohibited the state from infringing upon "the right of any person, who is willing or desires to sell, lease or rent any part or all of his real property, to decline to sell, lease or rent such property to such person or persons as he, in his absolute discretion, chooses."

The Mulkeys appealed Judge Thompson's decision to the California Supreme Court, which reversed. That court held that Proposition 14 violated the Equal Protection Clause of the Fourteenth Amendment because it placed the state's stamp of approval upon the property owner's decision to discriminate in the sale or rental of real property. The United States Supreme Court agreed, and affirmed.

Justice Byron White concluded for the majority: "Here we are dealing with a provision which does not just repeal an existing law forbidding private racial discriminations. [Proposition 14] ... was intended to authorize, and does authorize, racial discrimination in the housing market. The right to discriminate is now one of the basic policies of the State. The California Supreme Court believes that ... [Proposition 14] will significantly encourage and involve the State in private discriminations. We have been presented with no persuasive considerations indicating that these judgments should be overturned."

Justice Harlan saw the case differently. "In the case at hand California, acting through the initiative and referendum, has decided to remain 'neutral' in the realm of private discrimination affecting the sale or rental of private residential property; in such transactions private owners are now free to act in a discriminatory manner previously forbidden to them. In short, all that has happened is that California has effected a *pro tanto* repeal of its prior statutes forbidding private discrimination. This runs no more afoul of the Fourteenth Amendment than would have California's failure to pass any such antidiscrimination statutes in the first instance."

Justice Harlan, however, thought that Nellie Hunter's case was different. Hunter, a black, wanted to buy a home in Akron, Ohio, but was told by a real estate agent that "she could not show ... [her] any of the houses on the list she had prepared ... because all of the owners had specified they did not wish their houses shown to negroes."[53]

Hunter took the matter to court, only to be told that the city's fair housing laws were rendered ineffective by a new amendment. The Supreme Court of Ohio affirmed being of the opinion that the amendment did not violate the Equal Protection Clause.

The U.S. Supreme Court reversed. Justice White, again writing for the majority, pointed out that the Akron amendment specifically required that only "laws to end housing discrimination based on 'race, color, religion, national origin or ancestry'" had to be voted on by the people. This, White said "discriminates against minorities, and constitutes a real, substantial, and invidious denial of the equal protection of the laws."

Harlan agreed. This case, he said, was not the same as the Mulkeys. "Here, we have a provision that has the clear purpose of making it more difficult for certain racial and religious minorities to achieve legislation that is in their interest. Since the charter amendment is discriminatory on its face, Akron must 'bear a far heavier burden of justification' than is required in the normal case." And, he concluded, it had not done so.

For Illegitimate Children. The Supreme Court accepted as true "that the mother, Louise Levy, gave birth to these five illegitimate children and that they lived with her; that she treated them as a parent would treat any other child; that she worked as a domestic servant to support them, taking them to church every Sunday and enrolling them, at her own expense, in a parochial school."[54] When suit was brought on behalf of the children for the wrongful death of their mother, the courts in Louisiana denied recovery because under the law only legitimate children were given a right to sue for wrongful death of a parent. With Justices Harlan, Black and Stewart dissenting, the Supreme Court reversed.

When Minnie Brade Glona's son was killed in an auto accident in New Orleans, Louisiana, her suit for wrongful death of her son was dismissed by Federal District Judge Frederick J. R. Heebe because her son was illegitimate. The Court of Appeals affirmed, but the Supreme Court reversed. Justices Harlan, Black and Stewart again dissented.[55]

In reversing the *Levy* case, Justice Douglas declared: "Legitimacy or illegitimacy of birth has no relation to the nature of the wrong allegedly inflicted on the mother. These children, though illegitimate, were dependent on her; she cared for them and nurtured them; they were indeed hers in the biological and in the spiritual sense; in her death they suffered wrong in the sense that any dependent would."[56] It followed, therefore, that not extending wrongful death protection to the illegitimate children, denied then equal protection of the law.

In upholding the right of Minnie Brade Glona to recover for the wrongful death of her son, Justice Douglas wrote: "A law which creates an open season on illegitimates in the area of automobile accidents gives a windfall to tortfeasors. But it hardly has a causal connection with the 'sin,' which is, we are told, the historic reason for the creation of the disability. To say that the test of equal protection should be the 'legal' rather than the biological relationship is to avoid the issue. For the Equal Protection Clause necessarily limits the authority of a State to draw such 'legal' lines as it chooses."[57]

Writing for the dissenters, Harlan argued that there should be no recovery in either of these cases because there was no *formal* acknowledgment of paternity by either Louise Levy or Minnie Brade Glona. "The rights at issue here stem from the existence of a family relationship, and the State has decided only that it will not recognize the family relationship unless the formalities of marriage, or of the acknowledgment of children by the parent in question, have been complied with."

For New Political Parties and Voters. Under the laws of Ohio, candidates of the Republican and Democratic Parties for President and Vice President were automatically placed on the general election ballot if each Party had obtained at least ten percent of the votes cast for governor at the last election. Independent parties, however, were required to obtain more than 400,000 signatures on petitions before qualifying for a ballot spot.

In 1968, former Alabama Governor George C. Wallace's American Independent Party secured more than the required number of signatures, but did not do so before the Ohio statutory date for filing such petitions had passed. Having been refused a position on the ballot, the Party sought an order of the

Federal District Court placing it on the ballot, which was refused. Subsequently, Justice Potter Stewart granted the injunction, which the Supreme Court later upheld.[58]

Writing for the majority, Justice Black pointed out that: "In the present situation the state laws place burdens on two different, although overlapping, kinds of rights—the right of individuals to associate for the advancement of political beliefs, and the right of qualified voters, regardless of their political persuasion, to cast their votes effectively." And while placing a substantial burden on new parties, these laws "give the two old, established parties a decided advantage over any new parties struggling for existence and thus place substantially unequal burdens on both the right to vote and to associate." New parties, therefore, are denied equal protection of the law.

"I would rest this decision," Harlan declared in concurring, "entirely on the proposition that Ohio's statutory scheme violates the basic right of political association assured by the First Amendment which is protected against state infringement under the Due Process Clause of the Fourteenth Amendment."

Herbert Carrington's problem wasn't that his party was not on the ballot, but rather that Texas was not going to let him vote at all.

> Herbert N. Carrington, is a sergeant in the United States Army. He entered the military service in 1946, at which time he was a resident of Alabama. He has been stationed at White Sands, New Mexico, and has resided in El Paso County, Texas, since February, 1962. He has purchased a home in El Paso, pays taxes in El Paso, registers his automobile in El Paso, and has purchased a poll tax in El Paso. He says that El Paso County is his legal residence, and we assume that such is the case.[59]

But when Carrington informed Republican Party officials that he wanted to vote in their Party's primary election May 2, 1964, he was told that he could not do so because under Texas law members of the Armed Forces were permitted to vote only in the county in which they lived at the time he or she entered military service. Carrington, of course, had not lived in any county in Texas at that time. When Texas courts refused to order the Party to permit him to vote, he appealed to the Supreme Court which reversed.[60]

Texas made two arguments to support its classification denying service personnel the right to vote. First it argued that "it has a legitimate interest in immunizing its elections from the concentrated balloting of military personnel, whose collective voice may overwhelm a small local civilian community." And secondly, "it has a valid interest in protecting the franchise from infiltration by transients, and it can reasonably assume that those servicemen who fall within the constitutional exclusion will be within the State for only a short period of time."

Justice Stewart responded to these arguments. As to the first, he wrote:

"[T]he exercise of rights so vital to the maintenance of democratic institutions ... cannot constitutionally be obliterated because of a fear of the political views of a particular group of bona fide residents. Yet, that is what Texas claims to have done here."

With regard to the question of transient voters, Stewart pointed out that "Texas deals with particular categories of citizens who, like soldiers, present specialized problems in determining residence. Students at colleges and universities in Texas, patients in hospitals and other institutions within the State, and civilian employees of the United States Government may be as transient as military personnel. But all of them are given at least an opportunity to show the election officials that they are bona fide residents."

This discrimination against military personnel led the Court to conclude that: "[T]he uniform of our country ... [must not] be the badge of disfranchisement for the man or woman who wears it."

Justice Harlan made two arguments in support of his dissent from the Court's decision. He did not believe that the Equal Protection Clause was ever intended to apply to state election procedures. However, assuming that the equal protection principle does apply, "I think," he argued, "that Texas, given the traditional American notion that control of the military should always be kept in civilian hands, ... could rationally decide to protect state and local politics against the influences of military voting strength by, in effect, postponing the privilege of voting otherwise attaching to a service-acquired domicile until the serviceman becomes a civilian and by limiting Texas servicemen to voting in the counties of their original domicile. Such a policy on Texas' part may seem to many unduly provincial in light of modern conditions, but it cannot, in my view, be said to be unconstitutional."

It was the question of having to pay for the privilege of voting that was at issue in *Harper v. Virginia Bd. of Elections*.[61] The Twenty-Fourth Amendment to the Constitution had abolished all poll taxes in federal elections. In *Harper*, the Supreme Court did the same for poll taxes levied by states in state elections. "We conclude," Justice Douglas declared, "that a State violates the Equal Protection Clause of the Fourteenth Amendment whenever it makes the affluence of the voter or payment of any fee an electoral standard. Voter qualifications have no relation to wealth nor to paying or not paying this or any other tax."

Believing that he was bound by the Court's decision in the *Carrington* case, Justice Harlan reluctantly agreed that the Equal Protection Clause now applied to voter qualifications, but he also believed that it was being misapplied in this case. He pointed out that "[p]roperty qualifications and poll taxes have been a traditional part of our political structure," as well as have other restrictions on the right to vote, such as literacy tests and the exclusion of women. But even assuming that such qualifications "are not in accord with current egalitarian notions of how a modern democracy should be organized," he questioned whether the courts should be involved in making any changes. "It is of course entirely fitting that legislatures should modify the law to reflect such changes in popular attitudes. However, it is all wrong, in my view, for the Court to adopt the political doctrines popularly accepted at a particular moment of our history and to declare all others to be irrational and invidious, barring them from the range of choice by reasonably minded people acting through the political process."

In the Criminal Justice System. In *Griffin v. Illinois*,[62] Justice Black wrote: "Destitute defendants must be afforded as adequate appellate review as defendants who have money enough to buy transcripts."

In order to alleviate the disparity in the appeal process between those who can afford to pay for a transcript and those who cannot, the Court held that it would be a violation of equal protection not to provide the indigent person with a transcript paid for by the State. Harlan disagreed. "All that Illinois has done," he argued, "is to fail to alleviate the consequences of differences in economic circumstances that exist wholly apart from any state action." He saw no difference between not providing the indigent with a transcript to appeal a criminal conviction than not paying tuition for indigent students at colleges and universities. For him, the real question in this case was whether an indigent defendant, forced to appeal without a transcript of his or her trial, was being denied due process of law. He concluded that he was not, noting that due process is denied when there is a "denial of fundamental fairness, shocking to the universal sense of justice." But, he wrote: "I am unable to bring myself to say that Illinois' failure to furnish free transcripts to indigents in all criminal cases, is 'shocking to the universal sense of justice.'"

Harlan did not believe that it was "shocking to the universal sense of justice" to deny counsel to Bennie Will Meyes and William Douglas to assist them in appealing their convictions for having committed 13 crimes including robbery, assault, and assault to commit murder. Both petitioned the California Court of Appeal for review, a review granted as a matter of right by California law. Because they were indigent, they requested the court to appoint counsel to handle their appeals. The court concluded that counsel would not be helpful to the defendants and denied the request. That denial was upheld by the California Supreme Court without a hearing. Upon appeal to the United States Supreme Court, a majority voted to reverse.[63] "There is lacking," Justice Douglas noted, "that equality demanded by the Fourteenth Amendment where the rich man, who appeals as of right, enjoys the benefit of counsel's examination into the record, research of the law, and marshaling of arguments on his behalf, while the indigent, already burdened by a preliminary determination that his case is without merit, is forced to shift for himself. The indigent, where the record is unclear or the errors are hidden, has only the right of a meaningless ritual, while the rich man has a meaningful appeal."

Still being of the opinion that the disparity in the treatment of indigent criminal defendants was no different than government treatment of other poor persons, Harlan dissented. "Every financial exaction which the State imposes on a uniform basis is more easily satisfied by the well-to-do than by the indigent. Yet I take it that no one would dispute the constitutional power of the State to levy a uniform sales tax, to charge tuition at a state university, to fix rates for the purchase of water from a municipal corporation, to impose a standard fine for criminal violations, or to establish minimum bail for various categories. Nor could it be contended that the State may not classify as crimes acts which the poor are more likely to commit than are the rich."

The Bill of Rights and the States

In *Gideon v. Wainwright*,[64] the Court held that States must abide by the Sixth Amendment's guarantee of right to counsel in criminal cases, even to the extent of paying attorneys to represent indigent defendants.

At the time, Justice Black wrote:

> The right of one charged with crime to counsel may not be deemed fundamental and essential to fair trials in some countries, but it is in ours. From the very beginning, our state and national constitutions and laws have laid great emphasis on procedural safeguards designed to assure fair trials before impartial tribunals in which every defendant stands equal before the law. This noble ideal cannot be realized if the poor man charged with crime has to face his accusers without a lawyer to assist him.

Harlan agreed. He wanted it understood however, that by extending the right to counsel to state defendants, that does not necessarily mean that federal defendants and state defendants must be treated alike. "When we hold a right or immunity valid against the Federal Government, to be 'implicit in the concept of ordered liberty' and thus valid against the States, I do not read our past decisions to suggest that by so holding, we automatically carry over an entire body of federal law and apply it in full sweep to the States."

After many years of confronting the question, to what extent, if any, should states be required to follow the provisions of the Bill of Rights, the Justice summarized his views as follows: "A few members of the Court have taken the position that the intention of those who drafted the first section of the Fourteenth Amendment was simply, and exclusively, to make the provisions of the first eight Amendments applicable to state action. This view has never been accepted by this Court. In my view, often expressed elsewhere, the first section of the Fourteenth Amendment was meant neither to incorporate, nor to be limited to, the specific guarantees of the first eight Amendments."[65]

For the Justice, the Court's task was "to start with the words 'liberty' and 'due process of law' and attempt to define them in a way that accords with American traditions and our system of government." He acknowledges that, although this approach is a difficult one, the Bill of Rights does play a part in this process.

AS A JUSTICE FOR THE GOVERNMENT

Justice Harlan subscribed to the position that in adjudicating cases involving individual rights, the Court's approach should be different when the federal government is infringing upon those rights than when it is state action that is involved. The federal government must obey the commands of the Bill of Rights, while state actions are limited only by the restrictions gleaned from the word "liberty" found in the Due Process Clause of the Fourteenth Amendment. This requires the Court to recognize "what a reasonable and sensitive judgment must, that certain interests require particularly careful scrutiny of the state needs asserted to justify their abridgement."[66]

In scrutinizing "the state needs asserted" to infringe upon individual rights, the Justice often opted to uphold those "state needs" and to deny the freedom claimed by the individual. For example, the Justice voted to deny unemployment compensation to Adell Sherbert because she would not work on Saturday, even though her decision to do so was motivated by her religious convictions. He did not believe "that the State is constitutionally *compelled* to carve out an exception to its general rule of eligibility in the present case. Those situations in which the Constitution may require special treatment on account of religion are, in my view, few and far between, and this view is amply supported by the course of constitutional litigation in this area."[67]

He is, of course, right that the Court had previously upheld some state infringement upon the individual's free exercise of religion. But as Justice Brennan points out in *Sherbert*, the "conduct or actions so regulated [in those cases] posed some substantial threat to public safety, peace or order." In Sherbert's case, upholding her free exercise rights, posed no threat to public safety, peace or order. The state's arguments for not paying compensation to her related to the possibility of spurious claims, and budgetary matters, which the majority concluded were not sufficient to deny benefits to her.

Harlan also voted to uphold Sunday Closing Laws as against an argument that such laws imposed a heavy burden upon orthodox Jews who were required by their faith to close on Saturdays, and by the law to close on Sundays. In voting to uphold Sunday Closing Laws, Frankfurter and Harlan were willing to accord "to the legislature a wide range of power to classify and to delineate."[68]

The Justice made a spirited defense of Paul Cohen's right to protest against the draft by having the F-word on the back of his jacket while in the Los Angeles courthouse. His statement that "one man's vulgarity is another's lyric" is a far-reaching one insofar as protection for free speech is concerned.

But the Justice did not give the came consideration to David Paul O'Brien, who burned his draft card in protest of the draft, and he would have upheld the suspension of Mary Beth and John Tinker for wearing black armbands to school to protest the Vietnam War.

Harlan joined the majority opinion in O'Brien's case, which gave scant recognition to O'Brien's argument that he was making a speech by burning his draft card.[69]

In *Tinker*, instead of placing the burden upon school authorities to sustain the infringement upon the Tinker children's protest, Harlan would have required the students to justify their unpopular speech. The First Amendment, however, places the burden upon the government to produce sufficient evidence to outweigh the right to free expression before any infringement is upheld.

Justice Harlan also turned a deaf ear to the pleas of Ephram Nestor who had paid into the social security program for nineteen years prior to being deported for prior membership in the Communist Party. To uphold, as Harlan did, the termination of Nestor's retirement benefits after he was deported, was an act of gross injustice. As Justice Brennan pointed out: "The Framers ordained that even the worst of men should not be punished for their past acts or for any conduct without adherence to the procedural safeguards written into the Constitution."[70] He was of the opinion that the legislation which authorized the termination of benefits in cases such as Nestor's, was an *ex post facto* law and one that imposed punishment "without a judicial trial."

In the bar admission cases, *Konigsberg* and *Anastaplo*, the Justice showed an insensitivity to associational privacy. In both of these cases, the bar associations had substantial evidence of the good moral character of each of the applicants. And even if each had admitted membership in the Communist Party, that alone would not have allowed the state to deny them admission to practice law.

Condoning the kind of inquiry into personal beliefs and associations, as was done in these cases, would certainly have a chilling effect upon the activities of potential applicants to the bar.

Harlan's view of the laws of Virginia, Illinois and Michigan regulating the practice of law, was much narrower than that of the justices who voted to strike down those laws. In *Button*, he concluded that the regulations did no more than prevent the solicitation of legal business by lawyers subject to the control of the NAACP. The majority, however held that the rules infringed upon the freedom of speech and associational rights of NAACP members. In the *Mine Workers* and *Union Transportation Union* cases, the majority again found infringement upon First Amendment rights, whereas Harlan concluded that any First Amendment interests were "remote at best."

In cases involving freedom of the press, as he had in other First Amendment cases, Harlan wanted it understood that he was applying the Fourteenth

Amendment, not the First Amendment per se. This was important for him because when dealing with alleged state infringement upon First Amendment rights, he applied a less exacting standard than when applying the First Amendment to federal action.

Approaching the issue from this perspective allowed Harlan to extend less protection to the press than most of the other justices. For example, he was willing to allow a private individual to recover damages for libel upon proof that the press did not exercise "reasonable care," a much less exacting standard than requiring the complainant to prove the press acted "with malice." In arriving at that conclusion, he argued that the "publisher of a newspaper has no special immunity from the application of general laws. He has no special privilege to invade the rights and liberties of others." And furthermore, "it does no violence, in my judgment, to the value of freedom of speech and press to impose a duty of reasonable care upon those who would exercise these freedoms."[71]

Harlan applied this approach when dealing with obscenity. For example, in cases involving the federal government's attempt to regulate the distribution of obscene material, he applied the First Amendment and would have upheld the government's efforts only insofar as the material being prohibited was "hard core pornography." In *Alberts*, however, a case involving state obscenity laws, because it was the Fourteenth Amendment that was involved, he was willing to allow the state much greater leeway. "We do not decide," he argued, "whether the policy of the State is wise, or whether it is based on assumptions scientifically substantiated. We can inquire only whether the state action so subverts the fundamental liberties implicit in the Due Process Clause that it cannot be sustained as a rational exercise of power."[72]

The Justice voted consistently to strike down racial discrimination when it was clear that the discrimination was the result of government action. For example, he voted most of the time to integrate juries, public schools, and other public facilities. He was more cautious, however, when the discrimination was being done by private individuals or businesses. He saw these cases as a clash between the right of the private person to discriminate and the right to equal treatment by the person being discriminated against. "Freedom of the individual to choose his associates or his neighbors, to use and dispose of his property as he sees fit, to be irrational, arbitrary, capricious, even unjust in his personal relations are things all entitled to a large measure of protection from governmental interference. This liberty would be overridden, in the name of equality, if the strictures of the [Fourteenth] Amendment were applied to governmental and private action without distinction."[73] Using this approach, the Justice voted to reverse several cases in which blacks were convicted for their attempt to integrate segregated lunch counters.[74] He would have sent the cases back to the state courts to make a determination whether there was state action that would trigger the application of the Fourteenth Amendment.

The majority in each of these cases, however, concluded that there was state involvement in the continuation of segregated lunch counters, and therefore, there was a denial of equal protection and the convictions must be reversed.

Harlan would have upheld the discrimination against illegitimate children in the *Levy* and *Glona* cases. The majority, however, concluded that such children have the same rights as legitimate children. "We start from the premise," Justice Douglas declared, "that illegitimate children are not 'nonpersons.' They are humans, live and have their being. They are clearly 'persons' within the meaning of the Equal Protection Clause of the Fourteenth Amendment."[75]

The Court's decision in the *Levy* case allowed the five illegitimate children of Louise Levy to sue for damages for the wrongful death of their mother.

In addition to voting against potential voters, as he did in the *Carrington* and *Harper* cases, Harlan voted against providing absentee ballots to jail inmates, and against a non–property owning, non-parent who wanted to vote in a school election.[76] In the school election case, the majority concluded that when confronted with a classification of voters, the Court must give the classification a "close and exacting examination." Joining with Justice Potter Stewart, Harlan objected to the Court's approach. Writing for himself, Harlan and Justice Black, Stewart pointed out that the case did not involve a racial classification, and the law did not infringe upon any constitutional right. "For 'the Constitution of the United States does not confer the right of suffrage upon any one....'" Justice Stewart, of course, is correct; the Constitution does not protect a right to vote. Nevertheless, the Court has given voting a preferred place in our hierarchy of values. Harlan did not always agree.[77]

When the question before the Court was whether certain state criminal procedures denied a defendant equal protection of the law, Justice Harlan voted about as many times in support of the defendant as he did to uphold the state's procedures.[78] In voting to uphold some state procedures, he expressed the opinion that: "To be sure, a transcript of the prior hearing may be an incidental convenience—so, too, would a daily transcript at a criminal trial—but the Fourteenth Amendment does not require a State to furnish an indigent with every luxury that a wealthy litigant might conceivably choose to purchase."[79] Surely the command of the Equal Protection Clause is not to make rich and poor defendants equal in the defense of the criminal charge against them. Nevertheless, in most cases having competent counsel in the appellate process together with a complete transcript of the proceedings in the trial court, are the bare essentials for an adequate appeal. And only by giving great deference to the requests of defendants for these essentials, can any semblance of equality be attained.

As the Justice pointed out in his dissent in *Duncan v. Louisiana*,[80] he did not accept the proposition that the Fourteenth Amendment was a shorthand method of applying the Bill of Rights to the states. For him, the provisions of the Bill of Rights which were applicable to the states were those that came within the definition of the "words 'liberty' and 'due process of law' and attempt to define them in a way that accords with American traditions and our system of government." This case by case approach allowed him to accept as applicable to the states the command of the First Amendment.[81]

As this review of Harlan's opinions and voting record indicates, the Justice was not only willing to give government, especially state government, considerable leeway to legislate on matters effecting constitutional rights,[82] he also voted against the exercise of such rights, many times. For this reason, the Justice is included as a *Justice for the Government*.

5

JUSTICE BYRON R. WHITE

PERSONAL LIFE

Growing Up

"You started working early. A friend of mine who lived across the street and I went to work in the [sugar] beet fields when we were 7 or 8. In the spring you did a thing called blocking and thinning, which was clearing out all but one beet every few inches along the row. ... Then twice in the summer you did the handhoeing of the weeds, and in the fall you helped with the harvest. ... We might make a dollar a day or maybe even $2."[1]

The above is one of the memories Byron R. White has of his early childhood growing up in Wellington, Colorado. Later, in commenting upon his work in beet fields, he said: "Digging into the ground with your hands is not essential to a useful life. I had a very good time doing it, and I look back on it with some fondness."[2]

White was born in Fort Collins, Colorado, on June 8, 1917, the second son of Mr. and Mrs. Alpha Albert White. Albert White, as he was called, was the branch manager of a lumber supply company. The Whites' other son, Clayton (Sam), was four-and-a-half years older than Byron.

Graduating from high school first in his class, White earned a scholarship to the University of Colorado. He did not know at the time what he wanted to be, but he had an uncle in Iowa who was a lawyer. During the family's visits to Iowa, Byron "took a great shine to him." White's parents, however, did not direct him to law school. He remembers, however, that his "parents wanted me to be what I wanted to be. They had a pretty simple prescription for living. You worked hard, did as well as you could and were considerate of other people's feelings."

White had an outstanding academic record in college, sufficient to be elected to Phi Beta Kappa and secure for him a Rhodes Scholarship. His brother Sam was also a Rhodes Scholar.

JUSTICE BYRON R. WHITE (collection of the Supreme Court of the United States).

College and Professional Football

While White played football in high school, he was too small to do so during his freshman year, and recalls that he broke a shoulder and was unable to play one other year. He excelled in football and in other sports at the University, however, earning "three varsity letters in football, four in basketball, and three in baseball."³ He gained the nickname "Whizzer" while at the university, and attracted national attention as the football team's tailback.

Shortly after learning that he had been awarded a Rhodes Scholarship, White was offered an opportunity to play professional football for the Pittsburgh Steelers for a one-season contract of $15,000. He received permission to delay going to Oxford until after the 1938 football season.

> "Whizzer" White led the National Football League in rushing with 567 yards. No other rookie had ever before led the league in any department, and White did it with a last place team.

White went to Oxford in January 1939, and returned in September when the war began in Europe. He entered Yale Law School in October, and after his first year accepted a contract to play football with the Detroit Lions during the 1940 season. He also agreed to play during the 1941 season, but Pearl Harbor intervened and that ended his professional football career.

In commenting upon professional football, "'Whizzer' said: 'I liked pro ball better than the college game. ... In the professional league there is no such thing as a soft game.'"⁴

White thought that participating in sports was a great experience, and he recommended it to others. "The fundamental reason for playing competitive sports" he said, "is to get some experience. Sports constantly makes demands on the participant for top performance, and they develop integrity, self-reliance and initiative. They teach you a lot about working in groups without being unduly submerged in the group."

Law School, the Navy and Marriage

White excelled at Yale Law School as he had at the University, receiving "the Edgar Cullen Award for the highest scholastic grades achieved by a freshman."⁵ He graduated *magna cum laude*. White left Yale in July 1941, and upon being rejected by the Marines because of color-blindness enlisted in the Navy where he was assigned to Naval Intelligence and stationed in the South Pacific. During four years in the Navy, he earned two bronze stars.

> "It's hard to say that you had a good time in the war," White reminisced, "but, on the other hand, you couldn't say it was dull or purposeless. It's an experience I'd just as soon not have had but, having had it, I have to admit it was a very great experience."

After the war, White returned to Yale for his last year of law school. He married his college sweetheart, Marion Sterns, on June 15, 1946. The Whites had two children, Charles (Barney) and Nancy.

The Practice of Law

Upon graduation, White accepted a position as clerk for Chief Justice Fred Vinson of the United States Supreme Court. He was the first Supreme Court clerk to be later appointed to the Court.

Upon completing his term as clerk, White returned with his family to Colorado, where White accepted a position with the Denver law firm of Lewis, Grant and Davis. Describing his experience with the firm, White declared: "It had a typical practice for that kind of town—just the general practice of law—and it gave you a wide variety of experience."[6]

Active in Politics

In an interview given in 1962, the then Justice White had this to say about his involvement in politics.

> I was in local politics from the first moment I arrived in Denver. I served as a precinct committeeman every year for several years, and I was a ward captain after that. Every year after 1947, I worked on someone's committee. It might have been a judge, a candidate for the state legislature or someone running for local office.

White was also a great believer in all people participating in politics. "Everyone in this country has an obligation to take part in politics. That's the foundation, the most important principle, on which our system is built. If our system is to work, people must intelligently elect their representatives in the legislatures and the Congress. And the best way to do it is to get their feet wet in politics."

Friendship with John and Robert Kennedy

White and John Kennedy first met in Munich, Germany, during the time White was at Oxford. As White recalls the meeting: "He [Kennedy] was traveling around with some friends of his, and I think we had a couple of evenings together."[7]

The two men also met while serving in the Soloman Islands during World War II. And White was assigned to write a report on the sinking of Kennedy's PT-109. "As a result of these encounters with Kennedy, I began to get a strong feeling about what kind of fellow he was. He proved himself to be very intelligent in the way he ran his boat, as well as cool and courageous under fire. I concluded he was a pretty solid sort of person." They also met and talked when White was clerking for Chief Justice Vinson. At that time, John Kennedy was serving his first term as a member of the U.S. House of Representatives.

White tells of his decision to become involved in the presidential campaign of 1960: "I was driving back from an AAU track meet in Boulder and I got to thinking about the coming presidential campaign. I'd been reading about the various candidates and, shuffling through the names of these guys in my mind. I began to feel that Jack Kennedy would be my preference."[8]

Shortly thereafter, he organized the Colorado Committee for Kennedy. Later he was asked to head Kennedy's pre-convention organization in that state. "White organized Colorado-for-Kennedy clubs from the precinct level up—and successfully delivered thirteen and a half of the twenty-one votes at the 1960 Democratic convention."[9]

Following Kennedy's nomination, Robert Kennedy asked White to head up the National Citizens for Kennedy Committee. Robert Kennedy was so "[i]mpressed by White's persuasive and organizational abilities ... [that he] asked his brother to name White Deputy Attorney General—and this the President-elect did on December 16, 1960."

Dennis J. Hutchinson, in a biography, describes White's tenure as Deputy Attorney General: "He was widely praised for helping to recruit a uniformly talented and energetic team of young assistant attorneys general, many of whom went on to distinguished careers in both government and the private sector. He also was recognized for his courage and icy calm in personally addressing the riots that grew out of the 'freedom rides' from Birmingham to Montgomery, Alabama, in the spring of 1961."[10] White also was given the task of screening candidates for federal judgeships.

Justice Charles Whittaker tendered his resignation from the Court in March 1962. The names of three persons—Harvard professor Paul Freund, Secretary of Labor Arthur Goldberg, and Federal Judge William Hastie, a black—were at the top of the list to replace Whittaker. Hutchinson discusses the President's dilemma: "Kennedy told Arthur Schlesinger, Jr., 'But I didn't want to start off with a Harvard man and a professor; we've taken so many Harvard men that it's damn hard to appoint another. And we couldn't do Hastie this time; it was just too early.' Nor was Kennedy eager to lose Goldberg from the cabinet, and, in any event, he anticipated making several more appointments to the Court. Nicholas Katzenbach ... has reported that he suggested White's name to Robert Kennedy...."

President Kennedy nominated White on March 30, and the Senate confirmed the appointment 12 days later.

When White joined the Court, Earl Warren was Chief Justice. Other members of the Court were Justices Hugo L. Black, William O. Douglas, Felix Frankfurter, Tom C. Clark, William J. Brennan, Jr., John M. Harlan, and Potter Stewart. Justice White served as an Associate Justice from April 23, 1962, until his retirement on June 30, 1993.

As Associate Justice (1962–1993)

The Free Exercise of Religion

When the Supreme Court required the State of South Carolina to pay Ardell Sherbert unemployment benefits because her religion prevented her from working on Saturday, Justice White joined Justice Harlan's dissent.[11]

Harlan and White found the Court's decision "far more troublesome than its apparently narrow dimensions would indicate at first glance. ... The State ... must *single out* for financial assistance those whose behavior is religiously motivated, even though it denies such assistance to others whose identical behavior [in this case, inability to work on Saturdays] is not religiously motivated."

Following the *Sherbert* case, the Court required Indiana to pay unemployment benefits to Eddie C. Thomas, a Jehovah's Witness who quit work in an armament plant because working there conflicted with his religious beliefs,[12] and to Paula Hobbie, a Seventh-Day Adventist who refused Saturday work in a jewelry store because that was her Sabbath.[13] Justice White voted with the majority in both cases. And when William Frazee was denied unemployment benefits for not working on Sunday, which he called "the Lord's day,"[14] the Justice wrote the opinion for a unanimous Court requiring the State to grant him benefits.

White recognized the validity of prior cases, including *Sherbert*. In response to the argument that in each of the other cases, the employees had belonged to a religion whose tenets specifically conflicted with the work they were to perform, he pointed out: "Our judgments in those cases rested on the fact that each of the claimants had a sincere belief that religion required him or her to refrain from the work in question. Never did we suggest that unless a claimant belongs to a sect that forbids what his job requires, his belief, however sincere, must be deemed a purely personal preference rather than a religious belief."

Not being able to find any justification for the denial of benefits to Frazee, White concluded that "there may exist state interests sufficiently compelling to override a legitimate claim to the free exercise of religion. No such interest has been presented here."

The Justice also voted to uphold the right of the Amish not to send their children to school beyond the eighth grade. "Since the Amish children are permitted to acquire the basic tools of literacy to survive in modern society by attending grades one through eight and since the deviation from the State's compulsory-education law is relatively slight, I conclude that ... [the Amish] must prevail, largely because 'religious freedom—the freedom to believe and to practice strange and, it may be, foreign creeds—has classically been one of the highest values of our society.'"[15]

Justice White was not so accommodating, however, to Simcha Goldman, a rabbi serving in the Air Force who was prevented from wearing a
yarmulke, the traditional head covering of Orthodox Jews. White joined Justice John Paul Stevens's opinion, in which the two Justices argued that the
need for uniformity in appearance of Air Force personnel outweighed Goldman's right to free exercise of religion.[16] The majority, including White,
believed that the Air Force should be not be required to examine each request
for deviation from the rule, even though the request was a religious one.

Justice Sandra Day O'Connor argued, in dissent, that the asserted need
for uniformity insofar as Air Force uniforms were concerned did not justify
the Air Force's refusal to allow Goldman to wear the yarmulke. "In rare
instances where the military has not consistently or plausibly justified its
asserted need for rigidity of enforcement, and where the individual seeking
the exemption establishes that the assertion by the military of a threat to discipline or esprit de corps is in his or her case completely unfounded, I would
hold that the Government's policy of uniformity must yield to the individual's assertion of the right of free exercise of religion."

Freedom of Speech

Soliciting and Pamphleteering. "The issue is whether the Village has exercised
its power to regulate solicitation in such a manner as not unduly to intrude
upon the rights of free speech."[17] That was the question Justice White and
the Court confronted in an ordinance of the Village of Schaumburg, Illinois,
regulating solicitation by charitable organizations. The ordinance provided
that before a charity was granted a permit to solicit contributions, it had
to supply "proof that at least seventy-five per cent of the proceeds of such solicitation will be used directly for the charitable purpose of the organization."

Citizens for Better Environment [CBE] challenged the ordinance, arguing that it infringed upon its right to solicit which was protected by the free
speech clause of the First Amendment. Members argued that CBE was not
a traditional charitable organization, but rather was an "advocacy-oriented"
organization; that its primary purpose was to disseminate information and
advocate certain positions on environmental matters. It acknowledged that
approximately 40 percent of its funds were used for administration and
fundraising.

District Judge Prentice H. Marshall held that the ordinance was unconstitutional; the Circuit Court agreed and so did the Supreme Court. After
reviewing a number of prior cases dealing with solicitation, White pointed
out that the "issue before us, then, is not whether charitable solicitations in
residential neighborhoods are within the protections of the First Amendment.
It is clear that they are."

The Village argued that "any organization using more than 25 percent of its receipts on fundraising, salaries, and overhead is not a charitable, but a commercial, for-profit enterprise and that to permit it to represent itself as a charity is fraudulent." The Justice responded that "this cannot be true of those organizations that are primarily engaged in research, advocacy, or public education and that use their own paid staff to carry out these functions as well as to solicit financial support." Therefore, White concluded, "[t]he 75-percent requirement in the village ordinance plainly is insufficiently related to the governmental interests asserted in its support to justify its interference with protected speech."

The International Society for Krishna Conscience [Krishnas] did not fare as well as the CBE, in *Heffron v. Int'l. Soc. for Krishna Consc.*[18] The Krishnas are a religious organization having as one of its tenets "the practice of Sankirtan, ... which enjoins its members to go into public places to distribute or sell religious literature and to solicit donations for the support of the Krishna religion."

When confronted with a rule of the Minnesota State Fair limiting the distribution or sale of material at licensed locations only, the Krishnas brought an action seeking to have the rule declared unconstitutional as an infringement upon their right to distribute literature and solicit contributions. The Minnesota Supreme Court agreed that the rule, as applied to the Krishnas, violated their free exercise right to practice Sankirtan. The United States Supreme Court reversed, with the Justice writing the Court's opinion.

White focused on the fact that if the Krishnas were exempted from the rule "nonreligious organizations seeking support for their activities are entitled to rights equal to those of religious groups to enter a public forum and spread their views, whether by soliciting funds or distributing literature." He was, therefore, of the opinion that the Krishnas and their "ritual of Sankirtan have no special claim to First Amendment protection as compared to that of other religions who also distribute literature and solicit funds." And he did not agree with the Minnesota Supreme Court that the rule is "an unnecessary regulation because the State could avoid the threat to its interest posed by .... [Krishnas] by less-restrictive means, such as penalizing disorder or disruption, limiting the number of solicitors, or putting more narrowly drawn restrictions on the location and movement of ... [Krishnas'] representatives."

Justice Brennan took issue with White's conclusion that the Krishnas' practice of Sankirtan gave them no rights greater than other religions who solicit and distribute literature. Because Sankirtan is part of the Krishnas' "religious beliefs and principles," Brennan argued, they should be given consideration similar to that given the Amish for not sending their children to school beyond the eighth grade; to a Jehovah's Witness who could not work in an armament plant; and to Seventh-Day Adventists who could not work on Saturday, their Sabbath.

Picketing and Parading. Reverend B. Elton Cox, a representative of the Congress of Racial Equality [CORE], was arrested on December 15, 1961, and charged with "four offenses under Louisiana law—criminal conspiracy, disturbing the peace, obstructing public passages, and picketing before a courthouse."[19] These arrests occurred after Reverend Cox, and approximately 2,000 students from Southern University, Baton Rouge, a Negro college, participated in a demonstration near the State Capitol and a courthouse. The demonstration was a protest against the arrest of several persons being held in jail, as well as the "evil of discrimination."

Upon nearing the courthouse, a discussion took place between Reverend Cox and Police Chief Wingate White. Whether that discussion resulted in the Police Chief giving the protesters permission to continue the demonstration, became an issue at Cox's trial. The demonstrators had stopped across the street, approximately 101 feet from the courthouse.

> It was close to noon and, being lunch time, a small crowd of 100 to 300 curious white people, mostly courthouse personnel, gathered on the east sidewalk and courthouse steps, about 100 feet from the demonstrators. Seventy-five to eighty policemen, including city and state patrolmen and members of the Sheriff's staff, as well as members of the fire department and a fire truck were stationed in the street between the two groups.

Sheriff Clemmons urged the demonstrators to disperse, and when they did not do so immediately, two deputies started across the street. The crowd dispersed after a tear gas shell was exploded by a police officer. There were no further demonstrations. Reverend Cox was arrested the next day.

Cox was acquitted of the conspiracy charge, but the judge found him guilty of the other three charges. The Supreme Court, however, reversed all three, but for different reasons.

In an opinion written by Justice Arthur Goldberg, the Court reversed the breach of peace conviction because there was no evidence that the peace was breached. Furthermore, the Court found that the Louisiana breach of the peace statute was overly broad and therefore unconstitutional because "it sweeps within its broad scope activities that are constitutionally protected free speech and assembly. Maintenance of the opportunity for free political discussion is a basic tenet of our constitutional democracy."

The Court was of the opinion that the statute making it a crime to obstruct public passageways was constitutional. It found, however, "that the authorities in Baton Rouge permit or prohibit parades or street meetings in their completely uncontrolled discretion." In other words, the authorities seemed to be allowing certain groups to parade and demonstrate, but not others. This "unfettered discretion in local officials in the regulation of the use of the streets for peaceful parades and meetings is an unwarranted abridgment of ... [Cox's] freedom of speech and assembly secured to him by the First Amendment...."

Cox's conviction for picketing near the courthouse was also reversed by the Court.[20] The majority first concluded that the anti-courthouse picketing statute was constitutional. "A State may," Justice Goldberg acknowledged, "adopt safeguards necessary and appropriate to assure that the administration of justice at all stages is free from outside control and influence." But the conviction had to be reversed because the "record here clearly shows that the officials present gave permission for the demonstration to take place across the street from the courthouse."

Justice White concurred in the reversal of the breach of the peace conviction, but dissented in the reversal of the convictions for obstructing public passageways and picketing near the courthouse. He could find no evidence in the record that other parades and demonstrations had been approved in the past, at least, certainly not as large as the one engaged in by Cox and the students. For him, "at some point the authorities were entitled to apply the statute and to clear the streets. That point was reached here."

Insofar as the conviction for picketing near the courthouse was concerned, White joined Justice Black's dissent. Black expressed concern for the integrity of the judicial system. "The very purpose of a court system is to adjudicate controversies, both criminal and civil, in the calmness and solemnity of the courtroom according to legal procedures. Justice cannot be rightly administered, nor are the lives and safety of prisoners secure, where throngs of people clamor against the processes of justice right outside the courthouse or jailhouse doors."

For Justice White and a majority of the justices, the activities of Thaddeus Zywicki and Mary Grace near the Supreme Court building in Washington, D.C., was a different matter. Thaddeus Zywicki tried distributing literature about unfit judges on the sidewalk near the Supreme Court building. When told by a police officer that it was against the law to distribute material there, Zywicki left.

When Mary Grace heard about Zywicki, she made a sign with the First Amendment printed on it, and went to the place where Zywicki had been. When informed by a police officer that she could not picket there, Grace left the area. Later she and Zywicki brought suit to have the federal law which prohibited such picketing declared unconstitutional. The statute in question reads:

> Section 13K. It shall be unlawful to parade, stand, or move in processions or assemblages in the Supreme Court Building or grounds, or to display therein any flag, banner, or device designed or adapted to bring into public notice any party, organization, or movement.[21]

District Judge Louis F. Oberdorfer upheld the law and dismissed the case. The Circuit Court of Appeals reversed, concluding that the statute was unconstitutional as a violation of the First Amendment.

With Justice White writing the opinion, the Court held that the law was a legitimate exercise of the government's authority to regulate speech activities on the grounds of the Supreme Court, but concluded that the law did not apply to the public sidewalks surrounding the building. "As we have said, the building's perimeter sidewalks are indistinguishable from other public sidewalks in the city that are normally open to the conduct that is at issue here and that Section 13K forbids. A total ban on that conduct is no more necessary for the maintenance of peace and tranquillity on the public sidewalks surrounding the building than on any other sidewalks in the city."

Because the Court did not invalidate the statute, Justice Thurgood Marshall did reach that question and concluded that Section 13K was an unconstitutional infringement upon First Amendment rights. "Visitors to this Court," he argued, "do not lose their First Amendment rights at the edge of the sidewalks any more than 'students or teachers shed their constitutional rights to freedom of speech or expression at the schoolhouse gate.' ... Since the continuing existence of the statute will inevitably have a chilling effect on freedom of expression, there is no virtue in deciding its constitutionality on a piecemeal basis." Furthermore, "[s]o sweeping a prohibition is scarcely necessary to protect the operations of this Court, and in my view cannot constitutionally be applied either to the Court grounds or to the areas inside the Court building that are open to the public."

Sandra C. Schultz's problem was not concerned with demonstrating near a courthouse or the Supreme Court building, but rather the right to do so on the street in front of the residence of Dr. Bejamin M. Victoria, a doctor who performed abortions.

Schultz sought to enjoin a Brookfield, Wisconsin, ordinance that prohibited "picketing before ... the residence ... of any individual."[22]

District Judge John W. Reynolds held that the law violated the First Amendment right to picket and issued an injunction against its enforcement. The Supreme Court reversed, being of the opinion that because "the picketing prohibited by the Brookfield ordinance is speech directed primarily at those who are presumptively unwilling to receive it, the State has a substantial and justifiable interest in banning it."

White agreed and wrote: "I agree with the Court that an ordinance which only forbade picketing before a single residence would not be unconstitutional on its face." If, however, a law was "construed to forbid all picketing in residential neighborhoods, the overbreadth doctrine would render it unconstitutional on its face and hence prohibit its enforcement against those ... [like Schultz and others] who engage in single-residence picketing."

Unpopular Speech. Sidney Street was listening to the radio in his apartment in Brooklyn, New York, when he heard a news report that civil rights activist James Meredith had been shot in Mississippi. Street took his American flag, went down to the nearby street corner, and burned it. A police officer later testified that Street said: "We don't need no damn flag...."[23] Street denied that he made that statement, but did agree that the flag was his: "Yes; that is my flag, I burned it. If they let that happen to Meredith we don't need an American flag."

Street was charged with, and later convicted of, violating a New York statute making it a crime to "publicly mutilate, deface, defile, or defy, trample upon, or cast contempt upon either by words or act [any flag of the United States]." His conviction was upheld by the courts of New York, but reversed by the Supreme Court. Justice John M. Harlan wrote the majority opinion. White joined Chief Justice Earl Warren's dissent.

The majority was concerned that Street might have been punished for both what he said and what he did. Punishing him for what he said, according to the majority, would be an unconstitutional infringement upon his right to free speech. "We have no doubt," Justice Harlan pointed out, "that the constitutionally guaranteed 'freedom to be intellectually ... diverse or even contrary,' and the 'right to differ as to things that touch the heart of the existing order,' encompass the freedom to express publicly one's opinions about our flag, including those opinions which are defiant or contemptuous."

Not being able to determine whether Street may have been punished for what he said, the majority reversed and sent the case back to the New York courts.

Justice White disagreed. "I reject the proposition," he argued, "that if Street was convicted for both burning and talking, his conviction must be reversed if the speech conviction is unconstitutional."

Valarie Goguen also made an unpopular speech when he sewed a small United States flag to the seat of his trousers. "On January 30, 1970, two police officers in Leominster, Massachusetts, saw Goguen bedecked in this fashion."[24] Goguen was arrested the next day and charged with violating a Massachusetts statute which reads: "Whoever publicly mutilates, tramples upon, defaces or treats contemptuously the flag of the United States ... shall be punished...." Goguen was convicted but brought an action in the Federal District Court claiming that the law was unconstitutional under the Fourteenth Amendment Due Process Clause because it was vague and unconstitutional under the First Amendment because it infringed upon free speech. Judge Levin H. Campbell agreed that the phrase "treats contemptuously" was vague and did violate due process. The Appeals Court and the Supreme Court both affirmed.

Justice Lewis F. Powell, for the Court, acknowledged that it is sometimes difficult to define criminal actions with precision but concluded that the legislature could have done a better job with the flag desecration statute. "Indeed," he asserted, "because display of the flag is so common and takes so many forms, changing from one generation to another and often difficult to distinguish in principle, a legislature should define with some care the flag behavior it intends to outlaw. Certain nothing prevents a legislature from defining with substantial specificity what constitutes forbidden treatment of United States flags."

Justice White concurred in the judgment releasing Goguen. He believed that Goguen had been convicted because he treated the flag "contemptuously" and that was a violation of his right to freedom of speech. "It is ... clear under our cases that disrespectful or contemptuous spoken or written words about the flag may not be punished consistently with the First Amendment." "This is true," he concluded, "of Goguen's conviction."

Eighteen-year-old Robert Watts expressed an unpopular idea during a group discussion of police brutality. When one of the group suggested that "the young people present should get more education before expressing their views,"[25] Watts spoke up: "They always holler at us to get an education. And now I have already received my draft classification as 1-A and I have got to report for my physical this Monday coming. I am not going. If they ever make me carry a rifle the first man I want to get in my sights is L. B. J."

Watts's statement was heard by an Army Counter Intelligence Corps officer, and the next day he was arrested by Secret Service agents. He was charged with violating a federal law making it a crime to threaten the President of the United States. Watts was convicted by a jury, and that decision was affirmed by the Court of Appeals. The Supreme Court, in a *Per Curiam* opinion, reversed. The Court upheld the constitutionality of the statute but concluded that applying it to Watts was an infringement upon his free speech rights. "We do not believe that the kind of political hyperbole indulged in by ... [Watts] fits within the statutory term. For we must interpret the language Congress chose 'against the background of a profound national commitment to the principle that debate on public issues should be uninhibited, robust, and wide-open, and that it may well include vehement, caustic, and sometimes unpleasantly sharp attacks on government and public officials.'"

The majority concluded that the only offense which Watts had committed "was 'a kind of very crude offensive method of stating a political opposition to the President.'" Justice White dissented without opinion.

Public Employees' Right to Speak.

> The Hatch Act, [a federal law], provides in pertinent part that any employee of an Executive agency ... may not take an active part in political management or political campaigns of a partisan nature and ... [those who do are] subject to removal or suspension without pay for violation.[26]

The National Association of Letter Carriers brought an action in the District of Columbia Federal Court contending that the Act was an unconstitutional infringement upon federal employees' First Amendment rights. Judge Gerhard A. Gesell agreed and declared the law unconstitutional. Justice White, writing for a majority of the Supreme Court, held: "Our judgment is that neither the First Amendment nor any other provision of the

Constitution invalidates a law barring this kind of partisan political conduct by federal employees."[27]

White pointed out that historically it was thought that governmental employment should depend upon meritorious service rather than on an employee's political persuasion; that even Thomas Jefferson was concerned about the political activities of some government employees; and at the time of the enactment of the Hatch Act, President Franklin Roosevelt expressed the opinion that it was constitutional. Furthermore, government employees "are expected to enforce the law and execute the programs of the Government without bias or favoritism for or against any political party or group or members thereof." It is also critical, White wrote "not only ... that the Government and its employees in fact avoid practicing political justice, but it is also critical that they appear to the public to be avoiding it, if confidence in the system of representative Government is not to be eroded to a disastrous extent."

The Justice then examined the law and the regulations issued under it and concluded "the extent to which pure expression is impermissibly threatened, if at all, by ... [the law and regulations] does not in our view make the statute substantially overbroad and so invalid on its face."

On the same day that the Court upheld the Hatch Act, it also upheld Section 818 of Oklahoma's Merit System of Personnel Administration Act, which restricts political activities of state employees. Justice White, for the Court, concluded that the Oklahoma law did not violate the First Amendment rights of state employees.[28]

Justice Douglas dissented in both of these cases and wrote:

> But it is of no concern of Government what an employee does in his spare time, whether religion, recreation, social work, or politics is his hobby—unless what he does impairs efficiency or other facets of the merits of his job. Some things, some activities do affect or may be thought to affect the employee's job performance. But his political creed, like his religion, is irrelevant. In the areas of speech, like religion, it is of no concern what the employee says in private to his wife or to the public in Constitutional Hall.

Speaking out got Sheila Myers, an Assistant District Attorney in the Orleans Parish District Attorney's office, in trouble. Myers was assigned to Judge Ward's court but when District Attorney Harry Connick sought to transfer her to Judge Israel Augustine's court, she strongly objected. She enjoyed working in Judge Ward's court.

Being unable to reverse Connick's decision to transfer her, she distributed a questionnaire to the other employees in the office. The questionnaire dealt with office transfer policy, morale, confidence in other employees, whether the employees were required to work on political campaigns and whether the office should have a grievance committee. When Connick learned about Myers' activities, he discharged her.

Myers brought suit against Connick alleging that her termination had violated her right to free speech. She sought reinstatement to her job and back pay. District Judge Jack M. Gordon agreed that her termination was an unconstitutional infringement upon her right to free speech. He ordered Connick to reinstate her, give her back pay, and pay her damages in the amount of $1,500. Judge Gordon's decision was upheld by the Court of Appeals without opinion.

Five members of the Supreme Court voted to reverse with four justices dissenting. Writing for the majority, Justice White acknowledged that "it has been settled that a State cannot condition public employment on a basis that infringes the employee's constitutionally protected interest in freedom of expression."[30] Myers, however, did not fall within the protection of this rule because "when a public employee speaks not as a citizen upon matters of public concern, but instead as an employee upon matters only of personal interest, absent the most unusual circumstances, a federal court is not the appropriate forum in which to review the wisdom of a personnel decision taken by a public agency allegedly in reaction to the employee's behavior." Most of the questions on the questionnaire, the Justice concluded dealt only with matters personal to Myers and not of public concern.

The dissenters, in an opinion written by Justice Brennan, took a different view as to whether the questionnaire related to matters of public concern. "I would hold," Brennan argued, "that Myers' questionnaire addressed matters of public concern because it discussed subjects that could reasonably be expected to be of interest to persons seeking to develop informed opinions about the manner in which the Orleans Parish District Attorney, an elected official discharged with managing a vital governmental agency, discharges his responsibilities."

Brennan believed that if employees are prevented from expressing their opinions, "the public will be deprived of valuable information with which to evaluate the performance of elected officials."

Justice White participated in a case quite similar to the *Watts* case, except the person making the statement about the President's life, was a public employee. The Justice's response was the same, however, the speaker should be punished. In this case, punishment would have been discharge from government employment.

The case involved Ardith McPherson, a probationary deputy constable in Harris County, Texas. McPherson worked as a data processor, typing court data into a computer. She rarely had access to any member of the public and was not required to answer the phone. On March 30, 1981, McPherson and several other employees heard a radio broadcast that told of an attempt to assassinate President Ronald Reagan. During a conversation with another employee, McPherson mentioned the possibility that the assassin may have been black, as McPherson was, and that the President was cutting back on welfare, Medicaid and food stamps. And, as she later testified: 'I said, shoot, if they go for him again, I hope they get him.'[31] McPherson's statement was reported to Constable Walter Rankin. Rankin immediately confronted McPherson, who admitted making the statement, but said: "I didn't mean anything by it." Rankin, however, discharged her.

McPherson's suit against Rankin for reinstatement and back pay was dismissed by Judge Norman W. Black, but the Circuit Court held that the discharge violated McPherson's right to free speech, and ordered the trial to proceed. In an opinion written by Justice Marshall, the Supreme Court agreed.

The only real issue to be decided was whether McPherson's statement had a detrimental effect upon the functioning of the Constable's office. Justice Marshall acknowledged: "Interference with work, personnel relationships, or the speaker's job performance can detract from the public employer's function; avoiding such interference can be a strong state interest." There was, however, no evidence that McPherson's statement caused any of that to happen. "While McPherson's statement was made at the workplace, there is no evidence that it interfered with the efficient functioning of the office."

"Given the function of the agency, McPherson's position in the office, and the nature of her statement," Marshall wrote, "we are not persuaded that Rankin's interest in discharging her outweighed her rights under the First Amendment."

Justice Scalia wrote a dissenting opinion, which White joined. Scalia argued that the only speech of a government employee that is protected by the First Amendment is speech that relates to a matter of public concern. McPherson's speech, he concluded, was not of that kind.

Commercial Speech. The justices individually have had a difficult time with the issue of whether commercial advertising is speech and therefore protected by the First Amendment. For example, in *Valentine v. Chrestensen*,[32] the justices unanimously upheld a New York City ordinance which prohibited the distribution of handbills containing commercial advertising. Writing for the Court, Justice Owen J. Roberts stated: "We are equally clear that the Constitution imposes no ... restraint on government as respects purely commercial advertising." Later, again unanimously, the justices upheld another New York City law which prohibited trucks from having advertising on them, unless the advertising related to the owner's business.[33] In this case, Railway Express wanted to rent the sides of its trucks to businesses who wanted to put advertisements thereon. Railway Express was convicted for violating the ordinance, and the Court upheld the conviction without reference to the First Amendment.

When the Pittsburgh Press was ordered to stop carrying "sex-designated advertising columns," a majority of the justices agreed that the order did not violate the constitution.[34] Justice Lewis Powell, Jr., for the majority, discussed both the *Valentine* case, and *Railway Express* and concluded that a commercial advertisement placed in a sex-designated column is still commercial advertising. That, plus the fact that such an ad is also made illegal, is sufficient to outweigh any First Amendment interests of the publisher. Justice White joined Powell's opinion. Chief Justice Burger dissented, being of the opinion that the commission's order was a prior restraint on freedom of the press and therefore unconstitutional.

The Court finally came to grips with the commercial speech issue in *Bigelow v. Virginia.*[35] Jeffrey C. Bigelow, the managing editor of the *Virginia Weekly,* in Charlottesville, Virginia, printed an advertisement from the Women's Pavilion of New York City, offering to help women who were pregnant with an unwanted pregnancy. Bigelow was convicted for violating a Virginia statute making it a criminal offense to circulate any publication which encouraged women to seek an abortion. The Supreme Court reversed, holding that the advertisement was protected by the First Amendment.

After discussing prior commercial speech cases, Justice Harry Blackmun, for the majority, declared: "We conclude ... that the Virginia courts erred in their assumptions that advertising, as such, was entitled to no First Amendment protection and that appellant Bigelow had no legitimate First Amendment interest."

Furthermore, he pointed out: "Advertising is not ... stripped of all First Amendment protection. The relationship of speech to the market-place of products or of services does not make it valueless in the marketplace of ideas."

Justices Rehnquist and White dissented. They argued that "the advertisement appears ... to be a classic commercial proposition directed toward the exchange of services rather than the exchange of ideas."

It was the law prohibiting the advertising of prescription drug prices that caused the Virginia Citizens Consumer Council to bring an action against the Virginia State Board of Pharmacy. The Council sought a court order declaring the law to be unconstitutional. District Court Judge Albert S. Bryan held that the law violated the First Amendment and granted judgment for the Council, and the Supreme Court agreed. Justice Blackmun wrote the Court's opinion, in which Justice White concurred.

In addressing the question of whether, and to what extent, if any, commercial speech is protected by the First Amendment, Justice Blackmun noted that this case squarely presents that issue. "Our question is whether speech which does 'no more than propose a commercial transaction' ... is so removed from any 'exposition of ideas' ... and from 'truth, science, morality, and arts in general, ... that it lacks all protection. Our answer is that it is not."[36]

Having concluded that commercial speech is protected speech, the Court, with only Justice Rehnquist dissenting, affirmed Judge Bruan's decision, because Virginia had not presented sufficient evidence that the advertisement was false or misleading.

Much commercial advertising is done on billboards. The City of San

Diego, California, enacted a very comprehensive ordinance regulating such signs within the city. "[U]nder the ordinance (1) a sign advertising goods or services available on the property where the sign is located is allowed; (2) a sign on a building or other property advertising goods or services produced or offered elsewhere is barred; (3) noncommercial advertising ... [generally] is everywhere prohibited. The occupant of property may advertise his own goods or services; he may not advertise the goods or services of others, nor may he display most noncommercial messages."[37]

Justice White, writing for himself and Justices Stewart, Marshall and Powell agreed that the part of the ordinance regulating commercial signs did not violate the First Amendment.

The Justice acknowledged that prior cases established that commercial speech enjoyed First Amendment protection but not to the same degree as noncommercial speech, such as political or public service messages. In balancing the city's interests in traffic safety and general appearance, White concluded that those interests outweighed any First Amendment rights of persons wishing to erect signs. "The constitutional problem in this area requires resolution of the conflict between the city's land-use interests and the commercial interests of those seeking to purvey goods and services within the city. In light of the above analysis, we cannot conclude that the city has drawn an ordinance broader than is necessary to meet its interests, or that it fails directly to advance substantial government interests."

Justices Brennan and Blackmun were of the opinion that the parts of the ordinance relating to commercial advertising was unconstitutional because the city had failed to offer evidence that signs created a safety hazard or that its ordinance, under which some signs were allowed, really addressed the city's alleged aesthetic interests.

Prior to 1977, most lawyer's Codes of Professional Ethics prohibited them from advertising. In *Bates v. State Bar of Arizona*,[38] Justice White joined the majority in holding that a lawyer's First Amendment right to free speech included the right to advertise. However, in another case he voted to uphold public censure of lawyer Gary E. Peel whose letterhead carried the statement "Certified Civil Trial Specialist, by the National Board of Trial Advocacy."[39]

The National Board of Trial Advocacy [NBTA], certified attorneys as trial specialists if they met certain standards. Peel, who had practiced law in Illinois since 1968, met those standards and was certified in 1981 and again in 1986. He was listed in NBTA's 1985 Directory of Certified Specialists and Board Members. Peel was censured by the Illinois Disciplinary Commission for violating a rule which prohibited lawyers from holding themselves out as "certified" or as "a specialist." The censure was upheld by the Illinois Supreme Court but reversed by the United States Supreme Court.

Four of the justices, concluded that there was nothing misleading about Peel's letterhead. "The facts stated on petitioner's letterhead," Justice Stevens noted, "are true and verifiable. It is undisputed that NBTA has certified petitioner as a civil trial specialist and that three States have licensed him to practice law."

Justice White voted to uphold the censure, because he believed that the letterhead was *potentially* misleading and that was enough to override Peel's free speech rights. "As I see it, it is petitioner who should have to clean up his advertisement so as to eliminate its potential to mislead. Until he does, the State's Rule legally bars him from circulating the letterhead in its present form."

Places to Speak.

> This case presents the question whether peaceful picketing of a business enterprise located within a shopping center can be enjoined on the ground that it constitutes an unconsented invasion of the property rights of the owners of the land on which the center is situated.[40]

The Logan Valley Plaza opened with two businesses, Weis Markets, Inc. and Sears, Roebuck and Co. When Weis Market opened, its staff was entirely nonunion. Shortly thereafter, the Amalgamated Food Employees Union began picketing the market. The picketers handed out leaflets pointing out that Weis's employees did not belong to a union. The picketers were, at all times, peaceful. Weis and Logan Valley Plaza sought a court order prohibiting the picketing, which was granted. The court ordered the picketers off the mall and confined them to the berm along the street. The order was affirmed by the Pennsylvania Supreme Court.

Concluding that the answer to the question posed above should be no, i.e., that picketing on the mall could not be prohibited, a majority of the Supreme Court reversed.

Justice Marshall examined several prior cases dealing with First Amendment rights, specifically *Marsh v. Alabama*,[41] wherein the Court had held that soliciting and distributing literature on the streets of a company-owned town could not be prohibited. With regard to picketing on the mall, Marshall wrote: "All we decide here is that because the shopping center serves as the community business block 'and is freely accessible and open to the people in the area and those passing through,' ... the State may not delegate the power, through the use of its trespass laws, wholly to exclude those members of the public wishing to exercise their First Amendment rights on the premises in a manner and for a purpose generally consonant with the use to which the property is actually put."

Justice White however argued in dissent that Logan Valley Plaza was not the same as the company town in *Marsh*. People are invited to the shopping center for the purpose of shopping and nothing else. There is no general invitation to park there except while shopping. "I am fearful," he concluded, "that the Court's decision today will be a license for pickets to leave the public streets and carry out their activities on private property, as long as they are not obstructive. I do not agree that when the owner of private property invites the public to do business with him he impliedly dedicates his property for other uses as well. I do not think the First Amendment, which bars only official interferences with speech, has this reach."[42]

Whether all live entertainment could be prohibited in a commercial zone was the question before the Court in *Schad v. Mount Ephraim.*[43] In holding that it could not be, Justice White pointed out that "nude dancing is not without its First Amendment protections from official regulation."

The case arose when an adult bookstore installed a "coin-operated mechanism, permitting the customer to watch a live dancer, usually nude, performing behind a glass panel." Mt. Ephraim argued that the purpose of the ordinance was "to avoid the problems that may be associated with live entertainment, such as parking, trash, police protection, and medical facilities." The Borough, however, did not produce any evidence that live entertainment caused such problems nor did it explain why a theater, for example, would create any more problems than a restaurant. "[T]his ordinance," the Justice declared, "is not narrowly drawn to respond to what might be the distinctive problems arising from certain types of live entertainment, and it is not clear that a more selective approach would fail to address those unique problems if any there are." What disturbed the Justice most, however, was the fact that the ordinance excluded all live entertainment, even "non-obscene nude dancing that is otherwise protected by the First Amendment."

Generally speaking, streets and parks are considered as places where people can exercise their right to speak freely. However, Park Service regulations relating to the parks in the District of Columbia prohibit sleeping in a park "when it reasonably appears, in light of all the circumstances, that the participants, in conducting those activities, are in fact using the area as a living accommodation regardless of the intent of the participants or the nature of any other activities in which they may also be engaging."[44] The Community for Creative Non-Violence (CCNV) requested permission to set up tents on the mall and to sleep in them at night to draw attention to the plight of the homeless. The Park Service allowed CCNV to erect the tents, but denied permission to sleep in them overnight. Although the Service had previously allowed Vietnam veterans to sleep on the ground on the mall during a protest, the Service was of the opinion that sleeping on the ground was not "a living accommodation," while sleeping in tents would be.

The CCNV brought an action against the Park Service seeking a court order allowing them to sleep in tents. It argued that sleeping was an integral part of their demonstration because that drew attention to the fact that many of the homeless do not have a place to sleep at night. District Judge John H. Pratt dismissed the action, but the Circuit Court reversed, being of the opinion that under these circumstances sleeping was expressive conduct and an integral part of CCNV's protest, and therefore protected by the First Amendment.

Justice White, and a majority of the Court disagreed and reversed.[45] White assumed, for the purpose of the case, "that overnight sleeping in connection with the demonstration is expressive conduct protected to some extent by the First Amendment." The Justice was of the opinion, however, "that the [Park Service] regulation narrowly focuses on the Government's substantial interest in maintaining parks in the heart of our Capital in an attractive and intact condition, readily available to the millions of people who wish to see and enjoy them by their presence. To permit camping—using these areas as living accommodations—would be totally inimical to these purposes, as would be readily understood by those who have frequented the National Parks across the country and observed the unfortunate consequences of the activities of those who refuse to confine their camping to designated areas."

Justice Marshall, for himself and Justice Brennan, vigorously dissented. "The majority," Marshall declared, "cites no evidence indicating that sleeping engaged in as symbolic speech will cause *substantial* wear and tear on park property. ... The majority acknowledges that a proper time, place, and manner restriction must be 'narrowly tailored.' Here, however, the tailoring requirement is virtually forsaken inasmuch as the Government offers no justification for applying its absolute ban on sleeping yet is willing to allow ... [CCNV] to engage in activities—such as feigned sleeping—that is no less burdensome."

Miscellaneous Speech Cases. The First National Bank of Boston "wanted to spend money to publicize ... [its] views on a proposed constitutional amendment that was to be submitted to the voters ... at a general election on November 2, 1976. The amendment would have permitted the legislature to impose a graduated tax on income of individuals."[46] Francis X. Bellotti, the Massachusetts Attorney General, informed First National that such expenditure of funds would violate a state law prohibiting corporations from spending money to influence the vote "on any question submitted to the voters, other than one materially affecting any of the property, business or assets of the corporation."

In an action brought by the Bank, the Supreme Judicial Court of Massachusetts concluded that the law did not violate the First Amendment rights of corporations. Justice White dissented when the United States Supreme Court reversed.

"The proper question therefore," Justice Powell declared, "is not whether corporations 'have' First Amendment rights and, if so, whether they are coextensive with those of natural persons. Instead, the question must be whether ... [the law] abridges expression that the First Amendment was meant to protect. We hold that it does."

Powell expressed concern about giving a legislature power to dictate "the subjects about which persons may speak and the speakers who may address a public issue. ... Such power in government to channel the expression of views is unacceptable under the First Amendment."

Justice White argued, in dissent, that corporations do not have the same free speech rights as individuals. "It is clear," he asserted, "that the communications of profitmaking corporations are not 'an integral part of the development of ideas, of mental exploration and of the affirmation of self.' They do not represent a manifestation of individual freedom or choice." That being the case, then government has greater leeway to regulate corporate expressions.

Justice White dissented when the Court allowed Indiana to apply its public indecency statute to prohibit nude dancing in a bar lounge.[47] The Justice agreed that nude dancing was a type of expression that was protected by the First Amendment. But he disagreed that Indiana had offered sufficient evidence to outweigh the right of the dancers to express themselves in this manner. The Justice pointed out that there was a difference in prohibiting nudity in "parks, beaches, hot dog stands, and like public places ... [in order] to protect others from offense," as opposed to "preventing nude dancing in theaters and barrooms since the viewers are exclusively consenting adults who pay money to see these dances."

Freedom of Association

Punishment for Membership—Affidavits and Oaths. The Court has been plagued with the question whether a person should be criminally punished for membership in an alleged subversive organization, if the person does not have the specific intent to carry out the organization's illegal goals. The Court pointed out in *Scales v. United States*,[48] that a "blanket prohibition of association with a group having both legal and illegal aims ... would indeed ... [create] a real danger that legitimate political expression or association would be impaired...." Someone, therefore, who believes in the organization's legal aims should not be punished, for "he lacks the requisite specific intent 'to bring about the overthrow of the government as speedily as circumstances would permit.'" Such a person may be foolish but should not be made a criminal.

The Court applied that rule to protect Mr. Robel who worked as a machinist in a defense plant in Seattle, Washington. Because Robel was a member of the Communist Party, he was indicted for violating a federal law making it a criminal offense to be a member of a Communist organization and work in a defense plant.[49] The District Court dismissed the indictment, and the Government appealed. When the case reached the Supreme Court, Chief Justice Earl Warren wrote: "We affirm the judgment of the District Court, ... on the ground that ... [the law] is an unconstitutional abridgment of the right of association protected by the First Amendment."

The Chief Justice was of the opinion that the statute punished both active membership that could be punished as well as passive membership which could not be. "It is made irrelevant to the statute's operation that an individual may be a passive or inactive member of a designated organization, that he may be unaware of the organization's unlawful aims, or that he may disagree with those unlawful aims."

Justice White acknowledged in dissent that, although the right of association was not mentioned in the Constitution, if "men may speak as individuals, they may speak in groups as well. If they may assemble and petition, they must have the right to associate to some extent. In this sense the right of association simply extends constitutional protection to First Amendment rights when exercised with others rather than by an individual alone." He was of the opinion, however, that because the Communist Party had been found to be a Communist-action organization the government should be allowed to exclude Communist Party members from defense plants. "Congress should be entitled to take suitable precautionary measures. Some Party members may be no threat at all, but many of them undoubtedly are, and it is exceedingly difficult to identify those in advance of the very events which Congress seeks to avoid. If Party members such as Robel may be barred from 'sensitive positions,' it is because they are potential threats to security."

Lawrence W. Baggett's job, and that of more than 60 other employees of the University of Washington, was put in jeopardy when the Washington state legislature enacted laws requiring all state employees to take a loyalty oath.

Baggett and the others brought an action against University officials seeking a declaration that the loyalty oaths were unconstitutional.[50] The laws required each employee to swear that he or she was not "a subversive person" as defined by law and was "not a member of the Communist Party or knowingly of any other subversive organization." The District Court upheld the oath requirements, but the Supreme Court reversed.

The employees argued that the oaths were "unduly vague, uncertain and broad," and in an opinion written by Justice White, the Court agreed.

White was specifically concerned by the inability of one required to take the oath to understand what activities were prohibited. For example, he asks: "Does the statute reach endorsement or support for Communist candidates for office? Does it reach a lawyer who represents the Communist Party or its members or a journalist who defends constitutional rights of the Communist Party or its members or anyone who supports any cause which is likewise supported by Communists or the Communist Party?" Would it be a violation, he asks, to attend conventions and exchange views with scholars from Communist countries? Or would one violate the oath by inviting scholars from those countries to speak or teach at a University?

The justices were confronted with this kind of problem again in *Elfbrandt v. Russell*.[51] Barbara Elfbrandt, a Quaker and teacher in Tucson, Arizona, brought an action against her school district challenging the validity of an oath required by Arizona law. Although the oath was similar to one required of applicants for citizenship, anyone taking the oath was subject to "prosecution for perjury and for discharge from public office ... [if he or she] took the oath and ... 'knowingly and willfully becomes or remains a member of the communist party of the United States or its successors or any of its subordinate organizations' or 'any other organization' having for 'one of its purposes' the overthrow of the government ... where the employee had knowledge of the unlawful purpose."

The Supreme Court of Arizona upheld the oath, but the United States Supreme Court reversed, with Justice White dissenting. The difference between the majority and Justice White turned upon whether someone who took the oath could be punished if he or she did not have the specific intent to carry out the organization's illegal goals.

Justice Douglas declared in the Court's opinion that under this law "the 'hazard of being prosecuted for knowing but guiltless behavior' ... is a reality." Douglas concluded that a "law which applies to membership without the 'specific intent' to further the illegal aims of the organization infringes unnecessarily on protected freedoms. It rests on the doctrine of 'guilt by association' which has no place here."

Justice White approached the solution of the case differently. He pointed out that under prior case law "a State is entitled to condition public employment upon its employees abstaining from knowing membership in the Communist Party and other organizations advocating the overthrow of the government which employs them...." That being true he argued, then certainly the government can charge one with perjury if he "obtains employment by falsifying his present qualifications." Furthermore, he argued, if it is the fear of a criminal penalty for perjury that the majority finds makes the statute unconstitutional it should only strike down that part of the law.

Associational Privacy. In discussing the right of association in *Bates v. Little Rock*,[52] Justice Potter Stewart declared: "Freedoms such as these are protected not only against heavy-handed frontal attack, but also from being stifled by more subtle governmental interference." The "subtle governmental interference" to which he was referring was the government's demand that some organizations disclose their membership lists and that some individuals disclose the names of the organizations to which they belong.

Theodore R. Gibson faced that demand from the Florida Legislative Investigation Committee. Gibson, as President of the Miami Branch of the NAACP, was ordered to appear before the Committee and to bring the organization's membership list. When he appeared but did not bring the records, he was held in contempt, sentenced to six months in prison, and ordered to pay a fine of $1,200. His conviction was reversed by the Supreme Court.[53]

Florida argued that the purpose of the investigation was to find out if communists had infiltrated the NAACP. Justice Arthur Goldberg did not believe that was the principal purpose for the investigation. "There is no suggestion that the Miami branch of the N. A. A. C. P. or the national organization with which it is affiliated was, or is, itself a subversive organization. Nor is there any indication that the activities or policies of the N. A. A. C. P. were either Communist dominated or influenced. In fact, this very record indicates that the association was and is against communism and has voluntarily taken steps to keep Communists from being members."

This led Justice Goldberg to the following conclusion:

> To permit legislative inquiry to proceed on less than an adequate foundation would be to sanction unjustified and unwarranted intrusions into the very heart of the constitutional privilege to be secure in associations in legitimate organizations engaged in the exercise of First and Fourteenth Amendment rights; to impose a lesser standard than we here do would be inconsistent with the maintenance of those essential conditions basic to the preservation of our democracy.

For Justice White, the government's overriding concern for finding out who were members of the Communist Party, caused him to dissent. "I cannot join the Court in attaching great weight to the organization's interest in concealing the presence of infiltrating Communists, if such be the case. The net effect of the Court's decision is, of course, to insulate from effective legislative inquiry and preventive legislation the time-proven skills of the Communist Party in subverting and eventually controlling legitimate organizations."

Bar associations across the country were also seeking to find allegedly subversive persons and to prevent them from practicing law. Sarah Baird got caught up in that crusade.

> Sarah Baird graduated from law school at Stanford University in California in 1967. So far as the record shows there is not now and never has been a single mark against her moral character. She has taken the examination prescribed by Arizona, and the answer of the State admits that she satisfactorily passed it. Among the questions she answered was No. 25, which called on her to reveal all organizations with which she had been associated since she reached 16 years of age. This question she answered to the satisfaction of the Arizona Bar Committee. ... In addition, however, she was asked to state whether she had ever been a member of the Communist Party or any organization "that advocates overthrow of the United States Government by force or violence." When she refused to answer this question, the Committee declined to process her application further or recommend her admission to the bar.[54]

When the Arizona Supreme Court refused to order the Association to admit her, she appealed to the United States Supreme Court, which reversed.

Justice Black, writing for himself and three other justices, pointed out that under Arizona law a person committed perjury if he or she answered any of the questions on the application falsely. "In effect," he declared, "this young lady was asked by the State to make a guess as to whether any organization to which she ever belonged 'advocates overthrow of the United States Government by force or violence.'" Black then pointed out that the Court had previously held: "The First Amendment's protection of association prohibits a State from excluding a person from a profession or punishing him solely because he is a member of a particular political organization or because he holds certain beliefs." In other words, had Baird been a member of the Communist Party at the time of her application, Arizona could not have refused to admit her to the practice of law on that basis alone.

"It is my view," Justice White wrote in dissent, "that the Constitution does not require a State to admit to practice a lawyer who believes in violence and intends to implement that belief in his practice of law and advice to clients. I also believe that the State may ask an applicant preliminary questions that will permit further investigation and reasoned, articulated judgment as to whether the applicant will or will not advise lawless conduct as a practicing lawyer."

Political Parties and New Members. In cases involving political parties, voters and candidates there are "two different, although overlapping, kinds of rights—the right of individuals to associate for the advancement of political beliefs, and the right of qualified voters, regardless of their political persuasion, to cast their votes effectively. Both of these rights, of course, rank among our most precious freedoms."[55]

That statement was made by Justice Black when the Court struck down Ohio's laws which made it "virtually impossible for a new political party, even though it has hundreds of thousands of members, or an old party, which has a very small number of members, to be placed on the state ballot to choose electors pledged to particular candidates for the Presidency and Vice Presidency of the United States." The majority held, in that case, that the laws not only violated the right to freely associate for political purposes but the Equal Protection Clause of the Fourteenth Amendment as well, because the laws gave preference to the major established parties.

Justice White dissented. He did not believe that Ohio's laws, which required new parties to hold a primary election and to secure signatures of qualified electors equaling 15 percent of the number of votes cast for governor at the last election, were unreasonable.

The Justice was also of the opinion that certain election laws of California were reasonable and therefore wrote the Court's opinion denying Storer and Frommhagen places on the ballot to run for Congress from their respective districts.[56]

Storer and Frommhagen were kept off the ballot by Section 6830(d) of the California elections code which required that a person desiring to be an independent candidate must not have been a member of a qualified political party within one year prior to the primary election. In this case, both men had been members of the Democratic Party within that one year period.

The Justice, and the majority, upheld Section 6830(d) with very little discussion of any constitutional rights of Storer and Frommhagen or those who might wish to vote for them. The majority simply accepted California's arguments for the validity of the law. "The requirement that the independent candidate not have been affiliated with a political party for a year before the primary," White wrote, "is expressive of a general state policy aimed at maintaining the integrity of the various routes to the ballot. It involves no discrimination against independents."

Justice Brennan, in dissent, pointed out how burdensome California's law really was. "Both Storer and Frommhagen sought to run in their respective districts as independent candidates for Congress. The term of office for the United States House of Representatives, of course, is two years. Thus, Section 6830(d) ... required Storer and Frommhagen to disaffiliate from their parties within *seven months* after the preceding congressional election. Few incumbent Congressmen, however, declare their intention to seek reelection seven months after election and only four months into their terms. Yet ... Storer and Frommhagen were forced by Section 6830(d) ... to evaluate their political opportunities and opt in or out of their parties 17 months before the next congressional election."

Justice White also wrote the Court's opinion upholding a Washington state law which "requires that a minor-party candidate for partisan office receive at least 1% of all votes cast for that office in the State's primary election before the candidate's name will be placed on the general election ballot."[57]

Justice Marshall did not think that the majority was giving sufficient weight to the place that minority parties play in our democratic process, and he therefore dissented. "The minor party's often unconventional positions broaden political debate, expand the range of issues with which the electorate is concerned, and influence the positions of the majority, in some instances ultimately becoming majority positions. And its very existence provides an outlet for voters to express dissatisfaction with the candidates or platforms of the major parties."

Miscellaneous Association Cases. While Coates was involved in a student demonstration, he was arrested and convicted of violating a Cincinnati, Ohio, ordinance which made it a crime "for 'three or more persons to assemble ... on any of the sidewalks ... and there conduct themselves in a manner annoying to persons passing by...'"[58] Coates' conviction was upheld by a close vote of the Supreme Court of Ohio. The United States Supreme Court reversed, with Justice White dissenting.

In an opinion written by Justice Stewart, the majority held that the ordinance violated the Due Process Clause because it was too vague and the First Amendment because it infringed upon the right of free association and assembly.

"But the vice of the ordinance," Stewart declared, "lies not alone in its violation of the due process standard of vagueness. The ordinance also violates the constitutional right of free assembly and association. Our decisions establish that mere public intolerance or animosity cannot be the basis for abridgment of these constitutional freedoms."

White disagreed. He did not believe that the ordinance was "vague on its face." Nor did the Justice believe that the law violated the right of association. He argued that if Coates, and the others, had assembled for the purpose of picketing and demonstrating, the conduct aspect of those activities were subject to control by government. Here again, the record did not indicate just what Coates was doing. "The statute is not infirm on its face," he argued, "and since we have no information from this record as to what conduct was charged against these defendants, we are in no position to judge the statute as applied."

The extent of the right of association of union members came before the District of Columbia District Court in 1986. At issue was the constitutionality of a section of the Food Stamp Act which prohibited a "household from becoming eligible for food stamps if a member of that household is on strike because of a labor dispute."[59]

District Judge Lewis F. Oberdorfer declared the law unconstitutional as a violation of workers' right of association. Judge Oberdorfer wrote: "It may be that a striker would not live apart from close family members in order to provide them with food stamps. ... But as defendant [Secretary of Agriculture Richard E. Lyng] has bluntly stated, the striker has, as an alternative to leaving his family, the further options of quitting his job or returning to work. Pursuant of either of these alternatives would obviously sever or at least threaten his association with his union and fellow union members. Indeed, that is exactly what has happened to plaintiff Combs. Denial of food stamps to his family was a proximate cause of his disassociation from a strike, his fellow strikers and his union."

In reversing Judge Oberdorfer, Justice White, for the majority, wrote: "The statute certainly does not 'order' any individuals not to dine together; nor does it in any way 'directly and substantially' interfere with family living arrangements."[60]

Nor did the Justice believe that the law had any effect upon associational rights of the workers. "It does not 'order' ... [the workers] not to associate together for the purpose of conducting a strike ... and it does not 'prevent' them from associating together or burden their ability to do so in any significant manner."

Justice Marshall dissented, being of the opinion that the law discriminated against the striking worker and therefore was a denial of equal protection.

In several cases, beginning with *Roberts v. United States Jaycees*,[61] the Court held that certain all-male organizations, such as the Jaycees and Rotarians, can be required to accept females as members, even though requiring them to do so infringes upon their right of association.

In *Roberts*, the Court acknowledged that freedom of association included the "freedom not to associate," but pointed out that a State has a "compelling interest in eradicating discrimination against its female citizens" which was sufficient to require the Jaycees to admit females to membership. Justice White voted with the majority to require these all-male organizations to accept females as members.

Freedom of the Press

Libel. The Justice was on the Court in 1964 when it decided *New York Times Co. v. Sullivan.*[62] In that case, the Court held: "The constitutional guarantees require, we think, a federal rule that prohibits a public official from recovering damages for a defamatory falsehood relating to his official conduct unless he proves that statement was made with 'actual malice'—that is, with knowledge that it was false or with reckless disregard of whether it was false or not."

In the *Wally Butts* case, however, Butts was not a "public official." He was a well known college football coach and thus a "public figure." Applying the *Times* rule to "public figures" would mean that such a person could not recover damages for defamation unless he or she could prove that the press acted with "actual malice" in printing a story about them.

In concluding that the rule should apply to "public figures," Chief Justice Warren pointed out "that many who do not hold public office at the moment are nevertheless intimately involved in the resolution of important public questions or, by reason of their fame, shape events in areas of concern to society at large."[63] It is, therefore, in the public interest that the press be protected from libel actions from such persons, unless it acts with actual malice, or with reckless disregard of the truth. The Chief Justice was of the opinion that Curtis Publishing Co. had acted with "that degree of reckless disregard for the truth," and therefore, the award of damages to Butts should be upheld.

Justices Brennan and White agreed that Butts was a public figure and that the "actual malice" test was the proper one for his case. They were of the opinion, however, that the trial court's charge to the jury did not sufficiently explain that test to the jury, and therefore the case should be sent back for a new trial.

Although the *Times* rule protects the press from most libel actions brought by public officials and public figures, it leaves unanswered questions concerning libel actions brought by people who do not fall in either category, such as Elmer Gertz, a lawyer who represented the family of a boy killed by a police officer.

In 1968 a Chicago policeman named Nuccio shot and killed a youth named
Nelson. The state authorities prosecuted Nuccio for homicide and ultimately
obtained a conviction for murder in the second degree. The Nelson family
retained ... Elmer Gertz, a reputable attorney, to represent them in civil litigation against Nuccio.[64]

In March 1969, the *American Opinion*, published by the John Birch Soci-
ety, ran an article titled "FRAME-UP: Richard Nuccio and the war on police."
Although Gertz's only connection with Nuccio's case was as attorney for the
Nelsons, the article "stated that ... [Gertz] had been an official of the 'Marx-
ist League for Industrial Democracy'...." The article also "labeled Gertz a
'Leninist' and a 'Communist-fronter.'" None of these statements were true.

Gertz brought an action for libel against Robert Welch, Inc., the spon-
sor of the John Birch Society. A jury awarded him $50,000, but Judge Bernard
M. Decker set the verdict aside. He was of the opinion that because the article discussed a matter of public interest, the *Times* rule should apply and Gertz
was required to prove that the article was published with actual malice, or with
reckless disregard of the truth. The Supreme Court reversed. "The principal
issue in this case," Justice Powell wrote, "is whether a newspaper or broadcaster that publishes defamatory falsehoods about an individual who is neither a public official nor a public figure may claim a constitutional privilege
against liability for the injury inflicted by those statements."

After an extensive examination of the law of libel, and recognizing that
the "First Amendment requires that we protect some falsehood in order to
protect speech that matters," the Court adopted new rules that would apply
to persons defamed who are not *public officials* or *public figures*. Those rules allow
a State to "define for themselves the appropriate standard of liability for a
publisher or broadcaster of defamatory falsehood injurious to a private individual." However, recovery would be allowed only when the publisher or
broadcaster was at fault in some way, such as being negligent in publishing
the material. Furthermore, the defamed person could recover only such damages he or she actually suffered. And punitive damages were not to be given
unless the alleged defamatory material was known to be false, or was published with reckless disregard of its falsity.

White dissented. He criticized the majority for making "sweeping changes
[that] will be popular with the press, but this is not the road to salvation for
a court of law." He found the changes to "cut very deeply" into the law of
defamation. "No longer will the plaintiff be able to rest his case with proof of
a libel defamatory on its face or proof of slander historically actionable *per se*.
In addition, he must prove some further degree of culpable conduct on the
part of the publisher, such as intentional or reckless falsehood or negligence.
And if he succeeds in this respect, he faces still another obstacle: recover for
loss of reputation will be conditioned upon 'competent' proof of actual injury
to his standing in the community."

Furthermore, he wrote: "I fail to see how the quality or quantity of public debate will be promoted by further emasculation of state libel laws for the benefit of the news media."

The Justice's frustration with the Court's "emasculation" of the common law rules of defamation came to the fore again in a concurring opinion in a case decided in 1985.[65] He acknowledged that he had voted with the majority in the *New York Times* case and had agreed to the extension of its rule to later cases. "But," he declared, "I came to have increasing doubts about the soundness of the Court's approach and about some of the assumptions underlying it. ... I have also become convinced that the Court struck an improvident balance in the *New York Times* case between the public's interest in being fully informed about public officials and public affairs and the competing interest of those who have been defamed in vindicating their reputation."

The Justice recognized that "[i]n a country like ours, where the people purport to be able to govern themselves through their elected representatives, adequate information about their government is of transcendent importance. The flow of intelligence deserves full First Amendment protection. Criticism and assessment of the performance of public officials and of government in general are not subject to penalties imposed by law. But these First Amendment values are not at all served by circulating false statements of fact about public officials. On the contrary, erroneous information frustrates these values. They are even more disserved when the statements falsely impugn the honesty of those men and women and hence lessen the confidence in government."

White argued that in the case of an alleged defamation of a public official, rather than requiring the official to prove that the press acted with "actual malice", "we could have achieved our stated goal by limiting the recoverable damages to a level that would not unduly threaten the press." Nor should the official have to prove malice, if he or she seeks no damages, but desires "only to clear his [her] name." "I still believe," he notes, "the common-law rules should have been retained where the plaintiff is not a public official or public figure."

Prior Restraint of and Punishment for Publication. The Justice voted with the majority in the *Pentagon Papers* case.[66] That case came to the Court to test the validity of two lower court orders dealing with the publication of a Defense Department document titled: "*History of United States Decision Making Process on Viet-Nam Policy,*" commonly referred to as *The Pentagon Papers.* In seeking court orders barring the publication of the material, the government argued that publication would do irreparable damage to the interests of the United States.

Judge Murray F. Gurfein, in New York, had issued a preliminary injunction against the New York Times Company restraining the publication of parts of these *Papers.* Judge Gerhard A. Gessell, in Washington, D.C., however, had refused to issue an order preventing the *Washington Post* from publishing parts of the document. The Supreme Court ultimately decided that restraining the publication of the *Papers* would be a violation of these newspapers freedom of the press. "The Government," the Court wrote, "thus carries a heavy burden of showing justification for the imposition of such a restraint." But "the Government has not met that burden."

Justice White concurred "only because of the concededly extraordinary protection against prior restraints enjoyed by the press under our constitutional system." But he wanted it understood that the press was not immune from injunctions against publication under all circumstances. He voted not to allow injunctions against the *New York Times* and the *Washington Post* because "the United States has not satisfied the very heavy burden that it must meet to warrant an injunction against publication in these cases...." The Justice was of the opinion, however, that publication of the material at issue would cause some harm to the country.

Sometimes states have attempted to punish the publication of information which the press has legitimately obtained. For example:

> In August 1971, ... [Cohn's] 17-year-old daughter was the victim of a rape and did not survive the incident. Six youths were soon indicted for murder and rape. Although there was substantial press coverage of the crime ... the identity of the victim was not disclosed pending trial.... In April 1972, some eight months later, the six defendants appeared in court. Five pleaded guilty to rape or attempted rape, the charge of murder having been dropped.[67]

The sixth youth pleaded not guilty, and his case was set for trial at a later date. Wassel, a reporter for television station WSB-TV, attended the proceedings and learned the victim's name. During a newscast that same day, Wassel reported that the victim was Cynthia Cohn.

Cynthia Cohn's father brought an action against Cox Broadcasting Corp., the owner of WSB-TV, asserting that it had violated his right to privacy. He claimed his privacy was protected by a Georgia state law which made it a criminal offense to publish the "name or identity of any female who may have been raped." Although the station argued that its newscast was protected by the First Amendment, the Georgia courts disagreed, concluding that the station was liable, and that a trial by jury would be held to assess the damages Cohn had suffered.

Justice White authored the Court's opinion, which reversed. In support of its statute, Georgia argued that the purpose of the law was to protect the common-law right of privacy. White agreed that "powerful arguments can be made, and have been made, that however it may be ultimately defined, there *is* a zone of privacy surrounding every individual, a zone within which the State may protect him from intrusion by the press, with all its attendant publicity." But, the Justice pointed out, it is not necessary to consider, in this case, whether a state can ever subject the press to criminal or civil damages for violation of the right to privacy. The issue here is much narrower, he wrote. It is "whether the State may impose sanctions on the accurate publication of the name of a rape victim obtained from public records—more specifically, from judicial records which are maintained in connection with a public prosecution and which themselves are open to public inspection."

White's answer for the Court was: "We are convinced that the State may not do so." "At the very least," the Justice asserted, "the First and Fourteenth Amendments will not allow exposing the press to liability for truthfully publishing information released to the public in official court records. If there are privacy interests to be protected in judicial proceedings, the States must respond by means which avoid public documentation or other exposure of private information. Their political institutions must weigh the interests in privacy with the interests of the public to know and of the press to publish."

The case of *The Florida Star v. B. J. F.*[68] presented the Court with a problem similar to that in *Cohn*. And while a majority reached the same result, Justice White dissented because he believed that the facts of the case required a different result.

After B. J. F. was robbed and sexually assaulted, she reported the incident to the police. A police report was made and placed in the Department's pressroom. "A Florida Star reporter-trainee sent to the pressroom copied the police report verbatim, including B. J. F.'s full name..." Consequently, her name was included in a "Police Reports" story in the paper. This was a violation of a Florida statute that made it a criminal offense to "'print, publish, or broadcast ... in any instrument of mass communication' the name of the victim of a sexual offense." Relying on this statute, B. J. F. brought an action against the *Star*, claiming that by publishing her name, the newspaper violated her right to privacy. A jury agreed and awarded her $75,000 compensatory damages and $25,000 punitive damages.

In reversing the judgment, Justice Marshall, for the majority, concluded that this case was different than *Cohn* because B. J. F.'s name was not obtained from the records of a *judicial* proceeding. This case, therefore, called for a different analysis. The proper rule to be applied here, Marshal said, was: "[I]f a newspaper lawfully obtains truthful information about a matter of public significance then state officials may not constitutionally punish publication of the information, absent a need to further a state interest of the highest order." If the press does not have this protection, Marshall argued, it would have the "onerous obligation of sifting through government press releases, reports, and pronouncements to prune out material arguably unlawful for publication."

"We hold only," Marshall continued, "that where a newspaper publishes truthful information which it has lawfully obtained, punishment may be lawfully imposed, if at all, only when narrowly tailored to a state interest of the highest order, and that no such interest is satisfactorily served by imposing liability ... [on the *Star*] under the facts of this case."

Justice White did not agree that the reasons upon which the majority based its decision were sufficient to override B. J. F.'s right of privacy. He therefore dissented. The Justice expressed concern that the decision would make it almost impossible for individuals to recover damages from the media for invasion of privacy.

White was of the opinion that the majority was not drawing the proper line between the individual's right of privacy and the press's freedom to publish. He concluded his dissent: "I would find a place to draw the line higher on the hillside: a spot high enough to protect B. J. F.'s desire for privacy and peace-of-mind in the wake of a horrible personal tragedy. There is no public interest in publishing the names, addresses, and phone numbers of persons who are the victims of crime—and no public interest in immunizing the press from liability in the rare cases where a State's efforts to protect a victim's privacy have failed."

Hugo Zacchini's case presented the Court with a somewhat different kind of "privacy" question.

> Petitioner, Hugo Zacchini, is an entertainer. He performs a "human cannon-ball" act in which he is shot from a cannon into a net some 200 feet away. Each performance occupies some 15 seconds. In August and September 1972 ... [Zacchini] was engaged to perform his act on a regular basis at the Geauga County Fair in Burton, Ohio. ... Members of public attending the fair were not charged a separate admission fee to observe his act.[69]

A reporter for a television station videotaped Zacchini's performance, and that tape, together with favorable comments, was aired on the evening news.

Zacchini brought an action for damages against the station, "alleging that he is 'engaged in the entertainment business,' that the act he performs is one 'invented by his father and ... performed only by his family for the last fifty years,' that ... [the station] 'showed and commercialized the film of his act without his consent,' and that such conduct was 'an unlawful appropriation of ... [his] professional property.'" The Ohio Supreme Court gave judgment for the television station, being of the opinion that it was privileged to report matters of public interest so long as it was done for public consumption and without intent to injure anyone.

The United States Supreme Court reversed. Zacchini "is not contending," Justice White pointed out, "that his appearance at the fair and his performance could not be reported by the press as newsworthy items. His complaint is that ... [the station] filmed his entire act and displayed that film on television for the public to see and enjoy. This, he claimed, was an appropriation of his professional property."

In agreeing with Zacchini, White noted that the station is no more privileged to show his performance than it would be to show any copyrighted play, or to "film and broadcast a prize fight ... or a baseball game ... where the promoters or the participants had other plans for publicizing the event."

Justices Powell, Brennan and Marshall dissented."When a film is used, as here," Justice Powell argued, "for a routine portion of a regular news program, I would hold that the First Amendment protects the station from a 'right of publicity' or 'appropriation' suit, absent a strong showing by the plaintiff that the news broadcast was a subterfuge or cover for private commercial exploitation."

Obscenity. In *Memoirs v. Massachusetts*,[78] Justices Brennan and Abe Fortas and Chief Justice Warren concluded that there were three elements to the test for obscenity: "(a) the dominant theme of the material taken as a whole appeals to a prurient interest in sex; (b) the material is patently offensive because it affronts contemporary community standards relating to the description or representation of sexual matters; and (c) the material is utterly without redeeming social value."

Applying that test to the book *Memoirs of a Woman of Pleasure* (commonly known as *Fanny Hill)* the Court concluded that the book was not obscene.

In dissenting, Justice White took the Court to task for requiring that material is not obscene unless it "is utterly without redeeming social value." He saw that as making it more difficult for courts to conclude that a particular piece of material was obscene. "If 'social importance,'" he declared, "is to be used as the prevailing opinion uses it today, obscene material, however far beyond customary limits of candor, is immune if it has any literary style, if it contains any historical references or language characteristic of a bygone day, or even if it is printed or bound in an interesting way. Well written, especially effective obscenity is protected; the poorly written is vulnerable. And why shouldn't the fact that some people buy and read such material prove its 'social value?'"

White joined the Court when it discarded the three-part test put forth in *Memoirs* and adopted a new test in *Miller v. California*.[71] The new test for obscenity was to be: "(a) whether 'the average person, applying contemporary community standards' would find that the work, taken as a whole, appeals to prurient interest...; (b) whether the work depicts or describes, in a patently offensive way, sexual conduct specifically defined by applicable state law; and (c) whether the work, taken as a whole, lacks serious literary, artistic, political, or scientific value." In adopting this new three-part test the majority, including White, were of the opinion that it would be more reliable than the three-part *Memoirs* test.

Before the *Miller* case was decided, Wesley Ward was charged with selling two books—*Bizarre World* and *Illustrated Case Histories, a Study of Sado-*

Masochism[72]—alleged to be obscene under Illinois law. He was convicted, and appealed to the Illinois Supreme Court. By the time that court heard Ward's appeal, the United States Supreme Court had decided *Miller*. Ward therefore argued that his conviction should be reversed because the Illinois obscenity statute did not conform to the new, three-part *Miller* test. The Illinois court rejected that argument and upheld the conviction. The United States Supreme Court, in an opinion written by Justice White, affirmed.

White wrote: "Since it is plain enough from its prior cases and from its response to *Miller* that the Illinois court recognizes the limitations on the *kinds* of sexual conduct which may not be represented or depicted under the obscenity laws, we cannot hold the Illinois statute to be unconstitutionally overbroad."

Miscellaneous Press Cases.

> The issue in these cases is whether requiring newsmen to appear and testify before state or federal grand juries abridges the freedom of speech and press guaranteed by the First Amendment. We hold that it does not.[73]

In that statement, Justice White was referring to three cases involving newsmen who refused to testify before grand juries concerning information each had obtained during investigations made prior to their writing certain news stories. The reporters were Paul Branzburg, Paul Pappas and Earl Caldwell.

Branzburg, a reporter for the Louisville, Kentucky, *Courier-Journal*, was investigating the use of drugs in the county. He obtained permission from two men who were making hashish to watch their activities. He promised that he would not reveal their identities. Later, Branzburg wrote a story which his paper published together with a picture of a pair of hands working at a laboratory table. Branzburg also investigated drug use in Frankfort, Kentucky. While doing so, he interviewed a number of people smoking marijuana and wrote a story about them without revealing their identities.

When Branzburg was called to appear before grand juries investigating drug use, he refused to identify the individuals making hashish as well as the drug users he had interviewed. In both instances, he was cited for and convicted of contempt. He appealed to the Supreme Court.

Pappas, while working as a reporter for a television station in New Bedford, Massachusetts, was called to cover a civil disorder involving the Black Panthers, who were holed up in a barricaded store. He gained entrance to the store and recorded a statement of one of the Black Panther leaders which was telecast by the station. Later, Pappas returned to the store. "As a condition of entry, Pappas agreed not to disclose anything he saw or heard inside the store except an anticipated police raid, which Pappas, 'on his own,' was free to photograph and report as he wished."

Some months later, Pappas was called before a grand jury and asked to reveal the information he had obtained while with the Panthers. He refused, was charged and convicted of contempt, and appealed to the Supreme Court.

Caldwell, a reporter for the *New York Times* working in California, was assigned to cover the Black Panther Party and other black militant groups. Later, he was ordered to appear before a federal grand jury and bring his notes and any tape recordings he had made concerning the Party. When he refused to do so, he was given another subpoena which simply ordered him to appear and testify before the jury. Caldwell asked the District Court to quash the subpoena. District Judge Alfonso J. Zirpoli refused to do so, but did issue an order protecting Caldwell from being forced "to reveal confidential associations, sources or information received, developed or maintained by him as a professional journalist in the course of his efforts to gather news for dissemination to the public through the press or other news media." Judge Zirpoli was of the opinion that under the First Amendment, reporters were privileged to refuse to reveal their sources. The United States appealed to the Supreme Court.

The Supreme Court upheld the contempt charges against Branzburg and Pappas, and reversed Judge Zirpoli's order which protected Caldwell from revealing certain information he had obtained from the Black Panther Party.

In referring to the First Amendment, Justice White stated: "We do not question the significance of free speech, press, or assembly to the country's welfare. Nor is it suggested that news gathering does not qualify for First Amendment protection; without some protection for seeking out the news, freedom of the press could be eviscerated." But he did not find any infringement on freedom of the press in these cases. For the Justice, and the majority, reporters were no different than the average citizen who can be forced to testify before a grand jury. He pointed out that "the First Amendment does not invalidate every incidental burdening of the press that may result from the enforcement of civil or criminal statutes of general applicability." And, he said, the Court would not "grant newsmen a testimonial privilege that other citizens do not enjoy." Furthermore, "we cannot seriously entertain the notion that the First Amendment protects a newsman's agreement to conceal the criminal conduct of his source, or evidence thereof, on the theory that it is better to write about crime than to do something about it."

The Pursuit of Liberty

The Right of Privacy. The Justice concurred in *Griswold*[74] when the Court struck down a Connecticut law making it a criminal offense to use contraceptives. The Court held that there was a constitutional right of privacy, and this law infringed upon that right. White agreed.

White did not agree, however, that the right of privacy announced in *Griswold* included the right of a pregnant woman to make the choice whether or not to bear the child. He therefore dissented in *Roe v. Wade*. "I find nothing in the language or history of the Constitution to support the Court's judgment. The Court simply fashions and announces a new constitutional right for pregnant mothers and, with scarcely any reason or authority for its action, invests that right with sufficient substance to override most existing state abortion statutes."[75]

The Justice was of the opinion that in this sensitive area, the rules governing abortions should be left to state legislatures. This caused him to dissent when the Court struck down Missouri laws which required a married woman to secure the consent of her husband and an unmarried woman under the age of 18 to secure the consent of a parent before securing an abortion.[76]

On the question of the validity of the law requiring a woman to secure the consent of the husband, White wrote: "It is truly surprising that the majority finds in the United States Constitution ... a rule that the State must assign a greater value to a mother's decision to cut off a potential human life by abortion than to a father's decision to let it mature into a live child."

Subsequently, the Justice voted with the majority to uphold a Utah state law which required a physician, who is about to perform an abortion, to notify an unmarried minor's parents, or the husband of a minor who is married.[77] He also joined Justice O'Connor's concurring opinion when the Court upheld another Missouri law requiring a minor to obtain the consent of at least one parent or, in the alternative, secure a court order approving the abortion.[78]

By 1986, Justice White had become disillusioned with the Court's approach to abortion decisions, and thought it time to overrule *Roe v. Wade*. "In my view, the time has come to recognize that *Roe v. Wade* ... 'departs from a proper understanding' of the Constitution and to overrule it."[79] Upon examining the cases in which the Court had upheld a right of privacy, the Justice concluded that they did not support the right of a woman to make a decision whether or not to bear a child. "If the woman's liberty to choose an abortion is fundamental, then, it is not because any of our precedents ... command or justify that result; it can only be because protection for this unique choice is itself 'implicit in the concept of ordered liberty' or, perhaps, 'deeply rooted in this Nation's history and tradition.' It seems clear to me that it is neither."

While the Justice did not believe that the Constitution protected a woman's right to choose to abort a fetus, he strongly believed that the Constitution protected "the liberty interest of a father in his relationship with his child," and that interest does not depend "on the marital status of the mother or the biological father."[80]

Justice White made those statements in a case resembling a television soap opera. Some of the facts: While Carole and Gerald were married, she gave birth to a child named Victoria. Although Gerald was listed on the birth certificate as the father, bloodtests taken later indicated a 98.07 percent possibility that Michael was the biological father.

Carole and Victoria lived for a time with Gerald; thereafter they lived in succession with Michael, Scott, Gerald, Scott, Gerald, Michael and finally settled down with Gerald, where two other children were born to them. Meanwhile, Michael and Victoria joined in a lawsuit seeking to legally establish Michael's right of visitation with Victoria. Gerald entered the lawsuit claiming that under California law he was Victoria's father because a child born "of a wife cohabiting with her husband, who is not impotent or sterile, is conclusively presumed to be a child of the marriage." The courts agreed with Gerald and denied Michael visitation rights with Victoria because "allowing such visitation would 'violat[e] the intention of the Legislature by impugning the integrity of the family unit.'"

This case brought forth five separate opinions from the Supreme Court. Four justices concluded that Michael had no constitutionally protectable interest in Victoria. Justice Stevens, however, was willing "to assume ... that Michael's relationship with Victoria is strong enough to give him a constitutional right to try to convince a trial judge that Victoria's best interest would be served by granting him visitation rights." He concluded that Michael had his chance before the trial judge in this case, and that judge determined that visitation by Michael was not in Victoria's best interest.

Justice White also believed that prior cases clearly establish a "liberty interest of a father in his relationship with his child." And further: "In none of these cases did we indicate that the father's rights were dependent on the marital status of the mother or biological father." The Justice was of the opinion that the California law, and the Court's approval of it, was unrealistic in today's world. "It is hardly rare in this world of divorce and remarriage for a child to live with the 'father' to whom her mother is married and still have a relationship with her biological father." He therefore concluded that California's law was unfair to biological fathers like Michael.

A biological connection, however, was not enough in White's opinion to secure constitutional protection for Mrs. Inez Moore.[81] In addition to herself, Mrs. Moore's family consisted of her son, Dale, Sr., her grandson, Dale, Jr., and grandson, John, Jr. John, Jr.'s, father, however, did not live in the home. All of the Moores lived happily together in Mrs. Moore's home until she received a notice from the City of East Cleveland, Ohio, that John, Jr., was an "illegal occupant" and must be removed from the home. The City's definition of a family who could live together did not include grandson John, Jr. because his father, John, Sr., did not live there.

When Mrs. Moore refused to remove grandson John, Jr., from the home, she was charged with a violation of the law, convicted and sentenced to five days in jail and given a $25 fine. The courts of Ohio affirmed, but a majority of the Supreme Court voted to reverse.

Quoting from a prior case, Justice Powell declared: "This Court has long recognized that freedom of personal choice in matters of marriage and family life is one of the liberties protected by the Due Process Clause of the Fourteenth Amendment."

East Cleveland attempted to justify its definition of a family by arguing that too many people living together caused overcrowding, heavy traffic, parking congestion and placed an undue burden on the school system. Powell, however, pointed out that the law really didn't accomplish any of those goals. For example, a household consisting of husband, wife, and a half-dozen children, all licensed to drive, were considered a family. But an adult brother and sister were not, even if they both used public transportation. He also pointed out that, in Mrs. Moore's case, if her son Dale, Sr., had a dozen children, she, her son, and all those grandchildren could live together without violating the law.

"I cannot believe," Justice White wrote in dissent, "that the interest in residing with more than one set of grandchildren is one that calls for any kind of heightened protection under the Due Process Clause. To say that one has a personal right to live with all, rather than some, of one's grandchildren and that this right is implicit in ordered liberty is, as my Brother STEWART says, 'to extend the limited substantive contours of Due Process beyond recognition.'" Having concluded that Mrs. Moore did not have a constitutional right to live with her son and these two grandchildren, White voted to uphold the law.

Michael Hardwick, a homosexual, did not receive any more consideration for his constitutional claims from the Justice than he gave to Mrs. Moore. Hardwick brought an action in the Federal District Court seeking a declaration that the sodomy laws of Georgia were unconstitutional. Judge Robert H. Hall dismissed the suit, but the Court of Appeals reversed, holding that the statute violated Hardwick's constitutional right of privacy. In an opinion by Justice White, the Supreme Court reversed.[82]

The Justice framed the question for the Court as being whether the Constitution confers "a fundamental right upon homosexuals to engage in sodomy." To that question he gave a resounding no. For the Justice, rights which were entitled to heightened judicial protection were those "fundamental liberties that are 'implicit in the concept of ordered liberty,' such that 'neither liberty nor justice would exist if [they] were sacrificed.'" Or, they were "liberties that are 'deeply rooted in this Nation's history and tradition.'" Consensual sodomy, he said, did not fall into either of these categories. Furthermore, the Justice rejected the argument that homosexual conduct should be protected because it occurs in the privacy of the home.

Justice Blackmun did not believe that the case had anything to do with any alleged right to engage in sodomy. He argued that the Court "must analyze ... Hardwick's claim in the light of the values that underlie the constitutional right of privacy. If that right means anything, it means that, before Georgia can prosecute citizens for making choices about the most intimate

aspects of their lives, it must do more than assert that the choice they have
made is an 'abominable crime not fit to be named among Christians.'" Blackmun took issue with the majority's refusal to recognize that sexual intimacy
has been recognized as "a sensitive, key relationship of human existence, central to family life, community welfare, and the development of human personality." And he concluded: "The fact that individuals define themselves in
a significant way through their intimate sexual relationships with others suggests, in a Nation as diverse as ours, that there may be many 'right' ways of
conducting those relationships, and that much of the richness of a relationship will come from the freedom an individual has to *choose* the form and
nature of these intensely personal bonds."

Equal Protection of the Law

Blacks on Juries. Justice White accepted without question the principle that
racial discrimination in the selection of grand and petit jurors "not only violates our Constitution ... but is at war with our basic concepts of a democratic society and a representative government."[83] He also believed, however, that
the person claiming such discrimination has the burden of proving that it
existed in his or her case. When the Court heard Robert Swain's argument
that there was discrimination in the selection of jurors when he was convicted
of rape in 1962, Justice White and a majority of the Court concluded that he
had not proved that to be true.

Swain, a black, presented evidence which showed "that while Negro males
over 21 constitute 26% of all males in the county, ... only 10 to 15% of the
grand and petit jury panels drawn from the jury box since 1953 have been
Negroes.... In this period of time, Negroes served on 80% of the grand juries
selected, the number ranging from one to three. There were four or five
Negroes on the grand jury panel of about 33 in this case, out of which two
served on the grand jury which indicted ... [Swain]. Although there has been
an average of six to seven Negroes on petit jury venires in criminal cases, no
Negro has actually served on a petit jury since about 1950. In this case there
were eight Negroes on the petit jury venire but none actually served, two being
exempt and six being struck by the prosecutor in the process of selecting the
jury."

White responded to Swain's argument: "Undoubtedly the selection of
prospective jurors was somewhat haphazard and little effort was made to ensure
that all groups in the community were fully represented. But an imperfect
system is not equivalent to purposeful discrimination based on race. We do
not think that the burden of proof was carried by ... [Swain] in this case."

Justice Goldberg wrote in dissent: "The petitioner [Swain] established
by competent evidence and without contradiction that not only was there no
Negro on the jury that convicted and sentenced him, but also no Negro within

the memory of persons now living has ever served on any petit jury in any civil or criminal case tried in Talladega County, Alabama."

Swain also argued that he was the victim of discrimination when the prosecutor used peremptory challenges to strike all blacks from the jury which tried him. After examining the history of the use of peremptory challenges, Justice White concluded: "In the light of the purpose of the peremptory system and the function it serves in a pluralistic society in connection with the institution of jury trial, we cannot hold that the Constitution requires an examination of the prosecutor's reasons for the exercise of his challenges in any given case."

Some twenty years later, the Justice had a change of heart with regard to the use of peremptory challenges to eliminate blacks from trial juries. When the Court held that "the Equal Protection Clause forbids the prosecutor to challenge potential jurors solely on account of their race or on the assumption that black jurors as a group will be unable impartially to consider the State's case against a black defendant,"[84] White agreed. He declared: "It appears ... that the practice of peremptorily eliminating blacks from petit juries in cases with black defendants remains widespread, so much so that I agree that an opportunity to inquire should be afforded when this occurs. If the defendant objects, the judge, in whom the Court puts considerable trust, may determine that the prosecution must respond."

When there was strong evidence of discrimination in the jury selection process, the Justice voted to reverse the defendant's conviction. Such was the situation in Claude Alexander's case.

Before his trial for rape, Alexander, a black, moved to quash the indictment because blacks had been excluded from the grand jury. The motion was denied, and he was convicted and sentenced to life imprisonment. His conviction was upheld by the Louisiana Supreme Court, but with Justice White writing the opinion, the United States Supreme Court reversed.[85]

White describes the process by which the grand jury pool was selected: "In Lafayette Parish, 21% of the population was Negro and 21 or over, therefore presumptively eligible for grand jury service. Use of questionnaires by the jury commissioners created a pool of possible grand jurors which was 14% Negro, a reduction by one-third of possible black grand jurors. The commissioners then twice culled this group to create a list of 400 prospective jurors, 7% of whom were Negro—a further reduction by one-half. The percentage dropped to 5% on petitioner's grand jury venire and to zero on the grand jury that actually indicted him."

In addition to noting that the number of blacks selected for the grand jury venire was substantially below the number eligible, Justice White also pointed out that the "racial designation on both the questionnaire and information card provided a clear and easy opportunity for racial discrimination."

The question for the Court in *Rose v. Mitchell*[86] was not the racial composition of the grand jury but the alleged use of race in selecting the grand jury foreman. This question was raised by James E. Mitchell and James Nichols, Jr., both black, who were tried and convicted of murder in Tennessee.

Although the evidence indicated that there had never been a black jury foreman in the county, a majority of the Supreme Court did not believe that was enough to prove racial discrimination. White dissented. He believed that the defendants had made out a prima facie case of discrimination because at least during the prior 20 years no black had ever served as jury foreman; furthermore, the jury foreman was selected by the local circuit judge. "Although these facts are not necessarily inconsistent with an ultimate conclusion that ... [the foreman] was not chosen on racial grounds, they raise, in conjunction with the previously described statistical presentation, a strong inference of intentional racial discrimination, shifting the burden to the State."

Integration of Public Schools. Justice White was not on the Court when it decided *Brown v. Board of Education.* He joined a unanimous court, however, to strike down a proposed desegregation plan for the Knoxville, Tennessee, school system in *Goss v. Board of Education.*[87] Under the Knoxville plan, school districts were rezoned without reference to race; however, "a student, upon request would be permitted solely on the basis of his own race and the racial composition of the school to which he has been assigned ... to transfer from such school, where he would be in a racial minority, back to his former segregated school where his race would be in the majority." In striking down the plan, the Court declared: "The recognition of race as an absolute criterion for granting transfers which operate only in the direction of schools in which the transferee's race is in the majority is no less unconstitutional than its use for original admission or subsequent assignment to public schools."

Throughout the remainder of his tenure on the Court, Justice White consistently voted to force the integration of public schools.

Integration of Public Facilities. In 1962, Chief Judge Sidney C. Mize of the Federal District Court in Mississippi declared that the segregation that existed in the City of Jackson's recreational facilities violated the Equal Protection Clause. Accordingly, the City desegregated its parks, auditoriums, golf courses and zoo. However, the City decided against desegregating the public swimming pools and closed them. This action was upheld by the District Court, the Court of Appeals and the Supreme Court. In support of the Supreme Court's decision, Justice Black wrote: "Nothing in the history or language of the Fourteenth Amendment nor in any of our prior cases persuades us that the closing of the Jackson swimming pools to all its citizens constitutes a denial of 'the equal protection of the laws.'"[88]

This decision disturbed Justice White, who dissented. For him, the City closed the pools for only one reason. "Jackson, Mississippi, closed its swimming pools when a district judge struck down the city's tradition of segregation in municipal services and made clear his expectation that public facilities would be integrated. The circumstances surrounding this action and the absence of other credible reasons for the closings leave little doubt that shutting down the pools was nothing more or less than a most effective expression of official policy that Negroes and whites must not be permitted to mingle together when using the services provided by the city."

The Justice rejected the majority's contention that closing the pools should be permitted because it had the same effect upon whites as it did upon blacks. "Closing the pools without a colorable nondiscriminatory reason was every bit as much an official endorsement of the notion that Negroes are not equal to whites as was the use of state National Guard troops in 1957 to bar entry of nine Negro students into Little Rock's Central High School ..."

The position the Justice took in City of Jackson case, was consistent with the position he took in prior and subsequent cases involving integration of public facilities.

Integration of Private Facilities. The Equal Protection Clause was adopted to eliminate discrimination by *state* governments. State involvement in segregation is manifested many times by laws making it a criminal offense to serve both white and colored persons in private facilities such as restaurants.[89]

But even when government action is more subtle, segregation in private facilities may still be unconstitutional. Such was the case of *Lombard v. Louisiana*.[90] Although New Orleans did not have an ordinance prohibiting restaurant service to both whites and blacks, three black and one white college students were arrested and convicted for trespassing when they refused to leave a segregated lunch counter. Sit-in demonstrations held prior to the students being arrested, caused the police chief to issue the following statement: "We wish to urge the parents of both white and Negro students who participated in today's sit-in demonstration[s] to urge upon these young people that such actions are not in the community interest. ... [W]e want everyone to fully understand that the police department and its personnel is ready and able to enforce the laws of the City of New Orleans and the state of Louisiana."

The Mayor also issued a statement: "I have today directed the superintendent of police that no additional sit-in demonstrations ... will be permitted ... regardless of the avowed purpose or intent of the participants...."

These statements were enough government involvement for the Supreme Court to reverse the students' convictions. Chief Justice Earl Warren authored the Court's opinion. "As we interpret the New Orleans city officials' statements, they here determined that the city would not permit Negroes to seek desegregated service in restaurants. Consequently, the city must be treated exactly as if it had an ordinance prohibiting such conduct." And the "official command here was to direct continuance of segregated service in restaurants, and to prohibit any conduct directed towards its discontinuance; it was not restricted solely to preserve the public peace in a nondiscriminatory fashion in a situation where violence was present or imminent by reason of public demonstrations." Justice White joined that opinion.

Whether or not the government is involved in the segregation is a question of fact, and sometimes the same set of facts leads different people to different conclusions. *Griffin v. Maryland*[91] was such a case. Glen Echo Amusement Park, near Washington, D.C., allowed only whites to enjoy its facilities. In order to maintain its segregation policy, the Park arranged with the National Detective Agency, a private company, to have Francis J. Collins patrol the Park grounds. Although Collins was paid by the Agency, he was under the control of the Park management. Collins was also a county deputy sheriff.

When Collins saw five black youths sitting in the carousel waiting for it to start, he "told them that it was the park's policy, 'not to have colored people on the rides, or in the park.'" When the youths did not leave, Collins arrested them for trespassing and took them to the police station. All were subsequently convicted and ordered to pay a fine of $100. When the case reached the Supreme Court, it reversed. A majority of the justices believed that government was involved in the segregation of the park because not only was Collins a deputy sheriff, he had also been instructed by the president of the Park "to arrest Negroes for trespassing if they did not leave the park when he ordered them to do so."

Justice White joined Justices Harlan and Black in dissenting. They were of the opinion that all Collins was doing was arresting these youths for trespassing on private property just as any police officer who may have been dispatched from headquarters could legally have done.

Where Blacks Live and Who They Live With. Justice White wrote the majority opinions in *Reitman v. Mulkey*[92] and *Hunter v. Erickson*.[93] Both of these cases, which are discussed in Chapter 4, involve the repeal of fair housing statutes. In *Reitman*, the issue before the Court was whether or not a recent amendment to the California Constitution (Proposition 14) had repealed the state's guarantee of fair housing. When Lincoln W. Mulkey and his wife, who were black, were denied permission to rent an apartment by Neil Reitman they brought an action under California's fair housing laws seeking an order of the court prohibiting Reitman from discriminating against them because they were black. Reitman responded to the lawsuit by arguing that Proposition 14 made the fair housing laws void. The Supreme Court of California disagreed noting that if Proposition 14 repealed the fair housing statutes it would have the effect of making the state "at least a partner in the instant act of discrimination and that its conduct is not beyond the reach of the Fourteenth Amendment."[94]

In an opinion written by Justice White, the United States Supreme Court affirmed the California court's decision. In discussing the effect of Proposition

14, he wrote: "Here we are dealing with a provision which does not just repeal an existing law forbidding private racial discriminations. ... [Proposition 14] was intended to authorize, and does authorize, racial discrimination in the housing market. The right to discriminate is now one of the basic policies of the State. The California Supreme Court believes that the ... [Proposition] will significantly encourage and involve the State in private discriminations."[95]

The Justice also wrote the opinion in which the Court struck down a Florida law making it a crime for any mixed racial couple to "habitually live in and occupy in the nighttime the same room."[96] Dewey McLaughlin, a black man, and Connie Hoffman, a white woman, were convicted of violating the law, sentenced to 30 days in jail and each fined $150. All justices of the Supreme Court voted to reverse.

Florida argued that the purpose of the law "was to prevent breaches of the basic concepts of sexual decency" and to prevent "illicit extramarital and premarital promiscuity." But Justice White could not understand why it was so important to punish promiscuity of a mixed racial couple, but not of a couple of the same race. "There is no suggestion that a white person and a Negro are any more likely habitually to occupy the same room together than the white or the Negro couple or to engage in illicit intercourse if they do." He therefore concluded that there "is involved here an exercise of the state police power which trenches upon the constitutionally protected freedom from invidious official discrimination based on race."

Gender Discrimination. With few exceptions, Justice White voted to strike down discrimination against either men or women. Whether by design or coincidence, however, it was in cases involving discrimination against males that he wrote opinions. For example, when the Court upheld a Florida law giving widows, but not widowers, a $500 property tax exemption, White dissented. "I find the discrimination invidious and violative of the Equal Protection Clause. There is merit in giving poor widows a tax break, but gender-based classifications are suspect and require more justification than the State has offered."[97]

The Justice also disagreed with the Court in *Parham v. Hughes*[98] when it upheld a Georgia statute that gave the mother of an illegitimate child the right to sue for the wrongful death of the child, but did not allow the father to do so unless he legitimated the child. Lemuel Parham was the biological father of a child born out of wedlock with Cassandra Moreen. When Cassandra and the child were killed in an auto accident, Lemuel Parham brought suit for the wrongful death of the child. The Georgia Supreme Court denied the lawsuit, and the U.S. Supreme Court affirmed.

The state argued that before fathers who have not legitimated the child could sue for its wrongful death, they must first prove their paternity. By simply eliminating them by statute, the state forestalls the "difficult problems of proof of paternity." White responded: "Whatever may be the evidentiary problems associated with proof of parenthood where a father, but presumably not a mother, is involved, I am sure that any interest the State conceivably has in simplifying the determination of liability in wrongful-death actions does not justify the outright gender discrimination in this case."

For Aliens. When cases involving discrimination against aliens began to come before the Court in the early '70s, Justice White joined the majority in upholding their right to equal protection.[99] The Justice, however, voted with the majority to uphold a New York law which limited employment as a state police officer to United States citizens.[100] He also voted to uphold another New York law which prevented Susan M. Norwick, a British citizen, and Tarja U. Dachinger, a citizen of Finland, from becoming teachers.[101] In each of these cases, the majority was of the opinion that state police officers and teachers should be citizens because the position was one that "involves discretionary decision making, or execution of policy, which substantially affects members of the political community."[102]

The Justice was of the opinion that the position of County Deputy Probation Officer was similar to that of police officer and teacher and therefore voted to uphold Los Angeles County when it refused to employ Jose Chavez-Salido, Ricardo Bohorques and Pedro Luis Ybarra as Deputy Probation Officers. "Looking at the functions of California probation officers," White declared, "we conclude that they, like ... state troopers ..., sufficiently partake of the sovereign's power to exercise coercive force over the individual that they may be limited to citizens."[103] Justice Harry Blackmun dissented. "I find it ironic that the Court invokes the principle of democratic self-government to exclude from the law enforcement process individuals who have not only resided here lawfully, but who now desire merely to help the State enforce its laws."

For Voters and New Political Parties. The first case involving the classification of voters in which Justice White participated was that of Sergeant Herbert Carrington who had been prevented from voting in an election in Texas because he was in the army. In striking down the Texas law prohibiting members of the Armed Forces from voting, the majority pointed out that: "By forbidding a soldier ever to controvert the presumption of non-residence, the Texas Constitution imposes an invidious discrimination in violation of the Fourteenth Amendment."[104]

The Justice also voted to declare unconstitutional as a violation of equal protection, Tennessee's requirement that a person live in the state for one year and in the county for three months before being eligible to register to vote. The Court did, however, approve of the state closing its registration thirty days before the election.[105] This, the Court believed was necessary in order for the state to complete its administrative tasks before the election.

Justice White, and a majority, held that allowing only property owners to vote on the question of the issuance of general obligation bonds by a city, denied equal protection to non-property owning residents. They could find "no basis for concluding that non-property owners are substantially less interested in the issuance of these securities than are property owners."[106]

While the Justice voted consistently against discrimination against voters, he was not as concerned about the problems of independent political parties such as those George Wallace's Independent Party faced in Ohio in 1968. In order to be on the ballot in Ohio, independent parties had to obtain signatures from voters equal to 15 percent of the ballots cast for governor during the last election. And those signatures had to be obtained prior to February 7. In contrast, the Democratic and Republican Parties qualified for a ballot position without having to secure any signatures if each had received at least 10 percent of the votes cast in the last gubernatorial election.

Although Wallace's Independent Party was able to secure the required number of signatures, it was unable to meet the February 7 deadline, and was therefore refused a ballot position for the 1968 general election. The Party petitioned the Federal District Court, which agreed that the Ohio laws were discriminatory and therefore violated equal protection; but the Court did not order Ohio to place the Party's name on the ballot. The Supreme Court not only agreed that the laws discriminated against independent parties, but it also ordered that Wallace's Party be given a ballot position.

Writing for the majority, Justice Black declared: "[T]he State is left with broad powers to regulate voting, which may include laws relating to the qualification and functions of electors. But here the totality of the Ohio restrictive laws taken as a whole imposes a burden on voting and associational rights which we hold is an invidious discrimination, in violation of the Equal Protection Clause."[107]

Without discussing those issues White concluded in dissent, that the Ohio laws did not violate either the Due Process Clause nor the Equal Protection Clause. He argued that because the Ohio laws were not unreasonable the Independent Party should be required to comply with them.

In the Criminal Justice System. Before the Justice joined the Court, it had held that in most cases states must furnish a copy of the trial transcript to those convicted persons who desired to appeal, but did not have sufficient funds to pay for one. The Court did, however, allow states to substitute other information in lieu of a transcript if that information was adequate for the defendant's appeal. White agreed with this approach, and voted most of the time to require transcripts to be provided to indigent defendants.

In *Draper v. Washington*,[108] however, White dissented when a majority of the Court held that Washington must furnish a transcript to Robert A. Draper, James D. Long and Raymond L. Lorentzen, who had all been convicted of robbery. When the defendants asked for a transcript, the trial judge held a hearing at which the defendants were allowed to argue why they needed one. In denying the transcript, the judge concluded that the assignments of error made by the defendants were "patently frivolous," and that their guilt had been "established by overwhelming evidence."

Writing for the Supreme Court, Justice Arthur Goldberg declared: "We hold today that the conclusion of the trial judge that an indigent's appeal is frivolous is ... [an] inadequate substitute for the full appellate review available to nonindigents in Washington, when the effect of that finding is to prevent an appellate examination based upon a sufficiently complete record of the trial proceedings themselves."

Justice White thought that the record prepared by the trial judge was adequate. Furthermore: "While the court gave Draper every opportunity to represent himself and the other petitioners in connection with making this record, he also required petitioners' trial counsel to be present to support petitioners' position. This counsel did and it appears that both at the hearing and upon appeal where he orally argued, he placed his resources and abilities at the disposal of the petitioners."

For the Poor. Justice White voted about as many times to strike down discrimination against poor people as he did to uphold such discrimination.[109] He did, however, agree with Demetrio P. Rodriguez that the Texas system of financing public schools discriminated against students of poor families and was therefore unconstitutional as a violation of equal protection.

Rodriguez, and some other parents, brought an action against the San Antonio School District claiming that because they lived in a school district that had a low tax base, there was less money available for the education of their children, than was available to educate children who lived in wealthier districts. The District Court agreed that Texas' method of financing education did discriminate against children living in lesser affluent districts and was unconstitutional as a violation of equal protection. A majority of the Supreme Court reversed, concluding "to the extent that the Texas system of school financing results in unequal expenditures between children who happen to reside in different districts, we cannot say that such disparities are the product of a system that is so irrational as to be invidiously discriminatory."[110]

Justice White, in dissent, reviewed the disparity existing between the revenue of the Edgewood Independent School District, where the Rodriguez children attended school, and other districts within Texas. This led him to conclude that "the parents and children of Edgewood, and in like districts, suffer from an invidious discrimination violative of the Equal Protection Clause."

The Bill of Rights and the States

As Gary Duncan, a black aged 19, and two younger cousins broke off an encounter with several white boys, he either touched or slapped one of them, Herman Landry. The encounter was reported to the police, who arrested

Duncan and charged him with simple battery. Duncan asked for a jury trial which was denied, because under Louisiana law jury trials were given only for serious felonies. At the trial, the white youths testified that Duncan slapped Landry, but the blacks testified that Duncan had only touched Landry on the arm.

Duncan was found guilty, sentenced to sixty days in jail, and fined $150. The Supreme Court of Louisiana upheld Duncan's conviction, but the United States Supreme Court reversed.

The question before the Court was whether the right to a jury trial guaranteed by the Sixth Amendment applied to Duncan's case. With Justice White writing the opinion, the Court said that it did. "Because we believe that trial by jury in criminal cases is fundamental to the American scheme of justice," White declared, "we hold that the Fourteenth Amendment guarantees a right of jury trial in all criminal cases which—were they to be tried in a federal court—would come within the Sixth Amendment's guarantee."[111]

Louisiana argued that because this was only a petty offense, the Sixth Amendment should not apply. "We need not..." White responded, "settle in this case the exact location of the line between petty offenses and serious crimes. It is sufficient for our purposes to hold that a crime punishable by two years in prison is, based on past and contemporary standards in this country, a serious crime and not a petty offense."

On the broader issue of the extent to which states are bound by the provisions of the Bill of Rights, White wrote: "Because we believe that trial by jury in criminal cases is fundamental to the American scheme of justice, we hold that the Fourteenth Amendment guarantees a right to a jury trial in all criminal cases which—were they to be tried in a federal court—would come within the Sixth Amendment's guarantee."

AS A JUSTICE FOR THE GOVERNMENT

The Justice voted not to give unemployment benefits to Sabbatarian Ardell Sherbert when she could not find a job that allowed her to have Saturdays off. This, even though the only reason the state offered in support of its decision was an economic one, i.e., that unscrupulous claimants might file false claims and thus dilute the fund. In response to this argument, Justice Brennan pointed out that even if fraudulent claims were filed, "it would plainly be incumbent upon the [Department] ... to demonstrate that no alternative forms of regulation would combat such abuses without infringing First Amendment rights."[112] As noted above, however, when the *Thomas, Hobbie* and *Frazee* cases came to the Court, White had a change of heart and voted to uphold their right to unemployment compensation even though they too were all Sabbatarians.

Justice White, however, was not a strong supporter of religious freedom. White voted against Muslims in prison who were prevented from attending Jumu'ah their holy day services Friday noon, because they were assigned work away from the main prison building. The Justice and the majority believed that making accommodation for the Muslims "would have undesirable results in the institution."[113]

White voted with the majority to uphold the discharge of Native Americans Alfred Smith and Galen Black, who "were fired from their jobs with a private drug rehabilitation organization because they ingested peyote for sacramental purposes at a ceremony of the Native American Church, of which both are members."[114]

While peyote under Oregon law was considered a controlled substance, Justice Blackmun pointed out that "the State actually has not evinced any concrete interest in enforcing its drug laws against religious users of peyote. Oregon has never sought to prosecute [Smith and Black] ..., and does not claim that it has made significant enforcement efforts against other religious users of peyote. The State's asserted interest thus amounts only to the symbolic preservation of an unenforced prohibition."

The Justice voted to protect the right of solicitation most of the time, but not solicitation done by a member of the armed forces on a military base. In those instances, he voted to uphold regulations requiring prior approval from a superior officer before engaging in such solicitation.[115]

Some unpopular speech received First Amendment protection from Justice White. For example, he voted most of the time to protect those individuals who were charged with using "fighting words." He did not, however, vote to protect those who made speeches by burning the American flag. He also voted to affirm Harold O. Spence's conviction for flag desecration. On May 10, 1970, Spence, a Seattle college student, had sewn a peace sign on his own flag and flew it upside down from his apartment window in protest of the killing of several students during a peace demonstration on the campus of Kent State University in Ohio. The majority had reversed Spence's conviction.[116]

Public employees who claimed that their public speeches were protected by the First Amendment generally did not receive support from Justice White. He voted to restrict both federal and state employees from engaging in political activities. And, as noted above, he voted to approve the discharge of public employees Sheila Myers and Ardith McPherson. In voting to approve McPherson's discharge particularly, White and Scalia virtually ignored the existence of the First Amendment.

When voting on commercial speech cases, Justice White joined the majority in proclaiming: "The Constitution ... accords a lesser protection to commercial speech than to other constitutionally guaranteed expression."[117] Those who claimed protection of the First Amendment for their commercial speech, therefore, did not fare well with him.

Overall, Justice White was not a strong supporter of freedom of association, particularly for those persons associating with the Communist Party or other alleged subversive organizations. He voted to uphold Robel's conviction for being a member of the Communist Party and working in a defense plant even though Congress had never outlawed the Party. If Congress had passed such a law, it is almost certain that the Court would have declared it unconstitutional as a violation of the First Amendment, and White would have concurred. Although the Justice wrote the opinion striking down Washington State's loyalty oath, he voted to uphold New York's very comprehensive loyalty program. Although he voted to uphold the associational privacy of the NAACP when Florida sought to secure the NAACP's membership records, he dissented when the Court held that Theodore R. Gibson did not have to turn over the records of the Miami Branch of the NAACP. White accepted Florida's argument that it wanted the records to see if any NAACP members were also members of the Communist Party.

White consistently voted to require applicants for admission to the bar to declare if they were or ever had been a member of the Communist Party or any other organization which advocated the overthrow of the government by force. This approach allows the State to exclude an individual from the practice of law because of what he or she believes, not for any subversive action he or she may have taken.

In the four cases which came to the Court during his tenure, the Justice voted for protecting the rights of associations in the advancement of their legal goals.[118]

New political parties attempting to obtain a place on the ballot did not receive much consideration from Justice White. In addition to the cases discussed in the text above, he voted to uphold Ohio's laws effecting independent candidates when John Anderson became a candidate for the presidency in 1980.[119] Anderson obtained the necessary signatures to qualify for the ballot, but missed the filing deadline by 57 days. A majority of the justices held that the burden placed upon independent candidates by Ohio's laws violated "voters' freedom of choice and freedom of association, in an election of nationwide importance, [and] unquestionably outweigh[ed] the State's minimal interest in imposing a March deadline." White disagreed, and joined Justice Rehnquist's dissenting opinion.

When Alan B. Burdick was prohibited from casting a write-in ballot in an election in Hawaii, he sought to have the law declared unconstitutional. Justice White wrote the Court's opinion concluding that the law did not violate Burdick's First Amendment rights of expression or association.[120]

In voting to uphold a federal law which denied food stamps to workers on strike, White concluded that the law did not violate the associational rights of union members. He acknowledged, however, that: "Exercising the right to strike inevitably risks economic hardship, but we are not inclined to hold that the right of association requires the Government to minimize that result by qualifying the striker for food stamps."[121]

Justice White generally voted to protect the press from libel actions brought by public officials and public figures. As pointed out above, however, by 1985 he had become disenchanted with the Court's approach to defamation cases and argued that the Court should abandon the "actual malice" test for public officials. He claimed that requiring a public official to prove the press acted with "actual malice" was "severe overkill."[122] He suggested that if the press had circulated misinformation about a public official, he or she ought to be able to vindicate his or her reputation and recover any actual damages suffered.

In the cases involving prior restraint of publication of news or punishment after publication, Justice White voted many times to permit both. For example, he wrote the opinion upholding the censorship of the *Spectrum*, the Hazelwood High School student newspaper. When the principal saw the page proofs for an upcoming issue of the paper, he directed that two pages therein be omitted. The two pages deleted contained stories on pregnancy and divorce, as well as "articles on teenage marriage, runaways, and juvenile delinquents, as well as a general article on teenage pregnancy."[123] White and the majority believed that the principal had "acted reasonably" in censoring the paper.

The Justice also voted to uphold a Pittsburgh, Pennsylvania, ordinance prohibiting newspapers from carrying "'help-wanted' advertisements in sex-designated columns."[124]

Even though Justice White concurred when the Court created the right of privacy in *Griswold*, his vision of it was much narrower than that of the majority. He dissented in *Roe v. Wade*, when the Court upheld the right of a pregnant woman to make the choice whether or not to bear a child. He did not believe that the right of privacy included that choice, a position which he consistently maintained thereafter.

When the Court upheld Mrs. Moore's right to have her grandson John Moore, Jr., live with her even though his father did not, Justice Powell declared: "Our decisions establish that the Constitution protects the sanctity of the family precisely because the institution of the family is deeply rooted in this Nation's history and tradition."[125] White, however, thought that the majority should not be creating a new constitutional right for Mrs. Moore. He wrote: "That the Court has ample precedent for the creation of new constitutional rights should not lead it to repeat the process at will. The Judiciary, including this Court, is the most vulnerable and comes nearest to illegitimacy when it deals with judge-made constitutional law having little or no cognizable roots in the language or even the design of the Constitution." And as indicated in *Bowers v. Hardwick*, he could find no privacy right of any kind that protected homosexual lifestyle.

White did believe, however, that the right of privacy gave unwed fathers an interest in their children, and that before those rights could be cut off, these fathers were entitled to be heard. He also agreed that people had the right to refuse medical treatment, i.e., a right to die, but he joined the majority in holding that the State does not have to leave that decision to close family members alone.[126]

Justice White's voting record with regard to racial discrimination is consistent with his work in civil rights as Deputy Attorney General. He voted most of the time to integrate juries, schools, and other public facilities. Insofar as integration of private facilities, he voted to apply the Civil Rights Act of 1964 to Heart of Atlanta Motel[127] and Ollie's Barbecue,[128] both private facilities. He dissented, however, when the majority used the Civil Rights Act of 1964 to dismiss convictions of black persons who had been arrested for refusing to leave privately owned lunch counters where they were "sitting in."[129]

White was a strong supporter of equal rights for women, men, illegitimate children, voters, and those caught up in the criminal justice system. For example, he agreed with three other justices who were of the opinion that government treatment of people differently because of their sex was an "inherently suspect ... classification ... and so unjustifiably discriminatory" that such classifications violated the principle of equality.[130]

He also supported most aliens seeking equal treatment from the state in which they lived, but voted against allowing aliens to be a police officer, teacher or probation officer. And when the Court required Texas to educate children of "undocumented aliens," the Justice dissented.[131]

Sometimes governments enact laws that discriminate against persons with regard to the exercise of a fundamental right, and the Justice voted most of the time to strike down that kind of discrimination. That was true for Redhail, who wanted to get married but could not do so without permission of a court because he was under a court order to support a child born out of wedlock.[132] The law, therefore, treated Redhail differently than other people with regard to the fundamental right to marry. In striking down the law, the majority pointed out that "[w]hen a statutory classification significantly interferes with the exercise of a fundamental right, it cannot be upheld unless it is supported by sufficiently important state interests and is closely tailored to effectuate only those interests." The majority, including White, did not think that the law in this case met that test.

By the time Justice White joined the Court, it had held that the Fourteenth Amendment's Due Process Clause required states to abide by most of the provisions of the Bill of Rights just as the federal government was always required to do. After he joined the Court, he voted to require states to abide by the Sixth Amendment's requirement of compulsory process and trial by jury in cases for which the penalty could be incarceration. He also agreed that the double jeopardy provision of the Fifth Amendment applied to state criminal proceedings.[133]

With a few exceptions, Justice White had a good voting record in cases dealing with equal protection of the law. The same cannot be said, however, of his voting record on freedom of religion, speech, press and association or right of privacy issues. In such cases, he voted much of the time *for* the government and *against* these individual rights. He therefore is included as a *Justice for the Government.*

6

CHIEF JUSTICE
WARREN E. BURGER

PERSONAL LIFE

Growing Up

Justice Harry Blackmun, in an interview with the *New York Times* while he and Chief Justice Warren Burger were still on the Supreme Court, described his boyhood pal as "a pretty dominating person, and always has been." He went on to say, "The chief has a great heart in him, and he's a very fine human being when you get to know him, when the tensions are off."[1]

The Chief Justice was born September 17, 1907, to Charles and Katherine Burger in St. Paul, Minnesota, the fourth of seven children. Charles Burger "was a railway cargo inspector who turned occasionally to traveling as a salesman of coffee or candy or patent medicines: the Burger brood was raised largely by the mother.... Mrs. Burger insisted that all the children attend Methodist Sunday School."[2]

While growing up, Burger had a paper route with 265 customers, and he helped put together special sections of the *St. Paul Pioneer Press*, working until the early hours of the morning. He also worked in the fields on the family's small truck farm. "'Warren had to work hard for everything he's ever had,' his brother John once said."[3]

During his high school days, the future Chief Justice was president of the student council and editor of the newspaper. He earned letters in football, swimming, hockey and track. With the help of high school teacher Edna Moore he obtained a scholarship to Princeton University. The family's financial condition, however, prevented him from accepting it.

Burger "worked during the summer of 1925 as a laborer in the construction of St. Paul's Robert Street Bridge. Then he was hired by the Mutual Life Insurance Company of New York. He started as 'essentially an office boy' but

CHIEF JUSTICE WARREN E. BURGER (collection of the Supreme Court of the United States).

soon was promoted to more senior clerical work. He enrolled in the night school division of the University of Minnesota. Two years later he entered the St. Paul College of Law—now William Mitchell College of Law. He continued with evening classes at the University between law school sessions. He graduated *magna cum laude* from law school in 1931."[4]

In commenting upon Burger's attendance at St. Paul College of Law,

Everette E. Dennis has written: "It certainly didn't compare with Harvard, where his boyhood friend Harry Blackmun was studying law, but Burger did have the advantages of practical-minded teachers who were practicing lawyers and judges moonlighting as law teachers."[5]

Practice of Law and Marriage

Upon graduation from law school Burger joined the St. Paul law firm of Boyesen, Otis and Faricy, where he became a partner in less than three years. "Burger and the firm prospered even in the Great Depression years. His legal work covered a wide range of practice, and he developed a reputation as a skilled advocate."[6] He also taught Contracts at his alma mater for seventeen years.

The future Chief Justice married Elvira Stromberg in 1933. The couple met while both were attending night school at the University of Minnesota. Boyhood friend, and later a justice of the Supreme Court, Harry Blackmun was best man at the wedding. Two children were born of the marriage, son Wade Allen and daughter Margaret Elizabeth.

Politics and Public Service

"Burger took an interest in local bond issues and mayoral elections, but did not get into politics until he helped manage the successful gubernatorial campaign of another promising young local lawyer—Harold Stassen—in 1938. 'They called us the Boy Scout Brigade,' Stassen recalls. Burger, kept out of World War II by spinal trouble, which still requires him to wear a back brace, became the first president of the St. Paul Council on Human Relations."[7]

During the 1948 Republican Convention, Burger managed Stassen's unsuccessful attempt to gain the nomination for president. "At the GOP's convention four years later, Burger, still a Stassen lieutenant, offered a skilled defense of a Texas delegation that was pledged to Dwight Eisenhower. By helping repel an attack on Eisenhower's supporters by forces loyal to Robert Taft of Ohio, Burger is credited with having been a major figure in assuring Eisenhower's subsequent nomination."[8]

During this period, Burger was active in local civic activities, being president of the Junior Chamber of Commerce and the St. Paul Council on Human Relations. "When Japanese-Americans were forced to leave the West Coast during World War II, the council created a special committee to find housing and employment for those who came to St. Paul. Burger also played a leading role in reforming a notoriously corrupt police department, by making the police chief a career position and giving special training to police officers in dealing with minorities."[9]

Shortly after taking office in 1953, President Eisenhower named Burger to the post of assistant attorney general in the Civil Division of the Justice

Department, where he served until appointed to the District of Columbia Court of Appeals in 1955.

Judge on the District of Columbia Court of Appeals

At the time President Eisenhower offered him a position on the Court of Appeals, Burger had submitted his resignation from the Department of Justice, intending to return to the practice of law in St. Paul. "He had long before told friends [*Time* reports]: 'I never have had a passion to be a judge.'"[10]

Describing the Burgers' lifestyle while Burger was on the Court of Appeals, *Time* reports:

> [T]he Burgers ... led a quiet life in Washington, normally limiting their entertaining to small dinner parties at their 140-year-old farmhouse in nearby Arlington. He drives a five-year-old Volkswagen. His avocations are painting and sculpture. He has done some bas-relief for some of his friends, and tried — without success — to put some life into the dismal school of official portraiture that fills the corridors of his courthouse.[11]

Burger served on the Court of Appeals for 13 years. In addition to his court work, he spoke and wrote about the judicial system. "At this time," author Burnett Anderson notes, "Burger began speaking out on the growing problems of the American judicial system: inefficient management of the courts, the overload of cases, long delays in hearing and resolution, and inadequacies in the administration of the prison system. He advocated improving legal education with emphasis on practical skills and ethics."[12]

Nomination to Be Chief Justice of the United States

In an exchange of letters with newly elected President Richard Nixon, Chief Justice Earl Warren indicated that he would resign at the end of the Court's term in June 1969. The President, out of respect for the Court and Chief Justice Warren, delayed picking Warren's successor until late in May.

On May 21, 1969, in a ceremony attended by Vice President Spiro T. Agnew, the Cabinet, and other guests, President Nixon announced the nomination of Judge Warren E. Burger to be the next Chief Justice. In a biography of the new Chief Justice, John P. Mackenzie describes the scene at the White House.

> President Richard M. Nixon strode before the television cameras in the company of the man who was his choice to be the next Chief Justice of the United States. ... He would be President Nixon's "law and order" nominee, a jurist of "strict constructionist" views — at least as that phrase has become understood by persons of similar ideological bent. He was Warren E. Burger, sixty-one-year-old judge of the United States Court of Appeals for the District of Columbia, the fifteenth Chief Justice of the United States.[13]

During hearings on the nomination, Senate Minority leader Everett Dirksen gave three reasons why the Senate should promptly confirm Judge Burger: "No. 1, he looks like a Chief Justice. No. 2, he acts like a Chief Justice. No. 3, he talks like a Chief Justice."[14]

Burger was confirmed by a Senate vote of 74 to 3 on June 9, and took the oath of office June 23, 1969.

When Burger joined the Court as Chief Justice, other members of the Court were Justices Hugo L. Black, William O. Douglas, William J. Brennan, Jr., John M. Harlan (II), Potter Stewart, Thurgood Marshall, and Bryon R. White. Burger retired as Chief Justice on September 26, 1986.

AS CHIEF JUSTICE (1969–1986)

The Free Exercise of Religion

Frieda Yoder, age 15, Vernon Yutzy, age 14, and Barbara Miller, age 15, had completed the eighth grade at the New Glarus Public School in Wisconsin. Their parents, Jonas Yoder, Adin Yutzy and Wallace Miller, respectively, thereafter refused to enroll them in the public high school. Yoder and Yutzy were members of the Old Order Amish, and Miller was a member of the Conservative Amish Mennonite Church.

> The Old Order Amish religion dictates that the Amish child ... not attend high school since any high school, public or private, constitutes a deterrent to his [her] salvation. The period of adolescence is critical in the religious and cultural development of the child because at this time the child enters gradually into the fullness of Amish life, is given responsibilities which would be directly interfered with if he [she] were compelled to go to high school, and accepts adult baptism.[15]

The fathers of the three children were charged and convicted of violating a Wisconsin statute which required children between the ages of 7 and 16 to attend school regularly. The Supreme Court of Wisconsin reversed, being of the opinion that to apply the law to the Amish would be a violation of their right to free exercise of religion as protected by the First Amendment.

The United States Supreme Court, with Chief Justice Burger writing the opinion, affirmed.[16] The Chief Justice examined the precepts of the Amish religion, and concluded "that the record in this case abundantly supports the claim that the traditional way of life of the Amish is not merely a matter of personal preference, but one of deep religious conviction, shared by an organized group, and intimately related to daily living."

Wisconsin, however, asserted two interests in support of the law: "that some degree of education is necessary to prepare citizens to participate effectively and intelligently in our open political system, if we are to preserve freedom and independence. Further, education prepares individuals to be self-reliant and self-sufficient participants in society."

Agreeing that both interests were important and legitimate, Burger noted that these interests were not neglected in the Amish way of life. "The Amish alternative to formal secondary school education," he argued, "has enabled them to function effectively in their day-to-day life under self-imposed limitations on relations with the world, and to survive and prosper in contemporary society as a separate, sharply identifiable and highly self-sufficient community for more than 200 years in this country." The Chief Justice therefore concluded "that the First and Fourteenth Amendments prevent the State from compelling ... [the fathers] to cause their children to attend formal high school to age 16."

The Chief Justice also agreed with George and Maxine Maynard who claimed that being forced to have a car license plate bearing the motto "Live Free or Die," infringed upon their religious beliefs and therefore violated the First Amendment.[17]

The Maynards were Jehovah's Witnesses, and believed that "[i]t would be contrary to ... [their] belief to give up ... [their] life for the state, even if it meant living in bondage." Motivated by these religious beliefs, the Maynards covered the motto on their car licenses. As a result, George Maynard was cited several times for violating a New Hampshire state law which made it a crime to obscure any part of a license plate. After being found guilty the third time, Maynard brought an action in the Federal District Court seeking an injunction to prevent the state from forcing him to comply with the law. The court agreed that forcing the Maynards to abide by the law was a violation of their First Amendment rights and enjoined the state from arresting them again. The Supreme Court agreed and affirmed.

Burger framed and answered the question this way: "We are thus faced with the question of whether the State may constitutionally require an individual to participate in the dissemination of an ideological message by displaying it on his private property in a manner and for the express purpose that it be observed and read by the public. We hold that the State may not do so."

After noting that New Hampshire's interests in this case are not great, the Chief Justice concluded: "The First Amendment protects the right of individuals to hold a point of view different from the majority and to refuse to foster, in the way New Hampshire commands, an idea they find morally objectionable."

The free exercise of religion claim of Native Americans Stephen J. Roy and Karen Miller did not impress the Chief Justice as much as did the claims of the Amish and the Maynards. Roy and Miller brought suit to prevent the Secretary of Human Services from using the Social Security number of their daughter, Little Bird of the Snow.

The question presented is whether the Free Exercise Clause of the First Amendment compels the Government to accommodate a religiously based objection to the statutory requirements that a Social Security number be provided by an applicant seeking to receive certain welfare benefits and that the States use these numbers in administering the benefit programs.[18]

Based on recent conversations with an Abenaki chief, Roy believes that technology is "robbing the spirit of man." In order to prepare his daughter for greater spiritual power, therefore, Roy testified to his belief that he must keep her person and spirit unique and that the uniqueness of the Social Security number as an identifier, ... will serve to "rob the spirit" of his daughter and prevent her from attaining greater spiritual power.

District Judge Malcolm Muir accepted the argument of Roy and Miller and ordered the Secretary of Health and Human Services not to use Little Snow's number and to continue providing the Roy family with monetary and medical assistance until Little Snow's 16th birthday without requiring the family to furnish her Social Security number. With the Chief Justice writing the opinion, the Supreme Court reversed.

In overruling Judge Muir's order to the government not to use Little Snow's number, Burger wrote: "Never to our knowledge has the Court interpreted the First Amendment to require the Government *itself* to behave in ways that the individual believes will further his or her spiritual development or that of his or her family. The Free Exercise Clause simply cannot be understood to require the Government to conduct its own internal affairs in ways that comport with the religious beliefs of particular citizens. Just as the Government may not insist that ... [Roy and Miller] engage in any set form of religious observance, so ... [Roy and Miller] may not demand that the Government join in their chosen religious practices by refraining from using a number to identify their daughter."

Burger concluded that numbers were necessary for the smooth functioning of the system and to prevent fraud. Roy and Miller, therefore, "may not use the Free Exercise Clause to demand Government benefits, but only on their own terms, particularly where that insistence works a demonstrable disadvantage to the Government in the administration of the programs."

Only Justice Byron White dissented from this part of the Court's opinion. He was of the opinion that the cases of *Thomas v. Rev. Bd. of Indiana*[19] and *Sherbert v. Verner*[20] required a different result.

Freedom of Speech

Pamphleteering and Soliciting. Jerome M. Keefe, a real estate broker who lived in Westchester, Illinois, but whose office was in Austin, Illinois, was accused by the Organization for a Better Austin (OBA) of "panic peddling" and "blockbusting."[21] Keefe was specifically accused of arousing "the fears of the local white residents that Negroes were coming into the area and then, exploiting the reactions and emotions so aroused." Having aroused the local white residents, Keefe would then secure the listing of their homes, and sell to blacks. In an attempt to stop this practice, OBA prevailed upon several real estate brokers to sign a pledge not to engage in this kind of selling practice. Keefe, however, refused to sign and claimed that he did not engage in such practices.

The OBA then printed and began distributing leaflets in Westchester, calling attention to Keefe's real estate practices. The leaflets were distributed near Keefe's home, at a shopping center, and given to some of the parishioners who attended the same church as Keefe did.

Keefe secured an injunction from a local court, prohibiting OBA from "passing out pamphlets, leaflets, or literature of any kind, and from picketing, anywhere in the City of Westchester, Illinois." With the Chief Justice writing the opinion, the Supreme Court reversed.

The Chief Justice pointed out that pamphleteering is a form of speech protected by the free speech clause of the First Amendment, and that an injunction is a "prior restraint" upon such speech. "Any prior restraint on expression," Burger declared, "comes to this Court with a 'heavy presumption' against its constitutional validity," and therefore Keefe "carries a heavy burden of showing justification for the imposition of such a restraint." And in this case, Keefe has not done so. "No prior decisions support the claim that the interest of an individual in being free from public criticism of his business practices in pamphlets or leaflets warrants use of the injunctive power of a court."

The Chief Justice, however, did not vote to uphold the right of Captain Albert Glines of the Air Force Reserves to solicit signatures on a petition protesting Air Force grooming regulations. Glines had drafted a petition which he intended to send to several members of Congress and to the Secretary of Defense requesting that the regulations be changed.[22] At the time, Air Force regulations prohibited the circulation of petitions without prior approval of the base commander.

Immediately upon learning of the petition, and Glines's part in it, the base commander removed him from active duty and assigned him to the standby reserves. This prevented him from finishing his training. He also lost some of his military benefits.

Glines brought an action in the Federal District Court against his superior officer claiming the regulations were a violation of the First Amendment. He sought reinstatement and back pay. Judge William H. Orrick, Jr., agreed and ordered him reinstated with back pay. The Court of Appeals agreed with Judge Orrick that the regulations were unconstitutional but held that the order for back pay was improper under the law. The Government appealed to the Supreme Court, which reversed, with Justice Lewis F. Powell, Jr., writing the Court's opinion, which the Chief Justice joined. "Without the opportunity to review materials before they are dispersed throughout his base," Powell asserted, "a military commander could not avert possible disruption among his troops. Since a commander is charged with maintaining morale, discipline, and readiness, he must have authority over the distribution of materials that could affect adversely these essential attributes of an effective military force."[23]

Justice Brennan argued in dissent: "The Court unnecessarily tramels important First Amendment rights by uncritically accepting the dubious proposition that military security requires—or is furthered by—the discretionary suppression of a classic form of peaceful group expression. Service men and women deserve better than this."

Unpopular Speech. The Chief Justice did not believe that vulgar speech was protected by the First Amendment, and he therefore dissented when the Court reversed Paul Cohen's conviction for having the statement "Fuck the Draft" on the back of his jacket while in the Los Angeles County Courthouse. Burger joined Justice Harry Blackmun who wrote: "Cohen's absurd and immature antic, in my view, was mainly conduct and little speech."[24]

For the Chief Justice even "suggestive speech," particularly when used by a student at a school assembly, was speech that could be punished. Matthew N. Fraser, a student at Bethel High School, Pierce County, Washington, learned this the hard way.[25] Fraser was to make a nominating speech for a fellow student who was running for school office. He wrote out his speech and showed it to two of his teachers, who thought that it "was 'inappropriate and that he probably should not deliver it.'" Fraser, however, did deliver the speech and in it said:

> I know a man who is firm—he's firm in his pants, he's firm in his shirt, his character is firm—but most ... of all, his belief in you, the students of Bethel, is firm. ...
> Jeff Kuhlman is a man who will go to the very end—even the climax, for each and every one of you.

After the speech, Fraser was charged with violating a school rule prohibiting the use of "obscene, profane language or gestures" and was suspended for three days. His name was also removed from the list of potential graduation speakers.

Fraser brought an action in the Federal District Court, claiming that the punishment violated his First Amendment right to free speech, and Judge Jack E. Tanner agreed. Judge Tanner gave Fraser judgment for $278 in damages and $12,750 for costs and attorney's fees, and the Court of Appeals affirmed. The Supreme Court, with the Chief Justice writing the opinion, reversed, concluded that: "The First Amendment does not prevent the school officials from determining that to permit a vulgar and lewd speech such as ... [Fraser's] would undermine the school's basic educational mission. A high school assembly or classroom is no place for a sexually explicit monologue directed towards an unsuspecting audience of teenage students."

Justice Stevens thought differently. He pointed out that Fraser was an outstanding student and respected by other students to the extent that he was chosen to speak at commencement. And that, he argues "indicates that he was probably in a better position to determine whether an audience composed of 600 of his contemporaries would be offended by the use of a four-letter word— or a sexual metaphor—than is a group of judges who are at last two generations and 3,000 miles away from the scene of the crime."

Criminal conviction for "misuse" of an American flag in expressing an opinion, was also appropriate the Chief Justice believed. He dissented when the Court reversed the conviction of Valerie Goguen for flag desecration for sewing a flag on the seat of his pants.[26] He also believed that Harold Spence should be punished for attaching a "peace" sign to a flag and hanging it out the window of his apartment to protest the shooting of four students at Kent State University in Ohio.[27] The Chief Justice wrote: " If the constitutional role of this Court were to strike down unwise laws or restrict unwise application of some laws, I could agree with the result reached by the Court. That is not our function, however, and it should be left to each State and ultimately the common sense of its people to decide how the flag, as a symbol of national unity, should be protected."

Commercial Speech. In *Bigelow v. Virginia*,[28] Justice Blackmun wrote that "[o]ur cases clearly establish that speech is not stripped of First Amendment protection merely because it appears in" the form of a commercial advertisement. Burger agreed. The Chief Justice did not believe, however, that gave persons engaged in the professions, unrestricted authority to advertise their services. "I think it important to note also," he declared, "that the advertisement of professional services carries with it quite different risks from the advertisement of standard products."[29]

When the Court squarely faced the issue of lawyers' advertising their professional services, and upheld their right to do so, Burger dissented. "Because legal services can rarely, if ever, be 'standardized' and because potential clients rarely know in advance what services they do in fact need, price advertising can never give the public an accurate picture on which to base its selection of an attorney."[30]

The Chief Justice's concern about lawyers advertising caused him to dissent when the Court reversed disciplinary action given Ohio attorney Philip Q. Zauderer for an allegedly misleading advertisement.[31] Zauderer had placed an ad in a newspaper indicating that his firm was representing a number of women in cases against the maker of the Dalkon Shield Intrauterine Device. The ad did not directly solicit cases from other women, but did state that the firm's fees were on a contingent basis, and if there was no recovery there would be no fee.

The Office of Disciplinary Counsel concluded that the ad violated Ohio's disciplinary rules and issued a public reprimand. The Supreme Court held that the reprimand violated Zauderer's First Amendment rights, and reversed. Burger joined Justice Sandra Day O'Connor's dissent wherein she pointed out that the "Court's commercial speech decisions have repeatedly acknowledged that the differences between professional services and other advertised products may justify distinctive state regulation."

Places to Speak. "The fact that a form of expression enjoys some constitutional protection does not mean that there are not times and places inappropriate for its exercise."[32] With those words, the Chief Justice dissented when the Court struck down an ordinance of Mount Ephraim, New Jersey, which did not permit exhibition of live dancing within its borders. In concluding that the ordinance was a restriction on First Amendment activities, the majority pointed out that the "Borough has presented no evidence ... that live entertainment poses problems [such as parking, trash, or police protection] more significant than those associated with ... [other] permitted uses."

Burger saw the issue differently. "At issue here," he argued in dissent, "is the right of a small community to ban an activity incompatible with a quiet, residential atmosphere."

Although he acknowledged that the case presented a free speech issue, he was of the opinion that the desires of the people of Mount Ephraim to maintain a tranquil community were more important. "To say that there is a First Amendment right to impose every form of expression on every community, including the kind of 'expression' involved here, is sheer nonsense. ... To invoke the First Amendment to protect the activity involved in this case trivializes and demeans that great Amendment."

Burger also voted to uphold a ban on camping and sleeping in Lafayette Park and on the Mall in Washington, D.C. "The actions here claimed as speech entitled to the protections of the First Amendment," he asserted, "simply are not speech; rather, they constitute conduct."[33]

Freedom of Association

For Public Employees. When Richard Elrod, a Democrat, was elected Sheriff of Cook County, Illinois, he immediately discharged all Republicans then working in the Sheriff's office. John Burns, and several others who had been fired, brought an action against Elrod claiming that the discharge violated their First Amendment right to freedom of association. The case was dismissed by the District Court, but the Court of Appeals upheld the plaintiff's claims and reversed. The Supreme Court agreed and affirmed.[34]

Justice William J. Brennan, Jr., writing for himself, and Justices White and Marshall acknowledged that: "Patronage practice is not new to American politics." He pointed out, however, that the "cost of the practice of patronage is the restraint it places on freedoms of belief and association. In order to maintain their jobs, ... [Burns and the others] were required to pledge their political allegiance to the Democratic Party, work for the election of other candidates of the Democratic Party, contribute a portion of their wages to the Party, or obtain the sponsorship of a member of the Party, usually at the price of one of the first three alternatives." And while agreeing that there was "a vital need for government efficiency and effectiveness," those needs were not sufficient "to override their severe encroachment on First Amendment freedoms."

The Chief Justice disagreed, and dissented. "The Court strains," he argued, "the rational bounds of First Amendment doctrine and runs counter to longstanding practices that are part of the fabric of our democratic system to hold that the Constitution *commands* something it has not been thought to require for 185 years." He was of the opinion, that these matters should be left to the states and to Congress.

The Court reached the same conclusion and overturned the discharge of Aaron Finkel and Alan Tabakman from their positions as Assistant Public Defenders of Rockland County, New York, because they were not members of the same party as the newly appointed Public Defender. Burger joined the majority in this case. He gave no indication why he thought that the free associational rights of Finkel and Tabakman should be protected but those of Burns and his friends should not be.[35]

For Political Campaign Contributors. In *Buckley v. Valeo*,[36] the Court upheld that part of a federal law that placed limitations on political campaign contributions, but struck down limitations upon the amount of money a candidate can spend on his or her own campaign. The Court was of the opinion that the limitation of expenditures placed "substantial and direct restrictions on the ability of candidates, citizens, and associations to engage in protected political expression, restrictions that the First Amendment cannot tolerate."

Chief Justice Burger agreed that the limitation on expenditures infringed upon freedom of speech. He also believed that the limitation upon contributions had the same effect, and dissented on that issue. "I have long thought freedom of association and freedom of expression," he asserted, "were two peas from the same pod. The contribution limitations of the Act impose a restriction on certain forms of associational activity, that are for the most part, as the Court recognizes, ... harmless in fact."

The Chief Justice's views on limiting campaign contributions were vindicated in a slightly different context in *Citizens Against Rent Control v. Berkeley*.[37] In that case, the Court found unconstitutional a Berkeley, California, ordinance which limited contributions to a committee supporting or opposing a ballot measure. In writing the Court's opinion, Burger pointed out that: "The restraint imposed by the Berkeley ordinance on rights of association and in turn on individual and collective rights of expression plainly contravenes both the right of association and the speech guarantees of the First Amendment."

Freedom of the Press

Libel. "Because the threat or actual imposition of pecuniary liability for alleged defamation may impair the unfettered exercise of ... First Amendment freedoms, the Constitution imposes stringent limitations upon the permissible scope of such liability."[38] On that basis, Burger accepted the Court's rule that in defamation cases, public officials and public figures could not be awarded damages unless they were able to prove that the publisher acted with malice or with reckless disregard of the truth.

The Chief Justice parted company with the Court's majority, however, when the allegedly defamed person was a private citizen. He, therefore, dissented in the *Gertz* case, agreeing with much of what Justice White had written in that case. Burger, also, did not like the Court's decision to revamp the law of libel to the extent that, if the story relates to a matter of public concern, private citizens seeking damages for defamation must prove that the publisher was negligent in publishing the allegedly defamatory information. "I would prefer to allow this area of law to continue to evolve as it has up to now with respect to private citizens rather than embark on a new doctrinal theory which has no jurisprudential ancestry."[39]

The Chief Justice's desire to allow recovery of damages for alleged defamation of a private citizen not involved in a matter of public concern was partly fulfilled when the Court upheld an award of damages in the *Dun and Bradstreet, Inc.* case.[40] While he agreed with the result in that case, he wanted it understood that he still believed that *Gertz* was wrongly decided, and that he agreed with Justice White that *New York Times Co. v. Sullivan* should be reexamined.

Burger's (and White's) desire for a hands-off rule for private citizen's actions for defamation received a set-back when the Court held that a private person plaintiff, could not recover damages for defamation relating to a matter of public concern, unless he or she could prove that the publisher acted negligently and the published matter was false.[41]

Prior Restraint of and Punishment for Publication. "There is ... little variation among the members of the Court in terms of resistance to prior restraints against publication. Adherence to this basic constitutional principle, however, does not make these cases simple."[42] With those words, the Chief Justice approached the question of whether the prior restraints against the *Washington Post* and the *New York Times* for publishing parts of the *Pentagon Papers* should be upheld.

Because the answer to the question was a difficult one for him, and because he believed that the cases were brought to the Court too quickly, Burger voted to let the prior restraints stand and allow the cases to proceed through the lower courts. "This frenzied train of events took place in the name of the presumption against prior restraints created by the First Amendment. Due regard for the extraordinarily important and difficult questions involved in these litigations should have led the Court to shun such a precipitate timetable."

The Chief Justice had another opportunity to set forth his views on prior restraints when Judge Hugh Stuart's gag order on the press, in Erwin Charles Simants' trial for murder, came to the Court.[43] Simants was to be tried for allegedly killing six members of the Henry Kellie family near Southerland, Nebraska. Because of the extensive publicity surrounding the killings, and of his concern that Simants have a fair trial, Judge Stuart issued an order prohibiting the publication of certain information about the upcoming trial. The Nebraska Press Assn. applied to the Nebraska Supreme Court to stay Stuart's order. That court made some changes in the order, and let it stand as modified. The Press Assn. appealed to the United States Supreme Court, which reversed.

The gag order brought into conflict the First Amendment right of freedom of the press and Simants' Sixth Amendment right to a fair trial. After an extensive review of prior cases relating to prior restraints as well as those involving a defendant's Sixth Amendment right to a fair trial, Burger wrote: "We affirm that the guarantees of freedom of expression are not an absolute prohibition under all circumstances, but the barriers to prior restraint remain high and the presumption against its use continues intact. We hold that, with respect to the order entered in this case prohibiting reporting or commentary on judicial proceedings held in public, the barriers have not been overcome; to the extent that this order restrained publication of such material, it is clearly invalid."

In *Smith v. Daily Mail Publishing Co.*,[44] with Burger writing the majority opinion, the Court held that the media could not be punished for publishing the name of a minor which it had obtained from public records. The case involved the killing of a student, allegedly by another student whose name reporters obtained from witnesses, police and an assistant prosecutor. "At issue," the Chief Justice wrote, "is simply the power of a state to punish the truthful publication of an alleged juvenile delinquent's name lawfully obtained by a newspaper. The asserted state interest cannot justify the statute's imposition of criminal sanctions on this type of publication."

When the Court has been confronted with the question whether court proceedings should be closed to the press, Burger most often voted against closure, and wrote some of the Court's opinions upholding the right of the press to attend. "The right to an open public trial is a shared right of the accused and the public, the common concern being the assurance of fairness." And "these interests are not necessarily inconsistent. Plainly, the defendant has a right to a fair trial but, ... one of the important means of assuring a fair trial is that the process be open to neutral observers."[45]

But the Chief Justice voted to prohibit the press from being present at a rape trial during the testimony of the alleged victim.[46] The case arose when a trial judge, acting under a Massachusetts statute, closed the courtroom during the testimony of three girls who were minors and the alleged victims. The Globe Newspaper Co. asked the judge to change his ruling and allow it to attend the trial during the victims' testimony, but he refused to do so. The Supreme Judicial Court of Massachusetts agreed with the trial judge, but the United States Supreme Court reversed. By that time the trial had been held, and the defendant acquitted.

In an opinion written by Justice Brennan, the majority agreed that "safeguarding the physical and psychological well-being of a minor—is a compelling one. But as compelling as that interest is, it does not justify a *mandatory* closure rule, for it is clear that the circumstances of the particular case may affect the significance of the interest. A trial court can determine on a case-by-case basis whether closure is necessary to protect the welfare of a minor victim."

Burger disagreed. The press, he pointed out, still has access to the victim's testimony, and closure protects "the child from the severe—possibly permanent—psychological damage." And he did not accept the majority's view that the interests of the state would be served just as well with the trial judge making the decision to close or not on a case-by-case basis. While he agreed that most judges would do the right thing, "the victims and their families are entitled to assurance of such protection." And he expressed concern that newspaper and television "reports of a minor victim's testimony may very well be … [a deterrent] from reporting a crime on the belief that public testimony will be required."

Obscenity.

> Apart from the initial formulation in the Roth case, no majority of the Court has at any given time been able to agree on a standard to determine what constitutes obscene, pornographic material subject to regulation under the States' police power.[47]

With those words, the Chief Justice began a search for a standard of judging obscenity that would be acceptable to a majority of the justices. Burger started by acknowledging that the First Amendment did not protect obscene material. This led him to conclude "[t]hat basic guidelines for the trier of fact must be: (a) whether 'the average person, applying contemporary community standards' would find that the work, taken as a whole, appeals to prurient interest…; (b) whether the work depicts or describes, in a patently offensive way, sexual conduct specifically defined by the applicable state law; and (c) whether the work, taken as a whole, lacks serious literary, artistic, political, or scientific value."

In order to assist the states in defining what was "patently offensive,"

Burger suggested the following: "(a) Patently offensive representations or descriptions of ultimate sexual acts, normal or perverted, actual or simulated. (b) Patently offensive representations or descriptions of masturbation, excretory functions, lewd exhibition of the genitals."

By states using the above standard and describing the material prohibited as suggested, the Chief Justice concluded that only those dealing in "'hard core' sexual conduct" would be subject to prosecution.

Having developed this new standard for obscenity, the Court reversed and remanded five other cases to be reevaluated in view of thereof.[48]

Not only was the Chief Justice willing to punish the seller or distributor of materials found obscene under the new standard, he also voted to uphold a Jacksonville, Florida, ordinance that punished the exhibition of "any motion picture ... in which the human male or female bare buttocks, human female bare breasts or human pubic areas ... [are] visible from any public street or public place."[49]

The case arose when Richard Erznoznik, the manager of a drive-in theater whose screen was visible beyond the confines of the theater, was arrested for violating the ordinance. With the consent of the city prosecutor, Erznoznik brought an action against the city alleging that the law was unconstitutional as a violation of the First Amendment. Erznoznik lost in the trial court, and the Florida Supreme Court denied him a hearing. The United States Supreme Court reversed concluding that the ordinance was unconstitutional.

"We hold only," Justice Powell declared, "that the present ordinance does not satisfy the rigorous constitutional standards that apply when government attempts to regulate expression. Where First Amendment freedoms are at stake we have repeatedly emphasized that precision of drafting and clarity of purpose are essential. These prerequisites are absent here."

Chief Justice Burger dissented and responded. "In sum, the Jacksonville ordinance involved in this case, although no model of draftsmanship, is narrowly drawn to regulate only certain unique public exhibitions of nudity; it would be absurd to suggest that it operates to suppress expression of *ideas*."

The Pursuit of Liberty

The Right of Privacy. Chief Justice Burger joined the majority in *Roe v. Wade* to uphold the right of a woman to make the choice whether or not to bear a child. Thereafter, he generally supported state restrictions upon the exercise of that right. For example, he wrote the opinion upholding a Utah state law that required "a physician to '[n]otify, if possible,' the parents of a dependent, unmarried minor girl prior to performing an abortion on the girl."[50] The Chief Justice pointed out that giving notice provided the parents with an opportunity to provide the family doctor with relevant medical information about the minor. He therefore concluded that "the statute plainly serves important state interests, is narrowly drawn to protect those interests, and does not violate any guarantees of the Constitution."

When the Court struck down a number of provisions of Pennsylvania's abortion laws which it believed unduly restricted a woman's right to make the choice whether or not to carry the child to term, Burger dissented. Writing for the majority, Justice Blackmun declared: "Few decisions are more personal and intimate, more properly private, or more basic to individual dignity and autonomy, than a woman's decision—with the guidance of her physician and within the limits specified in *Roe*—whether to end her pregnancy. A woman's right to make that choice freely is fundamental."[51]

Burger expressed the opinion that in striking down the provisions of the law, the Court had "apparently ... passed the point at which abortion is available merely on demand. If the statute at issue here is to be invalidated, the 'demand' will not even have to be the result of informed choice." Furthermore, he declared, if "today's holding really mean[s] what ... [it] seem[s] to say, I agree we should reexamine *Roe*."

Although Burger was not on the Court at the time the *Griswold* case was decided, he halfheartedly accepted its holding that a law making the use of contraceptives or giving assistance to a user thereof a criminal offense was unconstitutional as a violation of the right of privacy. He objected, however, when the Court struck down a Massachusetts statute which provided that contraceptives could be distributed only to married persons and then only by a registered physician.[52]

Although the Court found the law to be unconstitutional as a violation of equal protection because it treated married and unmarried persons differently, Burger did not agree that it was unconstitutional under the Equal Protection Clause or any other part of the Constitution. He believed that the law was a health measure and regulated only those who were permitted to distribute contraceptives, and the fact that they could only be distributed to married persons was irrelevant. "The choice of a means of birth control, although a highly personal matter, is also a health matter in a very real sense, and I see nothing arbitrary in a requirement of medical supervision."

In addition to voting to uphold legislation restricting a woman's choice to seek an abortion, Chief Justice Burger wholeheartedly agreed with Justice White that "in constitutional terms there is no such thing as a fundamental right to commit homosexual sodomy."[53] He therefore voted to allow Georgia to apply its sodomy law to homosexual activities. For the Chief Justice, society's treatment of homosexuals throughout history was a sufficient reason for not granting them a right of privacy. "Decisions of individuals relating to homosexual conduct have been subject to state intervention throughout the history of Western civilization. Condemnation of those practices is firmly rooted in Judeao-Christian moral and ethical standards. Homosexual sodomy was a capital crime under Roman law."

Unwed fathers, like homosexuals, did not receive much empathy from Burger. Such was the case of Peter Stanley.

> Joan Stanley lived with Peter Stanley intermittently for 18 years, during which time they had three children. When Joan Stanley died, Peter Stanley lost not only her but also his children. Under Illinois law, the children of unwed fathers become wards of the State upon the death of the mother.[54]

Stanley appealed the ruling making the children wards of the state, but, even though there was no showing that Stanley was an unfit parent, the Illinois Supreme Court upheld the lower court's decision. The United States Supreme Court reversed, finding that Stanley had parental rights in his children, and that he was entitled to a hearing on his fitness as a parent before the children could be taken from him.

"The private interest here, that of a man in the children he has sired and raised," Justice White asserted, "undeniably warrants deference and, absent a powerful countervailing interest, protection."

The only issue that Burger saw in the case was whether Stanley was being denied equal protection by not receiving a hearing on his fitness to be a parent, when other parents were given such a hearing. On that issue, Burger pointed out that Stanley could have been identified as the father of the children by marrying the mother, or by a paternity suit against him to establish parenthood. This led the Chief Justice to conclude that there was no "ground for holding that Illinois' statutory definition of 'parents' on its face violated the Equal Protection Clause; I see no ground for holding that any constitutional right of Stanley has been denied in the application of that statutory definition in the case at bar."

Equal Protection of the Law

Blacks on Juries. "Today the Court sets aside the peremptory challenge, a procedure which has been part of the common law for many centuries and part of our jury system for nearly 200 years."[55] With those words, the Chief Justice dissented when the Court set aside the conviction of a black man who had been convicted by a white jury after the prosecutor had used peremptory challenges to strike all blacks on the venire.

In this case, after an extensive examination of prior cases, Justice Powell wrote for the majority that:

> Although a prosecutor ordinarily is entitled to exercise permitted peremptory challenges 'for any reason at all, as long as that reason is related to his view concerning the outcome' of the case to be tried, ... the Equal Protection Clause forbids the prosecutor to challenge potential jurors solely on account of their race or on the assumption that black jurors as a group will be unable impartially to consider the State's case against a black defendant.

The Chief Justice criticizes the majority for departing from the Court's decision in *Swain v. Alabama*,[56] a 1965 case wherein the Court affirmed the defendant's conviction because there was no proof that the prosecution was solely responsible for the fact that no black person had served on the jury. "Today," he asserted, "we mark the return of racial differentiation as the Court accepts a positive evil for a perceived one. Prosecutors and defense attorneys alike will build records in support of their claims that peremptory challenges have been exercised in a racially discriminatory fashion by asking jurors to state their racial background and national origin for the record, despite the fact that 'such questions may be offensive to some jurors and thus are not ordinarily asked on voir dire.'"[57]

Integration of Public Schools.

> The objective today remains to eliminate from the public schools all vestiges of state-imposed segregation. Segregation was the evil struck down by *Brown I* as contrary to the equal protection guarantees of the Constitution. That was the violation sought to be corrected by the remedial measures of *Brown II*. That was the basis for the holding in *Green* that school authorities are "clearly charged with the affirmative duty to take whatever steps might be necessary to convert to a unitary system in which racial discrimination would be eliminated root and branch."[58]

The Chief Justice wrote those words in a case in which a unanimous Court upheld a desegregation plan approved by Federal District Judge James B. McMillan, Charlotte, North Carolina. On the same day, Burger wrote the Court's unanimous opinions in three other cases upholding desegregation of public schools.[59]

In one of these cases, the Court struck down a North Carolina statute that prohibited bussing of children for the purpose of integrating schools. "But more important," the Chief Justice declared, "the statute exploits an apparently neutral form to control assignment plans by directing that they be 'color blind;' that requirement, against the background of segregation, would render illusory the promise of *Brown v. Board of Education*...."[60]

Chief Justice Burger also wrote the opinion striking down a Mississippi law under which the state purchased and loaned textbooks to students attending private schools, most of which were all-white. A Federal District Court had upheld the law being of the opinion that its purpose was to provide better education for students. Burger pointed out, however, that "the constitutional infirmity of the Mississippi textbook program is that it significantly aids the organization and continuation of a separate system of private schools which, under the District Court holding, may discriminate if they so desire."[61]

Miscellaneous Racial Discrimination Cases. Jackson, Mississippi, closed its swimming pools after being ordered by District Judge Sidney C. Mize to operate them on an integrated basis. Thereafter, Hazel Palmer and others brought an action seeking to have the pools opened. In support of its decision to close the pools, the city argued that it could not operate them economically on an integrated basis. The courts, including the Supreme Court, therefore sustained the city's decision to close the pools.[62]

In a concurring opinion, Burger supported that decision. For him, the issue in this case was nothing more than whether a public entity can close a public facility which it has previously opened, whether that be a swimming pool, golf course or tennis court. "We would do grave disservice," he said, "both to elected officials and to the public, were we to require that every decision of local governments to terminate a desirable service be subjected to a microscopic scrutiny for forbidden motives rendering the decision unconstitutional."

The case of *Palmore v. Sidoti*[63] presented the Court with an unusual discrimination case. Linda Sidoti, a white woman, was given custody of her three-year-old daughter Melanie, when she and the girl's father, Anthony J. Sidoti, were divorced. Subsequently, Linda Sidoti lived with and later married Clarence Palmore, Jr., a black. These events caused Anthony Sidoti to file a petition for custody of Melanie. After hearing the evidence and being of the opinion that it was in Melanie's best interests, the judge gave custody of Melanie to Anthony. He explained his decision: "This Court feels that despite the strides that have been made in bettering relations between the races in this country, it is inevitable that Melanie will, if allowed to remain in her present situation and attains [*sic*] school age and thus more vulnerable [*sic*] to peer pressures, suffer from the social stigmatization that is sure to come." The Florida Supreme Court affirmed, but a unanimous United States Supreme Court reversed, with the Chief Justice writing the opinion.

Burger acknowledged that a child living with a racially different stepfather "may be subject to a variety of pressures and stresses not present if the child were living with parents of the same racial or ethnic origin." But, he concluded: "The effects of racial prejudice, however real, cannot justify a racial classification removing an infant child from the custody of its natural mother found to be an appropriate person to have such custody."

Gender Discrimination. When Sally Reed filed a petition in the Ada County, Idaho, Probate Court to be appointed administratrix of her son's estate, Cecil Reed, the father, also filed a petition seeking his appointment as administrator. Under Idaho law, the court was required to appoint the male, when two persons male and female, were seeking appointment as representative of an estate. In compliance with the law, the court appointed Cecil Reed as the administrator and Sally Reed appealed that decision. The Supreme Court of Idaho upheld Cecil Reed's appointment, noting that the purpose of the law "was to eliminate one area of controversy when two or more persons, equally entitled ... [under the law to] seek letters of administration."[64]

The United States Supreme Court unanimously disagreed. "To give a mandatory preference to members of either sex over members of the other," the Chief Justice wrote, "merely to accomplish the elimination of hearings on the merits, is to make the very kind of arbitrary legislative choice forbidden by the Equal Protection Clause of the Fourteenth Amendment...."

That females could buy beer at age 18 while males had to wait until they were 21, was not, insofar as Burger was concerned, a violation of equal protection. Curtis Craig and Mark Walker brought an action seeking a declaration that the Oklahoma law which permitted that kind of discrimination was unconstitutional. The District Court upheld the law, but in an opinion written by Justice Brennan, the Supreme Court reversed. Oklahoma sought to justify the different treatment of males and females by offering statistics that indicated only .18 percent of females were arrested for driving under the influence as compared to two percent of males. Justice Brennan responded: "While such a disparity is not trivial in a statistical sense, it hardly can form the basis for employment of a gender line as a classifying device."[65] Particularly "when it is further recognized that Oklahoma's statute prohibits only the selling of 3.2% beer to young males and not their drinking the beverage once acquired (even after purchase by their 18–20 year-old female companions), the relationship between gender and traffic safety become far too tenuous to satisfy ... [the constitutional] requirement that the gender-based difference be substantially related to achievement of the statutory objective."

Chief Justice Burger dissented. He disagreed with the majority's conclusion that "classifications by gender must serve important governmental objectives and must be substantially related to achievement of those objectives." "Though today's decision," he argued, "does not go so far as to make gender-based classifications 'suspect,' it makes gender a disfavored classification." And he could find no support in the Equal Protection Clause for doing that. "I see no basis for striking down the statute as violative of the Constitution simply because we find it unwise, unneeded, or possibly even a bit foolish."

Joe Hogan, a male nurse, did not receive support from the Chief Justice when he attempted to enroll in the School of Nursing at the Mississippi University for Women. Although Hogan met all entrance requirements, he was denied admission because he was a male. Hogan sought an injunction from the Federal Court to force his admission to the nursing program, but Judge L. T. Senter, Jr., refused to issue one. The Court of Appeals reversed and ordered the University to admit Hogan, and the Supreme Court affirmed.

Justice Powell, in an opinion in which Burger joined, dissented. After reviewing single-sex education in the United States, Powell points out that "the practice of voluntarily chosen single-sex education is an honored tradition in our country, even if it now rarely exists in state colleges and universities. Mississippi's accommodation of such student choices is legitimate because it is completely consensual and is important because it permits students to decide for themselves the type of college education they think will benefit them most. Finally, Mississippi's policy is substantially related to its long respected objective."[66] And he concluded: "This simply is not a sex discrimination case. The Equal Protection Clause was never intended to be applied to this kind of case."

For Illegitimate Children. In 1971, Burger joined the majority in upholding a Louisiana law which prohibited illegitimate children from inheriting from their father.[67]

The Court had another opportunity to examine inheritance rights of illegitimate children in *Trimble v. Gordon*[68] and reached the opposite conclusion. That case concerned the denial of inheritance rights to Deta Mona Trimble, the illegitimate child of Sherman Gordon and Jessie Trimble. Under Illinois law, illegitimate children could inherit only from their mothers. Upon the death of Sherman Gordon, therefore, the Illinois courts upheld the denial of inheritance to Deta Mona. A majority of the justices of the Supreme Court reversed.

In support of its statute, Illinois argued that whether Deta Mona was to share in her father's estate was in the hands of her father because he could have written a will and included her as a beneficiary. In response the majority declared: "By focusing on the steps that an intestate might have taken to assure some inheritance for his illegitimate children, the analysis loses sight of the essential question: the constitutionality of discrimination against illegitimates in a state succession law."

After discussing the rights of illegitimate children, Justice Powell for the majority tried to distinguish Deta Mona's situation from the prior case, but finally concluded: "To the extent that our analysis in this case differs from that in ... [the Vincent case] the more recent analysis controls."

The Chief Justice dissented being of the opinion that the prior case had been correctly decided and controlled Deta Mona's case.

The case of Robert Lalli, the illegitimate son of Mario and Rosmond Lalli, brought the issue back to the Court again. Upon the death of his father, Robert's claim to inheritance rights was denied because under New York law an illegitimate child could inherit only if a court "has during the lifetime of the father, made an order of filiation declaring paternity in a proceeding instituted during the pregnancy of the mother or within two years from the birth of the child."[69]

Even though Robert Lalli produced a notarized document wherein Mario acknowledged Robert as his son, and affidavits made by friends to the effect that Mario had openly recognized Robert, the New York courts denied inheritance to Robert. A majority of the Supreme Court, including Burger, affirmed.

Writing for himself, the Chief Justice and Justice Stewart, Justice Powell expressed the opinion that the New York law would prevent "[f]raudulent assertions of paternity" after the death of a putative father. Justices Brennan, White, Marshall and Stevens would have followed the *Trimble* case, and struck down the New York law. "The present case," Justice Brennan declared, "illustrates the injustice of the departure from *Trimble* worked by today's decision sustaining the New York rule. All interested parties concede that Robert Lalli is the son of Mario Lalli. Mario Lalli supported Robert during his son's youth. Mario Lalli formally acknowledged Robert Lalli as his son. ... Yet, for want of a judicial order of filiation entered during Mario's lifetime, Robert Lalli is denied his intestate share of his father's estate."

Although voting consistently to deny inheritance rights to illegitimate children, the Chief Justice wrote an opinion upholding disability insurance benefits to the illegitimate children of a disabled worker. Ramon Jimenez became entitled to disability benefits in October 1963. Thereafter, while Jimenez was living with Elizabeth Hernandez, two children were born to the couple. "These children have lived in Illinois with ... [Jimenez] all their lives; he has formally acknowledged them to be his children, has supported and cared for them since their birth, and has been their sole caretaker since their mother left the household in late 1968."[70] However, because the children were illegitimate, and born after Jimenez became disabled, they were not entitled to benefits under the Social Security Act. In concluding that the denial of benefits to these children violated equal protection, the Chief Justice quoted from a prior case wherein the Court struck down a law prohibiting the payment of worker's compensation benefits to illegitimate children upon the death of their father.

> "The status of illegitimacy has expressed through the ages society's condemnation of irresponsible liaisons beyond the bonds of marriage. But visiting this condemnation on the head of an infant is illogical and unjust."

For Aliens. In *In re Griffiths,*[71] the Court examined the case of Fre Le Poole Griffiths, a citizen of the Netherlands, who applied for admission to the bar of Connecticut. Griffiths had met all qualifications but was refused admission because under Connecticut's rules only citizens of the United States were entitled to practice law in that state. The Supreme Court reversed, holding "that the rule unconstitutionally discriminates against resident aliens."

Commenting upon the place of aliens in our society, Justice Powell declared for the majority: "Resident aliens, like citizens, pay taxes, support the economy, serve in the Armed Forces, and contribute in myriad other ways to our society. It is appropriate that a State bear a heavy burden when it deprives them of employment opportunities."

In this case, Connecticut argued that "the maxim that a lawyer is an 'officer of the court' is given concrete meaning by a statute which makes every lawyer a 'commissioner of the Superior Court.'" The majority was not impressed. It could find nothing that a "commissioner of the Superior Court" did, that needed to be done only by citizens.

In dissent, Burger noted that "the question for the Court is not what is enlightened or sound *policy* but rather what the Constitution and its Amendments provide; I am unable to accord to the Fourteenth Amendment the expansive reading the Court gives it."

After reviewing the role lawyers have played in our history, the Chief Justice concluded that there "is a reasonable, rational basis for a State to conclude that persons owing first loyalty to this country will grasp these traditions and apply our concepts more than those who seek the benefits of American citizenship while declining to accept the burdens of citizenship of this country."

When Jean-Marie Mauclet was denied student tuition assistance by New York State because he was a French citizen, Burger voted to uphold the state's decision. A majority of the Court disagreed and held the law unconstitutional as a violation of equal protection.[72]

In support of its law, New York offered two reasons for excluding aliens from its assistance program: "First, the section is said to offer an incentive for aliens to become naturalized. Second, the restriction on assistance to only those who are or will become eligible to vote is tailored to the purpose of the assistance program, namely, the enhancement of the educational level of the electorate."

That did not satisfy the majority. "Resident aliens," Justice Harry Blackmun pointed out, "are obligated to pay their full share of the taxes that support the assistance programs. There thus is no real unfairness in allowing resident aliens an equal right to participate in programs to which they contribute on an equal basis."

But the Chief Justice saw the case differently. He believed that a state was "free to exercise its largesse in any reasonable manner." And he believed it was entirely reasonable for New York to exclude aliens. "Resident individuals," he declared, "who are citizens, or who declare themselves committed to the idea of becoming American citizens, are more likely to remain in the State of New York after their graduation than are aliens whose ties to their country of origin are so strong that they decline to sever them in order to secure these valuable benefits."

When Edmund Foley, an alien, was prevented from taking the examination to become a New York State Trooper, Burger was able to garner a majority to uphold that decision. He acknowledged that under the Court's prior decisions relating to aliens although they have "the right to education and public welfare, along with the ability to earn a livelihood and engage in licensed professions, the right to govern is reserved to citizens."[73]

The Chief Justice pointed out: "A discussion of the police function is essentially a description of one of the basic functions of government, especially in a complex modern society where police presence is pervasive. The police function fulfills a most fundamental obligation of government to its constituency. Police officers in the ranks do not formulate policy, *per se*, but they are clothed with authority to exercise an almost infinite variety of discretionary powers."

This led the Chief Justice to conclude: "A State may, therefore, consonant with the Constitution, confine the performance of this important public responsibility to citizens of the United States."

Justice John Paul Stevens agreed that "our society is governed by its citizens." He pointed out, however that "it is a government of and for all persons subject to its jurisdiction, and the Constitution commands their equal treatment."

For Voters. Chief Justice Burger voted to uphold a Texas system for voting on bond issues whereby "all persons owning taxable property rendered for taxation voted in one box, and all other registered voters cast their ballots in a separate box."[74] A bond issue would pass "only if it was approved by a majority vote both in the 'renders box' and in the aggregate of both boxes." Under this system, therefore, even if a majority of the "nonrenders" voted for a bond issue, it would not pass without a majority vote of the "renders."

In finding this scheme to be a violation of equal protection, the majority pointed out that "the Texas rendering requirement erects a classification that impermissibly disfranchises persons otherwise qualified to vote, solely because they have not rendered some property for taxation."

While Burger approved disfranchising nonproperty owners from voting in bond issue elections, he believed that a state was obligated to provide some method of voting for persons in jail awaiting trial or there because of misdemeanor convictions. The Chief Justice wrote the Court's opinion holding that New York's refusal to provide a method of voting for such persons denied them equal protection of the law.[75]

The case arose when Board of Elections of Monroe County refused to make arrangements for 72 inmates of the jail to vote, either by a mobile voter registration unit, by being transported to the polls, or allowing them to vote by absentee ballot. Burger, for the majority, pointed out that the inmates were "under no legal disability impeding their legal right to register or to vote; they are simply not allowed to use the absentee ballot and are denied any alternative means of casting their vote although they are legally qualified to vote." "We have no choice, therefore," he concluded, "but to hold that ... the New York statutes deny appellants the equal protection of the laws guaranteed by the Fourteenth Amendment."

For the Poor.

Victoria Keppler has a daughter with an acute hearing deficiency. The daughter requires special instruction in a school for the deaf. The school is located in an area in which [Keppler] ... could not ordinarily afford to live. Thus, in order to make the most of her limited resources, ... [Keppler] agreed to share an apartment near the school with a woman, who like [Keppler] ... is on public assistance. Since [Keppler] ... is not related to the woman, ... [her] food stamps have been, and will continue to be cut off if they continue to live together.[76]

Under federal law, persons living in a household consisting of unrelated individuals are ineligible for food stamps. Judge Carl McGowan, in an action brought by several persons living in households similar to Keppler's, held the law to be unconstitutional as a violation of equal protection. The Supreme Court agreed, with Chief Justice Burger joining Justice Rehnquist's dissent.

"Traditional equal protection analysis," Justice Brennan, in the Court's opinion, declared, "does not require that every classification be drawn with precise 'mathematical nicety.' … But the classification here in issue is not only 'imprecise,' it is wholly without any rational basis."

Even though admitting that "the limitation will make ineligible many households which have not been formed for the purpose of collecting federal food stamps," Rehnquist and Burger were of the opinion that the program was justifiable in order to "deny food stamps to those households which may have been formed in large part to take advantage of the program." Furthermore: "The fact that the limitation will have unfortunate and perhaps unintended consequences beyond this does not make it unconstitutional."

Following Keppler's case, Congress amended the food stamp rules so that only those groups that purchase and prepare their food together were considered a family, and thus eligible for stamps. Parents, children, and siblings were assumed to be a family that prepared their food together and therefore were entitled to food stamps. However, "more distant relatives, or groups of unrelated persons who live together, as a single household [were not considered a family] unless they also customarily purchase food and prepare meals together."[77]

Several families who live together, but "buy their food and prepare their meals as separate economic units" brought actions against the Department of Agriculture asserting that the classifications made by the rules, discriminated against them and were thus unconstitutional. The Federal District Court agreed, but the Supreme Court, with Burger joining the majority, reversed.

Stevens, writing for the majority, nevertheless concluded: "Under the proper standard of review, we agree with the District Court that Congress had a rational basis both for treating parents, children, and siblings who live together as a single 'household,' and for applying a different standard in determining whether groups of more distant relatives and unrelated persons living together constitute a 'household.'"

Justices White, Brennan, and Marshall did not believe that the classification was rational. "The Government," Marshall argued, "has thus chosen to intrude into the family dining room—a place where I would have thought the right to privacy exists in its strongest form. What possible interest can the Government have in preventing members of a family from dining as they choose? It is simply none of the Government's business."

In the Criminal Justice System. "The narrow issue raised is whether an indigent may be continued in confinement beyond the maximum term specified by statute because of his failure to satisfy monetary provisions of the sentence."[78] That was the problem facing appellant Willie E. Williams who, after being convicted of petty theft, was sentenced to one year in prison, given a $500 fine and ordered to pay court costs of five dollars. Because Williams was unable to pay the fine and costs, his sentence was extended 101 days. Not being able to secure consideration from the Illinois courts, he appealed to the Supreme Court which, in an opinion written by the Chief Justice, held "that the Equal Protection Clause of the Fourteenth Amendment requires that the statutory ceiling placed on imprisonment for any substantive offense be the same for all defendants irrespective of their economic status."

While the Chief Justice supported the requirement of furnishing transcripts for indigent defendants to assist them in their appeals, he expressed concern that lawyers representing such defendants might make excessive demands for transcripts and thus "postpone the day when the appeal is finally determined."[79] He thought that lawyers who engaged in such conduct were "guilty of unprofessional conduct."

Miscellaneous Equal Protection Cases. When Robert Murgia, a Massachusetts State Police officer, was forced to retire at age 50, he brought legal action contending that the state's mandatory retirement age for police officers denied him equal protection of the law. The District Court agreed, but the Supreme Court, including the Chief Justice, did not and reversed.

The Court acknowledged that Murgia was in excellent health, that the "problems of retirement have been well documented and are beyond serious dispute,"[80] and that the state "perhaps has not chosen the best means to accomplish" its purpose, which was to assure that its officers were physically fit. Despite those findings, the Court concluded that the law was rational and therefore did not violate the Equal Protection Clause.

Justice Marshall pointed out, in dissent, that mandatory retirement of physically fit persons generally had an adverse effect upon the well-being of such persons. "Ample clinical evidence," he declared, "supports the conclusion that mandatory retirement poses a direct threat to the health and life expectancy of the retired person, and these consequences of termination for age are not disputed by ... [the state]. Thus, an older person deprived of his job by the government loses not only his right to earn a living, but, too often, his health as well, in sad contradiction of Browning's promise: 'The best is yet to be,/ The last of life for which the first was made.'"

AS A JUSTICE FOR THE GOVERNMENT

In Chief Justice Burger's opinions upholding the free exercise of religion, he indicates strong support for the Free Exercise Clause. For example, in response to Wisconsin's argument, in the *Amish* case, "that 'actions,' even though religiously grounded, are outside the protection of the First Amendment," he responded, "[b]ut to agree that religiously grounded conduct must often be subject to the broad police power of the State is not to deny that there are areas of conduct protected by the Free Exercise Clause of the First Amendment and thus beyond the power of the State to control, even under regulations of general applicability."[81] Burger, however, voted much of the time to override the claim of religious freedom.[82] For example, he did not have a great deal of empathy for conscientious objectors. When the Court held that Elliott Ashton Welsh II, was entitled to be classified as a conscientious objector even though his opposition to war was not based upon a belief in a Supreme Being, Burger joined Justice White's dissenting opinion.[83] He also voted with the majority to deny William R. Robison educational benefits under the G.I. Bill of Rights. Robison, a conscientious objector, served two years' alternative service working in a hospital. Upon completion of this service he applied for, but was denied, the educational benefits given to those who served in the Armed Forces. The Court, including Burger, upheld the government's decision, being of the opinion that: "The withholding of educational benefits involves only an incidental burden upon ... [Robison's] free exercise of religion—if, indeed any burden exists at all."[84]

In the area of freedom of speech, the Chief Justice generally voted to uphold restrictions upon pamphleteering, soliciting, picketing and parading.[85] And he did not believe that the First Amendment protected vulgar or other scurrilous language nor the misuse of the American flag as a means of making a speech. He therefore dissented when the Court struck down a Georgia statute that made it a crime to use "opprobrious words or abusive language, tending to cause a breach of the peace."[86] A majority of the justices, however, agreed with District Judge Sidney O. Smith, Jr., that "[t]he fault of the statute is that it leaves wide open the standard of responsibility, so that it is easily susceptible to improper application."

In dissenting from the decision to reverse the conviction of Harold Spence for displaying a flag on the seat of his trousers, the Chief Justice declared that "it should be left to each State and ultimately the common sense of its people to decide how the flag, as a symbol of national unity, should be protected."[87] This approach, however, leaves to the vagaries of the legislative process protection for speech and abdicates the Court's responsibility to protect freedom of speech as well as other constitutional rights.

Although Chief Justice Burger joined two cases in which the Court unanimously upheld the right of teachers to speak freely, he voted most of the time against free speech for other public employees.[88]

Burger had a very narrow view of the places where one could speak. He voted to uphold restrictions on the exercise of First Amendment rights on malls and military bases, and supported zoning restrictions for adult theaters. For him, a person's mail box was not an open forum for receipt of information other than that placed there by the mail carrier, and he voted to uphold limiting the use of teacher's mail boxes only to the teacher's bargaining unit, thus excluding a competing teachers organization from communication with teachers through their boxes. The Chief Justice also approved a ban on political advertising on the public transit system in Shaker Heights, Ohio, and dissented when the Court struck down the refusal of the municipal auditorium in Chattanooga, Tennessee, to permit the showing of the musical production "Hair."[89]

Except for voting most of the time to uphold freedom of association rights for new political parties and voters, Chief Justice Burger was not a strong supporter of freedom of association. He approved of Richard Elrod discharging John Burns and other deputies from the Cook County Sheriff's office because they were not members of the Democratic Party, but he voted to uphold the associational rights of Alan Tabakman and Aaron Finkel when they were discharged from their positions as Assistant Public Defenders.[90]

The Chief Justice approved bar association rules requiring applicants to disclose their past affiliation, if any, with the Communist Party or any other organization that advocates the overthrow of the government.[91] And he wrote the majority opinion upholding the discharge of Lucretia Richardson as a research sociologist from the Boston State Hospital because she believed that the oath required by the state was unconstitutional. The state oath required each employee to swear that he or she would "oppose the overthrow of the government of the United States ... by force, violence, or by any illegal or unconstitutional method."[92] A three judge Federal District Court had held the oath to be "'fatally vague and unspecific,' and therefore a violation of First Amendment rights."

The Chief Justice was a strong advocate of courts being open, not only to the public but also to the press. He also believed that the Speech Clause and the Press Clause of the First Amendment gave the same rights to those "who seek to disseminate ideas by way of a newspaper and those who give lectures or speeches."[93] He was willing, however, to sometimes permit restrictions upon the press to publish. For example, he voted to continue the restraint on the publication of the *Pentagon Papers*. He also joined an opinion in which Justice Stewart wrote that "newsmen have no constitutional right of access to prisons or their inmates beyond that afforded the general public."[94]

Burger wrote the new standard for judging what is and what is not obscene and voted most of the time to prevent or punish the distribution of such material.[95]

The Court's use of the Due Process Clause to "create" new constitutional rights, such as the right of privacy, did not gain favor with the Chief Justice. When the Court upheld the right of individuals, married or single to use contraceptives, Burger protested. He believed that this decision "seriously invade[d] the constitutional prerogatives of the States and regrettably hark[s] back to the heyday of substantive due process."[96]

Despite his condemnation of the Court for "creating" new rights, a majority of the justices continued to do so, and Burger continued to dissent. Not only did he vote, most of the time, against the privacy right of a woman to make the choice whether or not to bear a child, he also dissented when the Court expanded the right of privacy to include family living arrangements. For example, when a majority of the justices held that the right of privacy protected Inez Moore's extended family which included two grandchildren who were cousins, although that violated an East Cleveland, Ohio ordinance, Burger dissented. And when the Court held that forcing teachers Jo Carol LaFleur and Ann Elizabeth Nelson to take pregnancy leave five months before the birth of their children violated their right of privacy, the Chief Justice joined Justice William Rehnquist's dissenting opinion. He also joined Rehnquist's dissent when the Court held that a state could not terminate parents' right to their children unless it could prove with "clear and convincing" evidence that the parents were unfit. Rehnquist and Burger thought that this decision was an intrusion into state control of domestic relations and would have allowed parental rights to be terminated "by a fair preponderance of the evidence."[97]

In the *Sally Reed* case, the Chief Justice wrote: "By providing dissimilar treatment for men and women who are thus similarly situated, the challenged section violates the Equal Protection Clause."[98] Burger did not apply that principle, however, in most of the gender discrimination cases in which he participated thereafter. He voted to uphold Navy rules that required mandatory discharge of Navy Officer Robert C. Ballard because he had not been promoted after nine years of service, while allowing female officers to remain in the Navy for 13 years before being discharged. And when the Court upheld Leon Goldfarb's right to social security survivor's benefits after the death of his wife, Burger dissented. He did not believe that denying benefits to a widower but granting them to a widow was a denial of equal protection even though the effect of the law was to discriminate against females because their surviving spouses received less protection that surviving spouses of males. Nor was it a denial of equal protection to prevent Lemuel Parham from suing for the wrongful death of his illegitimate child, although the child's mother, Cassandra Moreen, was permitted by law to bring such an action.[99]

Burger voted much of the time to deny equal protection to illegitimate children. He voted against inheritance rights for them, and when Ramon Fiallo, a citizen, wanted to have his father, an alien, immigrate to the United States from the Dominican Republic, Burger joined the Court in upholding the immigration authorities' decision not to grant a visa to the father because Ramon was an illegitimate son.[100]

Aliens fared no better from the Chief Justice. He did not believe that it was a denial of equal protection to prevent Fre Le Poole Griffiths from becoming a Connecticut lawyer, for Edmund Foley from becoming a New York state patrolman, for Susan Norwick from becoming a teacher in New York, or for

Jose Chavez-Salido from becoming a Los Angeles County probation officer because all of them were aliens. He did, however, believe that it would be a denial of equal protection not to let Margarita Vargas, an alien, become a notary public in Texas.[101]

Because Tillye Cornman and eleven others lived in a federal enclave they were denied the right to vote in Maryland. When a Federal District Court held that it was a denial of equal protection to prevent Cornman and the others from voting in Maryland elections, the Supreme Court, with Burger participating, unanimously affirmed.[102] Other voters, especially property owners, were not accorded the same privilege by the Chief Justice.[103]

Although Burger voted most of the time to uphold government regulations that discriminated against the poor,[104] he believed that it would be a denial of due process for the state not to pay for blood tests for a defendant in a paternity action who did not have funds to pay for such tests. "We hold," he asserted, "that, in these specific circumstances, the application of [Connecticut's law] ... to deny appellant grouping tests because of his lack of financial resources violated the due process guarantee of the Fourteenth Amendment."[105]

The Chief Justice's willingness to vote for and uphold government infringement upon constitutional rights requires that he be included as a *Justice for the Government.*

7

CHIEF JUSTICE
WILLIAM H. REHNQUIST

PERSONAL LIFE

Growing Up

William H. Rehnquist "and his sister, Jean, were raised in Shorewood, Wis., a peaceful, upscale well-to-do Milwaukee suburb. In contrast to the mansions bordering Lake Michigan, the William B. Rehnquists lived in a modest tan brick house. His father, a first-generation American born of Swedish parents, was a wholesale paper salesman who had not attended college. His mother, Margery, a housewife and civic activist, was proud of her University of Wisconsin degree and her fluency in five foreign languages. She earned money as a freelance translator for local companies."[1]

Rehnquist was born October 1, 1924 and attended Shorewood public schools. While feature editor of the high school paper he editorialized against "'self-styled news 'interpreters' [who] have been doing a little too much spouting of their own. There is no fault to be found with straight news broadcasts; they perform a valuable public service. But thorns to the 'commentators,' the overly dramatic Gabriel Heater, the pompous H. V. Kaltenborn, and Walter Winchell with his corps of tattlers."

The views of the Republican Party, especially those of Republicans Alf Landon, Wendell Wilkie, Herbert Hoover and Robert A. Taft, were topics of discussion in the Rehnquist household.

> When Rehnquist was asked (during the Democratic administration of Franklin D. Roosevelt) by his elementary teacher about his career plans, he replied, "I'm going to change the government."[2]

At the age of 17, Rehnquist served as a civil-defense officer for his neighborhood.

CHIEF JUSTICE WILLIAM H. REHNQUIST (collection of the Supreme Court of the United States).

College, the Army Air Force, and Law School

Having won a scholarship at Kenyon College in Ohio, Rehnquist attended one year when he joined the Army Air Force in 1943. He became a weather observer and was sent to North Africa, where he served until 1946.

When he returned from Africa, he knew he didn't want to suffer through any more frigid winters. "I wanted to find someplace like North Africa to go to school," he recalls. He used his G.I. Bill benefits to attend Stanford, in Palo Alto, Calif., and when they ended, he ran the breakfast program in the university dining hall. "I had so many other part-time jobs, I can't remember them all."[3]

Before entering law school, Rehnquist obtained master's degrees from Stanford and Harvard. He entered Stanford Law School in the fall of 1949 and graduated first in his class in 1952. Rehnquist was an editor of the law review, and "won such praise from his instructors as 'nothing short of brilliant' and 'the outstanding student of his law school generation.'"[4] Justice Sandra Day O'Connor, who was in the same class, graduated third.

Clerk for Justice Robert H. Jackson

Upon graduating from law school, Rehnquist obtained a clerkship in the office of Justice Robert H. Jackson for the 1952 term of the United States Supreme Court.

> During that term, while the issues of *Brown v. Board of Education* ... [the school desegregation case] were under consideration, a memorandum bearing Rehnquist's initials was written for Justice Jackson and stated:
> *I realize that it is an unpopular and unhumanitarian position, for which I have been excoriated by "liberal" colleagues, but I think* Plessy v. Ferguson [*the "separate but equal" decision*] *was right and should be reaffirmed....*

Justice Jackson did not heed the advice of his clerk. He joined a unanimous Court in declaring that segregation in public schools violated the Equal Protection Clause of the Fourteenth Amendment.

Among the positive things that happened to Rehnquist during his clerkship was meeting Natalie (Nan) Cornell, who worked for the Central Intelligence Agency and who, for weeks after their meeting, refused to tell him where she worked. They were married in August 1953. Three children were born to the marriage, James, Janet and Nancy.

The Practice of Law

It is reported that after the clerkship had ended, Rehnquist tossed a coin to see whether he should start the practice of law in Albuquerque (tails) or Phoenix (heads). When the coin came up heads Rehnquist and Nan headed west to Phoenix, where he joined the law firm of Evans, Kitchel and Jenckes. He stayed with the firm until 1956, when he formed a partnership with Keith W. Ragan. That partnership continued for about a year, when Rehnquist joined the firm of Cunningham, Carson, and Messenger. During this period he served as a special Arizona state prosecutor, bringing charges against state officials charged with state highway fraud. In 1960, he formed a partnership with James Powers, a former trial lawyer with the Internal Revenue Service.

A Conservative Is Born

> Around the same time Rehnquist started to become active in the ultraconservative wing of the Arizona Republican party that was then coming to power. "Unlike a lot of Arizona politicians who tried to follow the public thought, Rehnquist really is a deep philosophical conservative," a lawyer who knew him in Phoenix told Martin Waldron of the *New York Times....* "He apparently just sat down and thought it out and decided intellectually that he is against anything liberal."[5]

Rehnquist displayed his conservatism in several ways. For example, "In a September [1957] speech to the Maricopa County Young Republican League he called Justices Earl Warren, William O. Douglas, and Hugo L. Black the 'left-wing philosophers' of the Supreme Court and accused them of 'making the Constitution say what they wanted it to say.'" He also spoke out against a proposed Phoenix open-housing ordinance and a plan for the integration of Phoenix high schools.

Among those with whom he became associated politically were Arizona senator Barry Goldwater and Richard G. Kleindienst, chairman of the state Republican Party.

Assistant Attorney General

In 1968, at the request of Richard Kleindienst, then Deputy Attorney General in President Richard Nixon's administration, Rehnquist accepted the position of Assistant Attorney General in charge of the Office of Legal Counsel in Washington, D.C.

> The head of the Office of Legal Counsel interprets the Constitution and government statutes for the President and the Attorney General and gives legal advice to all departments of the government. Until Rehnquist took over the post, it had been a relatively obscure research job, but in his two and a half years in the Justice Department the former Arizona lawyer became a familiar Capitol Hill advocate of controversial Nixon administration policies, often serving as the administration's lightning rod for liberal and Democratic attacks.[6]

As President Nixon's chief legal officer, Rehnquist "vigorously supported the Nixon administration's tough law-and-order package, including 'no-knock' entries, pretrial detention, wiretapping, and electronic surveillance and often said that the Supreme Court in his view had gone too far in its concern for the rights of the accused."

Nomination to the Supreme Court

In 1972, with the resignations of Justices Hugo L. Black and John M. Harlan, President Richard Nixon had two positions to fill on the Supreme Court. He then appointed Virginia lawyer Lewis F. Powell, Jr., and William H. Rehnquist. In discussing his nominees, President Nixon said that both of them shared his judicial philosophy. He then described that philosophy: "As a judicial conservative I believe that some Court decisions have gone too far in the past in weakening the peace forces as against the criminal forces in our society. The peace forces must not be denied the legal tools they need to protect the innocent from criminal elements."[7]

Among those opposing Rehnquist's nomination were the Arizona chapter of the NAACP and the American Civil Liberties Union, which took a stand opposing a nominee for the first time in 52 years.[8] But Rehnquist also had supporters in the press, including the *National Review* and columnists Joseph Kraft and Robert Bartley.[9]

During his confirmation hearing, Rehnquist denied that he supported school segregation and explained that the memorandum he had written to Justice Jackson regarding the concept of "separate but equal" contained a summary of the views Jackson expressed at the conference of the justices. And as for as his opposition to the proposed Phoenix "open housing ordinance," the nominee said that the ordinance has worked well. And he continued, "I think I have come to realize since, more than I did at the time, the strong concern that minorities have for the recognition of these rights."[10]

Rehnquist's nomination was approved by the Senate Judiciary Committee, 12 to 4, and by the Senate, 68 to 26, on December 10, 1971.

A longtime friend of Rehnquist's said of him: "There is no question in my mind that he's a top-notch lawyer, both in his writing ability and his legal acumen. Plus, he's a hell of a nice guy who never blows up."[11]

When Rehnquist joined the Court, Warren E. Burger was Chief Justice. Other members of the Court were Justices William O. Douglas, William J. Brennan, Jr., Potter Stewart, Byron R. White, Thurgood Marshall, Harry Blackmun and Lewis F. Powell, Jr. Rehnquist served as an Associate Justice for fourteen years.

Nomination as Chief Justice of the United States

When Warren E. Burger resigned as Chief Justice in 1986, President Ronald Reagan nominated Justice Rehnquist to fill the vacancy. Many of the same questions that were raised in 1972 at Rehnquist's nomination for associate justice surfaced again. He was affirmed, however, by a Senate vote of 65 to 33.

When Justice Rehnquist took the oath of office as Chief Justice on September 26, 1986, the other members of the Court were Justices William J. Brennan, Jr., Byron R. White, Thurgood Marshall, Harry Blackmun, Lewis

F. Powell, Jr., John Paul Stevens, and Sandra Day O'Connor. Antonin Scalia was nominated by President Reagan to fill the seat vacated by the new Chief Justice. He, also, took the oath of office on September 26, 1986.

AS ASSOCIATE JUSTICE (1972–1986) AND CHIEF JUSTICE (1986–)

The Free Exercise of Religion

Fred A. Cruz, a prisoner in Texas, sued Dr. George J. Beto, Director of the Texas Department of Corrections, alleging that prison officials "were obstructing ... [his] efforts to adhere to the tenets of his religious faith, Buddhism, and were refusing to permit ... [him] and other imprisoned Buddhists to use the prison chapel and similar facilities for the practice of Buddhism, even though the prison authorities were actively encouraging the observance of Jewish, Roman Catholic, and Protestant rituals and practices among the prison population...."[12] Federal District Judge Ben C. Connally dismissed the case and the Court of Appeals affirmed, but the Supreme Court reversed in a *Per Curiam* decision.[13] Justice Rehnquist was the only dissenter.

The Court pointed out that "Federal courts sit not to supervise prisons but to enforce the constitutional rights of all 'persons,' including prisoners," and that "[i]f Cruz was a Buddhist and if he was denied a reasonable opportunity of pursuing his faith comparable to the opportunity afforded fellow prisoners who adhere to conventional religious precepts, then there was palpable discrimination by the State against the Buddhist religion, established 600 B. C., long before the Christian era. The First Amendment ... prohibits government from making a law 'prohibiting the free exercise' of religion."

Justice Rehnquist argued that because Cruz was in prison his ability to exercise his First Amendment rights was limited. "By reason of his status, petitioner is obviously limited in the extent to which he may *practice* his religion. He is assuredly not free to attend the church of his choice outside the prison walls. But the fact that the Texas prison system offers no Buddhist services at this particular prison does not, under the circumstances pleaded in his complaint, demonstrate that his religious freedom is being impaired."

The Justice also dissented when the Court upheld the right of George and Maxine Maynard not to have to display the New Hampshire State motto, "Live Free or Die," printed on the state's auto licenses. He did not believe that New Hampshire was forcing the Maynards "to affirm or reject that motto; they are simply required by the State ... to carry a state auto license tag for identification and registration purposes."[14]

The religious views of S. Simcha Goldman, Jr., an ordained rabbi and orthodox Jew, did not receive any greater consideration from Justice Rehnquist than did Fred Cruz or George and Maxine Maynard. Goldman, a Captain in the Air Force, was ordered not to wear a yarmulke while in uniform and on duty. From his early youth, Goldman had been taught that wearing of a yarmulke to keep one's head covered at all times was part of Jewish heritage.

When Goldman was ordered not to wear the yarmulke, he petitioned the Federal District Court for an injunction against the Air Force that would prevent them from disciplining him for wearing it. Judge Aubrey E. Robinson, Jr., granted the injunction, and concluded: "Should this Court deny injunctive relief, Plaintiff would in all likelihood suffer irreparable harm. He would be faced with a dubious choice indeed; complying to the dictates of his religion or facing the possibility of imminent court-martial. Because of the seriousness of the First Amendment allegations, and resulting pressure on Plaintiff to abandon his religious observances injunctive relief is appropriate."[15] The Court of Appeals and the Supreme Court disagreed and reversed, with Justice Rehnquist writing the Supreme Court's opinion.

"Our review of military regulations challenged on First Amendment grounds," the Justice wrote, "is far more deferential than constitutional review of similar laws or regulations designed for civilian society."[16]

Rehnquist then turned to the Air Force's justification for the order against wearing the yarmulke. "Uniforms encourage a sense of hierarchical unity," he noted, "by tending to eliminate outward individual distinctions except for those of rank. The Air Force considers them as vital during peacetime as during war because its personnel must be ready to provide an effective defense on a moment's notice; the necessary habits of discipline and unity must be developed in advance of trouble."

In response to Goldman's free exercise rights, the Justice recognized that wearing the yarmulke was a "silent devotion, akin to prayer" but concluded that it simply made "military life ... more objectionable for petitioner and probably others."

Freedom of Speech

Pamphleteering and Soliciting. Justice Rehnquist dissented when the Court held unconstitutional an ordinance of the Village of Schaumberg which "prohibited the solicitation of contributions by charitable organizations that do not use at least 75 percent of their receipts for 'charitable' purposes."[17]

The majority of the Court was concerned with the effect of the ordinance upon those "organizations whose primary purpose is not to provide money or services for the poor, the needy or other worthy objects of charity, but ... [for those that] gather and disseminate information about and advocate positions on matters of public concern."

In striking down the ordinance, Justice White declared: "We agree with the Court of Appeals that the 75-percent limitation is a direct and substantial limitation on protected activity that cannot be sustained unless it serves a sufficiently strong, subordinating interest that the Village is entitled to protect. We also agree that the Village's proffered justifications [that the ordinance will prevent fraud] are inadequate and that the ordinance cannot survive scrutiny under the First Amendment."

In dissent, Rehnquist wrote: "I would uphold Schaumberg's ordinance … because that ordinance, while perhaps too strict to suit some tastes, affects only door-to-door solicitation for financial contributions, leaves little or no discretion in the hands of municipal authorities to 'censor' unpopular speech, and is rationally related to the community's collective desire to bestow its largess upon organizations that are truly 'charitable.'"

Picketing and Parading. In January 1987, a civil rights demonstration took place in Forsyth County, Georgia. The march attracted approximately 20,000 demonstrators and upwards of 1,000 counterdemonstrators. More than 3,000 police officers were employed to control the crowds at a cost of nearly $670,000. The county paid only a small part of the cost, with the state paying the rest. Subsequently, the county enacted an ordinance requiring every permit applicant to pay up to $1,000 a day for a permit, and allowing the permit administrator to "adjust the amount to be paid in order to meet the expense incident to the administration of the Ordinance and to the maintenance of public order in the matter licensed."[18]

When the Nationalist Movement sought a permit to conduct a demonstration in protest of the federal holiday honoring Martin Luther King, Jr., the administrator assessed a fee of $100. No additional charges were made for anticipated law enforcement costs.

The Nationalist Movement, rather than pay the fee, sought relief from the local Federal District Court. Judge William C. O'Kelly dismissed the case; the Court of Appeals, however reinstated it, and the Supreme Court affirmed that decision.

The Nationalist Movement argued that the ordinance was "invalid because it does not prescribe adequate standards for the administrator to apply when he sets a permit fee." Justice Blackmun, for the majority, agreed. "The decision how much to charge for police protection or administrative time— or even whether to charge at all—is left to the whim of the administrator. There are no articulated standards either in the ordinance or in the county's established practice."

The Court was also concerned that persons expressing unpopular views, which the administrator thought might attract "bottle throwers," may have to pay a higher fee.

Chief Justice Rehnquist dissented, arguing that the case of *Cox v. New Hampshire*,[19] decided in 1941, required the Court to uphold this ordinance. In the *Cox* case, the Court upheld a New Hampshire statute requiring a fee of up to $300 for holding a "parade, procession or open-air public meeting."

Rehnquist could see no difference between the Forsyth County ordinance and the New Hampshire statute.

Blackmun noted, however, that the New Hampshire statute did not call "for charging a premium in the case of a controversial political message delivered before a hostile audience."[20]

It was not the payment of a fee for demonstrating that bothered the Court in *Madsen v. Women's Health Center, Inc.*[21] At issue in this case was the validity of an injunction issued by Florida Circuit Court Judge Robert B. McGregor to regulate picketing around an abortion clinic in Melbourne, Florida. Because Judge McGregor's first injunction did not curtail the demonstrations, he issued a second one which created "a 36-foot buffer zone around the clinic entrances and driveway and the private property to the north and west of the clinic ... and prohibit[ed] protesters within a 300-foot zone around the clinic from approaching patients ... who do not consent to talk; and create[d] a 300-foot buffer zone around the residences of clinic staff."

The Supreme Court held that the 36-foot buffer zone did not violate the First Amendment, but struck down a 30-foot zone as it applied to the private property north and west of the clinic, the 300-foot no-approach zone around the clinic and the 300-foot zone around the residences of the clinic staff as being too broad.

Writing for the majority, Chief Justice Rehnquist said: "The need for a complete buffer zone near the clinic entrances and driveway may be debatable, but some deference must be given to the state court's familiarity with the facts and background of the dispute between the parties...."

Addressing Judge McGregor's order prohibiting persons from approaching those individuals seeking the clinic's services within 300 feet of the clinic, the Chief Justice wrote: "The record ... does not contain sufficient justification for this broad ban on picketing; it appears that a limitation on the time, duration of picketing, and number of pickets outside a smaller zone could have accomplished the desired result."

Justice Scalia, writing for himself and Justices Kennedy and Thomas, declared: "Because I believe that the judicial creation of a 36-foot zone in which only a particular group, which had broken no law, cannot exercise its rights of speech, assembly, and association, and the judicial enactment of a noise prohibition, applicable to that group and that group alone, are profoundly at odds with our First Amendment precedents and traditions, I dissent."

Unpopular Speech. Unpopular speech was not popular with Chief Justice Rehnquist.[22] He particularly objected to giving protection to persons who used the American flag as a means of expressing an opinion. For example, he dissented when the Court struck down a Massachusetts flag desecration statute that made it a crime to treat a flag "contemptuously."[23] Valarie Goguen had been convicted of violating this statute because he had sewn a flag to the seat of his pants. A majority of the justices were of the opinion that the words "treats contemptuously" were so vague that they would not give fair notice and warning, and therefore were a denial of due process of law. Rehnquist, after commenting upon the reverence given the flag throughout our history, concluded that Goguen "was simply prohibited from impairing the physical integrity of a unique national symbol which has been given content by generations of his and our forebears, a symbol of which he had acquired a copy."

The Chief Justice would also have upheld the conviction of Harold Spence for placing a "peace symbol" on a flag and hanging it out his apartment window. Placing "any word, figure, mark, picture, design, [etc.]"[24] on a United States flag was a crime under Washington law. Spence had testified that by displaying the flag with the symbol on it he was protesting the killing of four students at Kent State University, Ohio. Because there was no evidence of adverse public reaction to Spence's flag, the state sought to justify the conviction on the ground that it had "an interest in preserving the national flag as an unalloyed symbol of our country." But the majority did not buy that argument. Spence was using the flag here to convey his feelings about the killings of the students. "[H]is message," the Court said, "was direct, likely to be understood, and within the contours of the First Amendment."

The fact that Spence was making a speech with his flag was not sufficient to protect him, insofar as Rehnquist was concerned, and he dissented. "What … [Spence] here seeks is simply license to use the flag however he pleases, so long as the activity can be tied to a concept of speech, regardless of any state interest in having the flag used only for more limited purposes. I find no reasoning in the Court's opinion which convinces me that the Constitution requires such license to be given."

Having dissented from reversal of Goguen's and Spence's conviction for their somewhat insignificant misuse of the flag, his dissent from reversal of Gregory Johnson's conviction for burning an American flag was to be expected.[25] Johnson was part of a demonstration at the 1984 Republican National Convention in Dallas, Texas. "The demonstration ended in front of the Dallas City Hall, where Johnson unfurled the American flag, doused it with kerosene, and set it on fire. While the flag burned, the protesters chanted: 'America, the red, white, and blue, we spit on you.'" There was, however, no evidence of disorderly conduct or breach of the peace by anyone watching the incident.

Not being able to sustain Johnson's conviction on the basis that he had breached the peace, Texas argued that it had the right to protect "the flag as a symbol of national unity." As it had in the *Goguen* and *Spence* cases, the majority held that while that was a valid state interest, it could not override Johnson's First Amendment right to use the flag to make a speech. Furthermore, the Court did not believe "that this one gesture of an unknown man will change our Nation's attitude towards its flag." "We can imagine no more appropriate response to burning a flag than waving one's own, no better way to counter a flag burner's message than by saluting the flag that burns, no surer means of preserving the dignity even of the flag that burned than by—as one witness did—according its remains a respectful burial."

The Chief Justice was not impressed. "For more than 200 years, the American flag has occupied a unique position as the symbol of our Nation, a uniqueness that justifies a governmental prohibition against flag burning in the way respondent Johnson did here."

For the Chief Justice, flag burning was no different than any other crime. "Surely one of the high purposes of a democratic society is to legislate against conduct that is regarded as evil and profoundly offensive to the majority of the people—whether it be murder, embezzlement, pollution, or flag burning." And he concludes: "The government may conscript men into the Armed Forces where they must fight and perhaps die for the flag, but the government may not prohibit the public burning of the banner under which they fight. I would uphold the Texas statute as applied in this case."

Captain Howard Levy's speech was very unpopular to the Army and Rehnquist as well. While serving as Chief of the Dermatological Service at Fort Jackson, South Carolina, Levy, in commenting on our involvement in the Vietnam War, said:

> The United States is wrong in being involved in the Viet Nam War. I would refuse to go to Viet Nam if ordered to do so. I don't see why any colored soldier would go to Viet Nam; they should refuse to go to Viet Nam and if sent should refuse to fight because they are discriminated against and denied their freedom in the United States, and they are sacrificed and discriminated against in Viet Nam by being given all the hazardous duty and they are suffering the majority of casualties.[26]

Levy was convicted at a court-martial for "conduct unbecoming an officer and a gentleman," and for engaging in conduct "to the prejudice of good order and discipline in the armed forces." The Supreme Court upheld the decision of the court-martial tribunal, with Justice Rehnquist writing the Court's opinion.

In response to Levy's argument that his comments were protected by the First Amendment, the Justice declared: "While the members of the military are not excluded from the protection granted by the First Amendment, the different character of the military community and of the military mission requires a different application of those protections." Furthermore: "His conduct, that of a commissioned officer publicly urging enlisted personnel to refuse to obey orders which might send them into combat, was unprotected under the most expansive notions of the First Amendment."

Justice William O. Douglas saw the First Amendment issue in a different light. "The power to draft an army includes, of course, the power to curtail considerably the 'liberty' of the people who make it up. ... Making a speech or comment on one of the most important and controversial public issues of the past two decades cannot by any stretch of dictionary meaning be included in 'disorders and neglects to the prejudice of good order and discipline in the armed forces.' ... He was uttering his own belief—an article of faith that he sincerely held. ... Many others who loved their country shared his views."

Public Employees Right to Speak. "That question of whether speech of a government employee is constitutionally protected expression necessarily entails striking 'a balance between the interests of the teacher, as a citizen, in commenting upon matters of public concern and the interest of the State, as an employer, in promoting the efficiency of the public services it performs through its employees.'"[27] With those words, Justice Rehnquist, writing for a unanimous Court, set forth the approach the Court has taken in cases involving the discharge or punishment of a public employee for speaking out.

The Justice used that approach in Bessie Givhan's case when she protested the non-renewal of her teaching contract by her school district in Mississippi. Givhan apparently was a "thorn in the side" of principal James Leach. In recommending non-renewal, Leach wrote the Superintendent that "Ms. Givhan is a competent teacher, however, on many occasions she has taken an insulting and hostile attitude towards me and other administrators. She hampers my job greatly by making petty and unreasonable demands. She is overly critical for a reasonable working relationship to exist between us. She also refused to give achievement tests to her homeroom students."[28] Whatever statements Givhan had made to Leach, however, were made in private conversation with him.

When Givhan sought reinstatement, Judge Orma R. Smith held that Givhan's private comments to Leach were protected by the First Amendment and ordered her reinstated. The Court of Appeals reversed, but the Supreme Court unanimously agreed with Judge Smith that Givhan's speech was protected by the Constitution.[29] Justice Rehnquist wrote: "The First Amendment forbids abridgment of the 'freedom of speech.' Neither the Amendment itself nor our decisions indicate that this freedom is lost to the public employee who arranges to communicate privately with his employer rather than to spread his views before the public. We decline to adopt such a view of the First Amendment."

The right of government employees to accept honoraria for off-duty activities came before Federal District Judge Thomas P. Jackson when several employees sued to have the federal law prohibiting such honoraria declared unconstitutional. These employees had all received honoraria for writing or lecturing and wished to continue to engage in these activities.

Judge Jackson found the law to be an infringement upon the employees' First Amendment rights and enjoined its enforcement. The Supreme Court affirmed, with Chief Justice Rehnquist dissenting.[30] The majority found two things wrong with the law: "By denying ... [the employees compensation] the honoraria ban induces them to curtail their expression if they wish to continue working for the Government." Also, "[t]he large-scale disincentive to Government employees' expression also imposes a significant burden on the public's right to read and to hear what the employees would otherwise have written and said."

The Chief Justice, using the "balancing of interests" test, would have balanced in favor of the government. "The Court," he argued, "largely ignores the Government's foremost interest—prevention of impropriety and the appearance of impropriety...."

Commercial Speech.

> I continue to believe that the First Amendment speech provision, long regarded by this Court as a sanctuary for expressions of public importance or intellectual interest, is demeaned by invocation to protect advertisements of goods and services. I would hold quite simply that the ... advertisement, however truthful or reasonable it may be, is not the sort of expression that the Amendment was adopted to protect.[31]

He said much the same thing in a prior case when the Court held unconstitutional a Virginia law prohibiting pharmacists from advertising the price of drugs. In that case the Court posed and answered its own question. "Our question is whether speech which does 'no more than propose a commercial transaction' ... is so removed from any 'exposition of ideas' ... and from 'truth, science, morality, and arts in general' ... that it lacks all protection. Our answer is that it is not."[32]

Rehnquist was not convinced. He agreed with the Court that "the First Amendment is 'primarily an instrument to enlighten public decisionmaking in a democracy.'" But he was of the opinion the public decisionmaking referred to related "to political, social, and other public issues," and not to the decision "to purchase one or another kind of shampoo." "It is undoubtedly arguable," he continued, "that many people in the country regard the choice of shampoo as just as important as who may be elected to local, state, or national political office, but that does not automatically bring information about competing shampoos within the protection of the First Amendment."

The Justice continued to believe "that the Court unlocked a Pandora's Box when it 'elevated' commercial speech to the level of traditional political speech by according it First Amendment protection...."[33] Recognizing that a majority of the justices were committed to giving First Amendment protection to commercial speech, Rehnquist nevertheless, upheld Puerto Rico's complete ban on advertising casino gambling to its residents.[34] "Once it is determined that the First Amendment applies to the particular kind of commercial speech at issue," he declared, "then the speech may be restricted only if the government's interest in doing so is substantial, the restrictions directly advance the gov-

ernment's asserted interest, and the restrictions are no more extensive than necessary to serve that interest." The Justice and a majority of the Court were of
the opinion that the Puerto Rico statute met all of these requirements.

Places to Speak. When John Flower, a member of American Friends Service Committee, was found distributing literature on New Braunfels Avenue,
which runs through Fort Sam Houston in San Antonio, Texas, he was ordered
by military authorities to stop. New Braunfels Avenue is used by the public
in the same way as any other street in San Antonio. When Flower later
returned to the Avenue, he was arrested and found guilty of reentering a military base after being ordered not to do so. The Supreme Court reversed, with
Justice Rehnquist dissenting.

The majority was of the opinion that "a base commander can no more
order ... [Flower] off this public street because he was distributing leaflets than
could the city police order any leafleteer off any public street."[35]

In dissenting, Justice Rehnquist set forth his views on the right of the government to control the use of its property. Prior case law, he wrote, "suggests
that civilian authorities may draw reasonable distinctions, based on the purpose
for which public buildings and grounds are used, in according the right to exercise First Amendment freedoms in such buildings and on such grounds."

The Justice's views prompted him to also dissent when the Court held
that a municipally owned auditorium must allow the musical *Hair* to be shown
there even though the auditorium directors believed that the "production would
not be 'in the best interest of the community.'"[36]

Even though the musical was not obscene, the Justice would have affirmed
the decision of the lower court which had found that *Hair* was "not entertainment designed for the whole family." Rehnquist also argued that a municipal auditorium was not the same as a public street, and therefore a rule
prohibiting pubic auditoriums from selecting who can use their premises could
have unforeseen consequences. "May an opera house limit its productions to
operas, or must it also show rock musicals? May a municipal theater devote
an entire season to Shakespeare, or is it required to book any potential pro-
ducer on a first come, first served basis?"

Justice Rehnquist also believed that the government had the right to prohibit personally owned mailboxes from being used by anyone other than post
office personnel. A group of organizations in Westchester County, New York,
sought a court order prohibiting the Postal Service from enforcing the federal law making it a crime to put material in a mail box which does not contain postage. Federal District Judge William C. Conner had concluded that
the law infringed upon the First Amendment right to communicate and
declared it unconstitutional. He pointed out that "use of the mails is financially burdensome to plaintiffs and constitutes a significant impediment to ...
[their] ability to communicate quickly with their constituents."[37]

The Supreme Court, with the Justice writing the opinion, reversed. After a lengthy review of the history of the Postal Service, Rehnquist concluded: "There is neither historical nor constitutional support for the characterization of a letterbox as a public forum."[38] Furthermore, he argued: "The [organizations] ... can deliver their messages either by paying postage, by hanging their notices on doorknobs, by placing their notices under doors or under a doormat, by using newspaper or nonpostal boxes affixed to houses or mailbox posts, by telephoning their constituents, by engaging in person-to-person delivery in public areas, by tacking or taping their notices on a door post or letterbox post, or by placing advertisements in local newspapers." And he again pointed out "that the First Amendment does not guarantee access to property simply because it is owned or controlled by the government."

In dissent, Justice Stevens pointed out that "[t]he mailbox is private property; it is not a public forum to which the owner must grant access. If the owner does not want to receive any written communications other than stamped mail, he should be permitted to post the equivalent of a 'no trespassing' sign on his mailbox."

For the Chief Justice, airport terminals were also off limits for those wishing to express themselves. "[W]e conclude," he noted, "that the terminals are nonpublic fora and that the regulation reasonably limits solicitation."[39] With those words, Rehnquist and a majority of the justices upheld a ban on members of the International Society for Krishna Consciousness, Inc., from soliciting and distributing literature in airport terminals controlled by the New York Port Authority.

Part of the Krishna religion requires its members to perform *sankirtan*, which is "going into public places, disseminating religious literature and soliciting funds to support the religion." When they were prohibited from doing *sankirtan* in the public areas of the airport terminals, the Krishnas brought an action seeking an injunction against the Port Authority.

Judge Mary Johnson Lowe concluded that the terminals were public forums, and because the regulations were not narrowly drawn they were unconstitutional as a violation of the Krishnas' First Amendment right to solicit and distribute literature. The Supreme Court disagreed, holding that the terminals were not forums open for the exercise of constitutional rights and that the prohibitions against solicitation and distribution were reasonable.

The Chief Justice declared: "Thus, we think that neither by tradition nor purpose can the terminals be described as satisfying the standards we have previously set out for identifying a public forum." That being the case, the Court examined the rule and found it to be a reasonable regulation to prevent congestion and possible duress to persons being confronted by solicitors and distributors.

Justices Souter, Blackmun and Stevens dissented from the Court's decision. Souter pointed out: "The First Amendment inevitably requires people to put up with annoyance and uninvited persuasion. Indeed, in such cases we need to scrutinize restrictions on speech with special care." Scrutinizing the restrictions here, the dissenters concluded that they were not narrowly drawn and were therefore unconstitutional.

Miscellaneous Speech Cases. "The principal question presented is whether the First Amendment imposes limitations upon the exercise by a local school board of its discretion to remove library books from high school and junior high school libraries."[40] Three justices were of the opinion "that local school boards may not remove books from school library shelves simply because they dislike the ideas contained in those books and seek by their removal to 'prescribe what shall be orthodox in politics, nationalism, religion, or other matters of opinion.'... Such purposes stand inescapably condemned by our precedents."

In dissenting, Justice Rehnquist took issue with the plurality's conclusion that students have a constitutional right to receive information. "It is the very existence of a right to receive information, in the junior high school and high school setting, which I find wholly unsupported by our past decisions and inconsistent with the necessarily selective process of elementary and secondary education." Furthermore, he did not believe that the action of the school board in removing the books prevented the students from access because "the removed books are readily available to students and nonstudents alike at the corner bookstore or the public library."

The Justice also dissented when the Court struck down a federal law that "forbids any 'noncommercial educational broadcasting station which receives a grant from the Corporation [for Public Broadcasting]' to 'engage in editorializing.'"[41] Rehnquist thought that the majority opinion developed "a scenario in which the Government appears as the 'Big Bad Wolf,' and appellee Pacifica [a noncommercial broadcaster] as 'Little Red Riding Hood.' In the Court's scenario the Big Bad Wolf cruelly forbids Little Red Riding Hood to take to her grandmother some of the food she is carrying in her basket."

A truer picture of the situation would show, he argues, "that some of the food in the basket was given to Little Red Riding Hood by the Big Bad Wolf himself, and that the Big Bad Wolf had told Little Red Riding Hood in advance that if she accepted his food she would have to abide by his conditions." Rehnquist agreed that "the Government [could not] attach *any* condition to its largess," but argued that in this case "the Government is simply exercising its power to allocate its own public funds...." He did not believe that "the First Amendment makes ... [that] unconstitutional."

Freedom of Association

Political Parties and New Voters. "Plaintiff John B. Anderson is an independent candidate for the office of President of the United States. He declared his independent candidacy on April 24, 1980. On May 16, seeking to place his name on the November ballot in Ohio, Anderson tendered to defendant Anthony J. Celebrezze, Jr., Secretary of State of Ohio, those documents required by Ohio law to effect Anderson's nomination as a candidate for that office. The defendant rejected Anderson's filing, citing as the sole ground therefor Anderson's failure to file by the deadline set by Ohio ... [law.] That deadline requires an independent to file his nomination papers 75 days before the primary election in June."[42] In order to qualify under Ohio, Anderson would have had to file his nominating petition not later than March 20, 229 days before the general election.

Federal District Judge Robert M. Duncan held that the Ohio law was a violation of Anderson's constitutional right of association and ordered defendant Celebrezze to place Anderson's name on the November general election ballot. Although the Secretary of State appealed, the case was not heard until after the election, when the Court of Appeals reversed. The Supreme Court accepted Anderson's appeal and agreed with Judge Duncan that the Ohio law unduly infringed upon the right of association of new political parties and their members.[43]

Ohio offered three justifications for the 75-day requirement: "voter education, equal treatment for partisan and independent candidates, and political stability." The majority did not believe that these reasons justified the impact that the law had upon freedom of association. "By limiting the opportunities of independent-minded voters to associate in the electoral arena," Justice Stevens declared, "to enhance their political effectiveness as a group, such restrictions threaten to reduce diversity and competition in the marketplace of ideas. Historically political figures outside the two major parties have been fertile sources of new ideas and new programs; many of their challenges to the status quo have in time made their way into the political mainstream."

Although Justice Rehnquist recognized that "Anderson and his supporters would have been injured by Ohio's ballot access requirements," he nevertheless dissented. He was of the opinion that "the Constitution does not require that a State allow any particular Presidential candidate to be on its ballot, and so long as the Ohio ballot access laws are rational and allow nonparty candidates reasonable access to the general election ballot, this Court should not interfere...."

When the Court upheld the right of Harriet G. Pontikes to vote in the March 1972 Democratic primary in Illinois, the Justice again dissented. Because Pontikes had voted in the Republican primary in February 1971, she was required by law to wait 23 months before voting in another party's primary. Acting on her complaint, the Federal District Court held that the Illinois law significantly burdened Pontikes right of association, and therefore was unconstitutional. A majority of the Supreme Court agreed. "By preventing [Pontikes] ... from participating at all in Democratic primary elections during the statutory period, the Illinois statute deprived her of any voice in choosing the party's candidates, and thus substantially abridged her ability to associate effectively with the party of her choice."[44]

Illinois argued that the law was necessary to prevent "'raiding'—the practice whereby voters in sympathy with one party vote in another's primary in order to distort that primary's results." But the Court thought that was too restrictive because it locked voters into one party "and the only way to break the 'lock' is to forgo voting in *any* primary for a period of almost two years."

Rehnquist agreed that the Illinois law restricted "voters' freedom to associate with the political party of their choice." But he was of the opinion that "the State's legitimate interest in preventing 'raiding,'" while not perfect, outweighed the individual's right of free association.

Miscellaneous Association Cases. The North Carolina Prisoners' Labor Union, Inc., is not a true labor union; rather, it is an association whose "stated purposes are to work legally and peacefully to alter or eliminate practices ... [in prisons] which are thought to be in conflict with the just, constitutional and social interests of all persons."[45]

Although North Carolina prison officials do not prohibit inmates from joining the Union, members are prevented from soliciting other inmates directly, by correspondence or by a newsletter. Meetings are forbidden, and prison officials cannot negotiate with any person acting as a Union representative.

Believing that these restrictions were a violation of their constitutional right to freedom of association, the Union brought an action seeking an injunction against enforcement of the rules. Because prison officials did not prevent prisoners from joining the Union, the District Court did not answer the question whether "prisoners of the state have a constitutional right to join a corporate association of inmates." The court, however, held that the prison rules violated the members' right of free association. In so doing, the court took notice of the fact that other organizations, such as the Junior Chamber of Commerce, Alcoholics Anonymous, and the Boy Scouts of America, were not subject to the same restrictive rules.

The Supreme Court, in an opinion written by Justice Rehnquist, reversed.[46] "The District Court, we believe," he wrote, "got off on the wrong foot in this case by not giving appropriate deference to the decisions of prison administrators and appropriate recognition to the peculiar and restrictive circumstances of penal confinement." And addressing the question of the associational rights of prisoners, the Justice pointed out: "Perhaps the most obvious of the First Amendment rights that are necessarily curtailed by confinement are those associational rights that the First Amendment protects outside of prison walls. The concept of incarceration itself entails a restriction on the freedom of inmates to associate with those outside of the penal institution. Equally as obvious, the inmate's 'status as a prisoner' and the operational realities of a prison dictate restrictions on the associational rights among inmates."

Although prisoners generally did not fare well with Rehnquist, he did believe that David Dawson, who had been convicted of murder, did have some associational rights. Before the hearing on whether Dawson should be sentenced to death, the "prosecution gave notice that it intended to introduce (1) expert testimony regarding the origin and nature of the Aryan Brotherhood, as well as the fact that Dawson had the words 'Aryan Brotherhood' tattooed on the back of his right hand, (2) testimony that Dawson referred to himself as 'Abaddon' and had the name 'Abaddon' tattooed in red letters across his stomach, and (3) photographs of multiple swastika tattoos on Dawson's back and a picture of a swastika he had painted on the wall of his prison cell."[47] Because Dawson objected to this evidence, arguing that the introduction thereof would violate his First Amendment rights, a statement was read to the jury concerning the Aryan Brotherhood, and evidence introduced "that Dawson had tattooed the words 'Aryan Brotherhood' on his hand." The jury also heard evidence concerning the name "Abaddon."

Acting on the jury's recommendation that Dawson be given the death sentence, the trial judge imposed that penalty. The Supreme Court, however, reversed, being of the opinion that the introduction of evidence about the Aryan Brotherhood violated Dawson's right to freely associate with that group.

In response to the state's argument that the evidence was relative to "Dawson's 'character,'" Chief Justice Rehnquist asserted: "Whatever label is given to the evidence presented, however, we conclude that Dawson's First Amendment rights were violated by the admission of the Aryan Brotherhood evidence in this case, because the evidence proved nothing more than Dawson's abstract beliefs."

Freedom of the Press

Libel.

> We hold that, so long as they do not impose liability without fault, the States may define for themselves the appropriate standard of liability for a publisher or broadcaster of defamatory falsehood injurious to a private individual.[48]

Justice Rehnquist agreed to that statement and applied it in upholding the right of Michael Milkovich to pursue a claim for damages against the Lorain [Ohio] Journal Co.

J. Theodore Diadiun, a reporter for a paper owned by the Journal, "authored an article in an Ohio newspaper implying that ... Michael Milkovich, a local high school wrestling coach, lied under oath in a judicial proceeding about an incident involving ... [himself] and his team which occurred at a wrestling match."[49]

Diadiun's article contained this statement: "'Anyone who attended the meet ... knows in his heart that Milkovich and Scott lied at the hearing after each having given his solemn oath to tell the truth. But they got away with it." After many years of litigating the issue, the Ohio Supreme Court dismissed the case, being of the opinion that Diadiun's statements were matters of opinion and therefore not subject to a claim of defamation. Chief Justice Rehnquist, and a majority of the U. S. Supreme, disagreed and reversed.

After reviewing the protections prior cases have created for the press in defamation cases, the Chief Justice concluded: "We are not persuaded that, in addition to these protections, an additional separate constitutional privilege for 'opinion' is required by the First Amendment." The only question to be answered is "whether a reasonable factfinder could conclude that the statements in the Diadiun column imply an assertion that ... Milkovich perjured himself in a judicial proceeding. We think this question must be answered in the affirmative."

The *Milkovich* case exposes the press to defamation actions where the language used by the reporter would indicate "that the writer was seriously maintaining that the ... [individual involved] committed the crime of perjury," or presumably any other crime.

While Justice Brennan did not quarrel with Rehnquist's analysis of the law in the case, he dissented because he was of the opinion that "the challenged statements cannot reasonably be interpreted as either stating or implying defamatory facts about ... [Milkovich]." And therefore, "[u]nder the rule articulated in the majority opinion, ... the statements are due 'full constitutional protection.'"

Punishment for and Prior Restraint of Publication. Justice Rehnquist concurred when the Court held unconstitutional a West Virginia statute making "it a crime for a newspaper to publish, without the written approval of the juvenile court, the name of any youth charged as a juvenile offender."[50] He did so, however, because the statute applied only to newspapers and not to radio and television stations. Had the law applied to all forms of mass communications, the Justice would have upheld it, being of the opinion that such a prohibition did not violate the First Amendment. "In my view," he argued, "a State's interest in preserving the anonymity of its juvenile offenders—an interest that I consider to be, in the words of the Court, of the 'highest order'—far outweighs any minimal interference with freedom of the press that a ban on publication of the youths' names entails."

Having approved giving the government authority to prevent the publication of some legitimately obtained news, it was an easy step for the Justice to uphold closing criminal trials to the press and public. This he did by dissenting when the Court held "that the right to attend criminal trials is implicit in the guarantees of the First Amendment; without the freedom to attend such trials, which people have exercised for centuries, important aspects of freedom of speech and 'of the press could be eviscerated'"[51]

"I do not believe," Rehnquist wrote in dissent, "that either the First or Sixth Amendment, as made applicable to the States by the Fourteenth, requires that a State's reasons for denying public access to a trial, where both the prosecuting attorney and the defendant have consented to an order of closure approved by the judge, are subject to any additional constitutional review at our hands."

The Chief Justice did, however, believe that some limitations upon freedom of the press were unconstitutional. The Court and the Justice found one of those unconstitutional limitations in the case of reporter Michael Smith. Smith, who had written several articles about alleged "improprieties committed by the Charlotte County [Florida] State Attorney's Office and Sheriff's Department," was called to testify before the grand jury.[52] Smith was told that it was against the law to disclose his testimony, and if he did so he would be subject to criminal prosecution.

After the grand jury had been discharged, Smith, who wanted to publish information about the grand jury's investigation, brought an action in Federal District Court seeking a declaration that the anti-disclosure law was unconstitutional. Judge Elizabeth A. Kovachevich did not agree and dismissed the suit. The Court of Appeals reversed, upholding Smith's right to publish the information, and the Supreme Court unanimously affirmed, with the Chief Justice writing the opinion.

Florida argued that it was important to preserve the secrecy of the grand jury to keep the information from the targeted individual to prevent his or her escape, to prevent importuning the grand jury, and to prevent bribery of witnesses who may be called to give evidence at the trial.

The Chief Justice concluded his opinion by stating: "We agree with the Court of Appeals that the interests advanced by the ... Florida statute ... are not sufficient to overcome ... [Smith's] First Amendment right to make a truthful statement of information he acquired on his own."

Obscenity. William L. Hamling and associates embarked upon what they thought was a legal venture when they published an illustrated version of the *Presidential Report of the Commission on Obscenity and Pornography* and mailed thousands of brochures advertising its sale. The brochures contained "a collage of photographs from the Illustrated Report."[53] Hamling and his associates were indicted for, and convicted of sending obscene material through the mail. The Supreme Court, in an opinion written by the Justice, upheld their convictions, being of the opinion that the obscenity standards announced in *Miller v. California*[54] were applicable to this case. The Court said that the *Miller* case permits "a juror sitting in obscenity cases to draw on knowledge of the community or vicinage from which he comes in deciding what conclusion 'the average person, applying contemporary community standards' would reach in a given case."[55]

The Justice and the Court treated Mr. Jenkins much better than it had

Hamling and his associates. Jenkins, a manager of a theater in Albany, Georgia, had been found guilty of violating the Georgia obscenity law when he exhibited the film *Carnal Knowledge* in his theater. In reversing Jenkins' conviction, a unanimous Court concluded that the film was not obscene under the *Miller* standards. About *Carnal Knowledge*, Rehnquist wrote: "Our own viewing of the film satisfies us that 'Carnal Knowledge' could not be found under the *Miller* standards to depict sexual conduct in a patently offensive way. Nothing in the movie falls within either of the two examples given in *Miller* of material which may constitutionally be found to meet the 'patently offensive' element of those standards, nor is there anything sufficiently similar to such material to justify similar treatment."[56]

The *Miller* case requires that the tier of facts [jury or judge] determine whether the material at issue is obscene under the standards set forth in that case. If found to be obscene, that decision must be reviewed by each appellate court to which the case is appealed, even if that court is the Supreme Court. That procedure was not followed in the case of Chester McKinney. Twelve days before he was arrested for selling obscene material, an Alabama court (in a proceeding to which McKinney was not a party) found certain magazines, including *New Directions*, to be obscene.

McKinney was arrested and charged with selling *New Directions*. At his trial, he argued that *New Directions* was not obscene, and that he was entitled to have that issue submitted to the jury. The trial court disagreed, and the Supreme Court of Alabama upheld that decision. The U.S. Supreme Court reversed.

McKinney "contends," Justice Rehnquist noted, "that the procedures utilized by the State of Alabama, insofar as they precluded him from litigating the obscenity *vel non* of New Directions as a defense to his criminal prosecution, violated the First and Fourteenth Amendments. We agree. While there can be no doubt under our cases that obscene materials are beyond the protection of the First Amendment ... [our] decisions have also consistently recognized that the procedures by which a State ascertains whether certain materials are obscene must be ones which ensure 'the necessary sensitivity to freedom of expression'.... The Alabama statutory scheme at issue here ... fails to meet this requirement."[57]

Miscellaneous Press Cases. Barbara Susan Papish was dismissed from the University of Missouri for distributing on the campus "a newspaper 'containing forms of indecent speech.'"[58] "[T]he issue contained an article entitled 'M——-f——- Acquitted,' which discussed the trial and acquittal on an assault charge of a New York City youth who was a member of an organization known as 'Up Against the Wall, M——-f——-.'"

Papish brought an action against the University seeking to have the dismissal set aside. Judge William H. Becker refused to do so concluding that the article was not protected by the First Amendment, and therefore Papish had been justifiably punished for violating school rules. In a short *Per Curiam* opinion, the Supreme Court reversed, holding that Papish "was expelled because of the disapproved *content* of the newspaper rather than the time, place or manner of distribution." This, the majority held, was a violation of her First Amendment rights.

Not only did Justice Rehnquist think that the language Papish used was "lewd and obscene," he expressed the opinion the that "notion that the officials lawfully charged with the governance of the university have so little control over the environment for which they are responsible that they may not prevent the public distribution of a newspaper on campus which contained the language described in the Court's opinion is quite unacceptable to me, and I would suspect would have been equally unacceptable to the Framers of the First Amendment."

It was not distribution of a newspaper that contained vulgar language that the City of Cincinnati tried to rid itself of, but rather newsracks containing commercial publications. In banning only newsracks dispensing commercial material, the City eliminated 62 racks, while leaving 1,500–2,000 that contained other kinds of newspapers. Cincinnati argued that the ban was necessary to improve the appearance of its streets and sidewalks.

In striking down the ban, the majority of the Court did not think that the elimination of only 62 racks did much to accomplish the city's goals.[59]

For Chief Justice Rehnquist, this was a case wherein the majority was striking down a small infringement upon the First Amendment, and ignoring the fact that a much greater burden on First Amendment rights was possible. "Today's decision ... places the city in the position of having to decide between restricting more speech—fully protected speech—and allowing the proliferation of newsracks on its street corners to continue unabated. ... In my view, the city may order the removal of *all* newsracks from its public right-of-ways if it so chooses."

The Pursuit of Liberty

The Right of Privacy. After concluding in *Roe v. Wade*[60] that the right of privacy protects a woman's right to make the choice whether or not to bear a child, Justice Blackmun wrote for the majority: "Where certain 'fundamental rights' are involved the Court has held that regulation limiting these rights may be justified only by a 'compelling state interest,' ... and that legislative enactments must be narrowly drawn to express only the legitimate state interests at stake."

Although Justice Rehnquist acknowledged in dissent that a pregnant woman may have a "liberty" interest in seeking an abortion, his conception of that interest was substantially different than the majority's. He believed that states should not be held to such a high standard when dealing with such liberty interests. "But that liberty," he declared, "is not guaranteed absolutely against deprivation, only against deprivation without due process of law. The test traditionally applied in the area of social and economic legislation is whether or not a law such as that challenged has a rational relation to a valid state objective."

The Justice also argued: "To reach its result, the Court necessarily has to find within the scope of the Fourteenth Amendment a right that was apparently completely unknown to the drafters of the Amendment."

In voting to uphold Pennsylvania laws requiring a minor to obtain the consent of one parent, or from a court, before undergoing an abortion and requiring a married woman to notify her husband, Rehnquist again reiterated his position "that the Constitution does not subject state abortion regulations to heightened scrutiny."[61]

The "liberty" discussed in *Roe* encompasses more than just the right of a woman to choose whether or not to bear a child. It includes the right of parents to the possession and control of their children. Therefore, when a state seeks to permanently terminate parental rights, it cannot do so without certain procedural safeguards. For example, when New York terminated the parental rights of John and Annie Santosky, its procedure allowed the court to find that the children were "permanently neglected," based upon "a 'fair preponderance of the evidence.'"[62] The Supreme Court reversed. In the words of Justice Blackmun: "Before a State may sever completely and irrevocably the rights of parents in their natural child, due process requires that the State support its allegations by at least clear and convincing evidence." This standard, Blackmun pointed out, "strikes a fair balance between the rights of the natural parents and the State's legitimate concerns."

In dissent, Justice Rehnquist acknowledged that parents do have rights in their children that states must recognize. "On one side is the interest of parents," he noted, "in a continuation of the family unit and the raising of their own children. The importance of this interest cannot easily be overstated. Few consequences of judicial action are so grave as the severance of natural family ties." He was of the opinion, however, that New York's use of the "fair preponderance of the evidence," a lesser standard, adequately balanced parental interests against the state's desire to protect neglected children.

In *Santosky*, the Court required a state to find "clear and convincing" evidence of neglect before taking away the right of parents in their children. In *Cruzan v. Dir., Missouri Dept. of Health*,[63] a majority upheld a Missouri requirement "that evidence of ... [an] incompetent's wishes as to the withdrawal of treatment be proved by clear and convincing evidence."

This case involved the question whether Nancy Cruzan, who had been in a coma for a number of years following an auto accident, should be permitted to die by the withdrawal of nutrition and hydration. A trial court found that prior to the accident, Cruzan had indicated that "she would not wish to continue her life unless she could live at least halfway normally." The court, therefore, authorized the withdrawal of life-giving support. The Missouri Supreme Court reversed, concluding that Cruzan's statements were unreliable.

With Chief Justice Rehnquist writing the opinion, the U.S. Supreme Court affirmed. It found that "for purposes of this case, we assume that the United States Constitution would grant a competent person a constitutionally protected right to refuse lifesaving hydration and nutrition." But in view of the fact that Cruzan was not competent, the majority concluded that Missouri's "interest in the protection and preservation of human life" was so important that requiring "clear and convincing" evidence of the incompetent person's desires was constitutionally permissible.

Justice Brennan, writing for himself and Justices Marshall and Blackmun, was of the opinion that the "clear and convincing standard ... [was] an obstacle to the exercise of a fundamental right," the right to die, and therefore unconstitutional.

The extent to which one's reputation was protected by the right of privacy was before the Court in *Paul v. Davis.*[64] Edward C. Davis III, had been arrested for shoplifting, but the case against him was dismissed. Shortly thereafter, his name and photo appeared on a flyer sent out by several police departments cautioning businesses to look out for Davis and the others listed. Davis's action against the Chief of Police of Louisville, Kentucky, was dismissed by the trial court, and that decision affirmed by the Supreme Court. In addressing the question whether the flyer infringed upon any right of Davis's, Justice Rehnquist concluded that it did not. "While there is no 'right of privacy' found in any specific guarantee of the Constitution, the Court has recognized that 'zones of privacy' may be created by more specific constitutional guarantees and thereby impose limits upon government power. ... [Davis's] case, however, comes within none of these areas."

Because Justices Brennan, Marshall and White believed that Davis had been injured by his name and picture being in the flyer, they dissented. Writing for the three of them, Brennan pointed out that: "The stark fact is that the police here have officially imposed on respondent the stigmatizing label 'criminal' without the salutary and constitutionally mandated safeguards of a criminal trial." And he pointed out that even the majority agreed that the flyer would "have deleterious consequences for ... [Davis]."

Many years later, in quoting from a prior case about a person's reputation, Rehnquist noted: "The right of a man to the protection of his own reputation from unjustified invasion and wrongful hurt reflects no more than our basic concept of the essential dignity and worth of every human being—a concept at the root of any decent system of ordered liberty."[65]

In the latter case, the Chief Justice upheld the right of wrestling coach Mike Milkovich to sue reporter J. Theodore Diadiun and the *News-Herald* for damages to his reputation.

Equal Protection of the Law

Blacks on Juries. In *Batson v. Kentucky*,[66] the Court held "that a defendant may establish a prima facie case of purposeful discrimination in selection of the petit jury solely on evidence concerning the prosecutor's exercise of peremptory challenges at the defendant's trial."

Justice Rehnquist, however, argued in dissent: "In my view, there is simply nothing 'unequal' about the State's using its peremptory challenges to strike blacks from the jury in cases involving black defendants, so long as such challenges are used to exclude whites in cases involving white defendants, Hispanics in cases involving Hispanic defendants, Asians in cases involving Asian defendants, and so on."

Integration of Private Facilities. "On Sunday, December 29, 1968, a Caucasian member in good standing ...[of Moose Lodge 107, Harrisburg, Pennsylvania] brought ... [K. Leroy Irvis] a Negro, to the Lodge's dining room and bar as his guest and requested service of food and beverages. The Lodge through its employees refused service to [Irvis] ... solely because he ... [was] a Negro."[67]

Irvis filed a complaint with the Pennsylvania Human Relations Commission. In upholding Irvis's complaint, the Commission concluded "that the dining room was a 'place of public accommodation,'" and therefore the Lodge could not operate it as a segregated dining room. Irvis also brought an action against the Lodge in Federal Court arguing that he had been denied equal protection of the law. That court "held that in view of continuing and pervasive state regulation of liquor licensees, license granted club governed by constitution restricting membership and entry on premise to Caucasians was invalid as violation of equal protection of the laws...." The court also pointed out that only a limited number of liquor licenses were available, and that licensees must comply with detailed regulations.

The Supreme Court, with Justice Rehnquist writing the opinion, reversed concluding "that Moose Lodge's refusal to serve food and beverages to a guest by reason of the fact that he was a Negro does not, under the circumstances here presented, violate the Fourteenth Amendment."[68]

The Justice did not believe that "the 'pervasive' nature of the regulation of private clubs by the Pennsylvania Liquor Control Board ... sufficiently implicate[s] the State in the discriminatory guest policies of Moose Lodge to make the latter 'state action' within the ambit of the Equal Protection Clause of the Fourteenth Amendment."

Gender Discrimination. "The Court's conclusion that a law which treats males less favorably than females 'must serve important governmental objectives and must be substantially related to achievement of those objectives' apparently comes out of thin air. The Equal Protection Clause contains no such language, and none of our previous cases adopt that standard." Those words appear in the Justice's dissenting opinion in *Craig v. Boren*.[69] At issue in that case was the constitutionality of an Oklahoma law which allowed females to purchase nonintoxicating 3.2 percent beer at age eighteen, while making males wait until they were twenty-one.

For Rehnquist, the proper standard for judging gender discrimination cases was whether the regulation was rationally related to a legitimate governmental goal, and he believed that the Oklahoma law met that test.

When Michael M's. conviction for "statutory rape" was upheld by the Supreme Court, Justice Rehnquist wrote the Court's opinion. The Justice acknowledged that in *Craig* "the Court restated the test [for gender classifications] to require the classification to bear a 'substantial relationship' to 'important governmental objections.'"[70] In this case, however, the Justice applied a somewhat broader test. "[T]his Court," he argued, "has consistently upheld statutes where the gender classification is not invidious, but rather realistically reflects the fact that the sexes are not singularly situated in certain circumstances."

The California statute at issue in *Michael M*'s case made it a crime for a male to have sexual intercourse with a female under the age of eighteen. It was not a crime, however, for females to have intercourse with a male under the age of eighteen. California argued that the purpose of the statute was "to prevent illegitimate teenage pregnancies." For the Justice and the majority, that justified the discrimination against males.

Rehnquist did not agree "that a gender-neutral statute would be as effective as the statute California has chosen to enact."

The Chief Justice dissented when the Court held that it was a violation of equal protection for the state's attorney to use peremptory challenges to strike men from a jury panel in a paternity case. The case involved J. E. B. against whom a complaint had been filed alleging that he was the father of a child born to T. B. After the exercise of peremptory challenges by both the state's attorney and J. E. B.'s attorney, all jurors selected were female. This jury found J. E. B. to be the father of the child, and that decision was affirmed by the state appeals court, but reversed by the Supreme Court.[71]

Justice Blackmun, writing for the majority, held that "[d]iscrimination in jury selection, whether based on race or on gender, causes harm to the litigants, the community, and the individual jurors who are wrongfully excluded from participation in the judicial process." Furthermore: "Equal opportunity to participate in the fair administration of justice is fundamental to our democratic system. It not only furthers the goals of the jury system. It reaffirms the promise of equality under the law—that all citizens, regardless of race, ethnicity, or gender, have the chance to take part directly in our democracy."

Chief Justice Rehnquist noted in his dissent that there was a substantial difference between the cases involving the use of race in peremptory challenges as compared to those in which the decision to strike a juror is based upon his or her gender. "[U]se of peremptory challenges on the basis of sex," he argued, "is generally not the sort of derogatory and invidious act which peremptory challenges directed at black jurors may be."

For Illegitimate Children. Henry Clyde Stokes died of injuries received while working at his job. At the time of his death, he was the father of four legitimate children, one illegitimate child, and another who was born after his death. When the workmen's compensation claim for Stokes' death was settled, the illegitimate children received nothing because under Louisiana law such funds were to be paid to illegitimate children "*only* if there were not enough surviving dependents ... to exhaust the maximum allowable benefits."[72] In this case, the surviving legitimate children exhausted the benefits available.

In an action brought on behalf of the illegitimate children, the courts of Louisiana upheld the law, but the Supreme Court reversed concluding that the disparate treatment of the illegitimate children violated equal protection of the law. "The status of illegitimacy," Justice Lewis Powell declared, "has expressed through the ages society's condemnation of irresponsible liaisons beyond the bonds of marriage. But visiting this condemnation on the head of an infant is illogical and unjust."

Justice Rehnquist dissented. "While the Court's opinion today is by no means a sharp departure from the precedents on which it relies, it is an extraordinary departure from what I conceive to be the intent of the framers of the Fourteenth Amendment and the import of the traditional presumption of constitutionality accorded legislative enactments. ... The traditional police power of the State has been deemed to embrace any measure thought to further the well-being of the State in question, subject only to the specific prohibitions contained in the Federal Constitution. That Constitution of course contains numerous guarantees of individual liberty, which I would have no trouble describing as 'fundamental personal liberties,' but the right of illegitimate children to sue in state court to recover workmen's compensation benefits is not among them."

The Justice also dissented in *Gomez v. Perez*[73] when the Court struck down a Texas law that granted "legitimate children a judicially enforceable right to support from their natural fathers and at the same time den[ied] that right to illegitimate children." Justices Stewart and Rehnquist were of the opinion that the case was not properly before the Court because the laws had not been the "subject of litigation in the courts of Texas."

Relying on the *Gomez* case some years later, the Court unanimously held that another Texas law, which required paternity actions, to obtain support for an illegitimate child, to be brought before the child was one year old, denied the child equal protection of the law.[74] Writing for the Court, Justice Rehnquist, referring to *Gomez*, stated: "Specifically, we held that a State which grants an opportunity for legitimate children to obtain paternal support must also grant that opportunity to illegitimate children." In concluding his opinion the Justice wrote: "Accordingly, we conclude that the one-year period for establishing paternity denies illegitimate children in Texas the equal protection of the law."

For Aliens. "It is established, of course, that an alien is entitled to the shelter of the Equal Protection Clause. … This protection extends, specifically, in the words of Mr. Justice Hughes, to aliens who 'work for a living in the common occupations of the community.'"[75] Justice Blackmun wrote this statement when the Court held unconstitutional a New York law which barred aliens from the state's civil service.

On the same day, the Court also held that a state violates the Equal Protection Clause when it denies aliens admission to practice law.[76]

Justice Rehnquist wrote an extensive dissenting opinion applicable to both of these cases. "The Court in these two cases," he argued, "holds that an alien is not really different from a citizen, and that any legislative classification on the basis of alienage is 'inherently suspect.' The Fourteenth Amendment, the Equal Protection Clause of which the Court interprets as invalidating the state legislation here involved, contains no such language concerning 'inherently suspect classifications,' or, for that matter, merely 'suspect classifications. The principal purpose of those who drafted and adopted the Amendment was to prohibit the States from invidiously discriminating by reason of race, … and, because of this plainly manifested intent, classifications based on race have rightly been held 'suspect' under the Amendment."[77]

The true test in judging classifications related to aliens, the Justice argued, "is whether any rational justification exists for prohibiting aliens from employment in the competitive civil service and from admission to a state bar." For the Justice, the answer was clear. "I do not believe that it is irrational for New York to require this class of civil servants to be citizens, either natural born or naturalized." And he did not believe that it was irrational for Connecticut to require lawyers to be citizens.

For the same reasons set forth in his dissenting opinion in these cases, Rehnquist dissented when the Court held that it was a violation of equal protection of the law for Texas to prohibit aliens from being notary publics.[78]

For Voters.

[Abran] Ramirez is a 43-year-old farmworker, married, with five children. Twenty-one years ago he was convicted in Texas of a felony entitled "robbery by assault." He avers that the offense arose out of an argument in a restaurant, and that at the trial he was without counsel and pleaded guilty on the advice of the judge. After serving only three months in jail he was released on parole. His parole successfully terminated 11 years ago.

In February 1972 petitioner applied to register to vote in San Luis Obispo County. He was refused registration by respondent San Luis Obispo County Clerk on the sole ground that he had been convicted of a felony and had spent some time in incarceration.[79]

The Supreme Court of California unanimously held that the California law violated the Equal Protection Clause. The United States Supreme Court, with Justice Rehnquist writing the opinion, reversed.

Ramirez, and others who had joined him in the lawsuit, argued that punishing felons by taking away their right to vote was "outmoded, and that the more modern view is that it is essential to the process of rehabilitating the ex-felon that he be returned to his role in society as a fully participating citizen when he has completed the serving of his term."[80]

Rehnquist accepted the arguments as valid and responded: "But it is not for us to choose one set of values over the other. If respondents [Ramirez and the others] are correct, and the view which they advocate is indeed the more enlightened and sensible one, presumably the people of the State of California will ultimately come around to that view. And if they do not do so, their failure is some evidence, at least, of the fact that there are two sides of the argument."

Voters in Holt, Alabama, received no greater consideration from the Justice than did the felons in California. Under Alabama law, the people of Holt, a small community near Tuscaloosa, are subject to the police and sanitary regulations of that city, and "Holt residents are also subject to the criminal jurisdiction of the city's court ... and to the city's power to license businesses, trades, and professions...."[81]

The Holt Civic Club brought an action against Tuscaloosa contending that Holt residents, "without a concomitant extension of the franchise on an equal footing with those residing within ... [Tuscaloosa's] corporate limits ... [are denied] rights secured by the Due Process and Equal Protection Clauses of the Fourteenth Amendments." Justice Rehnquist and a majority of the justices disagreed.

The Justice acknowledged: "Given this country's tradition of popular sovereignty, ... [Holt citizens] claimed right to vote in Tuscaloosa elections is not without some logical appeal." But you have to draw the line somewhere, and therefore the Justice declared: "The line heretofore marked by this Court's voting qualifications decisions coincide with the geographical boundary of the governmental unit at issue, and we hold that ... [Holt citizens'] case, like their homes, falls on the farther side."

The black citizens of Alabama fared better, when all participating justices found Section 182 of the Alabama Constitution to be a violation of equal protection. Section 182 disenfranchised all "persons convicted of, among other offenses, 'any crime ... involving moral turpitude.'"[82]

"Carmen Edwards, a black, Victor Underwood, a white, ... [had] been blocked from the voting rolls pursuant to Section 182 ... because they each ... [had] been convicted of presenting a worthless check." Edwards and Underwood brought an action claiming that by including misdemeanors within the purview of Section 182, Alabama intended to "disenfranchise blacks on account of their race and that their inclusion in Section 182 has had the intended effect."

After holding extensive hearings, Judge Frank H. McFadden concluded that Section 182 had been adopted with intent to disenfranchise blacks, but that was not a valid reason for concluding that the Section violated equal protection. Both the Court of Appeals and the Supreme Court disagreed, holding that Section 182 was a violation of the Equal Protection Clause.

Justice Rehnquist wrote: "Without deciding whether Section 182 would be valid if enacted today without any impermissible motivation, we simply observe that its original enactment was motivated by a desire to discriminate against blacks on account of race and the section continues to this day to have that effect."

AS A JUSTICE FOR THE GOVERNMENT

The theme that runs through Chief Justice Rehnquist's opinions on the free exercise of religion is one of deference to government laws and rules. In *Cruz*, the deference was to prison rules; in the *Maynard* case, it was to state rules governing car license plates; and in *Goldman* it was the military's desire for uniformity in military clothing. This type of deference makes it easy for the Chief Justice to tip the scales in favor of government, with little consideration for the true meaning of the free exercise clause.

As the lone dissenter in *Schaumburg*, Rehnquist asserted: "I believe that a simple request for money lies far from the core protections of the First Amendment as heretofore interpreted."[83] But a majority of the justices disagreed. They were of the opinion that there were substantial First Amendment values at stake here.

Although the Chief Justice voted to strike down parts of Judge McGregor's restrictive injunction in the *Madsen* case, he voted to approve Forsyth County's open-ended permit fee ordinance, and at times voted to uphold other restrictions on picketing and parading.[84]

When balancing the First Amendment right to espouse unpopular views, as against interests asserted by the government, Rehnquist, in almost all cases, chose to punish or restrict those views. That was true in the flag cases, in Captain Howard Levy's case, and in cases in which the speaker's speech contained vulgarity.[85]

Although the Chief Justice voted to uphold teacher Bessie Givhan's right to speak privately with her principal, he voted to uphold the ban prohibiting public employees from accepting honoraria. In other public employee cases, his balancing of interests also led to a vote to uphold government restrictions as against First Amendment rights.[86]

It appears that the Chief Justice really never did accept the Court's application of the First Amendment to commercial speech. For example, when the Court held unconstitutional a ban on an electric utility's advertising to promote the use of electricity, Rehnquist wrote in dissent: "Thus, even if I were to agree that commercial speech is entitled to some First Amendment protection, I would hold here that the State's decision to ban promotional advertising, in light of the substantial state interest at stake, is a constitutionally permissible exercise of its power to adopt regulations designed to promote the interests of its citizens."[87]

The Chief Justice has a very narrow view of where people can exercise their right of free speech. For him, military bases, malls, mailboxes, teacher's mailboxes, telephone poles, and the sidewalk near a post office are places where the government can prohibit the exercise of First Amendment rights.[88] He also voted to allow municipalities to limit adult bookstores and theaters to specific zones within a municipality.[89]

In both the case involving the removal of books from a school library, and the case involving grant of public money to noncommercial broadcasting stations, the Justice approves a form of censorship. In the library book case, Justice Blackmun, in voting to prevent school boards from removing library books they did not like, pointed out: "It does not seem radical to suggest that state action calculated to suppress novel ideas or concepts is fundamentally antithetical to the values of the First Amendment."[90]

Rehnquist's votes indicate that he did not give much weight to any right of association asserted by new political parties or voters wishing to associate with a different party. For example, in the *Anderson* case it was enough for him that the Constitution "grants an express plenary power to the States" insofar as regulating the election of a president.[91]

The Chief Justice upheld David Dawson's First Amendment right to associate with the Aryan Brotherhood, a white racist prison gang, and not to have that information used against him at his trial for murder.[92] The Chief Justice, however, had a very restricted view of First Amendment rights generally. For him, "[t]he government as an employer or school administrator [or prison official] may impose upon employees and students [and prisoners] *reasonable regulations* that would be impermissible if imposed by the government upon all citizens."[93] Throughout the years, however, the Court has required government to do more than just prove the *reasonableness* of the infringement upon First Amendment rights. For example, the Court has said: "Where there is a significant encroachment upon personal liberty, the State may prevail only upon showing a subordinating interest which is compelling."[94]

Although the Justice concurred in striking down the West Virginia law prohibiting the press from disclosing a juvenile's name, he would not have done so if the law had been one applicable to all forms of mass communication. And while he, at times, wrote of the values of the First Amendment, it is clear that he was willing to subordinate those values many times and uphold restrictions upon the press. He expressed such views in the West Virginia case. "So valued is the liberty of speech and of the press that there is a tendency in cases such as this to accept virtually any contention supported by a claim of interference with speech or the press. I would resist that temptation."[95]

The Chief Justice clearly resisted the temptation to uphold First Amendment values, in most of the obscenity cases in which he participated.[96]

In the right of privacy cases, the Chief Justice adhered to the view that when a person asserted a liberty interest, "[t]he constitutional issue to be decided by ... [the] courts is whether ... [the government's] determination that such regulations should be enacted is so irrational that it may be branded 'arbitrary,' and therefore a deprivation of ... [the individual's] 'liberty' interest...."[97] He wrote that statement in a case wherein the Court assumed that matters of an individual's personal appearance were protected as a "liberty" interest under the Due Process Clause, but nevertheless concluded that hair-grooming standards of a police department were rational and outweighed the patrolman's liberty interest. Almost all laws and regulations, of course, meet the test of rationality.

Following the *Batson* case, in which the Court prohibited prosecutors from using race as a criteria in exercising peremptory challenges, the Chief Justice voted against applying that holding retroactively to cases pending on appeal.[98] He also dissented when the Court held that a white man's right to equal protection prevented a prosecutor from exercising peremptory challenges to remove black jurors from the panel.[99]

Because the Fourteenth Amendment specifically prohibits states from denying equal protection, private discrimination is permitted unless there is some connection between the private entity and the government.

Rehnquist could not find that connection in the *Moose Lodge* case, and as a consequence permitted the Lodge to discriminate against Leroy Irvis.

The Chief Justice also believed that gender-based classifications, and especially those that discriminated against males, should be upheld if they are rationally related to a legitimate government goal.[100] But regardless of whether the discrimination was against males or females, he voted most of the time to uphold governmental classifications by gender.[101]

Although the Chief Justice voted to nullify the Texas statute limiting the time actions could be brought for support of an illegitimate child, he voted most of the time against extending equal protection to illegitimate children. When the Court struck down an Illinois law allowing illegitimate children to inherit only from their mothers, Rehnquist wrote in dissent: "The circumstances which justify the distinction between illegitimates and legitimates contained ... [in the law] are apparent with no great exercise of imagination; they are stated in the opinion of the Court, though they are there rejected as constitutionally insufficient."[102]

In support of his position that state discrimination against aliens does not violate the Fourteenth Amendment, Rehnquist noted "that the Constitution itself recognizes a basic difference between citizens and aliens. That distinction is constitutionally important in no less than 11 instances in a political document noted for its brevity."[103] But, as the Court pointed out earlier, the Fourteenth Amendment controls what *states* are prohibited from doing, and one of the things states are prohibited from doing is "deny to any *person* within its jurisdiction, the equal protection of the laws."

The people in the little town of Holt, Alabama, did not fare well with the Chief Justice either. He saw no violation of equal protection when Holt residents were excluded from voting in Tuscaloosa's city elections, even though they were subject to Tuscaloosa's laws.[104]

Poor people who suffered discrimination at the hands of the government did not receive much help from Rehnquist. He voted to uphold the Texas system of disbursing welfare funds even though Aid to Families with Dependent Children recipients received 75 percent of a standard payment, while aged persons received 100 percent, and the disabled and blind received 95 percent.[105] The Chief Justice also approved the Department of Agriculture's denial of food stamps to "individuals who live in households containing one or more members who are unrelated to the rest."[106] And when the Court upheld lower level federal AFDC payments to Puerto Rico than the government provides to states, the Chief Justice agreed that this was not a denial of equal protection.[107]

As the cases clearly indicate, the Chief Justice's constitutional philosophy in equal protection cases was one of deference to the legislative process. So long as the legislative action was "rational," there was no constitutional violation. For example, in dissenting when the Court struck down a classification that treated illegitimate children different than legitimate children, Rehnquist wrote: "When this Court expands the traditional 'reasonable basis' standard for judgment under the Equal Protection Clause into a search for 'legitimate' state interests that the legislation may 'promote,' and 'for fundamental personal rights' that it might 'endanger,' it is doing nothing less than passing judgments upon the acts of every state legislature."[108] This approach denigrates the Court's role in assuring that people receive the due process and equal protection which the Fourteenth Amendment guarantees.

But the Justice's deference to government regulation is not just in the areas of due process and equal protection; his views carry over into the areas of "fundamental personal liberties" such as freedom of religion, speech, press, association and privacy. The Chief Justice's record, therefore, requires that he be included as a *Justice for the Government.*

8

JUSTICE SANDRA DAY O'CONNOR

PERSONAL LIFE

Growing Up

Sandra Day O'Connor, the first child of Harry A. and Ada Mae Day, was born March 26, 1930, in El Paso, Texas.

> Day's sister and brother Ann and Alan, were born in 1938 and 1939; she therefore spent her first eight years as an only child, and most of these years on a remote ranch. Her early childhood friends were her parents, ranch hands, a bobcat, and a few javelina hogs. She learned to entertain herself and to find diversion in books. Her mother spent hours reading to her from the *Wall Street Journal*, the *Los Angeles Times*, the *New Yorker*, and the *Saturday Evening Post*. By the age of eight, she was also mending fences, riding with the cowboys, firing her own .22 rifle, and driving a truck.[1]

That is how writer Peter William Huber describes Justice Sandra Day O'Connor's childhood.

O'Connor's parents owned and operated the Lazy B ranch, located between Lordsburg, New Mexico, and Duncan, Arizona. Because there were no doctors near the ranch, Ada Mae went to El Paso where she stayed with her mother, Mamie Wilkey, until Sandra was born. The ranch house to which Ada Mae brought her newborn daughter was "a simple, four-room adobe building, [it] had neither running water nor electricity, until Sandra Day was seven. In the drought years of the Great Depression, her family confronted real hardship, but the ranch eventually prospered."

Because there was no school near the Lazy B, Sandra lived with her maternal grandmother Mamie and went to Radford School, a private institution in El Paso. Her cousin, Flournoy Davis, was also a student there, and

**JUSTICE SANDRA DAY O'CONNOR (collection of the Supreme Court of the
United States).**

they became lifelong friends. Author Judith Bentley writes: "Sandra's school
years were a tug between the ranch and El Paso. She was always homesick.
... During the summers Flournoy and Sandra took the train back to the ranch,
riding under the supervision of a hostess in the club car. ... Both girls were
avid readers and frequent cardplayers. Sandra was a whiz at games, very fast
and very quick, much to Flournoy's dismay. ... At the end of the summer,

Sandra was always reluctant to go back to El Paso, so she would hide. Once she and Flournoy refused to come down from the stock tank, where they were swimming away the vacation. Harry got his lariat and roped them both out."[2]

In an attempt to alleviate the homesickness Sandra experienced, her parents enrolled her in the Lordsburg school for her eighth grade. She rode a bus from before dawn until after dusk because Lordsburg was 22 miles away. This proved very unsatisfactory and the next year Sandra returned to Radford for one year. She then attended and graduated from Austin High School in El Paso.

In the book *Equal Justice, A Biography of Sandra Day O'Connor*, by Harold and Geraldine Woods, the justice is quoted describing her childhood: "It is very different from growing up in a city. When you grow up on a ranch, you tend to participate along with everyone else in whatever the activity is that's going on around you. If there's a roundup, then everyone gets involved in working on the roundup. If there's a fence to be fixed, or if there's a gate … or a well to be repaired, then everybody participates."[3]

When he was growing up, O'Connor's father Harry had hoped to attend Stanford University, but had to forgo those plans in order to take over the ranch when his father died. It was therefore a foregone conclusion that Sandra would go to Stanford upon graduation from high school, and that was the only school to which she applied. Author Bentley writes:

> Several factors were working against her acceptance [at Stanford], however: she was only sixteen; Austin [Texas] had neglected to give her a college entrance exam; and thousands of soldiers returning from World War II were competing for the same spots. A friend of her father's doubted she would ever get in (and he *knew* she wouldn't get into the law school when she applied three years later.) Not many girls from out in the boondocks were ever accepted without some kind of pull.[4]

As Bentley points out, however, "Sandra's pull was her academic record along with her list of extracurricular activities." And those credentials were sufficient to gain her admission to Stanford.

"College was never all study," Bentley writes. "Sandra was known for her great sense of humor and the twinkle in her eyes. She enjoyed doing things with people, whether going out to a drive-in to escape the dorm food or attending dances and movies. There were skiing weekends at Yosemite and vacations at the homes of new friends in California and Oregon."[5]

Law School

During her senior year at Stanford, O'Connor took a course in business law taught by Law School Professor Harry John Rathbun. She enjoyed the course and subsequently enrolled in the Law School.

Included among her friends at the Law School were Beatrice Challis, who became a lifelong friend; William H. Rehnquist, later Chief Justice of the United States; and John Jay O'Connor, who later became her husband. "Sandra," Harold and Geraldine Woods write, "dug into her legal studies with her usual enthusiasm. She earned membership in the Order of Coif, an honor society, and was appointed to the board of editors of the *Stanford Law Review*, a magazine of articles on legal affairs. These honors are only awarded to the best students from each class."[6]

Love, Marriage and Family

John O'Connor describes his meeting and subsequent friendship with the future justice:

> My wife and I met at Stanford Law School. We had not met each other there until we were given a joint assignment on the *Stanford Law Review*. Our job was to check the citations [list of quoted material] in an article written by someone else and to proofread the galley proof of the article. We had to do the citation checking in the library. ... After we finished checking the citations, I suggested that we could do the proofreading somewhere else. We went to a local restaurant, quickly did the proofreading, and then just began to talk. We liked each other immediately. We went out the next two or three nights, and then one night I asked for dates for the next five nights. She agreed. We ended up going out the next forty-two nights in a row! Neither one of us went out with another person after we met each other.[7]

The couple were married at the Lazy B on December 20, 1952, with a reception being held in a newly built barn. "Guests sat on hay bales," Bentley notes, "or danced to the music of a local band and ate Lazy B barbecued beef. The cowboys wore neckties and waltzed Stanford graduates around the floor, their arms pumping like crazy."[8]

The O'Connors have three children, Scott, Brian and Jay.

The Practice of Law

When the justice-to-be applied for jobs as a lawyer, she was confronted with the then existing discrimination against women lawyers. "Women lawyers were 'a bizarre thing' then, said Shirley Hufstedler, secretary of education in the Carter administration, who had graduated from Stanford three years before Sandra. Only about 4 percent of lawyers were women. The only law firms that offered them jobs were those owned by a father, brother, or husband."

One of the leading Los Angeles firms offered O'Connor a job as a legal secretary, which she refused. Instead, she accepted a position as deputy county attorney in San Mateo, California.

John O'Connor graduated from Stanford in 1953 and enlisted in the U.S. Army Judge Advocate General Corps. He was assigned to Frankfurt, Germany, where the couple spent three years. Sandra worked as an attorney for the Army Quartermaster Corps.

Upon completion of John's tour of duty with the Judge Advocate General Corps in 1957, the couple returned to the United States and settled in Phoenix, Arizona. After taking the Arizona bar examination, both were admitted to the practice of law. Their first son, Scott, was born three days later. John joined an established Phoenix law firm, and in the spring of 1958, Sandra and a friend of the family, Tom Tobin, opened the new law firm of Tobin and O'Connor.

"Tobin & O'Connor handled a variety of cases," Bentley reports. "Walk-in clients wanted advice on house purchases, landlord-tenant obligations, drunken driving tickets, and collecting damages for injuries from automobile accidents. The two young lawyers also signed up to defend indigents, people who had been accused of a crime who couldn't afford a lawyer. ... The defendant gained a lawyer, and the lawyer gained experience in trials, plea bargaining, and the sentencing procedure. Sandra began to experience the difference between the law school classroom and the courtroom." When second son Brian was born in 1960, O'Connor quit working to stay home and be a full-time mother. Third son Jay was born in May 1962.

O'Connor returned to work in 1965 when she accepted a position as an assistant state attorney general. "Lawyer O'Connor," according to the Woodses, "enjoyed the variety at the attorney general's office. 'I had a wonderful time,' she continues. 'It was a delightful period in my life. I liked the people with whom I worked very much. We were congenial ... and I learned so much. Part of the pleasure in being in a state attorney general's office is that you have so much responsibility at early age—much more so than might be true in a private practice where you might have to work many years before you can handle the type of cases that I was able to handle with relatively little experience.'"[9]

During this period in her life, O'Connor was a full-time mother, a practicing lawyer, and an active community worker. Author Peter Huber writes: "She wrote questions for the Arizona bar exam, helped start the state bar's referral service, sat on the local zoning commission, and served as a member of the Maricopa County Board of Adjustments and Appeals."[10] The future justice also served on the Governor's Committee on Marriage and Family and did volunteer work for the Salvation Army and for a school assisting minority children.

Politics and Public Service

Both of the O'Connors joined and became active in the Arizona Republican Party. She became a precinct committee member, a district chairperson, and was an alternate delegate to the 1972 Republican National Convention, where she supported Richard M. Nixon for president. In 1969, she was appointed by Governor Jack Williams to fill the unexpired term of State Senator Isabel A. Burgess, who had resigned to take a position in Washington, D.C.

An examination of O'Connor's record as a state senator would indicate that she was not committed to a specific ideology but was a person with independent views.

As a member of the State Senate Judiciary Committee, she voted to repeal Arizona's very restrictive abortion laws and opposed a resolution urging Congress to enact an anti-abortion constitutional amendment. She also co-sponsored a bill that would have made information concerning birth control methods available to those who wanted it. The bill was never enacted into law.

At the beginning of the 1973 session of the legislature, O'Connor was elected majority leader of the senate. She was the first woman to serve in that capacity in any state legislature.

As a Member of the Judiciary

In 1974, O'Connor ran for a position on the county Superior Court. That court handled all types of criminal and civil cases. After a hard-fought campaign, she won and served as a trial judge for five years. "She administered justice," Bentley states, "with an iron hand. She ran a tight courtroom, where all the formalities were observed, dignity was maintained, and no nonsense was tolerated. She was very much the judge in her demeanor. 'You have to say something awfully funny to get her to smile on the bench,' one lawyer said."[11]

Democratic Governor Bruce Babbitt appointed O'Connor to the Arizona Court of Appeals in 1979. When doing so, Governor Babbitt said: "I had to find the finest talent available to create confidence in our new merit system. Her intellectual ability and her judgment are astonishing."[12]

As an appeals court judge, she sat on cases involving appeals from convicted criminals, and in cases concerning workers' compensation, divorce, accidents and real property. She generally received high marks from lawyers for her work as a judge, but received some criticism for her impatience with lawyers and their clients.

Nomination to the Supreme Court

During the presidential campaign in 1980, Republican candidate Ronald Reagan, hoping to gain favor with women voters, pledged to name a woman to the Supreme Court if elected. Early in 1981, Justice Potter Stewart informed President Reagan that he intended to retire at the end of the Court's term in

June. A search began immediately for a qualified woman to replace him. O'Connor seemed to meet all of the President's requirements. "She was thoroughly Republican, with the solid support of a conservative senator, Barry Goldwater of Arizona. Her views on law and order, the family, the death penalty, federalism, busing, and the separation of lawmaking from law-interpreting seemed consistent with the President's."[13]

> No one championed O'Connor more forcefully than her longtime Arizona friend, Senator Barry Goldwater, whose early urging had helped her gain White House support. Noting the opposition from the far-right groups, Goldwater declared: "I don't like getting kicked around by people who call themselves conservatives on a nonconservative matter. It is a question of who is best for the court. If there is going to be a fight in the Senate, you are going to find 'Old Goldy' fighting like hell."[14]

Even though there was some opposition to the nomination because O'Connor had refused to condemn *Roe v. Wade*, the so-called abortion decision, she received 17 of the 18 votes of the Senate Judiciary Committee. The vote in the Senate to confirm was 99-0, and the new justice was sworn in on September 15, 1981.

When O'Connor joined the Court, Warren E. Burger was Chief Justice. Other members of the Court were Justices William J. Brennan, Jr., Byron R. White, Thurgood Marshall, Harry Blackmun, William H. Rehnquist, Lewis F. Powell, Jr., and John Paul Stevens.

AS ASSOCIATE JUSTICE (1981–)

The Free Exercise of Religion

"The issue posed in this case," Justice O'Connor asserted, "is whether, consistent with the Free Exercise Clause of the First Amendment, the Air Force may prohibit Captain Goldman, an Orthodox Jewish psychologist, from wearing a yarmulke while he is in uniform on duty inside a military hospital."[15] After criticizing the majority for not upholding Goldman's Free Exercise claim, the Justice in dissent, set forth what she believed was the proper approach to free exercise claims: "First, because the government is attempting to override an interest specifically protected by the Bill of Rights, the government must show that the opposing interest it asserts is of especial importance before there is any chance that its claim can prevail. Second, since the Bill of Rights is expressly designed to protect the individual against the aggregated and sometimes intolerant powers of the state, the government must show that the interest asserted will in fact be substantially harmed by granting the type of exemption requested by the individual."

Being unable to find any evidence that allowing Goldman to wear the yarmulke would "do substantial harm to military discipline and esprit de corps," the Justice concluded: "I would require the Government to accommodate the sincere religious belief of Captain Goldman."

The Justice also believed that the Court was wrong when it upheld denial of AFDC benefits and food stamps to Native Americans Stephen J. Roy and Karen Miller because they refused to give the government the social security number of their daughter Little Bird of the Snow.[16] "Based on recent conversations with an Abenaki chief, Roy believes that technology is 'robbing the spirit of man.'" Roy and Miller, therefore, argued that Little Snow's "spirit would be robbed ... by 'use' of the number," and forcing them to use the number violated their right to free exercise of religion.

The majority concluded, however, that requiring the applicant to furnish the social security number was "a reasonable means of promoting a legitimate public interest," that interest being the prevention of fraud in the welfare system. Justice O'Connor disagreed: "But the Government has failed to show that granting a religious exemption to those who legitimately object to providing a Social Security number will do any harm to its compelling interest in preventing welfare fraud."

The free exercise of religion claims asserted by Native Americans Alfred Smith and Galan Black also received little consideration from the Court. In this case, however, Justice O'Connor voted with the majority. Smith and Black "were fired from their jobs with a private drug rehabilitation organization because they ingested peyote for sacramental purposes at a ceremony of the Native American Church, of which both ... [were] members."[17]

Smith's and Black's applications for unemployment compensation were denied because, in the opinion of the Oregon Employment Division, they were discharged for "work-related 'misconduct.'" However, on appeal, the Oregon Supreme Court held that it would be a violation of the First Amendment to deny benefits to Smith and Black because of the sacramental use of peyote. The United States Supreme Court disagreed, and reversed. The majority held that because Oregon's law making it a crime to use drugs, including peyote, was "a neutral, generally applicable regulatory law" it could be applied to Smith and Black without offending the First Amendment. "There being no contention that Oregon's drug law represents an attempt to regulate religious beliefs, the communication of religious beliefs, or the raising of one's children in those beliefs, the rule to which we have adhered ... plainly controls."

Although O'Connor agreed with the result reached by the Court, she did not join its opinion. She wrote: "To reach this sweeping result, ... the Court must not only give a strained reading of the First Amendment but must also disregard our consistent application of free exercise doctrine to cases involving generally applicable regulations that burden religious conduct." As she had in previous cases, O'Connor argued that the proper approach to free exercise claims was to require "the government to justify any substantial burden on religiously motivated conduct by a compelling state interest and by means narrowly tailored to achieve that interest." The Justice thought that Oregon had done so in this case.

Freedom of Speech

Picketing and Parading.

> Sandra Schultz and Robert Braun believe that abortion is immoral and unjust. Between April 20 and May 20, 1985, Schultz, Braun and groups of pro-life demonstrators, ranging in size from 11 to more than 40 persons, have on at least six occasions picketed in front of the home of Dr. Benjamin M. Victoria [in Brookfield, Wisconsin] who performs abortions at facilities in Appleton and Milwaukee.[18]

Picketing in front of a person's residence was made unlawful in Brookfield by an ordinance enacted May 15, 1985. When threatened with arrest for violating the ordinance, Schultz and Braun brought an action seeking an injunction against enforcement of the law, arguing that it violated their First Amendment right of freedom of speech. District Judge John C. Reynolds granted a preliminary injunction against the enforcement of the ordinance, but the Supreme Court reversed with Justice O'Connor writing the Court's opinion.

"The antipicketing ordinance," the Justice wrote, "operates at the core of the First Amendment by prohibiting [Schultz and Braun] ... from engaging in picketing on an issue of public concern. Because of the importance of 'uninhibited, robust, and wide-open' debate on public issues, ... we have traditionally subjected restrictions on public issue picketing to careful scrutiny."[19]

After carefully examining the ordinance, O'Connor concluded that "only focused picketing taking place solely in front of a particular residence is prohibited," and that the purpose of the law was "the protection of residential privacy." Given these conclusions, and the fact that there were alternative means for the protesters to get their message across, it was not difficult for the Justice to uphold the ordinance.

Public Employees' Right to Speak. When the Court struck down the federal law banning the acceptance of honoraria by government employees, Justice O'Connor concurred.[20] Quoting from a prior case, the Justice pointed out that "the Court must balance 'the interests of the [employee], as a citizen, in commenting upon matters of public concern and the interest of the [Government], as an employer, in promoting the efficiency of the public services it performs through its employees.'" In this case, O'Connor did not believe that there was any evidence indicating that the balance of interests should favor the Government. "Congress assuredly was inspired by a worthy interest, but it made no effort to establish a connection between its interest and the large-scale inhibition of non-work-related speech by ... [government employees]. Our cases do not support the notion that the bare assertion of a laudable purpose justifies wide-ranging intrusions on First Amendment liberties."

The Justice's balancing approach to speech by public employees sometimes resulted in a vote to uphold the employee's discharge. Such was the case of Ardith McPherson. McPherson, a 19-year-old black woman, worked as a clerk in the Constable's Office of Harris County, Texas. "Her work station was a desk at which there was no telephone, in a room to which the public did not have ready access. Her job was to type data from court papers into a computer that maintained an automated record of the status of civil process in the county."[21] McPherson, together with some other employees, heard a radio broadcast of the assassination attempt on President Ronald Reagan's life on March 30, 1981. During the conversation which followed, comments were made about the President's "cutting back Medicaid and food stamps," to which McPherson responded: "if they go for him again, I hope they get him." When Constable Walter Rankin was informed of McPherson's statement, he discharged her.

McPherson brought an action seeking damages because she had been discharged for exercising her First Amendment right to free speech. Judge Norman D. Black gave judgment for Constable Rankin, which the Court of Appeals reversed, being of the opinion that there was no government interest here that outweighed McPherson's speech. The Supreme Court agreed. "Given the function of the ... [Constable's office], McPherson's position in the office, and the nature of her statement," Justice Thurgood Marshall declared, "we are not persuaded that Rankin's interest in discharging her outweighed her rights under the First Amendment."

Justice Antonin Scalia, writing for himself, Chief Justice Rehnquist, and Justices White and O'Connor concluded: "Because the statement at issue here did not address a matter of public concern, and because, even if it did, a law enforcement agency has adequate reason not to permit such expression, I would reverse the judgment of the court below."

Commercial Speech. Richard D. Shapero, a Kentucky lawyer, submitted to the Kentucky Bar Association a letter which he wanted to send to individuals who were involved in foreclosure proceedings. The letter contained the following paragraph:

> It has come to my attention that your home is being foreclosed on. If this is true, you may be about to lose your home. Federal law may allow you to keep your home by *ORDERING* your creditor ... to *STOP* and give you more time to pay them.[22]

The letter then suggested that the recipient call Shapero's office for some free information. Although the Bar Association did not find the letter false or misleading, it denied Shapero's request to distribute it because of a rule prohibiting "the mailing ... of written advertisements 'precipitated by a specific event or occurrence involving or relating to the addressee.'" The Kentucky Supreme Court upheld the Bar Association and Shapero appealed to the United States Supreme Court, which reversed.

Although the majority recognized that "a letter that is personalized ... to the recipient presents an increased risk of deception, intentional or inadvertent," it nevertheless concluded that "merely because targeted, direct-mail solicitation presents lawyers with opportunities for isolated abuses or mistakes does not justify a total ban on that mode of protected commercial speech." The solution, the Court suggested, was for the state to regulate the abuses.

In dissent, Justice O'Connor argued that the Court has "never held ... that commercial speech has the same constitutional status as speech on matters of public policy," and therefore "States should have considerable latitude to ban advertising that is '*potentially* or demonstrably misleading, ... *as well as* truthful advertising that undermines the substantial governmental interest in promoting the high ethical standards that are necessary in the legal profession.'" In applying that approach to the present case, the Justice concluded: "I think it clear that Kentucky has a substantial interest in preventing the potentially misleading effects of targeted, direct-mail advertising as well as the corrosive effects that such advertising can have on appropriate professional standards."

O'Connor expressed her continued dismay with the majority's decisions in cases involving personal solicitation and advertising by persons engaged in professional pursuits. For example, when the Court held that Florida could not apply its in-person solicitation ban to Certified Public Accountant Scott Fane, who wanted to solicit small businesses by phone, the Justice was the only dissenter. "I continue to believe," she declared, "that this Court took a wrong turn with *Bates v. State Bar of Arizona*,[23] ... and that it has compounded this error by finding increasingly unprofessional forms of attorney advertising to be protected speech."[24] She was of the opinion that there was danger of the solicitor overreaching even where the recipient was a businessman.

O'Connor gained a small victory when four justices joined her in upholding a Florida Bar rule prohibiting lawyers from direct-mail solicitation for thirty days following an accident resulting in personal injury or death.[25] "The Bar has substantial interest both in protecting injured Floridians from invasive conduct by lawyers and in preventing the erosion of confidence in the profession that such repeated invasions have engendered. ... The palliative devised by the Bar to address these harms is narrow both in scope and duration. The Constitution, in our view, requires nothing more."

Places to Speak. "On July 6, 1984, Alan Howard Snyder, a minister of the

Gospel for Jews for Jesus, was stopped by a Department of Airports peace officer while distributing free religious literature on a pedestrian walkway in the Central Terminal Area at LAX [the Los Angeles airport.] The officer showed Snyder a copy of ... [an Airport Commissioners' resolution prohibiting all First Amendment activities in that area], explained that Snyder's activities violated the resolution, and requested that Snyder leave LAX."[26] Jews for Jesus and Snyder filed suit against the Airport in Federal District Court. Judge Edward Rafeedie entered judgment for Jews for Jesus and Snyder, being of the opinion that the terminal area was a public forum and that the rule violated First Amendment rights. The Court of Appeals affirmed and so did the Supreme Court.

The Court did not address the question of whether the airport terminal was a public forum, open and available for First Amendment activities. Rather, it simply held that the regulation was too broad. "On its face, the resolution at issue in this case," Justice O'Connor noted, "reaches the universe of expressive activity, and, by prohibiting *all* protected expression, purports to create a virtual 'First Amendment Free Zone' at LAX. ... The resolution therefore does not merely reach the activity of ... [Jews for Jesus and Snyder] at LAX; it prohibits even talking and reading, or the wearing of campaign buttons or symbolic clothing."

The Justice also wrote the opinion in *Boos v. Barry*,[27] a case in which the constitutionality of a section of the District of Columbia Code was before the Court. The section prohibited "the display of any sign within 500 feet of a foreign embassy if that sign tends to bring that foreign government into 'public odium' or 'public disrepute.' It also prohibit[ed] any congregation of three or more persons within 500 feet of a foreign embassy."

Bridget M. Brooker and Michael Boos wished to demonstrate in front of the Soviet Embassy, and J. Michael Waller wanted to do the same in front of the Nicaraguan Embassy. They brought an action in Federal Court seeking a declaration that the ordinance was unconstitutional. District Judge Oliver Gasch upheld the ordinance, and the Court of Appeals affirmed. The Supreme Court, in an opinion written by Justice O'Connor, found the display part of the ordinance to be a violation of the First Amendment but held the prohibition against three or more persons congregating within 500 feet of an embassy to be valid.

The Government argued that the purpose of the display clause was to protect foreign diplomats from encountering unfavorable messages. "Since the dignity of foreign officials will be affronted by signs critical of their governments or governmental policies, we are told, these foreign diplomats must be shielded from such insults in order to fulfill our country's obligations under international law." But, O'Connor responded: "As a general matter, we have indicated that in public debate our own citizens must tolerate insulting, and even outrageous, speech in order to provide adequate 'breathing space' to the freedoms protected by the First Amendment."

With regard to the congregation clause the Justice pointed out that the Appeals Court held that police could disperse groups "only when the police reasonably believe that a threat to the security or peace of the embassy is present." "So narrowed," O'Connor wrote, "the congregation clause withstands First Amendment overbreadth scrutiny."

Justice O'Connor wrote the plurality opinion when the Court upheld a Postal Service regulation which prohibited solicitation on postal premises.[28]

> Marsha B. Kokinda and Kevin E. Pearl were volunteers for the National Democratic Policy Committee, who set up a table on the sidewalk near the entrance of the Bowie, Maryland, Post Office to solicit contributions, sell books and subscriptions to the organization's newspaper, and distribute literature addressing a variety of political issues.

When Kokinda and Pearl refused to leave the premises, they were arrested and later convicted of violating the regulation. Their convictions were reversed by the Court of Appeals because it concluded that the sidewalk was a traditional forum open for the exercise of First Amendment activities. The Supreme Court reversed.

In her opinion, the Justice wrote: "The postal sidewalk at issue does not have the characteristics of public sidewalks traditionally open to expressive activity. The municipal sidewalk that runs parallel to the road in this case is a public passageway. The Postal Service's sidewalk is not such a thoroughfare. Rather, it leads only from the parking area to the front door of the post office."

Based upon the conclusion that the postal sidewalk was not an open forum, the only question remaining was whether the regulation was reasonable. The Justice then concluded that "it is not unreasonable to prohibit solicitation on the ground that it is unquestionably a particular form of speech that is disruptive of business."

Miscellaneous Speech Cases. Justice O'Connor joined Justice Rehnquist's dissenting opinion when the Court held that school boards could not arbitrarily remove books from the school library. She wanted to make clear, however, that "[i]f the school board can set the curriculum, select teachers, and determine initially what books to purchase for the school library, it surely can decide which books to discontinue or remove from the school library so long as it does not also interfere with the right of students to read the material and to discuss it."[29]

The Justice was also of the opinion that prison officials have authority to regulate the correspondence of inmates. She, therefore, wrote the opinion upholding a regulation of the Missouri Divisions of Corrections which restricts correspondence between inmates at different institutions. Specifically the regulation "permits such correspondence 'with immediate family members who are inmates in other correctional institutions,' and it permits correspondence between inmates 'concerning legal matters.' Other correspondence between inmates, however, is permitted only if 'the classification/treatment team of each inmate deems it in the best interest of the parties involved.'"[30]

After reviewing prior cases, O'Connor concluded that "when a prison regulation impinges on inmates' constitutional rights, the regulation is valid if it is reasonably related to legitimate penological interests."

"Application of the [majority's] standard," Stevens argued in dissent, "would seem to permit disregard for inmates' constitutional rights whenever the imagination of the warden produces a plausible security concern and a deferential trial court is able to discern a logical connection between that concern and the challenged regulation."

Freedom of the Press

Libel and Punishment of the Press. Maurice S. Hepps brought an action against Philadelphia Newspapers, Inc., claiming that its newspaper, the *Philadelphia Inquirer*, had published false information about a chain of stores, known as "Thrifty," of which Hepps was the principal stockholder. "The stories reported that federal 'investigators have found connections between Thrifty and underworld figures,' ...; that 'the Thrifty Beverage beer chain ... had connections ... with organized crime,' ...; and that Thrifty had 'won a series of competitive advantages through rulings by the State Liquor Control Board.'"[31]

The trial judge instructed the jury that Hepps "bore the burden of proving [the] falsity" of the published material. The jury, therefore, found in favor of the *Inquirer* and awarded no damages to Hepps. The Pennsylvania Supreme Court reversed, concluding, that under Pennsylvania law "[s]tatements defaming ... [a] person are ... presumptively false" and therefore "plac[ing] the burden of showing truth on the ... [press] did not unconstitutionally inhibit free debate."

In an opinion written by Justice O'Connor, the Supreme Court reversed, being of the opinion that the First Amendment's protection of the press requires that the person alleging defamation must prove that the statements made were false.

"We recognize," the Justice declared, "that requiring the plaintiff to show falsity will insulate from liability some speech that is false, but unprovably so. Nonetheless, the Court's previous decisions on the restrictions that the First Amendment places upon the common law of defamation firmly support our conclusion here with respect to the allocation of the burden of proof."

New York sought to punish the press for publication by requiring "any entity contracting with an accused or convicted person for a depiction of the crime to submit a copy of the contract to ... [the] New York Crime Victims Board, ... and to turn over any income under that contract to the Board."[32] New York enacted this legislation in response to the criminal activities of a serial killer who came to be known as the "Son of Sam."

In 1981 Henry Hill, who had a criminal record spanning 25 years, entered into a contract with publisher Simon & Schuster to chronicle his years of crime. "The book [entitled *Wiseguy*, published in 1986] depicts, in colorful detail, the day-to-day existence of organized crime, primarily in Hill's first-person narrative. Throughout *Wiseguy*, Hill frankly admits to having participated in an astonishing variety of crimes." Hill had not been prosecuted for these crimes, because he was given immunity for testifying against other persons involved in the criminal activities.

After reviewing the matter, the Crime Victim's "Board ordered Hill to turn over the payments he had already received, and ordered Simon & Schuster to turn over all money payable to Hill at the time or in the future."

Simon & Schuster brought an action against the Board seeking a declaration that the law was unconstitutional as a violation of the First Amendment. Judge John F. Keenan, finding no violation of freedom of the press, dismissed the case. The Supreme Court disagreed and reversed, with Justice O'Connor writing the Court's opinion. "A statute is presumptively inconsistent with the First Amendment," the Justice wrote, "if it imposes a financial burden on speakers because of the content of their speech."

The Justice concluded: "The State's interest in compensating victims from the fruits of crime is a compelling one, but the Son of Sam law is not narrowly tailored to advance that objective. As a result, the statute is inconsistent with the First Amendment."

The Pursuit of Liberty

The Right to Travel.

> The question presented on this appeal is whether a statutory scheme by which a State [Alaska] distributes income derived from its natural resources to the adult citizens of the State in varying amounts, based on the length of each citizen's residence, violates the equal protection rights of newer state citizens.[33]

Under Alaska's distribution of income plan, individuals who had lived in Alaska at the time it became a state in 1959 would receive the most money, while those who came to the state in later years would receive a lesser amount.

Ronald M. Zobel and Patricia L. Zobel, residents of Alaska since 1978, filed suit to have the law declared unconstitutional as a violation of the Equal Protection Clause, and the Supreme Court agreed that it was.

Justice O'Connor concurred in the judgment but argued that the real issue was whether the distribution plan penalized the right of the more recent residents to travel, a right which she asserted is part of the Privileges and Immunities Clause of Article IV of the Constitution. That Clause guarantees that: "The Citizens of each State shall be entitled to all Privileges and Immunities of Citizens of the Several States."

"Accordingly," the Justice wrote, "I would measure Alaska's scheme against the principles implementing the Privileges and Immunities Clause. In addition to resolving the particular problems raised by Alaska's scheme, this analysis supplies a needed foundation for many of the 'right to travel' claims discussed in the Court's prior opinions."[34]

Although O'Connor found the Alaska natural resources distribution plan to be a violation of the right to travel, she did not believe that New York's plan of giving extra points on civil service examinations only to its own veterans unconstitutionally infringed on that right of others who move into the state thereafter. In striking down the New York plan, four members of the Court held that the New York plan infringed upon the right of out-of-state veterans to travel to New York. "[W]e conclude," Justice Brennan wrote, "that New York's veterans' preference violates ... [the] constitutionally protected rights to migrate and to equal protection of the law."[35]

In contrast to the Alaska plan, O'Connor did not see any infringement upon the right to travel. "[T]he New York scheme," she declared, "does not effectively penalize those who exercise their fundamental right to settle in the State of their choice by requiring newcomers to accept a status inferior to that of all old-time residents of New York upon their arrival." A new arrival in New York, the Justice argues, is in no different position than are all of the other citizens then living in New York who receive no preference on civil service exams.

The Right of Privacy. Justice O'Connor did not dispute the validity of the Court's decision to include the right of a woman to make the choice whether or not to bear a child to be within the parameters of the right to privacy. She was of the opinion, however, that "[t]he trimester or 'three-stage' approach adopted by the Court in *Roe*, and, in a modified form, employed by the Court to analyze the regulations in these cases, cannot be supported as a legitimate or useful framework for accommodating the woman's right and the State's interest."[36] She pointed out that under the Court's prior decisions, "the decision to perform an abortion 'must be left to the medical judgment of the pregnant woman's attending physician,'" during the first trimester. But, the Justice argued, the "difficulty with this analysis is clear: *potential* life is no less potential in the first weeks of pregnancy than it is at viability or afterward. At any state in pregnancy, there is the *potential* for human life. ... Accordingly, I believe that the State's interest in protecting potential human life exists throughout the pregnancy."

O'Connor was of the opinion that the "privacy right involved in the abortion context 'cannot be said to be absolute'"; therefore, restrictions on the right should not be struck down unless they present an "undue burden" on the exercise of the right.

She found no undue burden in the City of Akron, Ohio's ordinances which required that second-trimester abortions be performed in a hospital;

that a doctor not perform an abortion without the written consent of a minor's parent, or in lieu thereof, a court order permitting the abortion; that the doctor discuss at length with the patient such things as the development of the fetus, the date of possible viability, the physical and emotional impact of an abortion, and the availability of agencies to assist after birth; and that the abortion not be performed for 24 hours after the woman has given her consent.

In 1992, Justice O'Connor had the opportunity to be the fifth vote to overrule *Roe v. Wade*, but did not do so. Instead, she joined Justices Kennedy and Souter to affirm *Roe's* basic holding. Writing for the three of them, Justice O'Connor declared: "It must be stated at the outset and with clarity that *Roe's* essential holding, the holding we affirm, has three parts. First is a recognition of the right of the woman to choose to have an abortion before viability and to obtain it without undue interference from the State. Before viability, the State's interests are not strong enough to support a prohibition of abortion or the imposition of a substantial obstacle to the woman's effective right to elect the procedure. Second is a confirmation of the State's power to restrict abortions after fetal viability, if the law contains exceptions for pregnancies which endanger the woman's life or health. And third is the principle that the State has legitimate interests from the outset of the pregnancy in protecting the health of the woman and the life of the fetus that may become a child. These principles do not contradict one another; and we adhere to each."[37]

In addition to regulating the right of a woman to choose whether or not to bear a child, states also place restrictions upon the right to marry, a right included within the umbrella of the right of privacy. For example, among the regulations in effect at Missouri prisons was one requiring inmates to secure permission to marry from the prison superintendent. Such permission was to be granted "only 'when there are compelling reasons to do so.'"[38] When that regulation was challenged as being an unconstitutional infringement upon the right to marry, the Supreme Court struck it down. "[I]nmate marriages, like others," Justice O'Connor pointed out, "are expressions of emotional support and public commitment. These elements are an important and significant aspect of the marital relationship. In addition, many religions recognize marriage as having spiritual significance; for some inmates and their spouses, therefore, the commitment of marriage may be an exercise of religious faith as well as an expression of personal dedication."

Equal Protection of the Law

Blacks on Juries. When the Court held that it was a violation of Equal Protection of the Law for a prosecutor to use peremptory challenges to strike black persons from the jury, O'Connor concurred. "I concur in the Court's opinion and judgment, but also agree with the views of THE CHIEF JUS-

TICE and JUSTICE WHITE that today's decision does not apply retroactively."[39]

The Justice did not agree, however, that it was a violation of equal protection for lawyers to remove persons from juries because of their race in a civil case. She therefore dissented in *Edmonson v. Leesville Concrete Co.*[40]

Justice Kennedy wrote in the *Edmonson* case that "[r]acial bias mars the integrity of the judicial system and prevents the idea of democratic government from becoming a reality. ... To permit racial exclusion in this official forum compounds the racial insult inherent in judging a citizen by the color of his or her skin."

In dissent, Justice O'Connor wrote: "Racism is a terrible thing. It is irrational, destructive and mean. Arbitrary discrimination based on race is particularly abhorrent when manifest in a courtroom, a forum established by the government for the resolution of disputes through 'quiet rationality.'" But, she argued: "The Government is not responsible for everything that occurs in a courtroom. The Government is not responsible for a peremptory challenge by a private litigant."

When the Court considered "whether the Constitution prohibits a *criminal defendant* from engaging in purposeful discrimination in the exercise of peremptory challenges,"[41] O'Connor concluded that it did not. She therefore dissented when the Court gave an affirmative answer to the question.

The question arose in a case growing out of the trial of several white defendants accused of beating Jerry and Myra Collins, who were black. Because of the tension the beating created in the black community, the prosecution asked the trial judge to prohibit the defendants' attorney "exercising peremptory challenges in a racially discriminatory manner." That request was denied; the denial was upheld by the Georgia Supreme Court, but reversed by the United States Supreme Court, with Justice O'Connor dissenting.

The disagreement between the majority and the Justice was whether the action of the defendants' attorney in exercising peremptory challenges to strike certain persons from the jury panel is attributable to the state because it is only state discrimination that is prohibited by the Equal Protection Clause.

The majority held that allowing a defendant to determine, by peremptory challenges, who would be on the jury, was state action. This led the Court to conclude "that the Constitution prohibits a criminal defendant from engaging in purposeful discrimination on the ground of race in the exercise of peremptory challenges."

Justice O'Connor disagreed: "The government in no way influences the defense's decision to use a peremptory challenge to strike a potential juror."

Exclusion of Blacks from Universities. Although in 1954 the Court held in *Brown v. Board of Education*[42] that separate but equal schools violated equal protection, as late as 1992 Mississippi maintained "five almost completely white and three almost exclusively black universities."[43] In response to the state's argument that the admissions policies at these universities were neutral insofar as race is concerned, the Court noted: "We do not agree with the ... [lower courts] that the adoption and implementation of race-neutral policies alone suffice to demonstrate that the State has completely abandoned its prior dual system. ... Thus, even after a State dismantles its segregative *admissions* policy, there may still be state action that is traceable to the State's prior *de jure* segregation and that continues to foster segregation."

Justice O'Connor agreed and concurred. "I join the opinion of the Court, which requires public universities, like public elementary and secondary schools, to affirmatively dismantle their prior *de jure* segregation in order to create an environment free of racial discrimination and to make aggrieved individuals whole." And, she continued: "Only by eliminating a remnant that unnecessarily continues to foster segregation or by negating insofar as possible its segregative impact can the State satisfy its constitutional obligation to dismantle the discriminatory system that should, by now, be only a distant memory."

Gender Discrimination. "Respondent, Joe Hogan, is a registered nurse but does not have a baccalaureate degree in nursing. Since 1974, he has worked as a nursing supervisor in a medical center in Columbus, [Mississippi] the city in which MUW [Mississippi University for Women] is located. In 1979, Hogan applied for admission to the MUW School of Nursing's baccalaureate program. Although he was otherwise qualified, he was denied admission to the School of Nursing solely because of his sex."[44]

Hogan brought an action against MUW seeking a declaration that the University's single-sex policy denied him equal protection of the law. Judge L. T. Senter, Jr., disagreed and entered judgment for MUW. The Court of Appeals reversed, and, in an opinion written by Justice O'Connor, the Supreme Court affirmed. "The State's primary justification for maintaining the single-sex admissions policy of MUW's School of Nursing," the Justice noted, "is that it compensates for discrimination against women and, therefore, constitutes educational affirmative action. ... As applied to the School of Nursing, we find the State's argument unpersuasive." That led the Justice to conclude "that the State's policy of excluding males from MUW's School of Nursing violates the Equal Protection Clause of the Fourteenth Amendment...."

Justice O'Connor also found unpersuasive the argument that there was no violation of equal protection when "the State [Alabama] used 9 of its 10 peremptory challenges to remove male jurors"[45] from a case brought to establish the paternity of J.E.B. "I agree with the Court," O'Connor declared, "that the Equal Protection Clause prohibits the government from excluding a person from jury service on account of that person's gender."

For Illegitimate Children. Ten years after the birth of her daughter Tiffany, Cherlyn Clark filed a paternity action against Gene Jeter. Although a blood test indicated a 99.3 percent certainty that Jeter was the father of Tiffany, Pennsylvania courts dismissed the case because it had not been brought within six years after the child's birth, which the law required. A unanimous Supreme Court reversed, with Justice O'Connor writing the opinion.[46]

In examining statutes limiting the time for bringing paternity actions, O'Connor noted: "The unwillingness of the mother to file a paternity action on behalf of the child, which could stem from her relationship with the natural father or ... from the emotional strain of having an illegitimate child, or even from the desire to avoid community and family disapproval, may continue for years after the child is born. The problem may be exacerbated if, as often happens, the mother herself is a minor." These conclusions led the Court to "conclude that the Pennsylvania [six year limitation] statute does not withstand heightened scrutiny [and is therefore unconstitutional] under the Equal Protection Clause."

AS A JUSTICE FOR THE GOVERNMENT

Justice O'Connor strenuously argued that the majority's approach to free exercise of religion cases did not give due weight to that important right. For example, quoting from a prior case, she wrote: "'Only an especially important governmental interest pursued by narrowly tailored means can justify exacting a sacrifice of First Amendment freedoms as the price for an equal share of the rights, benefits and privileges enjoyed by other citizens.'[47] Nevertheless, even using an approach which required the government to justify its infringement on the free exercise of religion, she still voted much of the time to uphold governmental restrictions on religious beliefs and practices.[48]

Although the Justice wrote the opinion upholding the anti-residential picketing ordinance in *Schultz and Braun's* case, she voted much of the time to protect the right to picket and demonstrate.[49]

Justice O'Connor participated in only a few cases involving "unpopular speech." In both of the cases in which the Court held that flag burning was speech protected by the First Amendment, she voted with the dissenters.[50]

When balancing the right of public employees to speak on matters of public concern, against asserted governmental interests in punishing or restricting such speech, O'Connor generally found the government's interests outweighed the employee's First Amendment rights.[51] And that was her approach to commercial speech cases, as well, especially when the state was regulating the speech of professionals such as attorneys and accountants.[52] For example, when the Court held that an "attorney may not be disciplined for soliciting legal business through printed advertising containing truthful and nondeceptive information and advice regarding the legal rights of potential clients,"[53] the Justice dissented. She wrote: "In my view, state regulation of professional advice in advertisements is qualitatively different from regulation of claims concerning commercial goods and merchandise, and is entitled to greater deference than the majority's analysis would permit."

Although the Justice recognized that areas which were generally open to the public were also available for First Amendment activities, she was willing to deny the right to exercise speech activities at non-traditional forums.[54] Even though she held that the rule prohibiting First Amendment activities at the Los Angeles airport was unconstitutional, she left for another day the question of whether the terminal was a traditional open forum. And in the *Kokinda* case, she voted to uphold a postal regulation prohibiting the "[s]oliciting alms and contributions" on postal premises. The Justice wrote that even though some "groups have been permitted to leaflet, speak, and picket on postal premises, ... [the] practice of allowing some speech activities on postal property [does] not add up to the dedication of postal property to speech activities."[55]

With the exception of cases involving obscenity, the Justice's voting record in freedom of the press cases, indicate a fairly strong support for a free press.[56] For example, when confronted with the 1992 Cable Act, which "tells cable operators which programmers they must carry, and keeps cable operators from carrying others that they might prefer,"[57] O'Connor agreed that it was an unconstitutional infringement upon the press.

She was of the opinion that the law was content-based, and on that basis such "restrictions are generally unconstitutional unless they are narrowly tailored to a compelling state interest." Finding no such justification for the law, the Justice concluded that the must-carry rules "are an impermissible restraint on the cable operators' editorial discretion as well as on the cable programmer's speech."

In obscenity cases, however, O'Connor accepted the test formulated by the Court in the *Miller* case,[58] and thus voted most of the time to allow punishment for the dissemination of such material.

Although the Justice voted to permit a number of restrictions upon the right of a woman to make the choice whether or not to bear a child, she did not supply the fifth vote to overrule *Roe v. Wade*. Writing for herself and Justices Kennedy and Souter, she declared: "After considering the fundamental constitutional questions resolved by *Roe*, principles of institutional integrity, and the rule of *stare decisis*, we are led to conclude this: the essential holding of *Roe v. Wade* should be retained and once again reaffirmed."[59]

O'Connor joined a majority of the Court in holding that the biological connection between a father and his child, standing alone, did not give the father any rights in the child.[60]

She also joined a majority of the Court to uphold the application of Georgia's sodomy laws to homosexuals. The majority saw the issue as "whether the ...Constitution confers a fundamental right upon homosexuals to engage in sodomy."[61] Justice Blackmun, on the other hand, thought the "case ... [was] about 'the most comprehensive of rights and the right most valued by civilized men,' namely, 'the right to be let alone.'"

When confronted with the issue, Justice O'Connor agreed that there was "a protected liberty interest in refusing unwanted medical treatment,"[62] generally considered to be a right to die.

She voted, however, to uphold a Missouri requirement that before permitting the termination of life support, a patient's desire to have dehydration and nutrition withdrawn must be proved by "clear and convincing" evidence.

While the Justice voted to prohibit the use of peremptory challenges in a racial discriminatory manner in the *Batson* case, she dissented when the Court held that racially motivated peremptory challenges could not be used in civil cases, nor by criminal defendants.[63]

The Justice was a strong supporter of equal treatment for both men and women. She voted to prohibit the government from exercising peremptory challenges to strike persons from a jury because of their gender.[64]

In other equal protection cases, Justice O'Connor voted much of the time to uphold government classifications. For example, she voted to allow aliens to be Notary Publics in Texas, but voted not to permit them to be Deputy Probation Officers in California. Nor did she believe that the Equal Protection Clause required Texas to allow children of illegal alien parents to attend public school.[65]

In the area of criminal justice, O'Connor did not believe that Georgia's death penalty law violated equal protection, although statistics indicated that Georgia executed more blacks than whites. And she did not support appointing counsel for indigents in postconviction proceedings.[66]

Although there are some bright spots in Justice O'Connor's performance on the Court, as indicated above, she voted much of the time to permit government infringement on constitutional rights. O'Connor, therefore, is included as a *Justice for the Government*.

9

Justice Antonin Scalia

Personal Life

Growing Up

> This kid was a conservative when he was 17 years old. An archconservative Catholic. He could have been a member of the Curia. He was the top student in the class. He was brilliant, way above everybody else.[1]

That was William Stern's assessment of Antonin Scalia, his former classmate at Xavier High School, a Catholic military academy in Manhattan, New York. The statement was made in June 1986 when President Ronald Reagan nominated Scalia to be an associate justice of the Supreme Court.

Antonin Scalia was born March 11, 1936, in Trenton, New Jersey, to S. Eugene and Catherine Louise Scalia. Antonin, "Nino" as his friends called him, was an only child. His father was born in Sicily, came to the United States and became a professor of Romance languages. His mother, an elementary school teacher, was born in the United States of Italian parents who had immigrated to this country.

When Antonin was five years old, the family moved to Elmhurst, in the borough of Queens, New York, when Eugene became a professor at Brooklyn College. Biographer Sally Katzen writes: "Growing up in New York was stimulating and challenging, particularly when Scalia carried the French horn he played in band to and from school on the subway during rush hour. He was a good student, first in public school in Queens and later at St. Francis Xavier, a military prep school in Manhattan, where he graduated first in his class."[2]

Scalia attended Georgetown University in Washington, D.C., where he was class valedictorian. He also attended the University of Fribourg in Switzerland. He studied law at Harvard Law School, where he distinguished himself

JUSTICE ANTONIN SCALIA (photo by Joseph D. Lavenburg, National Geographic Society; collection of the Supreme Court of the United States).

by being a member of the Law Review and graduating magna cum laude in 1960. He was offered, and he accepted, the opportunity to stay at the Law School for a year as a Sheldon Fellow.

Love and Marriage

Author Katzen describes the Scalias' marriage as follows:

> While at Harvard, Scalia met and became engaged to Maureen McCarthy, an
> English major at Radcliffe College and the daughter of a Massachusetts physi-
> cian. The couple married in September 1960 and have nine children. The
> Scalias have enjoyed a strong and mutually supportive relationship, enriched
> by their deep faith in Catholicism. She has done volunteer work wherever they
> lived, including working with hospitalized children, helping retarded young
> adults, and teaching in the Sunday school at their parish church.

The Scalias' nine children are Ann Forrest, Eugene, John Francis, Catherine
Elizabeth, Mary Clare, Paul David, Matthew, Christopher James and Margaret Jane.

Lawyer and Professor of Law

In 1961, Scalia joined the Cleveland, Ohio, law firm of Jones, Day, Cockley
& Reavis, where he practiced business law. "Colleagues at the firm," Katzen
notes, "remember him as a 'brash, instantly likable' fellow who impressed them
with his legal abilities and warm, gregarious personality, often engaging other
lawyers in spirited debate over legal issues."

Richard W. Pogue, the managing partner of the law firm describes Scalia
as "a consensus builder despite his strongly held views."[3]

In 1967, Scalia turned down an offer to become a partner in the law firm
and accepted a position as a law professor at the University of Virginia where
he became an expert in administrative law.

Scalia left law teaching in 1971 to take various government positions, but
he returned to teaching in 1977 serving as a visiting professor at Georgetown
University National Law Center, Washington, D.C., in 1977; professor of law
at the University of Chicago Law School, Chicago, Illinois, 1977–82; and as
a visiting professor of law at Stanford Law School, Palo Alto, California,
1980–81. While on the staff at Georgetown University National Law Center,
Scalia was also scholar-in-residence at the American Enterprise Institute, a
conservative think tank in Washington.

It was during these years that Scalia's conservative judicial philosophy
became evident.

> Scalia invoked judicial restraint in mounting a vigorous attack on the Supreme
> Court's controversial 1973 *Roe v. Wade* decision recognizing a woman's con-
> stitutional right to ... [decide whether or not to carry a fetus to term.] Assail-
> ing what he called an "imperial judiciary," the professor decried a tendency in
> the courts to usurp what should be "societal" decisions, declare rights where
> society "never believed they existed," and write those rights into statutes

although there was no public consensus about them. Increasingly, Scalia declared, the judiciary had derailed the democratic process by settling major issues outside the arena of public debate.[4]

Government Service

In 1971, President Richard M. Nixon appointed Scalia as General Counsel in the Office of Telecommunications Policy where he "played a leading role in negotiating a compromise among industry groups to set the framework for the growth of cable television."[5]

For the years 1972–74, Scalia served as Chairman of the Administrative Conference of the United States. This agency was given the task of improving the administrative process within the government.

"From 1974 to 1977," Sally Katzen writes, "he served President Gerald Ford as assistant attorney general for the Office of Legal Counsel at the Justice Department. It was in this position, as legal advisor for the executive branch, that Scalia began to articulate his deep respect for the presidency as an institution—a respect that would later mark his judicial writings."

In his position as assistant attorney general, Scalia issued an opinion that former president Nixon owned the Watergate tapes and documents. The Supreme Court ultimately disagreed and held that the tapes belonged to the government.

Appointment to the United States Court of Appeals

President Ronald Reagan nominated Scalia for a position on the United States Court of Appeals for the District of Columbia Circuit in July of 1982. He was confirmed and assumed his duties August 17, 1982.

> He was regarded by those who argued before him as a well-prepared judge, who genuinely enjoyed using oral arguments as an opportunity to probe, to challenge, and to engage in dialogue with responsive counsel. Scalia also earned the reputation of being collegial—able and willing to work with the other judges on the court to produce agreement or, if not agreement, a clear statement of the differences for others to tackle. As in his previous positions, his judicial colleagues, whether liberal or conservative, became his friends, and he was admired for his legal intellect, earthy wit, and "mean piano."[6]

Furthermore, Sally Katzen writes: "On the Court of Appeals, Scalia began to expound on his longstanding belief that courts and judges have a limited role in the three-branch system of government established by the Framers of the Constitution."

Nomination to the Supreme Court

When Chief Justice Warren E. Burger resigned in 1986, President Reagan nominated Justice William H. Rehnquist to fill the position of chief justice. This left a vacancy on the Court which Reagan sought to fill by nominating Scalia. Although the nomination was opposed by civil rights groups and feminist organizations, the two-day hearing was described as "'tepid' and 'cordial.'"[7] The American Bar Association gave Scalia its highest rating, and the Senate confirmed his nomination by a 98–0 vote on September 17. William H. Rehnquist was confirmed as Chief Justice the same day.

The other members of the Court were Justices William J. Brennan, Jr., Byron R. White, Thurgood Marshall, Harry Blackmun, Lewis F. Powell, Jr., John Paul Stevens and Sandra Day O'Connor.

A biography of Scalia states: "For recreation, the justice plays popular tunes on the piano and enjoys jogging, tennis, squash, and monthly games of five-card stud poker with an informal circle that includes Chief Justice Rehnquist."[8]

AS ASSOCIATE JUSTICE (1986–   )

The Free Exercise of Religion

Galen W. Black, who had a history of drug and alcohol abuse, was employed as a resident assistant in a drug and alcohol treatment clinic. He was drug and alcohol free at the time of his employment in 1982, and continued that way until September, 1983 when, as part of a Native American Church ceremony, he used a small amount of peyote "for spiritual reasons, as a communion."[9] Because his employer was of the opinion that the use of the drug was a relapse of his prior afflictions, Black's employment was terminated. Black then applied for unemployment compensation which was denied. The Court of Appeals of Oregon reversed, being of the opinion that the denial of benefits was an unconstitutional infringement upon his right to the free exercise of religion. The Supreme Court of Oregon agreed and affirmed.[10]

On the same date, the Oregon Supreme Court upheld the free exercise right of Alfred L. Smith to use peyote in a Native American Church ceremony, in circumstances similar to that of Galen W. Black.[11]

Oregon appealed both cases to the United States Supreme Court which reversed, because the record did not indicate whether the use of peyote in a religious ceremony was illegal in Oregon. Justice Stevens, writing for the majority held: "Because we are uncertain about the legality of the religious use of peyote in Oregon, it is not now appropriate for us to decide whether the practice is protected by the Federal Constitution."[12]

Upon hearing the case the second time, the Oregon Supreme Court wrote:

"We conclude that the Oregon statute against the possession of controlled substances, which include peyote, makes no exception for the sacramental use of peyote, but that outright prohibition of good faith religious use of peyote by adult members of the Native American Church would violate the First Amendment...."[13]

On that basis, the Oregon court concluded that Black and Smith were entitled to unemployment compensation.

Oregon again appealed to the United States Supreme Court which disagreed with the Oregon court and reversed, being of the opinion that because the Oregon law makes the use of peyote a crime and does not exempt its use in a religious ceremony, it does not violate the First Amendment.[14] "We have never held," Justice Antonin Scalia declared, "that an individual's religious beliefs excuse him from compliance with an otherwise valid law prohibiting conduct that the State is free to regulate. On the contrary, the record of more than a century of our free exercise jurisprudence contradicts that proposition."

Scalia then distinguished a number of other cases in which the Court had reversed criminal convictions of persons whose actions were religiously motivated. "The only decisions in which we have held that the First Amendment bars application of a neutral, generally applicable law to religiously motivated action have involved not the Free Exercise Clause alone, but the Free Exercise Clause in conjunction with other constitutional protections, such as freedom of speech and of the press...." He then cites a number of such cases, and concludes: "The present case does not present such a hybrid situation, but a free exercise claim unconnected with any communicative activity or parental right."

In response to Black's and Smith's argument "that when otherwise prohibitable conduct is accompanied by religious convictions, not only the convictions but the conduct itself must be free from government regulation," Scalia asserted, "[w]e have never held that, and decline to do so now." Scalia also argued that the Court's use of a "balancing of interests" approach in many free exercise of religion cases, should not be used in this case. "We conclude today," he declared, "that the sounder approach, and the approach in accord with the vast majority of our precedents, is to hold the test inapplicable to such challenges."

Justice O'Connor signed on to the judgment of the Court, but did not concur in Scalia's opinion. For her, Scalia had overlooked much free exercise jurisprudence. "To reach this sweeping result, however," she argued, "the Court must not only give a strained reading of the First Amendment but must also disregard our consistent application of free exercise doctrine to cases involving generally applicable regulations that burden religious conduct."

For O'Connor, the proper focus of the case should be upon the effect that the law has upon the individual's free exercise rights. "We have respected," O'Connor noted, "both the First Amendment's express textual mandate and the governmental interest in regulation of conduct by requiring the government to justify any substantial burden on religiously motivated conduct by a compelling state interest and by means narrowly tailored to achieve that interest."

Freedom of Speech

Picketing and Pamphleteering. When the Supreme Court upheld part and struck down part of the injunction issued by Judge Robert B. McGregor in *Madsen v. Women's Health Center, Inc.*,[15] Justice Scalia dissented. He was of the opinion that excluding the demonstrators from gathering within 36 feet of the clinic, and the ban on excessive noise were a violation of their constitutional rights. "Because I believe," he declared, "that the judicial creation of a 36-foot zone in which only a particular group, which had broken no law, cannot exercise its rights of speech, assembly, and association, and the judicial enactment of a noise prohibition, applicable to that group and that group alone, are profoundly at odds with our First Amendment precedents and traditions, I dissent."

While the Justice was greatly concerned about the First Amendment rights of the abortion protesters in *Madsen*, he did not express the same concern for Margaret McIntyre, who distributed a leaflet which did not contain her name, stating her opposition to a proposed tax levy. The distribution of anonymous literature was a violation of Ohio law. When she continued to distribute the material after being informed that it did not comply with the law, she was convicted and fined $100. Although McIntyre passed away during the pendency of the appeal of her conviction, the executor of her estate brought the case to the Supreme Court, which reversed.[16]

One of the issues discussed by the majority, Justice Clarence Thomas in a concurring opinion, and Justice Scalia in dissent was whether anonymity in the dissemination of information was protected by the First Amendment. The majority and Justice Thomas concluded that it was and voted to reverse McIntyre's conviction. Justice Scalia agreed insofar as anonymity being protected by the First Amendment, but argued that Ohio's interest in the integrity of its election process outweighed any rights which McIntyre had.

In concluding that anonymity was necessary to promote public debate during election campaigns, Justice Stevens for the majority pointed out that: "Under our Constitution, anonymous pamphleteering is not a pernicious, fraudulent practice, but an honorable tradition of advocacy and of dissent." And in this case, "Ohio has not shown that its interest in preventing misuse of anonymous election-related material justifies a prohibition of all uses of that speech."

Scalia posed, and answered, three questions in his dissenting opinion. "The first question is whether protection of the election process justifies limitations upon speech that cannot constitutionally be imposed generally." His answer was yes. "The State has a 'compelling interest in preserving the integrity of the election process.'"

"The second question relevant to our decision is whether a 'right to anonymity' is such a prominent value in our constitutional system that even protection of the electoral process cannot be purchased at its expense. The answer ... is clear: no."

"The third and last question relevant to our decision is whether the prohibition of anonymous campaigning is effective in protecting and enhancing democratic elections." In criticizing the majority for not answering this question, Scalia seeks support from the innumerable state and federal legislators who have voted for laws similar to that in Ohio. "How is it, one must wonder," he argues, "that all of these elected legislators, from around the country, and around the world, could not see what six Justices of this Court see so clearly that they are willing to require the entire Nation to act upon it: that requiring identification of the source of campaign literature does not improve the quality of the campaign?"

Unpopular Speech. Justice Scalia started his opinion in *R. A. V. v. St. Paul*[18] as follows: "In the predawn hours of June 21, 1990, petitioner, [R. A. V.] and several other teenagers allegedly assembled a crudely made cross by taping together broken chair legs. They then allegedly burned the cross inside the fenced yard of a black family that lived across the street from the house where petitioner was staying."

R. A. V. was charged and convicted of violating a St. Paul, Minnesota, ordinance making it a crime "to place on public or private property ... a burning cross ... which one knows ... arouses anger, alarm or resentment in others on the basis of race, color, creed, religion or gender...."

Although all justices voted to reverse R. A. V.'s conviction, not all joined Scalia's opinion. Scalia and the majority found the ordinance unconstitutional because it made only certain kinds of messages illegal. "[W]e conclude," he asserted, "that the ordinance is facially unconstitutional in that it prohibits otherwise permitted speech solely on the basis of the subjects the speech addresses." The disfavored subjects being "race, color, creed, religion or gender."

Public Employees Right to Speak. As noted in Chapter 8, Ardith McPherson was discharged as a clerical employee in Constable Rankin's office for speaking out after learning that President Ronald Reagan had been shot. McPherson concluded her remarks about the President with the words, "if they go for him again, I hope they get him."[18]

In concluding that McPherson's discharge was improper, the majority noted that her statement did not amount to the kind of threat against the President's life that would be punishable under federal law. Furthermore, the majority pointed out, she was not a law enforcement officer, rarely came in contact with the public, did not have access to any sensitive information, and her statement related to a matter of public interest.

Justice Scalia did not agree that McPherson's statement related to a matter of public concern. "Once McPherson stopped explicitly criticizing the President's policies and expressed a desire that he be assassinated, she crossed the line."

However, even if the last part of the statement was related to a matter of public concern, Scalia argued, it was not protected speech. "In sum, since Constable Rankin's interest in maintaining both an esprit de corps and a public image consistent with his office's law enforcement duties outweighs any interest his employees may have in expressing on the job a desire that the President be killed, even assuming that such an expression addresses a matter of public concern it is not protected by the First Amendment from suppression."

Commercial Speech. In 1980, the Court fashioned a rule to guide lower courts in determining when a government restriction on commercial speech is permissible and when it is a violation of the First Amendment. That rule requires that government regulation of commercial speech "directly advance the governmental interest asserted, and ... is no more extensive than is necessary to serve that interest."[19]

With that as its starting point, the Court of Appeals sought a solution to the case of *Fox v. Bd. of Trustees of State Univ. of N.Y.*[20] This case involved the validity of a regulation of the State University of New York (SUNY) prohibiting all "private commercial enterprises ... [from] operat(ing) on State University campuses..." Basing its decision on this regulation, SUNY prohibited the American Future Systems, Inc., from selling "cookware, china, crystal, and silverware to ... [SUNY] students through group demonstrations arranged by students," on campus.

Student Todd Fox brought an action against the University, seeking a declaration that the regulation was a violation of students' free speech and association rights. Although the trial court dismissed the case, the Court of Appeals reversed.

In applying the Supreme Court's rule regulating commercial speech to SUNY's regulation, the Appeals Court concluded that the lower court, in determining "whether ... [the regulation] is not more extensive than is necessary to serve ... [the state's] interest" should have examined the regulation to see if it was "the least restrictive means to accomplish [the] state's interest." The Appeals Court sent the case back to the lower court requesting it to re-examine SUNY's regulation.

The university appealed to the Supreme Court, which reversed.[21] Justice Scalia and the majority held that a state regulation of commercial speech need not be "the least restrictive" means available. They were of the opinion that because "'commercial speech [enjoys] a limited measure of protection, commensurate with its subordinate position in the scale of First Amendment values,' and is subject to 'modes of regulation that might be impermissible in the realm of noncommercial expression'.... [A] least restrictive-means requirement ... imposes a heavy burden on the State." The Court then sent the case back to the lower court for consideration in light of the Court's opinion.

Because they were of the opinion that SUNY's regulation could restrict both commercial and noncommercial speech, Justices Blackmun, Brennan and Marshall dissented:

> We have been told by authoritative university officials that the resolution prohibits a student from meeting with his physician or lawyer in his dorm room, if the doctor or lawyer is paid for the visit. We have similarly been told that the resolution prohibits a student from meeting with a tutor or job counselor in his dorm room. ... Presumably, then, the resolution also forbids a music lesson in the dorm, a form of tutoring. A speech therapist would be excluded, as would an art or drama coach.

A public university cannot categorically prevent these fully protected activities from occurring in a student's dorm room.

Insofar as lawyers' advertising is concerned, Justice Scalia shared Justice O'Connor's position and joined her dissent in *Peel v. Attorney Reg. & Disciplinary Com'n.*[22] At issue in that case was the letterhead of attorney Gary E. Peel which contained the following information:

> "Gary E. Peel
> "Certified Civil Trial Specialist
> "By the National Board of Trial Advocacy
> "Licensed: Illinois, Missouri, Arizona."

The Illinois Disciplinary Commission found that Peel's letterhead was misleading and censured him for it. The Illinois Supreme Court agreed, and Peel appealed to the U.S. Supreme Court which reversed. A majority of the justices were of the opinion that the letterhead was "neither actually nor inherently misleading."

Writing for himself, and Justices Brennan, Blackmun and Kennedy, Justice Stevens pointed out: "The facts stated on petitioner's letterhead are true and verifiable."

Justices O'Connor and Scalia, and Chief Justice Rehnquist were of the opinion that the letterhead was "inherently misleading" and that therefore the state could prohibit it without violating Peel's First Amendment rights.

Places to Speak.

> The question presented is whether a provision of the Tennessee Code, which prohibits the solicitation of votes and the display or distribution of campaign

materials within 100 feet of the entrance to a polling place, violates the First and Fourteenth Amendment.[23]

Mary Rebecca Freeman thought that the answer was yes, that the law did violate her First Amendment rights. She therefore brought an action seeking a declaration of the court to that effect. The court dismissed the case, but the Tennessee Supreme Court reversed being of the opinion "that the statute was not the least restrictive means to serve the State's interest" of protecting the integrity of the voting process, and therefore was unconstitutional as a violation of the First Amendment. Five justices, including Scalia reversed.

For Justice Scalia, this was a very simple case. He argued that because the area around polling places, even though in this case that included part of the street and sidewalk, had been regulated ever since the secret ballot was adopted, the area was not a "traditional public forum." If the area is not a "traditional public forum," free speech activities can be prohibited there so long as the prohibition is viewpoint neutral. And in this case, of course, it was. "It is doctrinally less confusing to acknowledge that the environs of a polling place, on election day, are simply not a 'traditional public forum'—which means that they are subject to speech restrictions that are reasonable and viewpoint neutral."

Miscellaneous Speech Cases. Justice Scalia wrote a lengthy dissent in two cases concerning the question whether the First Amendment protects speech and associational rights of independent contractors from retaliation by government officials. In the first case, a majority of the Court upheld "the right of independent government contractors not to be terminated for exercising their First Amendment rights."[24]

In one case, Keen A. Umbehr's trash hauling contract was terminated by County Commissioners because he had been publicly critical of them.

In one other case, the name of O'Hare Truck Service, Inc., was stricken from a police department rotation list of companies furnishing towing services,[25] because O'Hare's owner, John Gratzianna, refused to make a contribution to Mayor Reid Paxson's re-election campaign, and in fact supported Paxson's opponent.

Writing for the majority, Justice Anthony M. Kennedy declared: "We decline to draw a line excluding independent contractors from the First Amendment safeguards of political association afforded to [government] employees."

Scalia argued, in dissent, that tradition should be the basis for deciding cases such as these, and those involving speech by public employees. "There can be no dispute that, like rewarding one's allies, the correlative act of refusing to reward one's opponents—and at the bottom *both* of today's cases involve exactly that—is an American political tradition as old as the Republic. ... If that long and unbroken tradition of our people does not decide these cases, then what does?"

The Justice then criticizes the majority for extending constitutional protection beyond the text of the Constitution. "What secret knowledge, one must wonder, is breathed into lawyers when they become Justices of this Court, that enables them to discern that a practice which the text of the Constitution does not clearly proscribe, and which our people have *regarded* as constitutional for 200 years, is in fact unconstitutional?"

Scalia then takes the majority to task for the decisions in these two cases:

> The Court must be living in another world. Day by day, case by case, it is busy designing a Constitution for a country I do not recognize. Depending upon which of today's cases one chooses to consider authoritative, it has either (*O'Hare*) thrown out a vast number of practices that are routine in American political life in order to get rid of a few bad apples; or (*Umbehr*) with the same purpose in mind subjected those routine practices to endless, uncertain, case-by-case, balance-all-the-factors-and-who-knows-who-will-win litigation.

Freedom of Association

Public Employees' Right to Political Association.

> Cynthia B. Rutan has been working for the State [of Illinois] since 1974 as a rehabilitation counselor. She claims that since 1981 she has been repeatedly denied promotions to supervisory positions for which she was qualified because she had not worked for or supported the Republican Party. Franklin Taylor, who operates road equipment for the Illinois Department of Transportation, claims that he was denied a promotion in 1983 because he did not have the support of the local Republican Party. ... James W. Moore claims that he has been repeatedly denied state employment as a prison guard because he did not have the support of Republican Party officials.[26]

These individuals brought an action against Illinois and the Republican Party claiming that they had been discriminated against because they were not supporters of the Party. Judge Harold A. Baker dismissed the case, being of the opinion that no First Amendment rights were being violated by the state's practices. The Court of Appeals reversed except as to Moore, concluding that no rights of his were violated by the decision not to hire him as a prison guard because of his lack of support for the Republican Party.

The Supreme Court held that not only was the freedom of associational rights of Rutan and Taylor being infringed upon by their not being promoted, but so was Moore's rights by not being hired because he did not support the Party.

In discussing Rutan's and Taylor's situations, Justice Brennan for the majority declared: "The First Amendment prevents the government, except in the most compelling circumstances, from wielding its power to interfere with its employees' freedom to believe and associate, or not to believe and associate." And insofar as Moore is concerned, Brennan noted that if "Moore's employment application was set aside because he chose not to support the Republican Party, as he asserts, then Moore's First Amendment rights have been violated. Therefore, we find that Moore's complaint was improperly dismissed."

This decision found no favor with Justice Scalia and he faulted the Court for it. "Thus, a new principle that the Court today announces will be enforced by a corps of judges (the Members of this Court included) who overwhelmingly owe their office to its violation. Something must be wrong here, and I suggest it is the Court."

The Justice's criticism of the Court focused upon what he considered the error in extending the reach of the Constitution to invalidate traditionally accepted political norms. "The provisions of the Bill of Rights were designed to restrain majorities from impairing long-recognized personal liberties. They did not create by implication novel individual rights overturning accepted political norms. Thus, when a practice is not expressly prohibited by the text of the Bill of Rights bears the endorsement of a long tradition of open, widespread, and unchallenged use that dates back to the beginning of the Republic, we have no proper basis for striking it down."

In concluding his dissent, the Justice noted that even if he did not think that the Court was wrong, he "would go no further than to allow a cause of action when the employee has lost his position, that is, his formal title and salary. That narrow ground alone is enough to resolve the constitutional claims in the present case." Applying that concession to the petitioners in this case, he would have upheld the dismissal of all claims because none of the petitioners had actually been discharged.

Association With a Political Party. In an effort to attract voters, the Republican Party of Connecticut adopted a rule permitting persons, not registered in a political party, to vote in the Republican primary election.

This was contrary to Connecticut law which required persons wishing to vote in a party primary to be a member of that party. In an action brought by the Republican Party, Judge José A. Cabranes held the law to be unconstitutional as a violation of the First Amendment's right of association. The Court of Appeals and the Supreme Court agreed and affirmed. In upholding the Party's right to have nonmembers vote in their primary election, Justice Thurgood Marshall pointed out: "The Party's attempt to broaden the base of public participation in and support of its activities is conduct undeniably central to the exercise of the right of association."[27]

Connecticut justified the law by arguing that allowing others to vote in a party's primary would add to the burden of administering the election; that the measure prevented party raiding; that closed primaries avoid voter confusion; and that the law protected the integrity of the two-party system. None of these, nor all of them together, the majority concluded, were sufficient to outweigh the Party's freedom of association rights. Justice Scalia did not believe that there was much of an associational interest here and therefore dissented. "In my view," he declared, "the Court's opinion exaggerates the importance of the associational interest at issue, if indeed it does not see one where none exists." Furthermore: "The Connecticut voter who, while steadfastly refusing to register as a Republican, casts a vote in the Republican primary, forms no more meaningful an 'association' with the Party than does the independent or the registered Democrat who responds to questions by a Republican Party pollster."

Freedom of the Press

Obscenity. In 1986, Dallas, Texas enacted a comprehensive ordinance regulating "sexually oriented businesses." Sexually oriented businesses included "an adult arcade, adult bookstore or adult video store, adult cabaret, adult motel, adult motion picture theater, adult theater, escort agency, nude model studio, or sexual encounter center."[28]

Before engaging in any of these kinds of businesses, the owner/operator was required to obtain a license from the city. Several such businesses brought an action seeking a declaration that the ordinance was unconstitutional, contending "that the licensing scheme fails to set a time limit within which the licensing authority must issue a license and, therefore, creates the likelihood of arbitrary denials and concomitant suppression of speech."

A majority of the Supreme Court agreed that the ordinance was unconstitutional, but were unable to agree on the reasons for that result. Justice Scalia, however, would have upheld the law "in all respects." For him, all that Dallas was doing was licensing certain types of "commercial activities," and he therefore did "not think the details of its licensing scheme had to comply with First Amendment standards." "The Constitution," he declared, "does not require a State or municipality to permit a business that intentionally specializes in, and holds itself forth to the public as specializing in, performance or portrayal of sex acts, sexual organs in a state of arousal, or live human nudity. In my view that suffices to sustain the Dallas ordinance."

Miscellaneous Press Cases. "The question presented in this case," Justice Marshall wrote, "is whether a state sales tax scheme that taxes general interest magazines, but exempts newspapers and religious, professional, trade, and sports journals, violates the First Amendment's guarantee of freedom of the press."[29] Marshall and a majority of the justices concluded that the tax was unconstitutional in an action brought by Arkansas Writer's Project, Inc. That group, publisher of a general interest magazine sold in Arkansas, had been assessed the tax for the year 1980 by the Commissioner of Revenue. When the Project was unsuccessful in having the tax declared unconstitutional by Arkansas courts, it appealed to the Supreme Court which agreed with the Project that the law was a violation of the First Amendment.

This was not a difficult case for the majority. Citing prior case law, Marshall declared: "Our cases clearly establish that a discriminatory tax on the press burdens rights protected by the First Amendment." This is true "because selective taxation of the press—either singling out the press as whole or targeting individual members of the press—pose a particular danger of abuse by the State."

Justice Scalia did not see this as a discriminatory tax. For him, the tax was simply a subsidy for those magazines not required to pay the tax. "I dissent from today's decision," he stated, "because it provides no rational basis for distinguishing the subsidy scheme here under challenge from many others that are common and unquestionably lawful."

The Pursuit of Liberty

The Right of Privacy. Justice Scalia had little empathy for the predicament in which Michael H. found himself as the biological father of Victoria whose mother was married to Gerald D. At issue in the case was whether a man who fathers a child born to a woman married to another man has any constitutional rights in the child. In California, the biological father had no rights, because under the law "a child born to a married woman living with her husband is presumed to be a child of the marriage."[30]

When Michael, joined by Victoria's guardian, sought to obtain visiting rights with Victoria, Gerald intervened claiming that because he and Carole were married and living together at the time of Victoria's conception and birth, he was conclusively presumed to be her father. California courts agreed and Michael appealed to the Supreme Court which affirmed. Scalia wrote an opinion which Chief Justice Rehnquist joined. Justices O'Connor and Kennedy signed on to the opinion, but did not entirely agree with Scalia's discussion of issues involved.

In addressing the question of whether Michael had any "liberty" interest as the biological father of Victoria, Scalia asserted that "the legal issue in the present case reduces to whether the relationship between persons in the situation of Michael and Victoria has been treated as a protected family unit under the historic practices of our society, or whether on any other basis it has been accorded special protection. We think it impossible to find that it has. In fact, quite to the contrary, our traditions have protected the marital family (Gerald, Carole, and the child they acknowledge to be theirs) against the sort of claim Michael asserts."

The Justice then concluded: "Where ... the child is born into an extant marital family, the natural father's unique opportunity conflicts with the similarly unique opportunity of the husband of the marriage; and it is not unconstitutional for the State to give categorical preference to the latter."

Five of the justices were of the opinion that Michael H. did have a constitutional liberty interest in his daughter Victoria. Justice Stevens, one of the five however, accepted the trial judge's decision that it would not be in Victoria's best interest to allow visitation rights by Michael.

Justice Scalia was just as adamant in his conclusion that the Constitution does not give a woman the right to abort an unborn child, which right the Court upheld in *Roe v. Wade*.[31] When the Court upheld several Missouri laws restricting abortions, Scalia concurred but criticized the Court for not facing up to the real issue and overrule *Roe*. He wrote, "what will it take, one must wonder, to permit us to reach that fundamental question? The result of our vote today is that we will not reconsider ... [*Roe v. Wade*] even if most of the Justices think it is wrong, unless we have before us a statute that in fact contradicts it...."[32]

Each time thereafter that the Court was faced with state laws restricting a woman's right to make the choice whether or not to bear a child, Scalia voted to uphold the regulations, but continued to insist that *Roe* be overruled. "I continue to believe ... that the Constitution contains no right to an abortion. It is not to be found in the longstanding traditions of our society, nor can it be logically deduced from the text of the Constitution—not, that is, without volunteering a judicial answer to the nonjusticiable question of when human life begins. Leaving this matter to the political process is not only legally correct, it is pragmatically so. That alone—and not lawyerly dissection of federal judicial precedents—can produce compromises satisfying a sufficient mass of the electorate that this deeply felt issue will cease distorting the remainder of our democratic process. The Court should end its disruptive intrusion into this field as soon as possible."[33]

The Justice believed that the issue in the abortion cases was "not whether the power of a woman to abort her unborn child is a 'liberty' in the absolute sense; or even whether it is a liberty of great importance to many women. Of course it is both. The issue is whether it is a liberty protected by the Constitution of the United States. I am sure it is not."[34]

Equal Protection of the Law

Blacks on Juries. In striking down the practice of using peremptory challenges to remove potential jurors because of their race, in *Batson v. Kentucky*[35] Justice Lewis F. Powell, Jr., wrote: "The harm from discriminatory jury selection extends beyond that inflicted on the defendant and the excluded juror to touch the entire community." Justice Scalia was not on the Court when this case was decided.

Scalia was on the Court, however, when it decided *Powers v. Ohio*.[36] In that case, the question to be answered was whether a white man on trial for murder could object to the prosecutor's use of peremptory challenges to strike black persons from the jury. When the prosecutor removed the first black person, Powers asked the trial judge to require the prosecutor to explain why he had struck the black person from the jury. The judge refused the request, and thereafter the prosecutor struck six more blacks from the panel. Powers was convicted, and his conviction was upheld by Ohio courts. The Supreme Court, however, reversed.

Because Powers was white, Ohio argued that he could not raise the equal protection claim because people of his race were not being excluded from the jury. In an opinion written by Justice Anthony M. Kennedy, the Court rejected Ohio's argument.

> We hold that the Equal Protection Clause prohibits a prosecutor from using the State's peremptory challenges to exclude otherwise qualified and unbiased persons from the petit jury solely by reason of their race, a practice that forecloses a significant opportunity to participate in civic life. An individual juror does not have a right to sit on any particular petit jury, but he or she does possess the right not to be excluded from one on account of race.

Scalia, in dissent, expressed the opinion that "today's holding cannot be considered in accordance with our prior law. It is a clear departure." After a review of a number of cases involving selection of jurors, the Justice concluded: "In sum, we have *never* held, or even said, that a juror has an equal protection right not to be excluded from a particular case through peremptory challenge; and the existence of such a right would call into question the continuing existence of a centuries-old system that has important beneficial effects."

The Court expanded the *Batson* rule to prohibit a private litigant to use peremptory challenges to remove black persons from a jury in a civil case.[37] The Court also held that white defendants cannot peremptorily strike black persons from a jury in a case in which the defendants are charged with assaulting black persons.[38] Scalia dissented in both of these cases. In the latter case he wrote: "Today's decision gives the lie once again to the belief that an activist, 'evolutionary' constitutional jurisprudence always evolves in the direction of greater individual rights. In the interest of promoting the supposedly greater good of race relations in the society as a whole (make no mistake that is what underlies all of this), we use the Constitution to destroy the ages-old right of criminal defendants to exercise peremptory challenges as they wish, to secure a jury that they consider fair."

Gender Discrimination. In J. E. B.'s trial to establish his paternity and for child support, Alabama, acting on behalf of the mother, used all of its peremptory challenges to strike men from the jury. The jury, which was eventually chosen, consisted only of women. J. E. B. objected, arguing that the elimination of males was a denial of equal protection of the law. The trial court disagreed, and J. E. B. was found to be the father of the child and ordered to pay child support. The Alabama appellate courts affirmed, but the Supreme Court reversed with an opinion written by Justice Blackmun. He wrote:

> Today we reaffirm what, by now, should be axiomatic: Intentional discrimina-
> tion on the basis of gender by state actors violates the Equal Protection Clause,
> particularly where, as here, the discrimination serves to ratify and perpetuate
> invidious, archaic, and overbroad stereotypes about the relative abilities of men
> and women.[39]

In an opinion very critical of the majority's decision, Scalia dissented.
He expressed the view "that most of the opinion is quite irrelevant to the case
at hand." He did not believe that J. E. B. had been harmed by the exclusion
of men from the jury, and that the scientific evidence clearly established that
he was the father of the child. Furthermore, he argued the only thing the decision does is "to pay conspicuous obeisance to the equality of the sexes ... [and]
imperils a practice that has been considered an essential part of a fair jury trial
since the dawn of the common law. The Constitution neither requires nor
permits this vandalizing of our people's traditions."

Justice Scalia was no happier with the Court's decision in *United States
v. Virginia*.[40] In that case, a majority of the justices held that the males-only
policy of Virginia Military Institute (VMI) was a violation of the Equal Protection Clause. After reviewing prior cases which dealt with gender-based
discrimination, Justice Ruth Bader Ginsburg pointed out that "the Court has
repeatedly recognized that neither federal nor state government acts compat-
ibly with the equal protection principle when a law or official policy denies to
women, simply because they are women, full citizenship stature—equal opportunity to aspire, achieve, participate in and contribute to society based on their
individual talents and capacities."

Concluding her opinion, Justice Ginsburg wrote: "A prime part of the
history of our Constitution, historian Richard Morris recounted, is the story
of the extension of constitutional rights and protections to people once ignored
or excluded. ... There is no reason to believe that the admission of women
capable of all the activities required of VMI cadets would destroy the Institute rather than enhance its capacity to serve the 'more perfect Union.'"[41]

Scalia started his dissent as follows: "Today the Court shuts down an
institution that has served the people of the Commonwealth of Virginia with
pride and distinction for over a century and a half. To achieve that desired
result, it rejects (contrary to our established practice) the factual findings of
two courts below, sweeps aside the precedents of this Court, and ignores the
history of our people."

The Justice acknowledges that the "question to be answered, ... is whether
the exclusion of women from VMI is 'substantially related to an important
governmental goal.'" He did not believe, however, that the majority really
applied that test, and he proceeded to do so. For him, the test was satisfied by
the findings made by the District Court concerning the value of single-sex
education. "'[I]n the light of this very substantial authority favoring single-
sex education,' the District Court concluded that 'the VMI Board's decision

to maintain an all-male institution is fully justified even without taking into consideration the other unique features of VMI's teaching and training.' ... This finding alone, which even this Court cannot dispute, ... should be sufficient to demonstrate the constitutionality of VMI's all-male composition."

The Justice believed that this decision would be the end of government sponsored single-sex education. "The enemies of single-sex education have won; by persuading only seven Justices (five would have been enough) that their view of the world is enshrined in the Constitution, they have effectively imposed that view on all 50 States."

For Fundamental Rights. Amendment 2 to the Colorado Constitution "prohibits all legislative, executive, or judicial action at any level of state or local government designed to protect the named class, a class we shall refer to as homosexual persons or gays and lesbians."[42]

A number of individuals, school districts, cities and counties brought suit seeking a declaration that Amendment 2 was unconstitutional as a violation of equal protection of the law and an injunction against its enforcement. After conducting an evidentiary hearing, Judge H. Jeffrey Bayless agreed with the plaintiffs that the Amendment was unconstitutional and granted the injunction. The Supreme Court of Colorado affirmed, as did the United States Supreme Court.

Justice Kennedy wrote:

> The State's principal argument in defense of Amendment 2 is that it puts gays and lesbians in the same position as all other persons. So, the State says, the measure does no more than deny homosexuals special rights. This reading of the amendment's language is implausible. We rely not upon our own interpretation of the amendment but upon the authoritative construction of Colorado's Supreme Court. The state court, deeming it unnecessary to determine the full extent of the amendment's reach, found it invalid even on a modest reading of its implications.

Kennedy points out that Colorado and some of its cities have enacted broad anti-discrimination laws, which make it unlawful for certain persons and entities to discriminate. These laws also "set forth an extensive catalogue of traits which cannot be the basis for discrimination, including age, military status, marital status, pregnancy, parenthood, custody of a minor child, political affiliation, physical or mental disability of an individual or of his or her associates—and, in recent times, sexual orientation." He then points out that Amendment 2 would prohibit homosexuals from securing the same protection against discrimination that these laws provide for other persons.

Kennedy ends his opinion:

> We must conclude that Amendment 2 classifies homosexuals not to further a proper legislative end but to make them unequal to everyone else. This

Colorado cannot do. A State cannot so deem a class of persons a stranger to its laws. Amendment 2 violates the Equal Protection Clause, and the judgment of the Supreme Court of Colorado is affirmed.

Scalia's disdain for the Court's decision and opinion is evident throughout his dissent. "Since the Constitution of the United States says nothing about this subject," he argues, "it is left to be resolved by normal democratic means, including the democratic adoption of provisions in state constitutions. This Court has no business imposing upon all Americans the resolution favored by the elite class from which Members of this institution are selected, pronouncing that 'animosity' toward homosexuality, ... is evil. I vigorously dissent."

The case of *Bowers v. Hardwick*,[43] the Justice insisted, requires that Amendment 2 be upheld. "If it is constitutionally permissible for a State to make homosexual conduct criminal, surely it is constitutionally permissible for a State to enact other laws merely *disfavoring* homosexual conduct."[44] And while agreeing that the law did discriminate against homosexuals, the Justice was of the opinion that "Coloradans are ... *entitled* to be hostile toward homosexual conduct." He was of the opinion, however, "that the degree of hostility reflected by Amendment 2 is the smallest conceivable."

Scalia criticizes the majority for taking sides "in this culture war."

> When the Court takes sides in the culture wars, it tends to be with the knights rather than the villains—and more specifically with the Templars, reflecting views and values of the lawyer class from which the Court's Members are drawn. How that class feels about homosexuality will be evident to anyone who wishes to interview job applicants at virtually any of the Nation's law schools. The interviewer may refuse to offer a job because the applicant is a Republican; because he is an adulterer; because he went to the wrong prep school or belongs to the wrong country club; because he eats snails; because he is a womanizer; because she wears real-animal fur; or even because he hates the Chicago Cubs. But if the interviewer should wish not to be an associate or partner of an applicant because he disapproves of the applicant's homosexuality, *then* he will have violated the pledge which the Association of American Law Schools requires of all its member-schools to exact from job interviewers: "assurance of the employer's willingness" to hire homosexuals.

AS A JUSTICE FOR THE GOVERNMENT

The theme that runs through Justice Scalia's opinion in *Employment Div., Ore. Dept. of Human Res. v. Smith*, is deference to government regulation, in this case the regulation of the use of peyote as part of a religious ritual, and little concern for the religious beliefs of the individuals involved. "Respondents [Smith and Black]" he argues, "urge us to hold, quite simply, that when otherwise prohibitable conduct is accompanied by religious convictions, not only the convictions but the conduct itself must be free from governmental regulation. We have never held that, and decline to do so now."[45]

But that's not really what the respondents assert. They argue, as does Justice O'Connor, that the Court has "respected both the First Amendment's express textual mandate and the governmental interest in regulation of conduct by requiring the government to justify any substantial burden on religiously motivated conduct by a compelling state interest and by means narrowly tailored to achieve that interest." The respondents, therefore, argue that there is no compelling state interest to justify making criminal the use of peyote as part of a religious ritual. And clearly there was no state compelling interest here, because, as Justice Blackmun pointed out "the State actually has not evinced any concrete interest in enforcing its drug laws against religious users of peyote. Oregon has never sought to prosecute respondents, and does not claim that it has made significant enforcement efforts against other religious users of peyote. The State's asserted interest thus amounts only to the symbolic preservation of an unenforced prohibition."

In voting to uphold Ohio's law prohibiting the distribution of anonymous campaign literature, the Justice criticizes the majority for not deferring to the judgment of legislators that requiring the distributor to provide his or her name is necessary to inform the recipient about the distributor and to prevent fraud in the election process. "Such a universal and long established American legislative practice," he argues, "must be given precedence, I think, over historical and academic speculation regarding a restriction that assuredly does not go to the heart of free speech."[46]

For the majority, however, the real issue was whether McIntyre's First Amendment right to distribute the information anonymously was outweighed by the interests of the state in providing the recipient with McIntyre's name. The Court's answer was that the state's asserted interests did not outweigh McIntyre's First Amendment right to distribute the leaflet anonymously.

In dissenting in the *McPherson's* case, Scalia started his opinion as follows: "I agree with the proposition, felicitously put by Constable Rankin's counsel, that no law enforcement agency is required by the First Amendment to permit one of its employees to 'ride with the cops and cheer for the robbers.'"[47] While he acknowledges that this statement was made felicitously, the thought that pervades his dissent is that when McPherson said, "If they go for him [the president] again, I hope they get him," she really meant it.

The majority in this case placed the burden upon Constable Rankin to justify his discharge of McPherson for her speech, and concluded that he had not met that burden, considering the minor position she held in the Constable's office. Scalia, on the other hand, did not believe that McPherson even had any right to say what she did.

Justice Scalia and the Court, in the *Fox* case, held that the government could regulate commercial speech but did not have to do so by "the least restrictive means,"[48] which the government must do when it regulates other kinds of speech. This, of course, will make it much easier for government to regulate such speech.

In dissenting in the *Rutan* case, Scalia wrote that "traditions are themselves the stuff out of which the Court's principles are to be formed." And he continues, "I know of no other way to formulate a constitutional jurisprudence that reflects, as it should, the principles adhered to, over time, by the American people, rather than those favored by the personal (and necessarily shifting) philosophical dispositions of a majority of this Court."[49]

Justice Stevens responded to Scalia's argument by quoting from an opinion he [Stevens] had written in 1972 while a member of the Court of Appeals. "In the *Lewis* case, I noted the obvious response to this position: '[I]f the age of a pernicious practice were a sufficient reason for its continued acceptance, the constitutional attack on racial discrimination would, of course, have been doomed to failure.' ... See, e.g., *Brown v. Board of Education*, 347 U.S. 483 (1954)."[50]

Scalia disagreed: "I argue for the role of tradition in giving content to *ambiguous* constitutional text; no tradition can supersede the Constitution."[51] And, he continued, even if "separate but equal" facilities had been a "tradition," its validity had been challenged as far back as Justice John M. Harlan's dissenting opinion in *Plessy v. Ferguson*.[52]

While Justice Harlan did indeed challenge the validity of the "separate but equal" doctrine in 1896, the doctrine was approved by the Supreme Court following *Plessy*, up to and including two cases decided in 1950.[53] Both cases involved the constitutionality of state-operated separate graduate schools for blacks. The Supreme Court specifically refused to reverse the "separate but equal" doctrine and instead concluded that the respective states had violated the Equal Protection Clause because neither school provided *equal* facilities for black students. Separate but equal educational facilities was the norm throughout a large part of the United States until the Court struck down that concept in *Brown v. Board of Education* in 1954.

Scalia reiterated his position that where the text of the Constitution is ambiguous, the Court should defer to tradition in deciding cases when he voted to uphold the Tennessee law prohibiting solicitation of votes and display of campaign material within 100 feet of a polling place. He argued that the 100-foot area was not a "traditional public forum," and therefore speech activities could be prohibited there. He reached this conclusion even though in many instances a 100-foot buffer zone would encompass streets and sidewalks which are "traditional public forums." His conclusion is based upon the fact that many states ban electioneering near polling places, and therefore those areas have not been traditionally used for speech activities.

Justice Stevens answers this argument by pointing out that "[w]e have never regarded tradition as a proxy for necessity where necessity must be demonstrated. To the contrary, our election-law jurisprudence is rich with examples of traditions that, though long standing, were later held to be unnecessary."[54] Furthermore, a majority of the justices have chosen not to accept Scalia's position that the Constitution should be interpreted by following long-standing traditions.[55]

No opinion fully expresses Scalia's views on freedom of the press. With the exception of the obscenity cases, he voted a few more times for freedom of the press than he voted against it. However, shortly after he joined the Court, he suggested that the test for obscenity as developed in *Miller v. California*[56] needed reexamination, presumably to make it easier to apply to the allegedly obscene materials.[57]

The Justice did not believe that a woman had any kind of a constitutional right to abort a child, and therefore consistently voted to uphold laws regulating that procedure. And he did not believe that a biological father had a liberty interest in the child he fathered with a then married woman.[58] However, when the Court struck down a requirement that prisoners obtain permission from the prison superintendent before they marry, Scalia agreed.[59]

Justice Scalia was not on the Court when the Court held, in *Batson*, that it was a violation of equal protection to peremptorily strike jurors because of their race. However, as the text above indicates, he thereafter consistently voted not to extend the holding of that case. And as the text also points out, Scalia was not a supporter of equal rights for women, men or for gays and lesbians.[60]

At the end of his concurring and dissenting opinion in the *Madsen* case, Justice Scalia indicated that "all friends of liberty" should be concerned with the majority's decision to uphold the injunction prohibiting demonstrators from entering a 36-foot buffer zone around an abortion clinic.

The Justice's rigid adherence, however, to the philosophy of judicial restraint, should concern "all friends of liberty" even much more so. By using that philosophy as the basis for his votes in cases involving individual liberty, the Justice, much of the time, upholds governmental infringement upon the freedoms guaranteed by the Constitution. Justice Scalia is therefore included as a *Justice for the Government*.

EPILOGUE

Justice Potter Stewart, during an address at a *Seminar on Media and the Law*, said to his audience composed of many members of the press:

> Where, ladies and gentlemen ..., do you think these great constitutional rights that you were so vehemently asserting, and in which you were so conspicuously wallowing yesterday, where do you think they come from? The stork didn't bring them. These came from the judges of this country, from these villains here sitting at the table. That's where they came from. They came because the courts of this country at some time or place when some other agency of government was trying to push the press around or, indeed, may be trying to do you in, it's the courts that protected you. And that's where all these constitutional rights come from .... It's not that it was done for you or that it was done for ourselves. It happened because it is our understanding that that's what the Constitution provides and protects. But let me point out that the Constitution of the United States is not a self-executing document...[1]

While Justice Stewart was referring to freedom of the press as guaranteed by the First Amendment, his statement is true with regard to all rights protected by the Constitution. It is judges, (and more specifically justices of the Supreme Court), that have given substance to the rights of freedom of religion, speech, press, assembly, and association in the First Amendment; the rights of privacy, travel and work, in the Due Process Clauses of the Fifth and Fourteenth Amendments; and the requirement of Equal Protection of the Laws in the Fourteenth Amendment.

Justice Stewart was certainly aware, of course, that not all "judges (and justices) of this country" have voted all of the time to uphold constitutional rights. Our history is to the contrary. Many judges and justices, for example, have voted much of the time to permit government to restrict the exercise of these rights. Among them are the justices profiled herein, who have not been at the vanguard of protecting constitutional liberties.

It is clear, therefore, that because the "Constitution of the United States is not a self-executing document," the extent to which we enjoy the rights guaranteed therein depends upon the decisions made by our judges and justices.

Justice Hugo Black summed up the responsibility of the judiciary this way:

> Finally, our Constitution was the first to provide for a really independent judiciary. ... In this country the judiciary was made independent because it has, I believe, the primary responsibility and duty of giving force and effect to constitutional liberties and limitations upon the executive and legislative branches.[2]

APPENDIX: VOTING RECORDS OF THESE NINE JUSTICES FOR THE GOVERNMENT

Column headings correspond to justices' last names; i.e., Ho is Justice Oliver Wendell Holmes, Jr.; F is Justice Felix Frankfurter; J is Justice Robert H. Jackson; and Ha is Justice John M. Harlan.
F indicates a vote For individual freedoms over government restrictions and A indicates a vote Against.

	Ho	F	J	Ha

THE CONSTITUTION FOLLOWS THE FLAG

	Ho	F	J	Ha
Hawaii v. Mankicki, 190 U.S. 197 (1903)	A			
Kepner v. United States, 195 U.S. 100 (1904)	F			
Dorr v. United States, 195 U.S. 138 (1904)	A			
Rassmussen v. United States, 197 U.S. 516 (1905)	F			
Trono v. United States, 199 U.S. 521 (1905)	A			
Weems v. United States, 217 U.S. 349 (1910)	F			
Dowdell v. United States, 221 U.S. 325 (1911)	A			

CIVIL RIGHTS ACTS

	Ho	F	J	Ha
James V. Bowman, 190 U.S. 127 (1903)	A			
Hodges v. Unites States, 203 U.S. 1 (1906)	A			

THE PURSUIT OF LIBERTY

The Right to Work

	Ho	F	J	Ha
Atkin v. Kansas, 191 U.S. 207 (1903)	A			
Lochner v. New York, 198 U.S. 45 (1905)	A			

	Ho	F	J	Ha
Adair v. United States, 208 U.S. 161 (1908)	A			
Muller v. Oregon, 208 U.S. 412 (1908)	A			
Smith v. Texas, 233 U.S. 630 (1914)	A			
Coppage v. Kansas, 236 U.S. 1 (1915)	F			
Adams v. Tanner, 244 U.S. 590 (1917)	A			
Barsky v. Regents, 347 U.S. 442 (1954)		F	A	

The Right to Travel

	Ho	F	J	Ha
Edwards v. California, 314 U.S. 160 (1941)		F	F	
Kent v. Dulles, 357 U.S. 116 (1958)		F		A
Dayton v. Dulles, 357 U.S. 144 (1958)	F			A
New York v. O'Neil, 359 U.S. 1 (1959)		A		A
Aptheker v. Secretary of State, 378 U.S. 500 (1964)				A
Zemel v. Rusk, 381 U.S. 1 (1965)				A
United States v. Guest, 383 U.S. 745 (1966)				F
Shapero v. Thompson, 394 U.S. 618 (1969)				A

The Right of Privacy

	Ho	F	J	Ha
Jacobson v. Massachusetts, 197 U.S. 11 (1905)	A			
Poe v. Ullman, 367 U.S. 497 (1961)				F
Armstrong v. Manzo, 380 U.S. 545 (1965)				F
Griswold v. Connecticut, 381 U.S. 479 (1965)				F
Wisconsin v. Constantineau, 400 U.S. 433 (1971)				F

Miscellaneous Liberty Cases

	Ho	F	J	Ha
Int. Postal Supply Co. v. Bruce, 194 U.S. 601 (1904)	A			
Chambers v. B. & O. R. R. Co, 207 U.S. 142 (1907)	A			
Meyer v. Nebraska, 262 U.S. 390 (1923)	A			
Bartels v. Iowa, 262 U.S. 404 (1923	A			
Pierce v. Society of Sisters, 268 U.S. 510 (1925)	F			
Yu Cong Eng v. Trinidad, 271 U.S. 500 (1926)	F			
Farrington v. Tokushige, 273 U.S. 284 (1927)	F			
Buck v. Bell, 274 U.S. 200 (1927)	A			

THE FREE EXERCISE OF RELIGION

	Ho	F	J	Ha
Selective Service Draft Cases, 245 U.S. 366 (1918)	F			
United States v. Schwimmer, 279 U.S. 644 (1929)	F			
United States v. Macintosh, 283 U.S. 605 (1931)	F			
United States v. Bland, 283 U.S. 636 (1931)	F			
Cantwell v. Connecticut, 310 U.S. 296 (1940)		F		
Minersville District v. Gobitis, 310 U.S. 586 (1940)		A		
Jones v. Opelika, 316 U.S. 584 (1942)			A	
Jamison v. Texas, 318 U.S. 413 (1943)		F	F	
Largent v. Texas, 318 U.S. 418 (1943)			F	
Jones v. Opelika, 319 U.S. 103 (1943)		A	A	

	Ho	F	J	Ha
Murdock v. Pennsylvania, 319 U.S. 105 (1943)			A	
Bd. of Education v. Barnette, 319 U.S. 624 (1943)	A	F		
Falbo v. United States, 320 U.S. 549 (1944)	A	A		
Prince v. Massachusetts, 321 U.S. 158 (1944)	F	F		
Follett v. McCormick, 321 U.S. 573 (1944)	A	A		
United States v. Ballard, 322 U.S. 78 (1944)	A	F		
In re Summers, 325 U.S. 561 (1945)	A	A		
Marsh v. Alabama, 326 U.S. 501 (1946)	F			
Tucker v. Texas, 326 U.S. 517 (1946)	F			
Estep v. United States, 327 U.S. 114 (1946)	F			
Girouard v. United States, 328 U.S. 61 (1946)	A			
Cleveland v. United States, 329 U.S. 14 (1946)	A		F	
Niemotko v. Maryland, 340 U.S. 268 (1951)	F	F		
Kunz v. New York, 340 U.S. 290 (1951)	F	A		
Kredroff v. St. Nicholas Cath. Church, 344 U.S. 94 (1952)	F	A		
Fowler v. Rhode Island, 345 U.S. 67 (1953)	F	F		
Poulos v. New Hampshire, 345 U.S. 395 (1953)	A	A		
Dickinson v. United States, 346 U.S. 389 (1953)	F	A		
Witmer v. United States, 348 U.S. 375 (1955)	A			
Sicurella v. United States, 348 U.S. 385 (1955)	F			
First Unit. Church v. Los Angeles, 357 U.S. 545 (1958)	F			F
Kreshik v. St. Nicholas Cath. Church, 363 U.S. 190 (1960)	F			F
McGowan v. Maryland, 366 U.S. 420 (1961)	A			A
Braunfeld v. Brown, 366 U.S. 599 (1961)	A			A
Gallagher v. Crown Kosher Mkt., 366 U.S. 617 (1961)	A			A
Torcaso v. Watkins, 367 U.S. 488 (1961)	F			F
Sherbert v. Verner, 374 U.S. 398 (1964)				A
United States v. Seeger, 380 U.S. 163 (1965)				F
Presbyterian Church v. Hull Church, 393 U.S. 440 (1969)				F
Welsh v. United States, 398 U.S. 333 (1970)				F
Gillette v. United States, 401 U.S. 437 (1971)				A

FREEDOM OF SPEECH

Pamphleteering and Soliciting

	Ho	F	J	Ha
Fox v. Washington, 236 U.S. 273 (1915)	A			
Abrams v. United States, 250 U.S. 616 (1919)	F			
Pierce v. United States, 252 U.S. 239 (1920)	F			
Gitlow v. New York, 268 U.S. 652 (1925)	F			
Schneider v. State, 308 U.S. 147 (1939)			F	
Martin v. Struthers, 319 U.S. 141 (1943)		A	A	
Hartzel v. United States, 322 U.S. 680 (1944)		A	A	
Beauharnais v. Illinois, 343 U.S. 250 (1952)		A	F	
Staub v. Baxley, 355 U.S. 313 (1958)		A		F
Talley v. California, 362 U.S. 60 (1960)		A		F
Ashton v. Kentucky, 384 U.S. 195 (1966)				F
O.B.A. v. Keefe, 402 U.S. 415 (1971)				A

Picketing and Parading

	Ho	F	J	Ha
Thornhill v. Alabama, 310 U.S. 88 (1940)		F		
Carlson v. California, 310 U.S. 106 (1940)		F		

	Ho	F	J	Ha
Drivers Union v. Meadowmoor, 312 U.S. 287 (1941)		A		
A. F. of L. v. Swing, 312 U.S. 321 (1941)		F		
Cox v. New Hampshire, 312 U.S. 569 (1941)		A		
Carpenters Union v. Ritter's Cafe, 315 U.S. 722 (1942)		A	A	
Bakery Drivers Local v. Wohl, 315 U.S. 769 (1942)		F	F	
Cafeteria Workers Union v. Angelos, 320 U.S. 293 (1943)		F	F	
Giboney v. Empire Storage, 336 U.S. 490 (1949)		A	A	
Hughes v. Superior Ct., 339 U.S. 460 (1950)		A	A	
Teamsters Union v. Hanke, 339 U.S. 470 (1950)		A	A	
Building & Service Union v. Gazzam, 339 U.S. 532 (1950)		A	A	
Plumbers Union v. Graham, 345 U.S. 192 (1953)		A	A	
Teamsters Union v. Vogt, Inc., 354 U.S. 284 (1957)		A		A
Edwards v. South Carolina, 372 U.S. 229 (1963)				F
Henry v. Rock Hill, 376 U.S. 776 (1964)				F
Cox v. Louisiana, 379 U.S. 536 (1965)				F
Cox v. Louisiana, 379 U.S. 559 (1965)				A
Adderley v. Florida, 385 U.S. 39 (1966)				A
Cameron v. Johnson, 390 U.S. 611 (1968)				A
Shuttlesworth v. Birmingham, 394 U.S. 147 (1969)				F

Unpopular Speech

	Ho	F	J	Ha
Turner v. Williams, 194 U.S. 279 (1904)	A			
Halter v. Nebraska, 205 U.S. 34 (1907)	A			
Schenck v. United States, 249 U.S. 47 (1919)	A			
Frohwerk v. United States, 249 U.S. 204 (1919)	A			
Debs v. United States, 249 U.S. 211 (1919)	A			
Gilbert v. Minnesota, 254 U.S. 325 (1920)	A			
Whitney v. California, 274 U.S. 357 (1927)	A			
Stromberg v. Carlson, 283 U.S. 359 (1931)	F			
Chaplinsky v. New Hampshire, 315 U.S. 568 (1942)		A	A	
Taylor v. Mississippi, 319 U.S. 583 (1943)		F	F	
Bridges v. Wixon, 326 U.S. 135 (1945)		A		
Terminiello v. Chicago, 337 U.S. 1 (1949)		A	A	
Feiner v. New York, 340 U.S. 315 (1951)		A	A	
Dennis v. United States, 341 U.S. 494 (1951)		A	A	
Yates v. United States, 354 U.S. 298 (1957)		F		F
United States v. O'Brien, 391 U.S. 367 (1968)				A
Tinker v. Des Moines Sch. Dist., 393 U.S. 503 (1969)				A
Cohen v. California, 403 U.S. 15 (1971)				F

Public Employees' Right to Speak

	Ho	F	J	Ha
United Public Workers v. Mitchell, 330 U.S. 75 (1947)	A			
Pickering v. Bd. of Education, 391 U.S. 563 (1968)				F

Commercial Speech

	Ho	F	J	Ha
Valentine v. Chrestensen, 316 U.S. 52 (1942)		A	A	
Railway Express v. New York, 336 U.S. 106 (1949)		A	A	

Ho F J Ha

Places to Speak

	Ho	F	J	Ha
Amalg. Food Employ. Union v. Logan Valley Plaza, 391 U.S. 308 (1968)		F		

Miscellaneous Speech

	Ho	F	J	Ha
Thomas v. Collins, 323 U.S. 516 (1945)	A	F		
Saia v. New York, 334 U.S. 558 (1948)	A	A		
Kovacs v. Cooper, 336 U.S. 77 (1949)	A	A		
Public Utilities Comm'n. v. Pollak, 343 U.S. 451 (1949)		A		
United States v. Harriss, 347 U.S. 612 (1954)	A	F		
Garrison v. Louisiana, 379 U.S. 64 (1964)			F	
Stanford v. Texas, 379 U.S. 476 (1965)			F	
Lamont v. Postmaster General, 381 U.S. 301 (1965)			F	
Carroll v. President and Comm. of Princes Anne, 393 U.S. 175 (1968)			F	
Schacht v. United States, 398 U.S. 58 (1970)			F	

FREEDOM OF ASSOCIATION

Affidavits and Oaths

	Ho	F	J	Ha
Communications Assn. v. Douds, 339 U.S. 382 (1950)	A	A		
Gerende v. Election Board, 341 U.S. 56 (1951)	A	A		
Garner v. Los Angeles Board, 341 U.S. 716 (1951)	A	A		
Wieman v. Updegraff, 344 U.S. 183 (1952)	F			
Speiser v. Randall, 357 U.S. 513 (1958)	F		F	
First Unit. Chruch v. Los Angeles, 357 U.S. 545 (1958)	F		F	
Cramp v. Bd. of Ed., 368 U.S. 278 (1961)	F		F	
Baggett v. Bullitt, 377 U.S. 360 (1964)			A	
Elfbrandt v. Russell, 384 U.S. 11 (1966)			A	
Keyishian v. Bd. of Regents, 385 U.S. 589 (1967)			A	
Whitehill v. Elkins, 389 U.S. 54 (1967)			A	
Schneider v. Smith, 390 U.S. 17 (1968)			F	

Blacklisting and Punishment for Membership

	Ho	F	J	Ha
Joint Anti-Fascist Committee v. McGrath, 341 U.S. 123 (1951)	F	F		
Dennis v. United States, 341 U.S. 494 (1951)	A	A		
Adler v. Bd. of Ed., 342 U.S. 485 (1952)	A	A		
Carlson v. Landon, 342 U.S. 524 (1952)	F	A		
Harisiades v. Schaughnessy, 342 U.S. 580 (1952)	A	A		
Galvin v. Press, 347 U.S. 522 (1954)	A	A		
Fleming v. Nestor, 363 U.S. 603 (1960)	A		A	
Communist Party v. Control Board, 367 U.S. 1 (1961)	A		A	
Scales v. United States, 367 U.S.203 (1961)	A		A	
Noto v. United States, 367 U.S. 290 (1961)	F		F	
United States v. Robel, 389 U.S. 258 (1967)			A	

Ho F J Ha

Associational Privacy

Case	Ho	F	J	Ha
United States v. Rumely, 345 U.S. 41 (1953)	F	F		
Schware v. Bd. of Bar Examiners, 353 U.S. 232 (1957)	F			F
Konigsberg v. State Bar, 353 U.S. 252 (1957)	A			A
Watkins v. United States, 354 U.S. 178 (1957)	F			F
Sweezy v. United States, 354 U.S. 234 (1957)	F			F
Beilan v. Board of Education, 357 U. 399 (1958)	A			A
NAACP v. Alabama, 357 U.S. 449 (1958)	F			F
Uphaus v. Wyman, 360 U.S. 72 (1959)	A			A
Barenblatt v. United States, 360 U.S. 109 (1959)	A			A
Bates v. Little Rock, 361 U.S. 516 (1960)	F			F
Uphaus v. Wyman, 364 U.S. 388 (1960)	A			A
Shelton v. Tucker, 364 U.S. 479 (1960)	A			A
Wilkinson v. United States, 365 U.S. 399 (1961)	A			A
Braden v. United States, 365 U.S. 431 (1961)	A			A
Konigsberg v. State Bar, 366 U.S. 36 (1961)	A			A
In re Anastaplo, 366 U.S. 82 (1961)	A			A
Louisiana v. NAACP, 366 U.S. 293 (1961)	F			F
Gibson v. Florida Leg. Committee, 372 U.S. 539 (1963)				A
NAACP v. Alabama, 377 U.S. 288 (1964)				F
DeGregory v. New Hampshire Atty. Gen., 383 U.S. 825 (1966)				A
Baird v. State Bar of Arizona, 401 U.S. 1 (1971)				A
In re Stolar, 401 U.S. 23 (1971)				A
Law Students Res. Council v. Wadmond, 401 U.S. 154 (1971)				A

For Advancement of Legal Goals

Case	Ho	F	J	Ha
NAACP v. Button, 371 U.S. 415 (1963)				A
Railroad Trainmen v. Virginia Bar, 377 U.S. 1 (1964)				A
United Mine Workers v. Illinois Bar, 389 U.S. 217 (1967)				A
United Transp. Union v. Michigan Bar, 401 U.S. 576 (1971)				A

Political Parties: Ballot Access and New Members

Case	Ho	F	J	Ha
Williams v. Rhodes, 393 U.S. 23 (1968)				F

Miscellaneous Association Cases

Case	Ho	F	J	Ha
Waugh v. Mississippi University, 237 U.S. 589 (1915)	A			
American Foundries v. Tri City Council, 257 U.S. 184 (1921)	F			
Texas & N. O. R. Co. v. Railway Clerks, 281 U.S. 548 (1930)	F			
United States v. Auto Workers, 352 U.S. 567 (1957)			A	A

FREEDOM OF THE PRESS

Contempt of Court for Publication

Case	Ho	F	J	Ha
Patterson v. Colorado, 205 U.S. 454 (1907)	A			
Toledo Newspaper Co. v. United States, 247 U.S. 402 (1918)	F			

Ho F J Ha

	Ho	F	J	Ha
Bridges v. California, 314 U.S. 252 (1941)		A	F	
Pennekamp v. Florida, 328 U.S. 331 (1946)		F		
Craig v. Harney, 331 U.S. 367 (1947)		A	A	
Wood v. Georgia, 370 U.S. 375 (1962)				A

Libel

	Ho	F	J	Ha
New York Times Co. v. Sullivan, 376 U.S. 254 (1964)				F
Linn v. Plant Guard Workers, 383 U.S. 53 (1966)				A
Rosenblatt v. Baer, 383 U.S. 75 (1966)				A
Time, Inc. v. Hill, 385 U.S. 374 (1967)				A
Curtis Publishing Co. v. Butts, 388 U.S. 130 (1967)				A
Beckley Newspapers v. Hanks, 389 U.S. 81 (1967)				F
St. Amant v. Thompson, 390 U.S. 727 (1968)				F
Greenbelt Pub. Assn. v. Bresler, 398 U.S. 6 (1970)				F
Monitor Patriot Co. v. Roy, 401 U.S. 265 (1971)				F
Time, Inc. v. Pape, 401 U.S. 279 (1971)				A
Ocala Star-Banner Co. v. Damron, 401 U.S. 295 (1971)				F
Rosenbloom v. Metromedia, 403 U.S. 29 (1971)				A

Punishment for and Prior Restraint of Publication

	Ho	F	J	Ha
Fox v. Washington, 236 U.S. 273 (1915)	A			
Near v. Minnesota, 283 U.S. 697 (1931)	F			
Mills v. Alabama, 384 U.S. 214 (1966)				F
Pickering v. Bd. of Education, 391 U.S. 563 (1968)				F
Red Lion Broadcasting Co. v. FCC, 395 U.S. 367 (1969)				A
New York Times Co. v. United States, 403 U.S. 713 (1971)				A

Obscenity

	Ho	F	J	Ha
Winters v. New York, 333 U.S. 507 (1948)	A			
Gelling v. State, 343 U.S. 960 (1952)	F	F		
Butler v. Michigan, 352 U. S 380 (1957)	F			F
Kingsley Books, Inc. v. Brown, 354 U.S. 436 (1957)	A			A
Roth v. United States, 354 U.S. 476 (1957)	A			F/A
Kingsley Pictures Corp. v. Regents, 360 U.S. 684 (1959)	F			F
Smith v. California, 361 U.S. 147 (1959)	F			F
Times Film Corp. v. Chicago, 365 U.S. 43 (1981)	A			A
Marcus v. Search Warrant, 367 U.S. 717 (1961)	F			F
Bantam Books, Inc. v. Sullivan, 372 U.S. 58 (1963)				A
Jacobellis v. Ohio, 378 U.S. 184 (1964)				A
A Quantity of Books v. Kansas, 378 U.S. 205 (1964)				A
Freedman v. Maryland, 380 U.S. 51 (1965)				F
Memoirs v. Massachusetts, 383 U.S. 413 (1966)				A
Ginzburg v. United States, 383 U.S. 463 (1966)				F
Mishkin v. New York, 383 U.S. 502 (1966)				A
Redrup v. New York, 386 U.S. 767 (1967)				A
Teitel Film Corp. v. Cusack, 390 U.S. 139 (1968)				F
Ginsberg v. New York, 390 U.S. 629 (1968)				A
Interstate Circuit v. Dallas, 390 U.S. 676 (1968)				A

	Ho	F	J	Ha
Rabeck v. New York, 391 U.S. 462 (1968)				A
Lee Art Theatre v. Virginia, 392 U.S. 636 (1968)				A
Stanley v. Georgia, 394 U.S. 557 (1969)				F
Blount v. Rizzi, 400 U.S. 410 (1971)				F
United States v. Reidel, 402 U.S. 351 (1971)				A
United States v. 37 Photographs, 402 U.S. 363 (1971)				A

Miscellaneous Press Cases

	Ho	F	J	Ha
Mutual Film Corp. v. Ohio Industrial Comm., 236 U.S. 230 (1915)	A			
Mutual Film Co. v. Ohio Industrial Comm. 236 U.S. 247 (1915)	A			
Mutual Film Corp. v. Kansas, 236 U.S. 248 (1915)	A			
Milwaukee Pub. Co. v. Burleson, 255 U.S. 407 (1921)	F			
Associated Press v. United States, 326 U.S. 1 (1945)		A		
Breard v. Alexandria, 341 U.S. 622 (1951)		A	A	
Joseph Burstyn, Inc. v. Wilson, 343 U.S. 495 (1952)		F	F	

EQUAL PROTECTION OF THE LAW

Blacks and Hispanics on Juries

	Ho	F	J	Ha
Brownfield v. South Carolina, 189 U.S. 426 (1903)	A			
Rogers v. Alabama, 192 U.S. 226 (1904)	F			
Martin v. Texas, 200 U.S. 316 (1906)	A			
Thomas v. Texas, 212 U.S. 278 (1909)	A			
Franklin v. South Carolina, 218 U.S. 161 (1910)	A			
Aldridge v. United States, 283 U.S. 308 (1931)	F			
Pierre v. Louisiana, 306 U.S. 354 (1939)		F		
Smith v. Texas, 311 U.S. 128 (1940)		F		
Hill v. Texas, 316 U.S. 400 (1942)		F	F	
Akins v. Texas, 325 U.S. 398 (1945)		A	A	
Patton v. Mississippi, 332 U.S. 463 (1947)		F	F	
Cassell v. Texas, 339 U.S. 282 (1950)		F	A	
Avery v. Georgia, 345 U.S. 559 (1953)		F		
Hernandez v. Texas, 347 U.S. 475 (1954)		F	F	
Reece v. Georgia, 350 U.S. 85 (1955)		F		F
Michel v. Louisiana, 350 U.S. 91 (1955)		A		A
Eubanks v. Louisiana, 356 U.S. 584 (1958)		F		F
Arnold v. North Carolina, 376 U.S. 773 (1964)				F
Swain v. Alabama, 380 U.S. 202 (1965)				A
Whitus v. Georgia, 385 U.S. 545 (1967)				F
Coleman v. Alabama, 389 U.S. 22 (1967)				F
Jones v. Georgia, 389 U.S. 24 (1967)				F
Carter v. Jury Com., 396 U.S. 320 (1970)				F
Turner v. Fouche, 396 U.S. 346 (1970)				F

Exclusion of Blacks from Universities

	Ho	F	J	Ha
Sipuel v. Regents, 332 U.S. 631 (1948)			F	F
Sweatt v. Painter, 339 U.S. 629 (1950)			F	F

	Ho	F	J	Ha
McLaurin v. Oklahoma St. Regents, 339 U.S. 637 (1950)		F	F	
Lucy v. Adams, 350 U.S. 1 (1955)		F		F
Hawkins v. Board of Control, 350 U.S. 413 (1956)		F		F

Integration of Public Schools

	Ho	F	J	Ha
Gong Lum v. Rice, 275 U.S. 78 (1927)	A			
Brown v. Board of Education, 347 U.S. 483 (1954)		F	F	
Bolling v. Sharp, 347 U.S. 497 (1954)		F	F	
Brown v. Board of Education, 349 U.S. 294 (1955)		F		F
Cooper v. Aaron, 358 U.S. 1 (1958)		F		F
Goss v. Bd. of Education, 373 U.S. 683 (1963)				F
Griffin v. School Board, 377 U.S. 218 (1964)				A
Rogers v. Paul, 382 U.S. 198 (1965)				A
Green v. County School Board, 391 U.S. 430 (1968)				F
Raney v. Board of Education, 391 U.S. 443 (1968)				F
Monroe v. Bd. of Comm'rs., 391 U.S. 450 (1968)				F
United States v. Montgomery County, 395 U.S. 225 (1969)				F
Swann v. Bd. of Education, 402 U.S. 1 (1971)				F
Davis v. School Comm'rs., 402 U.S. 33 (1971)				F
McDaniel v. Barresi, 402 U.S. 39 (1971)				F
Bd. of Education v. Swann, 402 U.S. 43 (1971)				F

Integration of Public Facilities

	Ho	F	J	Ha
Muir v. Louisville Park Theatrical Assoc., 347 U.S. 971 (1954)		F		
Mayor, et al v. Dawson, 350 U.S. 877 (1955)		F		F
Holmes v. City of Atlanta, 350 U.S. 879 (1955)		F		F
Gayle v. Members of Bd. of Comm'rs., 352 U.S. 903 (1956)		F		F
New Orleans City Park Impr. Assoc. v. Detiege, 358 U.S. 54 (1958)		F		F
State Athletic Com. v. Dorsey, 359 U.S. 533 (1959)		F		F
Johnson v. Virginia, 373 U.S. 61 (1963)				F
Wright v. Georgia, 373 U.S. 284 (1963)				F
Watson v. Memphis, 373 U.S. 526 (1963)				F
Schiro v. Bynum, 375 U.S. 395 (1964)				F
Evans v. Newton, 382 U.S. 296 (1966)				A
Evans v. Abney, 396 U.S. 435 (1970)				A
Palmer v. Thompson, 403 U.S. 217 (1971)				A

Integration of Private Facilities

	Ho	F	J	Ha
Burton v. Wilmington Pkg. Auth., 365 U.S. 715 (1961)		A		A
Turner v. City of Memphis, 369 U.S. 350 (1962)		F		F
Peterson v. Greenville, 373 U.S. 244 (1963)				F
Shuttlesworth v. Birmingham, 373 U.S. 262 (1963)				A
Lombard v. Louisiana, 373 U.S. 267 (1963)				A
Gober v. City of Birmingham, 373 U.S. 374 (1963)				F
Avent v. North Carolina, 373 U.S. 375 (1963)				F
Griffin v. Maryland, 378 U.S. 130 (1964)				A
Robinson v. Florida, 378 U.S. 153 (1964)				F

	Ho	F	J	Ha
Bell v. Maryland, 378 U.S. 226 (1964)				A
Hamm v. Rock Hill, 379 U.S. 306 (1964)				A
Adickes v. Kress & Co., 398 U.S. 144 (1970)				F

Where Blacks Live and Whom They Live With

	Ho	F	J	Ha
Buchanan v. Warley, 245 U.S. 60 (1917)	F			
Corrigan v. Buckley, 271 U.S. 323 (1926)	A			
Shelley v. Kraemer, 334 U.S. 1 (1948)		F		
Hurd v. Hodge, 334 U.S. 24 (1948)		F		
Barrows v. Jackson, 346 U.S. 249 (1964)		F		
McLaughlin v. Florida, 379 U.S. 184 (1964)				F
Reitman v. Mulkey, 387 U.S. 369 (1967)				A
Loving v. Virginia, 388 U.S. 1 (1967)				F
Jones v. Mayer Co., 392 U.S. 409 (1968)				A
Hunter v. Erickson, 393 U.S. 385 (1969)				F
James v. Valtierra, 402 U.S. 137 (1971)				A

Separate but Equal Facilities

	Ho	F	J	Ha
Berea College v. Kentucky, 211 U.S. 45 (1908)	A			
McCabe v. A.T.& S.F. Ry., 235 U.S. 151 (1914)	A			
S. Covington & Cincinnati Str. Ry. Co. V. Kentucky, 252 U.S. 399 (1920)	A			
Cincinnati Str. Ry. Co. v. Kentucky, 252 U.S. 408 (1920)	A			
Mitchell v. United States, 313 U.S. 80 (1941)		F		

Gender Discrimination

	Ho	F	J	Ha
Quong Wing v. Kirkendall, 223 U.S. 59 (1912)	A			
Mackenzie v. Hare 239 U.S. 299 (1915)	A			
Ballard v. United States, 329 U.S. 187 (1946)		A		
Goesaert v. Cleary, 335 U.S. 464 (1948)		A	A	

For Illegitimate Children

	Ho	F	J	Ha
Levy v. Louisiana, 391 U.S. 68 (1968)				A
Glona v. Am. Guarantee & Liab. Co., 391 U.S. 73 (1968)				A
Lavine v. Vincent, 401 U.S. 532 (1971)				A

For Aliens

	Ho	F	J	Ha
Truax v. Raich, 239 U.S. 33 (1915)	F			
Heim v. McCall, 239 U.S. 175 (1915)	A			
Crane v. New York, 239 U.S. 195 (1915)	A			
Terrace v. Thompson, 263 U.S. 197 (1923)	A			
Porterfield v. Webb, 263 U.S. 225 (1923)	A			
Webb v. O.Brien, 263 U.S. 313 (1923)	A			
Frick v. Webb, 263 U.S. 326 (1923)	A			
Cockrill v. California, 268 U.S. 258 (1925)	A			

	Ho	F	J	Ha
Oyama v. California, 332 U.S. 633 (1948)		F	A	
Takashi v. Fish Comm'n., 334 U.S. 410 (1948)		F	A	
Johnson v. Eisentrager, 339 U.S. 763 (1950)		A	A	
Graham v. Richardson, 403 U.S. 365 (1971)				F

In Classification of Voters

	Ho	F	J	Ha
Giles v. Harris, 189 U.S. 475 (1903)	A			
Guinn v. United States, 238 U.S. 347 (1915)	F			
Nixon v. Herndon, 273 U.S. 536 (1927)	F			
Smith v. Allwright, 321 U.S. 649 (1944)		F	F	
Butler v. Thompson, 341 U.S. 937 (1951)		A	A	
Terry v. Adams, 345 U.S. 461 (1953)		F	F	
Lassiter v. Northampton Elections Bd., 360 U.S. 45 (1959)		A		A
Gomillion v. Lightfoot, 364 U.S. 339 (1960)		F		F
Carrington v. Rash, 380 U.S. 89 (1965)				A
Harman v. Forssenius, 380 U.S. 528 (1965)				F
Harper v. Virginia Bd. of Elections, 383 U.S. 663 (1966)				A
McDonald v. Bd. of Elections, 394 U.S. 802 (1969)				A
Kramer v. Union Sch. Dist., 395 U.S. 621 (1969)				A
Cipriano v. City of Houma, 395 U.S. 701 (1969)				F
Evans v. Cornman, 398 U.S. 419 (1970)				F
Phoenix v. Kolodziejski, 399 U.S. 204 (1970)				A

For New Political Parties

	Ho	F	J	Ha
MacDougall v. Green, 335 U.S. 281 (1948)		A	A	
Williams v. Rhodes, 393 U.S. 23 (1968)				F
Hadnott Amos, 394 U.S. 358 (1969)				F
Moore v. Ogilvie, 394 U.S. 814 (1969)				A
Jenness v. Fortson, 403 U.S. 431 (1971)				A

For the Poor

	Ho	F	J	Ha
Dandridge v. Williams, 397 U.S. 471 (1970				A
Boddie v. Connecticut, 401 U.S. 371 (1971)				F

For Fundamental Rights

	Ho	F	J	Ha
Niemotko v. Maryland, 340 U.S. 268 (1951)		F	F	
Fowler v. Rhode Island, 345 U.S. 67 (1953)		F		
Martin v. Walton, 368 U.S. 25 (1961)		A		A
Baxstrom v. Herold, 383 U.S. 107 (1966)				F

In the Criminal Justice System

	Ho	F	J	Ha
Skinner v. Oklahoma, 316 U.S. 535 (1942)		F	F	
Fay v. New York, 332 U.S. 261 (1947)		A	A	
Moore v. New York, 333 U.S. 565 (1948)		A	A	
Dowd v. Cook, 340 U.S. 206 (1951)		F	F	

	Ho	F	J	Ha
Griffin v. Illinois, 351 U.S. 12 (1956)		F		A
Johnson v. United States, 352 U.S. 565 (1957)		F		F
Eskridge v. Washington Prison Board, 357 U.S. 214 (1958)				A
Burns v. Ohio, 360 U.S. 252 (1959)		A		A
McCray v. Indiana, 364 U.S. 277 (1960)		F		F
Smith v. Bennett, 365 U.S. 708 (1961)		F		F
Beck v. Washington, 369 U.S. 541 (1962)				A
Douglas v. California, 372 U.S. 353 (1963)				A
Lane v. Brown, 372 U.S. 477 (1963)				F
Draper v. Washington, 372 U.S. 487 (1963)				A
Rinaldi v. Yeager, 384 U.S. 305 (1966)				A
Long v. Dist. Ct. of Iowa, 385 U.S. 192 (1966)				A
Swenson v. Bosler, 386 U.S. 258 (1967)				F
Anders v. California, 386 U.S. 738 (1967)				A
Entsminger v. Iowa, 386 U.S. 748 (1967)				F
Roberts v. LaValle, 389 U.S. 40 (1967)				A
Gardner v. California, 393 U.S. 367 (1969)				A
Williams v. Oklahoma, 395 U.S. 458 (1969)				F
Williams v. Illinois, 399 U.S. 235 (1970)				F
Tate v. Short, 401 U.S. 395 (1971)				F

Miscellaneous Equal Protection Cases

	Ho	F	J	Ha
Anderson v. Martin, 375 U.S. 399 (1964)				F

THE BILL OF RIGHTS AND THE STATES

	Ho	F	J	Ha
West v. Louisiana, 194 U.S. 258 (1904)		A		
Lloyd v. Dollison, 194 U.S. 445 (1904)		A		
Patterson v. Colorado, 205 U.S. 454 (1907)		A		
Ughbanks v. Armstrong, 208 U.S. 481 (1908)		A		
Twining v. New Jersey, 211 U.S. 78 (1908)		A		
Ensign v. Pennsylvania, 227 U.S. 592 (1913)		A		
Mineapolis & St. Louis R. Co. v. Bombolis, 241 U.S. 211 (1916)		A		
Gilbert v. Minnesota, 254 U.S. 325 (1920)		F		
Prudential Ins. Co. v. Cheek, 259 U.S. 530 (1922)		A		
Gitlow v. New York, 268 U.S. 652 (1925)		F		
Whitney v. California, 274 U.S. 357 (1927)		F		
Fiske v. Kansas, 274 U.S. 380 (1927)		F		
Gaines v. Washington 277 U.S. 81 (1928)		A		
Stromberg v. Carlson, 283 U.S. 359 (1931)		F		
Near v. Minnesota, 283 U.S. 697 (1931)		F		
Schneider v. State, 308 U.S. 147 (1939)			F	
Cantwell v. Connecticut, 310 U.S. 296 (1940)			F	
Betts v. Brady, 316 U.S. 455 (1942)			A	A
Francis v. Resweber, 329 U.S. 459 (1947)			A	F
Everson v. Bd. of Education, 330 U.S. 1 (1947)			F	F
Adamson v. California, 332 U.S. 46 (1947)			A	A
Foster v. Illinois, 332 U.S. 134 (1947)			A	A
Wolf v. Colorado, 338 U.S. 25 (1949)			F	F

Ho F J Ha

Case	Ho	F	J	Ha
Beauharnais v. Illinois, 343 U.S. 250 (1952)		F	A	
Bartkus v. Illinois, 359 U.S. 121 (1959)		A		A
Mapp v. Ohio, 367 U.S. 643 (1961)		A		A
Gideon v. Wainwright, 372 U.S. 335 (1963)				F
Malloy v. Hogan, 378 U.S. 1 (1964)				A
Pointer v. Texas, 380 U.S. 400 (1965)				F
Klopfer v. North Carolina, 386 U.S. 213 (1967)				A
Washington v. Texas, 388 U.S. 14 (1947)				A
Duncan v. Louisiana, 391 U.S. 145 (1968)				A
Benton v. Maryland, 395 U.S. 784 (1969)				A

Involuntary Servitude

Case	Ho
Bailey v. Alabama, 211 U.S. 452 (1908)	A
Bailey v. Alabama, 219 U.S. 219 (1911)	A
United States v. Reynolds, 235 U.S. 133 (1914)	F
Butler v. Perry, 240 U.S. 328 (1916)	A

The Japanese Cases

Case	F	J
Hirabayashi v. United States, 320 U.S. 81 (1943)	A	A
Yasui v. United States, 320 U.S. 115 (1943)	A	A
Korematsu v. United States, 323 U.S. 214 (1944)	A	F
Ex Parte Endo, 323 U.S. 283 (1944)	F	F

Column headings correspond to justices' last names; i.e., W is Justice Byron R. White; B is Chief Justice Warren E. Burger; R is Chief Justice William H. Rehnquist; O'C is Justice Sandra Day O'Connor, and S is Justice Antonin Scalia.

W B R O'C S

THE FREE EXERCISE OF RELIGION

Case	W	B	R	O'C	S
Sherbert v. Verner, 374 U.S. 380 (1965)	A				
United States v. Seeger, 380 163 (1965)	F				
Presbyterian Church v. Hull Church, 393 U.S. 440 (1969)	F				
Welsh v. United States, 398 U.S. 333 (1970)	A	A			
Gillette v. United States, 401 U.S. 437 (1971)	A	A			
Cruz v. Beto, 405 U.S. 319 (1992)	F	F			
Wisconsin v. Yoder, 406 U.S. 205 (1972)	F	F	A		
Johnson v. Robison, 415 U.S. 361 (1974)	A	A	A		
Serbian Eastern Orthodox Church v. Milivojevich, 426 U.S. 696 (1976)	F	F	A		
Wooley v. Maynard, 430 U.S. 705 (1977)	F	F	A		
Trans World Airlines, Inc. v. Hardison, 432 U.S. 63 (1974)	A	A	A		

	W	B	R	O'C	S
McDaniel v. Paty, 435 U.S. 618 (1978)	F	F	F		
Jones v. Wolf, 443 U.S. 595 (1979)	F	F	A		
Thomas v. Rev. Bd., Ind. Emp. Sec. Div., 450 U.S. 707 (1981)	F	F	A		
United States v. Lee, 455 U.S. 252 (1982)	A	A	A	A	
Bob Jones University v. United States, 461 U.S. 574 (1983)	A	A	F	A	
Goldman v. Weinberger, 475 U.S. 503 (1986)	A	A	A	F	
Bowen v. Roy, 476 U.S. 693 (1986)	F	A	A	F	
Hobbie v. Unemployment App. Comm'n., 480 U.S. 136 (1987)	F		A	F	F
O'Lone v. Estate of Shabazz, 482 U.S. 342 (1987)	A		A	A	A
Lyng v. N. S. Indian Cemetery Pro. Assn., 485 U.S. 439 (1988)	A		A	A	A
Employment Div. v. Smith, 485 U.S. 660 (1988)	A		A	A	A
Frazee v. Illinois Empl. Sec. Dept., 489 U.S. 829 (1989)	F		F	F	F
Employment Div. v. Smith, 494 U.S. 872(1990)	A		A	A	A
Church of the Lukumi Babalu Aye, Inc. V. Hialeah, 508 U.S. 520 (1993)	F		F	F	F
City of Boerne v. Flores, 117 S. Ct. 2157 (1997)			A	F	A

FREEDOM OF SPEECH

Pamphleteering and Soliciting

	W	B	R	O'C	S
Ashton v. Kentucky, 384 U.S. 195 (1966)	F				
Organization for a Better Austin v. Keefe, 402 U.S. 415 (1971)	F	F			
Hynes v. Mayor of Oradell, 425 U.S. 610 (1976)	F	F	A		
Brown v. Glines, 444 U.S. 348 (1980)	A	A	A		
Secretary of the Navy v. Huff, 444 U.S. 453 (1980)	A	A	A		
Schaumberg, Village of v. Citizens for Better Environment, 444 U.S. 620 (1980)	F	F	A		
Heffron v. Int. Soc. for Krishna Consc., Inc., 452 U.S. 640 (1981)	A	A	A		
Sec. of State, Maryland v. J. H. Monson Co., Inc., 467 U.S. 947 (1988)	F	A	A	A	
Riley v. Nat. Fed. of Blind, 487 U.S. 781 (1988)	F		A	A	
IKON v. Lee, 505 U.S. 672 (1992)	A		A	A	A
Lee v. IKON, 505 U.S. 830 (1992)	A		A	F	A
McIntyre v. Ohio Elections Comm'n., 514 U.S. 334 (1995)			A	F	A

Picketing and Parading

	W	B	R	O'C	S
Edwards v. South Carolina, 372 U.S. 229 (1963)	F				
Henry v. Rock Hill, 376 U.S. 776 (1964)	F				
Cox v. Louisiana, 379 U.S. 536 (1965)	F				
Cox v. Louisiana, 379 U.S. 559 (1965)	A				
Adderley v. Florida, 385 U.S. 39 (1966)	A				

	W	B	R	O'C	S
Cameron v. Johnson, 390 U.S. 611 (1968)	A				
Shuttlesworth v. Birmingham, 394 U.S. 147 (1969)	F				
Am. Radio Assoc., Inc. v. Mobile S. S. Assn., 419 U.S. 215 (1974)	A	A	A		
National Socialist Party v. Skokie, 432 U.S. 43 (1977)	A	A	A		
NAACP v. Claiborne Hdwe. Co., 458 U.S. 886 (1982)	F	F	F	F	
United States v. Grace, 461 U.S. 171 (1983)	F	F	F	F	
Frisby v. Schultz, 487 U.S. 474 (1988)	A		A	A	A
Forsyth Co. v. National Movement, 505 U.S. 123 (1992)	A		A	F	A
Madsen v. Women's Health Center, Inc., 512 U.S. 753 (1994)			A\F	A\F	F
Hurley v. Irish-American Gay Group, 515 U.S. 557 (1995)			F	F	F
Schenck v. Pro-Choice Network of W. New York, 117 S. Ct. 855 (1997)			F\A	F\A	F

Unpopular Speech

	W	B	R	O'C	S
Brown v. Louisiana, 383 U.S. 131 (1966)	F				
Bond v. Floyd, 385 U.S. 116 (1966)	F				
United States v. O'Brien, 391 U.S. 367 (1968)	A				
Tinker v. Des Moines Sch. Dist., 393 U.S. 503 (1969)	F				
Street v. New York, 394 U. S. 576 (1969)	A				
Watts v. United States, 394 U. S. 705 (1969)	A				
Brandenburg v. Ohio, 395 U. S. 444 (1969)	F				
Bachellar v. Maryland, 397 U. S. 564 (1970)	F	F			
Cohen v. California, 403 U. S. 15 (1971)	A	A			
Gooding v. Wilson, 405 U. S. 518 (1972)	F	A			
Colton v. Kentucky, 407 U. S. 104 (1972)	A	A	A		
Plummer v. City of Columbus, 414 U. S. 2 (1973)	F	A	A		
Norwell v. City of Cincinnati, 414 U. S. 14 (1973)	F	F	F		
Hess v. Indiana, 414 U. S. 105 (1973)	F	A	A		
Lewis v. New Orleans, 415 U. S. 130 (1974)	F	A	A		
Smith v. Goguen, 415 U. S. 566 (1974)	F	A	A		
Eaton v. City of Tulsa, 415 U. S. 697 (1974)	F	A	A		
Parker v. Levy, 417 U. S. 733 (1974)	A	A	A		
Spence v. Washington, 418 U. S. 405 (1974)	A	A	A		
FCC v. Pacifica Foundation, 438 U. S. 726 (1978)	A	A	A		
Consolidation Edison v. PSC, 447 U. S. 531 (1980)					
Bethel School Dist. v. Fraser, 478 U. S. 675 (1986)	A	A	A	A	
Houston v. Hill, 482 U. S. 451 (1987)	F		A	F	F
Texas v. Johnson, 491 U. S. 397 (1989)	A		A	A	F
United States v. Eichman, 496 U. S. 310 (1990)	A		A	A	F

	W	B	R	O'C	S
R. A. V. v. St. Paul, 505 U. S. 377 (1992)	F		F	F	F
Wisconsin v. Mitchell, 508 U. S. 476 (1993)	A		A	A	A

Public Employees' Right to Speak

	W	B	R	O'C	S
Pickering v. Board of Education, 391 U. S. 563 (1968)	A				
CSC v. Letter Carriers, 413 U. S. 548 (1973)	A	A	A		
Broadrick v. Oklahoma, 413 U. S. 601 (1973)	A	A	A		
Mt. Healthy City Bd. of Ed. v. Doyle, 429 U. S. 274 (1977)	F	F	F		
Givhan v. Western Line Consol. Sch. Dist., 439 U. S. 410 (1979)	F	F	F		
Smith v. Arkansas St. Highway Employees, 441 U. S. 463 (1979)	A	A	A		
Connick v. Myers, 461 U. S. 138 (1983)	A	A	A	A	
Minn. Bd. for Com. Colleges v. Knight, 465 U. S. 271 (1984)	A	A	A	A	
Rankin v. McPherson, 483 U. S. 378 (1987)	A		A	A	A
Waters v. Churchill, 511 U. S. 661 (1994)			A	F/A	A
United States v. Nat. Treas. Employees Union, 513 U. S. 454 (1995)			A	F	A

Commercial Speech

	W	B	R	O'C	S
Bigelow v. Virginia, 421 U. S. 809 (1975)	A	F	A		
Va. Pharmacy Bd. v. Va. Cit. Consumer Council, 425 U. S. 748 (1976)	F	F	A		
Linmark Assoc., Inc. v. Willingboro, 431 U. S. 85 (1977)	F	F			
Bates v. State of Arizona, 433 U. S. 350 (1977)	F	A	A		
In re Primus, 436 U. S. 412 (1978)	F	F	A		
Freedoman v. Rogers, 440 U. S. 1 (1979)	A	A	A		
Central Hudson G. & E. Corp. v. Pub. Ser. Com., 447 U. S. 557 (1980)	F	F	A		
Metromedia, Inc. v. San Diego, 453 U. S. 490 (1981)	A	A	A		
In re R. M. J., 455 U. S. 191 (1982)	F	F	F	F	
Zauderer v. Off. of Disc. Counsel, 471 U. S. 626 (1985)	F/A	A	A	A	
Posadas de Puerto Rico Assoc. v. Tourism Co., 478 U. S. 328 (1986)	A	A	A	A	
Shapero v. Kentucky Bar Assn., 486 U. S. 466 (1988)	F		A	A	A
Board of Trustees, St. Univ. of N. Y. v. Fox, 492 U. S. 469 (1989)	A		A	A	A
Peel v. Atty. Reg. & Disc. Comm'n., 496 U. S. 91 (1990)	A		A	A	A
City of Cincinnati v. Discover Network, Inc., 507 U. S. 410 (1993)	A		A	F	F
Edenfield v. Fane, 507 U. S. 761 (1993)	F		F	A	F

W B R O'C S

	W	B	R	O'C	S
United States v. Edge Broadcasting, Co., 509 U. S. 418 (1993)	A		A	A	A
Ibanez v. Florida Dept. Bus. & Prof. Reg., 512 U. S. 136 (1994)			A	A	F
Florida Bar v. Went For It, Inc., 515 U. S. 618 (1995)			A	A	A
Ruben v. Coors Brewing Co., 514 U. S. 476 (1995)			F	F	F
44 Liquormart, Inc. v. Rhode Island, 116 S. Ct. 1495 (1996)			F	F	F
Glickman v. Wileman Bros. & Elliott, 117 S. Ct. 2130 (1997)			F	A	F

Places to Speak

	W	B	R	O'C	S
Amalg. Food Empl. Union v. Logan Valley Plaza, 391 U. S. 308 (1968)	A				
Flower v. United States, 407 U. S. 197 (1972)	F	A	A		
Lloyd Corp. v. Tanner, 407 U. S. 551 (1972)	A	A	A		
Lehman v. Shaker Heights, 418 U. S. 298 (1974)	A	A	A		
S. E. Promotions, Ltd. v. Conrad., 420 U. S. 546 (1975)	A	A	A		
Greer v. Spock, 424 U. S. 828 (1976)	A	A	A		
Young v. American Mini Theatres, 427 U. S. 50 (1976)	A	A	A		
Madison Sch. Dist. v. Wisc. Empl. Rel. Com'n. 429 U. S. 167 (1976)	F	F	F		
Pruneyard Shopping Center v. Robbins, 447 U. S. 74 (1980)	F	F	F		
Shad v. Mt. Ephraim, 452 U. S. 61 (1981)	F	A	A		
U. S. Postal Service v. Greenburgh Civic Assn., 453 U. S. 114 (1981)	A	A	A		
Widman v. Vincent, 454 U. S. 263 (1981)...	A	F	F	F	
Perry Ed. Assn. v. Perry Local Ed. Assn., 460 U. S. 37 (1983)	A	A	A	A	
City Council v. Taxpayers for Vincent, 466 U. S. 789 (1984)	A	A	A	A	
Clark v. Com. for Creative Non-Violence, 468 U. S. 288 (1984)	A	A	A	A	
United States v. Albertina, 472 U. S. 675 (1985)	A	A	A	A	
Cornelius v. NAACP Leg. Def. & Ed. Fund, 473 U. S. 788 (1985)	A	A	A	A	
Renton v. Playtime Theatres, 475 U. S. 41 (1986)	A	A	A	A	
Airport Comm'rs. v. Jews for Jesus, 482 U. S. 569 (1987)	F		F	A/F	A/F
Boos v. Barry, 485 U. S. 312 (1988)	A		A	F	F
United States v. Kokinda, 497 U. S. 720 (1990)	A		A	A	A
Burson v. Freeman, 504 U. S. 191 (1992)	A		A	F	A

	W	B	R	O'C	S
Lamb's Chapel v. Center Moriches Sch. Dist., 508 U. S. 384 (1993)	F		F	F	F
City of Ladue v. Gilleo, 512 U. S. 43 (1994)			F	F	F

Miscellaneous Speech Cases

	W	B	R	O'C	S
Garrison v. Louisiana, 379 U. S. 64 (1964)	F				
Stanford v. Texas, 379 U. S. 476 (1965)	F				
Carroll v. Pres. & Com'rs. of Princess Anne, 393 U. S. 175 (1968)	F				
Schacht v. United States, 398 U. S. 58 (1970)	F	F			
California v. LaRue, 409 U. S. 109 (1972)	A	A	A		
Procunier v. Martinez, 416 U. S. 396 (1974)	F	F	F		
Doran v. Salem Inn, Inc., 422 U. S. 922 (1975)	F	F	F		
Buckley v. Valeo, 424 U. S. 1 (1976)	A	F	A/F		
Abood v. Det. Bd. of Ed., 431 U. S. 209 (1977)	F	F	F		
First Nat. Bank of Boston v. Bellotti, 435 U. S. 765 (1978)	A	F	A		
Bell v. Wolfish, 441 U. S. 520 (1979)	A	A	A		
Cons. Edison Co. v. Pub. Ser. Comm'n., 447 U. S. 530 (1980)	F	F	A		
Brown v. Hartlage, 456 U. S. 45 (1982)	F	F	F	F	
Board of Ed. v. Pico, 457 U. S. 853 (1982)		A	A	A	
FCC v. League of Women Voters, 468 U. S. 364 (1984)	A	A	A	F	
FEC v. Nat. Conservative PAC, 470 U. S. 480 (1985)	A	F	F	F	
Wayte v. United States, 470 U. S. 598 (1985)	A	A	A	A	
Pacific G. & E. Co. v. Pub. Util. Comm'n., 475 U. S. 1 (1986)	A	F	A	F	
FEC v. Massachusetts Citizens for Life, 479 U. S. 238 (1986)	A		A	F	F
Meese v. Keene, 481 U. S. 465 (1987)	A		A	A	
Turner v. Safley, 482 U. S. 78 (1987)	A		A	A	A
Keller v. State Bar of California, 496 U. S. 1 (1990)	F		F	F	F
Rust v. Sullivan, 500 U. S. 173 (1991)	A		A	F	A
Barnes v. Glen Theatre, Inc., 501 U. S. 560 (1991)	F		A	A	A
Gentile v. State Bar of Nevada, 501 U. S. 1030 (1991)	A		A	F	A
Bd. of County Commissioners v. Umbehr, 116 S. Ct. 2342 (1996)			F	F	A
O'Hare Truck Service, Inc. v. City of Northlake, 116 S. Ct. 2353 (1996)			F	F	A
Colorado Republican Campaign Com., 116 S. Ct. 2309 (1996)			F	F	F

W B R O'C S

FREEDOM OF ASSOCIATION

Affidavits and Oaths

	W	B	R	O'C	S
Baggett v. Bullitt, 377 U. S. 360 (1964)	F				
Elfbrandt v. Russell, 384 U. S. 11 (1966)	A				
Keyishian v. Board of Regents, 385 U. S. 589 (1967)	A				
Whitehill v. Elkins, 389 U. S. 54 (1967)	A				
Schneider v. Smith, 390 U. S. 17 (1968)	F				
Cole v. Richardson, 405 U. S. 676 (1972)	A	A			
Socialist Labor Party v. Gilligan, 406 U. S. 583 (1972)	A	A	A		
Communist Party of Indiana v. Whitcomb, 414 U. S. 441 (1974)	F	F	F		

Blacklisting and Punishment for Membership

	W	B	R	O'C	S
United States v. Robel, 389 U. S. 258 (1967)	A				
Kleindienst v. Mandel, 408 U. S. 753 (1972).	A	A	A		

Associational Privacy

	W	B	R	O'C	S
Gibson v. Florida Leg. Committee, 372 U. S. 539 (1964)	A				
NAACP v. Alabama, 377 U. S. 288 (1964)	F				
DeGregory v. New Hampshire Atty. Gen., 383 U. S. 825 (1966)	A				
Baird v. State Bar of Arizona, 401 U. S. 1 (1971)	A	A			
In re Stolar, 401 U. S. 23 (1971)	A	A			
Law Students Res. Council v. Wadmond, 401 U. S. 154 (1971)	A	A			
Brown v. Socialist Workers Party, 459 U. S. 87 (1982)	F	F	A	A	
Seattle Times Co. v. Rhinehart, 467 U. S. 20 (1984)	F	F	F\A	F\A	

For Advancement of Legal Goals

	W	B	R	O'C	S
NAACP v. Button, 371 U. S. 515 (1963)	F				
Railroad Trainmen v. Virginia Bar, 377 U. S. 1 (1964)	F				
United Mine Workers v. Illinois Bar, 389 U. S. 217 (1967)	F				
United Transp. Union v. Michigan Bar, 401 U. S. 576 (1971)	F	F			

W B R O'C S

Public Employees and Political Association

	W	B	R	O'C	S
Elrod v. Burns, 427 U. S. 347 (1976)	F	A	A		
Branti v. Finkel, 445 U. S. 507 (1980)	F	F	A		
Rutan v. Republican Pty. of Illinois, 497 U. S. 62 (1990)	F		A	A	A

Political Parties: Ballot Access and New Members

	W	B	R	O'C	S
Williams v. Rhodes, 393 U. S. 23 (1968)	A				
Rosario v. Rockefeller, 410 U. S. 752 (1973)	A	A	A		
Kusper v. Pontikes, 414 U. S. 51 (1973)	F	F	A		
Storer v. Brown, 415 U. S.724 (1974)	A	A	A		
Cousins v. Wigoda, 419 U. S. 477 (1975)	F	F	F		
Democratic Party of U. S. v. Wisconsin, 450 U. S. 107 (1981)	F	F	A		
Anderson v. Celebrezze, 460 U. S. 780 (1983)	A	F	A	A	
Monro v. Socialist Workers Party, 479 U. S. 189 (1986)	A		A	A	A
Tashjian v. Republican Party of Conn., 479 U. S. 208 (1986)	F		A	A	A
Eu v. San Francisco Dem. County Central Committee, 489 U. S. 214 (1989)	F			F	F
Norman v. Reed, 502 U. S. 279 (1992)	F		F	F	A
Burdick v. Takushi, 504 U. S. 428 (1992)	A		A	A	A
Timmons v. Twin Cities Area New Party, 117 S. Ct. 1364 (1997)			A	A	A

Miscellaneous Association Cases

	W	B	R	O'C	S
Stanford v. Texas, 379 U. S. 476 (1965)	F				
Coates v. Cincinnati, 402 U. S. 611 (1971)	A	A			
Healy v. James, 408 U. S. 169 (1972)	F	F	F		
Jones v. N. C. Prisoners' Union, 433 U. S. 119 (1977)	A	A	A		
Citizens Against Rent Control v. Berkeley, 454 U. S. 290 (1981)	A	F	F	F	
FEC v. Nat. Right to Work Com., 459 U. S. 197 (1982)	A	A	A	A	
Roberts v. United States Jaycees, 468 U. S. 609 (1984)	A		A	A	
Bd. of Directors of Rotary Club v. Rotary Club, 481 U. S. 537 (1987)	A		A		A
Lyng v. UAW, 485 U. S. 360 (1988)	A		A	A	A
N. Y. State Club Assn. v. New York City, 487 U. S. 1 (1988)	A		A	A	A
Dallas v. Stanglin, 490 U. S. 19 (1989)	A		A	A	A
Dawson v. Delaware, 503 U. S. 159 (1982)	F		F	F	F

W B R O'C S

FREEDOM OF THE PRESS

Libel

	W	B	R	O'C	S
New York Times Co. v. Sullivan, 376 U. S. 254 (1964)	F				
Linn v. Plant Guard Workers, 383 U. S. 53 (1966)	A				
Rosenblatt v. Baer, 383 U. S. 75 (1966)	F				
Time, Inc. v. Hill, 385 U. S. 374 (1967)	F				
Curtis Pub. Co. v. Butts, 388 U. S. 130 (1967)	F				
Beckley Newspapers v. Hanks, 389 U. S. 81 (1967)	F				
St. Amant v. Thompson, 390 U. S. 727 (1968)	F				
Greenbelt Pub. Assn. v. Bresler, 398 U. S. 6 (1970)	F	F			
Monitor Patriot Co. v. Roy, 401 U. S. 265 (1971)	F	F			
Time, Inc. v. Pape, 401 U. S. 279 (1971)	F	F			
Ocala Star-Banner Co. v. Damron, 401 U. S. 295 (1971)	F	F			
Rosenbloom v. Metromedia, 403 U. S. 29 (1971)	F	F			
Letter Carriers v. Austin, 418 U. S. 264 (1974)	F	A	A		
Gertz v. Robert Welch, Inc., 418 U. S. 323 (1974)	A	A	A		
Cantrell v. Forest City Pub. Co., 419 U. S. 245 (1974)	A	A	A		
Time, Inc. v. Firestone, 424 U. S. 448 (1976)	A	F	F		
Herbert v. Lando, 441 U. S. 153 (1979)	A	A	A		
Bose Corp. v. Consumer Union, 466 U. S. 485 (1984)	A	F	A	A	
Dun and Bradstreet, Inc. v. Greenmoss Bldrs., Inc., 472 U. S. 749 (1985)	A	A	A	A	
Philadelphia Newspapers, Inc. v. Hepps, 475 U. S. 767 (1986)	A	A	A	F	
Hustler Magazine v. Falwell, 485 U. S. 46 (1988)	F		F	F	F
Harte-Hanks Comm. v. Connaughton, 491 U. S. 657 (1989)	A		A	A	A
Milkovich v. Lorain Journal Co., 497 U. S. 1 (1990)	A		A	A	A
Masson v. New Yorker Magazine, Inc., 501 U. S. 496 (1991)	A		A	A	A

Prior Restraint of and Punishment for Publication

	W	B	R	O'C	S
Mills v. Alabama, 384 U. S. 214 (1966)	F				
Pickering v. Bd. of Education, 391 U. S. 563 (1968)	F				

	W	B	R	O'C	S
Red Lion Broadcasting Co. v. FCC, 395 U. S. 367 (1969)	A				
New York Times Co. v. United States, 403 U. S. 713 (1971)	F	A			
Pittsburgh Press Co. v. Human. Rel. Comm'n., 413 U. S. 376 (1973)	A	F	A		
Pell v. Procunier, 417 U. S. 817 (1974)	A	A	A		
Saxbe v. Washington Post, 417 U. S. 843 (1974)	A	A	A		
Miami Herald Pub. Co. v. Tornillo, 418 U. S. 241 (1974)	F	F	F		
Cox Broadcasting Corp. v. Cohn, 420 U. S. 469 (1975)	F	F	A		
Nebraska Press Assn. v. Stuart, 427 U. S. 539 (1976)	F	F	F		
Oklahoma Publishing Co. v. District Court, 430 U. S. 308 (1977)	F	F	F		
Zacchini v. Scripps-Howard Broadcasing Co., 433 U. S. 562 (1977)	A	A	A		
Landmark Com., Inc. v. Virginia, 435 U. S. 829 (1978)	F	F	F		
Houchins v. KQED, Inc., 438 U. S. 1 (1978)	A	A	A		
Smith v. Daily Mail Pub. Co., 443 U. S. 97 (1979)	F	F	F		
Gannett Co. v. DePasquale, 443 U. S. 368 (1979)	F	A	A		
Snepp v. United States, 444 U. S. 507 (1980)	A	A	A		
Richmond Newspapers, Inc. v. Virginia, 448 U. S. 555 (1980)	F	F	A		
Globe Newapaper Co. v. Superior Court, 457 U. S. 596 (1982)	F	A	A	F	
Press-Enterprise Co. v. Superior Court, 464 U. S. 501 (1984)	F	F	F	F	
Seattle Times Co. v. Rhinehart, 467 U. S. 20 (1984)	A	A	A	A	
FCC v. League of Women Voters, 468 U. S. 364 (1984)	A	A	A	F	
Reagan v. Time, Inc., 468 U. S. 641 (1984)	A	A	A	A	
Press-Enterprise Co. v. Superior Court, 478 U. S. 1 (1986)	F	F	A	F	
Hazelwood Sch. Dist. v. Kuhlmeier, 484 U. S. 260 (1988)	A		A	A	A
City of Lakewood v. Plain Dealer Pub., 486 U. S. 750 (1988)	A			A	F
The Florida Star v. B. J. F., 491 U. S. 524 (1989)	A		A	A	F
Butterworth v. Smith, 494 U. S. 625 (1990)	F		F	F	F
Simon and Schuster, Inc. v. Crime Victims, 502 U. S. 105 (1991)	F		F	F	F
El Vocero de Puerto Rico v. Puerto Rico, 508 U. S. 147 (1993)	F		F	F	F

W B R O'C S

Obscenity

Case	W	B	R	O'C	S
Bantam Books, Inc. v. Sullivan, 372 U. S. 58 (1963)	F				
Jacobellis v. Ohio, 378 U. S. 184 (1964)	F				
A Quantity of Books v. Kansas, 378 U. S. 205 (1964)	F				
Freedman v. Maryland, 380 U. S. 51 (1965)	F				
Memoirs v. Massachusetts, 383 U. S. 413 (1966)	A				
Miskin v. New York, 383 U. S. 502 (1966)	A				
Ginzburg v. United States, 383 U. S. 463 (1966)	A				
Redrup v. New York, 386 U. S. 767 (1967)	F				
Teitel Film Corp. v. Cusack, 390 U. S. 1319 (1968)	F				
Ginsberg v. New York, 390 U. S. 629 (1967)	A				
Interstate Circuit v. Dallas, 390 U. S. 629 (1968)	F				
Rabeck v. New York, 391 U. S. 462 (1968)	F				
Lee Art Theatre v. Virginia, 392 U. S. 636 (1968)	F				
Stanley v. Georgia, 394 U. S. 557 (1969)	F				
Blount v. Rizzi, 400 U. S. 410 (1971)	F	F			
United States v. Reidel, 402 U. S. 351 (1971)	A	A			
United States v. 37 Photographs, 402 U. S. 363 (1971)	A	A			
Kois v. Wisconsin, 408 U. S. 229 (1972)	F	F	F		
Miller v. California, 413 U. S. 15 (1973)	A	A	A		
Paris Adult Theatre I v. Slaton, 413 U. S. 49 (1973)	A	A	A		
Kaplan v. California, 413 U. S. 115 (1973)	A	A	A		
United States v. 12-200 ft. Reels of Film, 413 U. S. 123 (1973)	A	A	A		
United States v. Orito, 413 U. S. 139 (1973)	A	A	A		
Heller v. New York, 413 U. S. 483 (1973)	A	A	A		
Roeden v. Kentucky, 413 U. S. 496 (1973)	F	F	F		
Hamling v. United States, 418 U. S. 87 (1974)	A	A	A		
Jenkins v. Georgia, 418 U. S. 153 (1974)	F	F	F		
Erznoznik v. City of Jacksonville, 422 U. S. 205 (1975)	A	A	A		
McKinney v. Alabama, 424 U. S. 669 (1976)	F	F	F		
Marks v. United States, 430 U. S. 188 (1977)	F\A	F\A	F/A		
Smith v. United States, 431 U. S. 291 (1977)	A	A	A		
Splawn v. California, 431 U. U. S. 595 (1977)	A	A	A		
Ward v. Illinois, 431 U. S. 767 (1977)	A	A	A		
Vance v. Universal Amusement Co., 445 U. S. 308 (1980)	A	A	A		
Flynt v. Ohio, 451 U. S. 619 (1981)	A	A	A		
California v. Mithcell Bros. Santa Anna Theater, 454 U. S. 90 (1981)	A	A	A	A	

	W	B	R	O'C	S
New York v. Ferber, 458 U. S. 747 (1982)	A	A	A	A	
Maryland v. Macon, 472 U. S. 463 (1985)	A	A	A	A	
Brockett v. Spokane Arcades, Inc., 472 U. S. 491 (1985)	A	A	A	A	
New York v. P. J. Video, Inc., 475 U. S. 868 (1986)	A	A	A	A	
Arcara v. Cloud Books, Inc., 478 U. S. 697 (1986)	A	A	A	A	
Pope v. Illinois, 481 U. S. 497 (1987)	A		A	A	A
Massachusetts v. Oakes, 491 U. S. 576 (1989)	A		A	A	A
Sable Com. of Cal., Inc. v. FCC, 492 U. S. 115 (1989)	F\A		F\A	F\A	F\A
FW/PBS, Inc. v. Dallas, 493 U. S. 215 (1990)	A		A	F	A
Osborne v. Ohio, 495 U. S. 103 (1990)	A		A	A	A
Alexander v. United States, 509 U. S. 544 (1993)	A		A	A	A
Denver Area Ed. Tele. Com. v. FCC, 116 S. Ct. 2374 (1996)		A	F/A	A	
Reno v. ACLU. 117 S. Ct. 2329 (1997)			F\A	F\A	F\A

Miscellaneous Press Cases

	W	B	R	O'C	S
Brandzburg v. Hayes, 408 U. S. 665 (1972)	A	A	A		
Papish v. Univ. of Missouri Curators, 410 U.S. 667 (1973)	F	A	A		
Zurcher v. Stanford Daily, 436 U. S. 547 (1978)	A	A	A		
Minneapolis Star v. Minnesota Comm'r. of Rev., 460 U. S. 575 (1983)	F\A	F	A	F	
Arkansas Writer's Proj., Inc. v. Ragland, 481 U. S. 221 (1987)	F		A	F	A
Cohen v. Cowles Media Co., 501 U. S. 663 (1991)	A		A	F	A
Leathers v. Medlock, 499 U. S. 439 (1991)	A		A	A	A
Turner Broadcasting Sy., Inc. v. FCC, 114 S. Ct. 2445 (1994)	A		A	F	F
Rosenberger v. Rector & Visitors of U. of Virginia, 515 U. S. 819 (1995)			F	F	F
Turner Broadcasting Sy., Inc. v. FCC, 512 U. S. 662 (1997)			A	F	F

THE PURSUIT OF LIBERTY

The Right to Travel

	W	B	R	O'C	S
Zemel v. Rusk, 381 U. S. 1 (1965)	A				
United States v. Guest, 383 U. S. 745 (1966)	F				
Shapero v. Thompson, 394 U. S. 618 (1969)	F				
Sosna v. Iowa, 419 U. S. 393 (1975)	A	A	A		
California v. Torres, 435 U. S. 1 (1978)	A	A	A		
California v. Azavorian, 439 U. S. 170 (1978)	A	A	A		

W B R O'C S

	W	B	R	O'C	S
Haig v. Agee, 453 U. S. 280 (1981)	A	A	A		
Zobel v. Williams, 457 U. S. 55 (1982)				F	
Atty. Gen. of N. Y. v. Soto-Lopez, 476 U. S. 898 (1986)	A		A	A	

The Right of Privacy

	W	B	R	O'C	S
Armstrong v. Manzo, 380 U. S. 545 (1965)	F				
Griswold v. Connecticut, 381 U. S. 479 (1965)	F				
Wisconsin v. Constantineau, 400 U. S. 433 (1971)	F	A			
Eisenstadt v. Baird, 405 U. S. 438 (1972)	F	A			
Stanley v. Illinois, 405 U. S. 645 (1972)	F	A			
Morrissey v. Brewer, 408 U. S. 471 (1972)	F	F	F		
Roe v. Wade, 410 U. S. 113 (1973)	A	F	A		
Cleveland Bd. of Ed. v. La Fleur, 414 U. S. 632 (1974)	F	A	A		
Wolff v. McDonnell, 418 U. S. 539 (1974)	A	A	A		
O'Connor v. Donaldson, 422 U. S. 563 (1975)	F	F	F		
Turner v. Dept. Employ. Sec. 423 U. S. 44 (1975)	F	A	A		
Paul v. Davis, 424 U. S. 693 (1976)	F	A	A		
Kelly v. Johnson, 425 U. S. 238 (1976)	A	A	A		
Meachum v. Fano, 427 U. S. 215 (1976)	A	A	A		
Planned Parenthood of Missouri v. Danforth, 428 U. S. 52 (1976)	A	A	A		
Whalen v. Roe, 429 U. S. 589 (1977)	A	A	A		
Moore v. East Cleveland, 431 U. S. 494 (1977)	A	A	A		
Carey v. Population Ser. Int., 431 U. S. 678 (1977)	F	A	A		
Beal v. Doe, 432 U. S. 438 (1977)	A	A	A		
Maher v. Doe, 432 U. S. 464 (1977)	A	A	A		
Bellotti v. Baird, 443 U. S. 622 (1979)	A	F	F		
Vitek v. Jones, 445 U. S. 480 (1980)	F	A	A		
Harris v. McRae, 448 U. S. 297 (1980)	A	A	A		
H. L. v. Matheson, 450 U. S. 398 (1981)	A	A	A		
Santosky v. Kramer, 455 U. S. 745 (1982)	A	A	A	A	
Youngberg v. Romeo, 457 U. S. 307 (1982)	F	F	F	F	
Akron v. Akron Center, 462 U. S. 416 (1983)	A	F	A	A	
Planned Parenthood Assn. v. Ashcroft, 462 U. S. 476 (1983)	A	A	A	A	
Simpoulos v. Virginia, 462 U. S. 506 (1983)	A	A	A	A	
Lehr v. Robertson, 463 U. S. 248 (1983)	F	A	A	A	
Seattle Times Co. v. Rhinehart, 467 U. S. 20 (1984)	F	F	F	F	
Thornburgh v. Am. Coll. of Obst. & Gyn., 476 U. S. 747 (1986)	A	A	A	A	
Bowers v. Hardwick, 478 U. S. 186 (1986)	A	A	A	A	
Turner v. Safley, 482 U. S. 78 (1987)	F	F	F	F	F
DeShaney v. Winnebago Co. Soc. Ser. Dept., 489 U. S. 189 (1989)	A	A	A	A	A

	W	B	R	O'C	S
Michael H. v. Gerald D., 491 U. S. 110 (1989)	F		A	A	A
Webster v. Reproductive Health Ser., 492 U. S. 490 (1989)	A		A	A	A
Washington v. Harper, 494 U. S. 210 (1990)	A		A	A	A
Cruzan v. Dir., Missouri Dept. of Health, 497 U. S. 261 (1990)	A		A	A	A
Hodgson v. Minnesota, 497 U. S. 417 (1990)	A		F	F	A
Ohio v. Akron Center, 497 U. S. 502 (1990)	A		A	A	A
Planned Parenthood v. Casey, 505 U. S. 833 (1992)	A		A	F	A

EQUAL PROTECTION OF THE LAW

Blacks on Juries

	W	B	R	O'C	S
Arnold v. North Carolina, 376 U. S. 773 (1964)	F				
Swain v. Alabama, 380 U. S. 202 (1965)	A				
Whitus v. Georgia, 385 U. S. 545 (1967)	F				
Jones v. Georgia, 389 U. S. 24 (1967)	F				
Coleman v. Alabama, 389 U. S. 22 (1967)	F				
Carter v. Jury Com., 396 U. S. 320 (1970)	F	F			
Turner v. Fouche, 396 U. S. 346 (1979)	F				
Alexander v. Louisiana, 405 U. S. 625 (1972)	F	F			
Rose v. Mitchell, 443 U. S. 545 (1979)	F	A	A		
Vasquez v. Hillery, 474 U. S. 254 (1986)	F	A	A	F	
Batson v. Kentucky, 476 U. S. 79 (1986)	F	A	A	F	
Allen v. Hardy, 478 U. S. 255 (1986)	A	A	A	A	
Griffin v. Kentucky, 479 U. S. 314 (1987)	A		A	A	F
Powers v. Ohio, 499 U. S. 400 (1991)	F		A	F	A
Ford v. Georgia, 498 U. S. 411 (1991)	F		F	F	F
Edmonson v. Leesville Concrete Co., 500 U. S. 614 (1991)	F		A	A	A
Trevino v. Texas, 503 U. S. 562 (1992)	F		F	F	F
Georgia v. McCollum, 505 U. S. 42 (1992)	F		F	A	A

Hispanics on Juries

	W	B	R	O'C	S
Castaneda v. Partida, 430 U. S. 482 (1977)	F	A	A		
Hernandez v. New York, 500 U. S. 352 (1991)	A		A	A	A

Integration of Public Schools and Universities

	W	B	R	O'C	S
Goss v. Bd. of Education, 373 U. S. 683 (1963)	F				
Griffin v. School Board, 377 U. S. 218 (1964)	F				
Rogers v. Paul, 382 U. S. 198 (1965)	A				
Green v. County School Board, 391 U. S. 430 (1968)	F				

	W	B	R	O'C	S
Raney v. Board of Education, 391 U. S. 443 (1968)	F				
Monroe v. Bd. of Comm'rs., 391 U. S. 450 (1968)	F				
United States v. Montgomery County, 395 U. S. 225 (1969)	F				
Swann v. Bd. of Education, 402 U. S. 1 (1971)	F	F			
Davis v. School Comm'rs., 402 U. S. 33 (1971)	F	F			
Bd. of Education v. Swann, 402 U. S. 43 (1971)	F	F			
McDaniel v. Barresi, 402 U. S. 39 (1971)	F	F			
Wright v. Council of City of Emporia, 407 U. S. 451 (1972)	F	A	A		
United State v. Scotland Neck Bd. of Ed., 407 U. S. 484 (1972)	F	F	F		
Norwood v. Harrison, 413 U. S. 455 (1973)	F	F	F		
Washington v. Seattle Sch. Dist. No. 1, 458 U. S. 457 (1982)	F	A	A	A	
Crawford v. Los Angeles Bd. of Ed., 458 U. S. 527 (1982)	A	A	A	A	
United States v. Fordice, 505 U. S. 717 (1992)	F		F	F	A

Integration of Public Facilities

	W	B	R	O'C	S
Johnson v. Virginia, 373 U. S. 61 (1963)	F				
Wright v. Georgia, 373 U. S. 284 (1963)	F				
Watson v. Memphis, 373 U. S. 526 (1963)	F				
Schiro v. Bynum, 375 U. S. 395 (1964)	F				
Evans v. Newton, 382 U. S. 296 (1966)	F				
Evans v. Abney, 396 U. S. 435(1970)	A	A			
Palmer v. Thompson, 403 U. S. 217 (1971)	F	A			
Gilmore v. City of Montgomery, 417 U. S. 556 (1974)	F	F	F		

Integration of Private Facilities

	W	B	R	O'C	S
Peterson v. Greenvillle, 373 U. S. 244 (1963)	F				
Shuttlesworth v. Birmingham, 373 U. S. 262 (1963)	F				
Lombard v. Louisiana, 373 U. S. 267 (1963)	F				
Gober v. City of Birmingham, 373 U. S. 374 (1963)	F				
Avent v. North Carolina, 373 U. S. 375 (1963)	F				
Griffin v. Maryland, 378 U. S. 130 (1964)	A				
Robinson v. Florida, 378 U. S. 153 (1964)	F				
Bell v. Maryland, 378 U. S. 226 (1964)	A				
Hamm v. Rock Hill, 379 U. S. 306 (1964)	A				

	W	B	R	O'C	S
Adickes v. Kress & Co., 398 U. S. 144 (1970)	F				
Moose Lodge #107 v. Irvis, 407 U. S. 163 (1972)	A	A	A		

Where Blacks Live and Whom They Live With

	W	B	R	O'C	S
McLaughlin v. Florida, 379 U. S. 184 (1964)	F				
Reitman v. Mulkey, 387 U. S. 369 (1967)	F				
Loving v. Virginia, 388 U. S. 1 (1967)	F				
Jones v. Mayer Co., 392 U. S. 409 (1968)	A				
Hunter v. Erickson, 393 U. S. 385 (1969)	F				
James v. Valtierra, 402 U. S. 137 (1971)	A				
Palmore v. Sidoti, 466 U. S. 429 (1984)	F	F	F	F	

Gender Discrimination

	W	B	R	O'C	S
Reed v. Reed, 404 U. S. 71 (1971)	F	F	F		
Frontiero v. Richardson, 411 U. S. 677 (1973)	F	F	A		
Kahn v. Shevin, 416 U. S. 351 (1974)	F	A	A		
Geduldig v. Aiello v. 417 U. S. 484 (1974)	A	A	A		
Schlesinger v. Ballard, 419 U. S. 498 (1975)	F	A	A		
Weinberger v. Wiesenfeld, 420 U. S. 636 (1975)	F	F	F		
Stanton v. Stanton, 421 U. S. 7 (1975)	F	F	A		
Craig v. Boren, 429 U. S. 190 (1976)	F	A	A		
Califano v. Goldfarb, 430 U. S. 199 (1977)	F	A	A		
Quillion v. Walcott, 434 U. S. 246 (1978)	A	A	A		
Orr v. Orr, 440 U. S. 268 (1979)	F	A	A		
Parham v. Hughes, 441 U. S. 347 (1979)	F	A	A		
Caban v. Mohammed, 441 U. S. 380 (1979)	F	A	A		
Davis v. Passman, 442 U. S. 228 (1979)	F	A	A		
Personnel Adm. of Massachusetts, v. Feeney, 442 U. S. 256 (1979)	A	A	A		
Califano v. Westcott, 443 U. S. 76 (1979)	F	F	F		
Wengler v. Druggists Mut. Ins. Co., 446 U. S. 142 (1980)	F	F	A		
Kirchberg v. Feenstra, 450 U. S. 455 (1981)	F	F	F		
Michael M. v. Sonoma Co. Sup. Ct., 450 U. S. 464 (1981)	F	A	A		
Rostker v. Goldberg, 453 U. S. 57 (1981)	F	A	A		
Mississippi Univ. for Women v. Hogan, 458 U. S. 718 (1982)	F	A	A	F	
Roberts v. United States Jaycees, 468 U. S. 468 U. S. 609 (1984)	F		F	F	
Bd. of Dir., Rotary Int. v. Rotary Club, 481 U. S. 537 (1987)	F		F		F
N. Y. State Club Assn. v. New York City, 487 U. S. 1 (1988)	F		F	F	F
United States v. Virginia, 116 S. Ct. 2264 (1996)		F	F	A	

W   B   R   O'C   S

For Illegitimate Children

	W	B	R	O'C	S
Levy v. Louisiana, 391 U. S. 68 (1968)	F				
Glona v. Am. Guarantee & Liab. Co., 391 U. S. 73 (1968)	F				
Labine v. Vincent, 401 U. S. 532 (1971)	F	A			
Weber v. Aetna Cas. & Sur. Co., 406 U. S. 164 (1972)	F	F	A		
Gomez v. Perez, 409 U. S. 535 (1973)	F	F	A		
Linda R. S. v. Richard D., 410 U. S. 614 (1973)	F	A	A		
New Jersey Welfare Rights Org. v. Cahill, 411 U. S. 619 (1973)	F	F	A		
Jimenez v. Weinberger, 417 U. S. 628 (1974)	F	F	A		
Mathews v. Lucas, 427 U. S. 495 (1976)	A	A	A		
Norton v. Mathews, 427 U. S. 524 (1976)	A	A	A		
Trimble v. Gordon, 430 U. S. 762 (1977)	F	A	A		
Fiallo v. Bell, 430 U. S. 787 (1977)	F	A	A		
Lalli v. Lalli, 439 U. S. 259 (1978)	F	A	A		
Califano v. Boles, 443 U. S. 282 (1979)	F	A	A		
Mills v. Habluetzel, 456 U. S. 91 (1982)	F	F	F	F	
Pickett v. Brown, 462 U. S. 1 (1983)	F	F	F	F	
Reed v. Campbell, 476 U. S. 852 (1986)	F	F	F	F	
Clark v. Jeter, 486 U. S. 456 (1908)	F	F	F	F	F

For Aliens

	W	B	R	O'C	S
Graham v. Richardson, 403 U. S. 365 (1971)	F	F			
Sugarman v. Dougal, 413 U. S. 634 (1973)	F	F	A		
In re Griffiths, 413 U. S. 717 (1973)	F	A	A		
Hampton v. Mow Sun Wong, 426 U. S. 88 (1976)	A	A	A		
Examining Board v. Flores de Otero, 426 U.S. 572 (1976)	F	F	A		
Nyquist v. Mauclet, 432 U. S. 1 (1977)	F	A	A		
Foley v. Connelie, 435 U. S. 291 (1978)	A	A	A		
Ambach v. Norwick, 441 U. S. 68 (1979)	A	A	A		
Cabell v. Chavez-Salido, 454 U. S. 432 (1982)	A	A	A	A	
Plyler v. Doe, 457 U. S. 202 (1982)	A	A	A	A	
Bernal v. Fainter, 467 U. S. 216 (1984)	F	F	A	F	

In Classification of Voters

	W	B	R	O'C	S
Carrington v. Rash, 380 U. S. 89 (1965)	F				
Harman v. Forssenius, 380 U. S. 528 (1965)	F				
Harper v. Virginia Bd. of Elections, 383 U. S. 663 (1966)	F				
McDonald v. Bd. of Elections, 394 U. S. 802 (1969)	A				
Kramer v. Union Sch. Dist., 395 U. S. 621 (1969)	F				

	W	B	R	O'C	S
Cipriano v. City of Houma, 395 U. S. 701 (1969)	F				
Evans v. Cornman, 398 U. S. 419 (1970)	F	F			
Phoenix v. Kolodziejski, 399 U. S. 204 (1970)	F	A			
Goosby v. Osser, 409 U. S. 512 (1972)	F	F	F		
Marston v. Lewis, 410 U. S. 679 (1973)	A	A	A		
Burns v. Fortson, 410 U. S. 686 (1973)	A	A	A		
O'Brien v. Skinner, 414 U. S. 524 (1974)	F	F	A		
Richardson v. Ramirez, 418 U. S. 24 (1974)	A	A	A		
Hill v. Stone, 421 U. S. 289 (1975)	F	A	A		
Holt Civic Club v. Tuscaloosa, 439 U. S. 60 (1978)	F	A	A		
Hunter v. Underwood, 471 U. S. 222 (1985)	F	F	F	F	
Quinn v. Millsap, 491 U. S. 95 (1989)	F	F	F	F	F

For New Political Parties

	W	B	R	O'C	S
Williams v. Rhodes, 393 U. S. 23 (1968)	A				
Hadnott v. Amos, 394 U. S. 358 (1969)	A				
Moore v. Ogilvie, 394 U. S. 814 (1969)	F				
Jenness v. Fortson, 403 U. S. 431 (1971)	A	A			
American Party of Texas v. White, 415 U. S. 767 (1974)	F\A	F\A	F\A		
Illinois Election Bd. v. Socialist Wkrs. Party, 440 U. S. 173 (1979)	F	F	F		

For the Poor

	W	B	R	O'C	S
Dandridge v. Williams, 397 U. S. 471 (1970)	A	A			
Boddie v. Connecticut, 401 U. S. 371 (1971)	F	F			
Bullock v. Carter, 405 U. S. 134 (1972)	F	F			
Jefferson v. Hackney, 406 U. S. 535 (1972)	A	A	A		
United States v. Kras, 409 U. S. 434 (1973)	A	A	A		
Ortwein v. Schwab, 410 U. S. 656 (1973)	A	A	A		
San Antonio Sch. Dist. v. Rodriquez, 411 U. S. 1 (1973)	F	A	A		
U. S. Dept. of Agric. v. Moreno, 413 U. S. 528 (1973)	F	A	A		
Memorial Hospital v. Maricopa Co., 415 U. S. 250 (1974)	F	F	A		
Lubin v. Panish, 415 U. S. 709 (1974)	F	F	F		
Beal v. Doe, 432 U. S. 438 (1977)	A	A	A		
Maher v. Doe, 432 U. S. 464 (1977)	A	A	A		
Harris v. Rosario, 446 U. S. 651 (1980)	A	A	A		
Little v. Streater, 452 U. S. 1 (1981)	F	F	F		
Lassiter v. Dept. of Soc. Services, 452 U. S. 18 (1981)	A	A	A		
Lyng v. Costello, 477 U. S. 635 (1986)	F	A	A	A	
Kadramas v. Dickinson Sch. Dist., 487 U. S. 450 (1988)	A		A	A	A
M. L. B. v. S. L. J., 117 S. Ct. 555 (1996)			A	F	A

W B R O'C S

For Fundamental Rights

Case	W	B	R	O'C	S
Baxstrom v. Herold, 383 U. S. 107 (1966)	F				
Dunn v. Blumstein, 405 U. S. 330 (1972)	F	A			
Eisenstadt v. Baird, 405 U. S. 438 (1972)	F	A			
Police Dept. of Chicago v. Mosley, 408 U. S. 92 (1972)	F	F	F		
Grayned v. City of Rockford, 408 U. S. 104 (1972)	F	F	F		
Village of Belle Terre v. Borass, 416 U. S. 1 (1974)	A	A	A		
Califano v. Jobst, 434 U. S. 47 (1977)	A	A	A		
Zablocki v. Redhail, 434 U. S. 374 (1978)	F	F	A		
Clement v. Fashing, 457 U. S. 957 (1982)	F	A	A	A	
Hooper v. Bernalillo Co., 472 U. S. 612 (1985)	F	F	A	A	
Romer v. Evans, 116 U. S. 1620 (1996)			A	F	A

In the Criminal Justice System

Case	W	B	R	O'C	S
Douglas v. California, 372 U. S. 353 (1963)	F				
Lane v. Brown, 372 U. S. 477 (1963)	F				
Draper v. Washington, 372 U. S. 487 (1963)	A				
Rinaldi v. Yeager, 384 U. S. 305 (1966)	F				
Long v. Dist. Ct. of Iowa, 385 U. S. 192 (1966)	F				
Swenson v. Bosler, 386 U. S. 258 (1967)	F				
Anders v. California, 386 U. S. 738 (1967)	F				
Entsminger v. Iowa, 386 U. S. 748 (1967)	F				
Roberts v. LaValle, 389 U. S. 40 (1967)	F				
Gardner v. California, 393 U. S. 367 (1969)	F				
Williams v. Oklahoma, 395 U. S. 458 (1969)	F				
Williams v. Illinois, 399 U. S. 235 (1970)	F	F			
Tate v. Short, 401 U. S. 395 (1971)	F	F			
Mayer v. City of Chicago, 404 U. S. 189 (1971)	F	F	F		
Britt v. North Carolina, 404 U. S. 226 (1971)	A	A	A		
James v. Strange, 407 U. S. 128 (1972)	F	F	F		
McGinnis v. Royster, 410 U. S. 263 (1973)	A	A	A		
Fuller v. Oregon, 417 U. S. 40 (1974)	A	A	A		
Ross v. Moffit, 417 U. S. 600 (1974)	A	A	A		
Estelle v. Dorrough, 420 U. S. 534 (1975)	A	A	A		
United States v. MacCollom, 426 U. S. 317 (1976)	F	A	A		
McClesky v. Kemp, 481 U. S. 279 (1987)	A		A	A	A
Pennsylvania v. Finley, 481 U. S. 551 (1987)	A		A	A	A

Miscellaneous Equal Protection Cases

Case	W	B	R	O'C	S
Anderson v. Martin, 375 U. S. 399 (1964)	F				
Richardson v. Belcher, 404 U. S. 78 (1971)	A	A			

	W	B	R	O'C	S
Lindsey v. Normet, 405 U. S. 56 (1972)	F	F			
Massachusetts Bd. of Retirement v. Murgia, 427 U. S. 307 (1976)	A	A	A		
Vance v. Bradely, 440 U. S. 93 (1979)	A	A	A		
New York Transit Auth. v. Beazer, 440 U. S. 568 (1979)	F	A	A		
Schweiker v. Wilson 450 U. S. 221 (1981)	A	A	A		
Memphis v. Greene, 451 U. S. 100 (1981)	A	A	A		
Martinez v. Bynum, 461 U. S. 321 (1983)	A	A	A	A	
Williams v. Vermont, 472 U. S. 14 (1985)	F	F	A	A	
Bowers v. Owens, 476 U. S. 340 (1986)	A	A	A	A	
Heller v. Doe, 509 U. S. 312 (1993)	A		A	F	A

THE BILL OF RIGHTS AND THE STATES

Gideon v. Wainwright, 372 U. S. 335 (1963)	F
Malloy v. Hogan, 378 U. S. 1 (1964)	F
Pointer v. Texas, 380 U. S. 400 (1965)	F
Klopfer v. North Carolina, 386 U. S. 213 (1967)	F
Washington v. Texas, 388 U. S. 14 (1967)	F
Duncan v. Louisiana, 391 U. S. 145 (1968)	F
Benton v. Maryland, 395 U. S. 784 (1969)	F

NOTES

A note regarding citations of court cases. "X v. Y, 25 U.S. 372, 376 (19nn)" means that the X v. Y opinion appears in volume 25 of the *United States* reports at page 372; that a quotation from the case appears at page 376, and that the case was decided in the year 19nn.

Preface

1. Address at Cooper Union, New York, February 27, 1860.
2. Definition contributed to "Nine Definitions of Liberalism," the *New Republic* (July 22, 1946).
3. James E. Leahy, *Freedom Fighters of the United States Supreme Court: Nine Who Championed Individual Liberty* (Jefferson, NC: McFarland, 1996).

Prologue

1. 1 Annals of Congress 439 (1789).
2. 347 U.S. 483 (1954).
3. Brown v. Board of Education, 349 U.S. 294 (1955).
4. See James E. Leahy, *Freedom Fighters of the United States Supreme Court: Nine Who Championed Individual Liberty* (Jefferson, NC: McFarland, 1996).

1. Justice Oliver Wendell Holmes, Jr.

1. Sheldon M. Novick, *Honorable Justice,* *The Life of Oliver W. Holmes* (Boston, Toronto, and London: Little Brown, 1981), p. 7.
2. Liva Baker, *The Justice from Beacon Hill: The Life and Times of Oliver Wendell Holmes* (New York: HarperCollins, 1991), p. 47.
3. Novick, note 1, p. 15.
4. Baker, note 2, p. 54.
5. Novick, note 1, p. 10.
6. Baker, note 2, p. 75.
7. Baker, note 2, p. 95.
8. Novick, note 1, p. 48.
9. Baker, note 2, pp. 148–49.
10. Mark DeWolfe Howe, *Justice Oliver Wendell Holmes: The Shaping Years, 1841–1870* (Cambridge, MA: Belknap Press, Harvard University Press, 1957), p. 176.
11. Baker, note 2, pp. 169–70.
12. Leon Friedman and Fred L. Israel, *The Justices of the United States Supreme Court, 1789–1969* (New York: Chelsea House, 1969), vol. III; article by Paul A. Freund, p. 1756.
13. Baker, note 2, p. 259.
14. Howe, note 10, p. 199.
15. Novick, note 1, p. 368.
16. *Ibid.*, p. 173.
17. Baker, note 2, p. 279.
18. McAuliffe v. New Bedford, 155 Mass. 216 (1892).
19. 162 Mass. 510 (1895).
20. Davis v. Massachusetts, 165 U.S. 43 (1897).
21. Baker, note 2, p. 308.
22. Oliver Wendell Holmes, Jr., *The Common Law* (Boston, Toronto and London: Little Brown, 1881); Howe, note 10, chapter 6; Novick, note 1, chapter 11; Baker, note 2, chapter 13; Robert W. Gordon, *The Legacy of Oliver Wendell Holmes, Jr.* (Stanford, CA: Stanford Press, 1992).

23. Gordon, note 22, p. 3.
24. Novick, note 1, p. 236.
25. Schwimmer v. United States, 27 F. 2d 742, 743 (1928).
26. United States v. Schwimmer, 279 U.S. 644, 651–52 (1929).
27. Schenck v. United States, 249 U.S. 47, 48–49 (1919).
28. Frohwerk v. United States, 249 U.S. 204 (1919).
29. Debs v. United States, 249 U.S. 211, 212–13 (1919).
30. Abrams v. United States, 250 U.S. 616, 617–18 (1919).
31. Pierce v. United States, 252 U.S. 239 (1920).
32. Gitlow v. New York, 268 U.S. 652 (1925).
33. Patterson v. Colorado, 205 U.S. 454, 458–59 (1907).
34. 247 U.S. 402 (1918).
35. United States v. Burleson, 258 Fed. Rpts. 282, 283 (1919).
36. Milwaukee Pub. Co. v. Burleson, 255 U.S. 407, 414 (1921).
37. Butcher's Union Co. v. Crescent City Co., 111 U.S. 746, 764 (1884).
38. 198 U.S. 45 (1905).
39. Adair v. United States, 208 U.S. 161, 168 (1908). The Court affirmed the *Adair* case in Coppage v. Kansas, 236 U.S. 1 (1915). Holmes dissented.
40. Meyer v. Nebraska, 262 U.S. 390, 397 (1923).
41. Bartels v. Iowa, 262 U.S. 404 (1923).
42. Buck v. Bell, 274 U.S. 200, 205 (1927).
43. 189 U.S. 426 (1903).
44. Rogers v. Alabama, 192 U.S. 226 (1904).
45. 200 U.S. 316 (1906).
46. Aldridge v. United States, 283 U.S. 308 (1931).
47. Giles v. Harris, 189 U.S. 475, 482 (1903).
48. Nixon v. Herndon, 273 U.S. 536, 540 (1927).
49. Truax v. Raich, 239 U.S. 33, 35 (1915).
50. Heim v. McCall, 239 U.S. 175, 176 (1915); and Crane v. New York, 239 U.S. 195 (1915).
51. Terrace v. Thompson, 263 U.S. 197 (1923); Porterfield v. Webb, 263 U.S. 225 (1923); Webb v. O'Brien, 263 U.S. 313 (1923); Frisk v. Webb, 263 U.S. 326 (1923): and Cockrill v. California, 268 U.S. 258 (1925).
52. 263 U.S. at 221.
53. Bailey v. Alabama, 219 U.S. 219, 229 (1911).
54. United States v. Reynolds, 235 U.S. 133, 150 (1914).
55. International Postal Supply Co. v. Bruce, 194 U.S. 601, 601–02 (1904).
56. Chambers v. Baltimore & Ohio R. R. Company, 207 U.S. 142, 149–50 (1907).
57. Barron v. Baltimore, 32 U.S. 242, 243 (1833).
58. Hurtado v. California, 110 U.S. 516, 538–58 (1884). See also Justice John M. Harlan's dissent in Twining v. New Jersey, 211 U.S. 78, 114–27 (1908).
59. Twining v. New Jersey, 211 U.S. 78, 90 (1908).
60. Gitlow v. New York, 268 U.S. 652, 672 (1925).
61. Downes v. Bidwell, 182 U.S. 244, 378 (1901).
62. 190 U.S. 197 (1903).
63. 109 U.S. 3 (1883).
64. 203 U.S. 1 (1906).
65. Jones v. Alfred H. Mayer, Co., 392 U.S. 409, 441–43 (1968).
66. 279 U.S. at 654–55.
67. Feiner v. New York, 340 U.S. 315 (1951) and Dennis v. United States, 341 U.S. 494 (1951).
68. 205 U.S. at 462. Shortly before Justice Holmes retired from the Court, he voted with the majority in recognizing that the First Amendment prevents states from restricting freedom of the press. See Near v. Minnesota, 283 U.S. 697 (1931).
69. 247 U.S. at 425–26.
70. Adair v. United States, 208 U.S. 45 (1908). See Appendix, *The Pursuit of Liberty— The Right to Work.*
71. See Griswold v. Connecticut, 381 U.S. 479 (1965) and Roe v. Wade, 410 U.S. 113 (1973) for establishing a constitutional right of privacy.
72. 262 U.S. at 400. See Appendix, *The Pursuit of Liberty— Teachers and Parents*; and *Miscellaneous Liberty* cases.
73. Jacobson v. Massachusetts, 197 U.S. 11 (1905).
74. 274 U.S. at 207.
75. Berea College v. Kentucky, 211 U.S. 45 (1908).
76. McCabe v. A. T. & S. F. Ry. Co., 235 U.S. 151 (1914); South Covington & Cincinnati Street Railway Company v. Kentucky, 252 U.S. 399 (1920); and Cincinnati Street Railway Company v. Kentucky, 252 U.S. 408 (1920).
77. Gong Lum v. Rice, 275 U.S. 78 (1927).
78. See Appendix, *Equal Protection of the Law—Blacks on Juries.*

79. See Appendix, *Equal Protection of the Law—for Aliens.*
80. 219 U.S. at 244.
81. Maxwell v. Dow, 176 U.S. 581 (1900).
82. See Appendix, *The Pursuit of Liberty—Miscellaneous Liberty* cases.

2. Justice Felix Frankfurter

1. Joseph P. Lash, *From the Diaries of Felix Frankfurter* (New York: Norton, 1975), p. 3.
2. Dr. Harlan B. Phillips, *Felix Frankfurter Reminisces* (New York: Reynal, 1960), p. 9.
3. Michael E. Parrish, *Felix Frankfurter and His Times* (New York: Free Press, 1982), p. 13.
4. Phillips, note 2, pp. 4–5.
5. Parrish, note 3, pp. 14–15.
6. Phillips, note 2, p. 14.
7. Parrish, note 3, p. 19.
8. Phillips, note 2, p. 31.
9. Parrish, note 3, p. 38.
10. Phillips, note 2, p. 62.
11. Parrish, note 3, p. 60.
12. Lash, note 1, p. 13.
13. Phillips, note 2, p. 84.
14. Parrish, note 3, p. 160.
15. Parrish, note 3, p. 76.
16. Lash, note 1, p. 30.
17. Leon Friedman and Fred L. Israel, *The Justices of the United States Supreme Court, 1789–1969, Felix Frankfurter* (New York: Chelsea House, 1969), vol. III; article by Albert M. Sacks, p. 2404.
18. Parish, note 3, pp. 66–67.
19. Bunting v. Oregon, 243 U.S. 426 (1917).
20. Settler v. O'Hara, 243 U.S. 629 (1917); Adkins v. Children's Hospital, 261 U.S. 525 (1923).
21. Lash, note 1, p. 34.
22. Phillips, note 2, p. 199.
23. Parrish, note 3, p. 178.
24. Parrish, note 3, p. 129.
25. Lash, note 1, p. 26.
26. Hirsch, note 16, p. 31–32.
27. Hirsch, note 16, p. 99.
28. Parrish, note 3, p. 275.
29. Parrish, note 3, p. 6.
30. Minersville District v. Gobitis, 310 U.S. 586, 591 (1940).
31. 319 U.S. 624 (1943).
32. Jones v. Opelika, 319 U.S. 103 (1943).
33. 319 U.S. at 108–09.
34. 319 U.S. at 135.
35. 366 U.S. 420 (1961).

36. 366 U.S. 599, 605 (1961).
37. 366 U.S. at 504–05.
38. 366 U.S. at 616.
39. Drivers Union v. Meadowmoor, 312 U.S. 287, 293 (1941).
40. 312 U.S. 287 (1941).
41. A. F. of L. v. Swing, 312 U.S. 321 (1941).
42. 315 U.S. 722 (1942).
43. 354 U.S. 284 (1957).
44. Beauharnais v. Illinois, 343 U.S. 250 (1952).
45. Staub v. City of Baxley, 355 U.S. 313 (1958).
46. Feiner v. New York, 340 U.S. 315, 316–17 (1951).
47. United States v. Dennis, 183 F. 2d 201, 206 (1950).
48. Dennis v. United States, 341 U.S. 494, 496 (1951).
49. Saia v. New York, 334 U.S. 558, 559 (1948).
50. Lovell v. Griffin, 303 U.S. 444 (1938); Hague v. C. I. O., 307 U.S. 496 (1939); and Cantwell v. Connecticut, 310 U.S. 296 (1940).
51. 336 U.S. 77 (1949).
52. Communications Assn. v. Douds, 339 U.S. 382, 416–17 (1950).
53. Garner v. Los Angeles, 341 U.S. 716, 726 (1951).
54. Wieman v. Updegraff, 344 U.S. 183, 186 (1952).
55. Anti-Fascist Committee v. McGrath, 341 U.S. 123, 124 (1951).
56. 342 U.S. 580 (1952).
57. 367 U.S. 1 (1961).
58. Schware v. Board of Bar Examiners, 353 U.S. 232, 234 (1957).
59. Sweezy v. New Hampshire, 354 U.S. 234, 238 (1957).
60. Beilan v. Board of Education, 357 U.S. 399, 405 (1958).
61. Frankfurter's opinion also related to the case of Lerner v. Casey, 357 U.S. 468 (1958).
62. 357 U.S. at 410.
63. Shelton v. Tucker, 364 U.S. 479, 482–83 (1960).
64. 314 U.S. 252 (1941).
65. 328 U.S. 331 (1946).
66. Kingsley Pictures Corp. v. Regents, 360 U.S. 684, 685 (1959).
67. 333 U.S. 507 (1948).
68. 314 U.S. 160 (1941).
69. 357 U.S. 116 (1958).
70. 357 U.S. 144 (1958).
71. 359 U.S. 1 (1959).
72. 316 U.S. 400 (1942).

73. Cassel v. Texas, 339 U.S. 282, 287–88 (1950).
74. 347 U.S. 483 (1950).
75. Cooper v. Aaron 358 U.S. 1, 8 (1958).
76. See Appendix, *Equal Protection of the Law—Integration of Public Facilities.*
77. 365 U.S. 715 (1961).
78. Goesaert v. Cleary, 335 U.S. 464, 465 (1948).
79. Terry v. Adams, 345 U.S. 461, 463 (1953).
80. Gomillion v. Lightfoot, 167 F. Supp. 405, 407 (1958).
81. Gomillion v. Lightfoot, 364 U.S. 339, 347 (1960).
82. Griffin v. Illinois, 351 U.S. 12, 13–14 (1956).
83. Burns v. Ohio, 360 U.S. 252, 256, note 8 (1959).
84. Adamson v. California, 332 U.S. 46, 62 (1947).
85. 338 U.S. 25 (1949).
86. Weeks v. United States, 232 U.S. 383 (1914).
87. Cantwell v. Connecticut, 310 U.S. 296, 303 (1940); Everson v. Bd. of Education, 330 U.S. 1, 26–27 (1947).
88. 330 U.S. at 26–27.
89. Hirabayshi v. United States, 320 U.S. 81, 86 (1943).
90. Korematsu v. United States, 323 U.S. 214 (1944).
91. Minersville District v. Gobitis, 310 U.S. 586, 600 (1940).
92. West Virginia St. Bd. of Ed. v. Barnette, 319 U.S. 624, 647 (1943).
93. Martin v. Struthers, 319 U.S. 141, 153–54 (1943).
94. Marbury v. Madison, 5 U.S. 137, 176 (1803).
95. 341 U.S. at 548–49. See also Communications Assn. v. Douds, 339 U.S. 382, 418 (1950).
96. 336 U.S. at 90.
97. McKay, *The Preference for Freedom,* 34 NYU Law Review 1182 (1959).
98. 364 U.S. at 494.
99. See Appendix, *Freedom of Association—Associational Privacy.*
100. See Appendix, *Freedom of the Press—Contempt of Court for Publication.*
101. 354 U.S. 476 (1957).
102. 360 U.S. at 696.
103. 350 U.S. 91 (1955).
104. 358 U.S. 1, 26 (1958). See Appendix, *Equal Protection of the Law—Integration of Public Schools.*

105. 334 U.S. 1 (1948).
106. 334 U.S. 24 (1948).
107. Goesaert v. Cleary, 315 U.S. 464 (1948).
108. 332 U.S. 46 (1947).
109. Mapp v. Ohio, 367 U.S. 643, 672 (1961).
110. Drivers Union v. Meadowmoor, 312 U.S. 287 (1941); Hughes v. Superior Court, 339 U.S. 460 (1950); Teamsters Union v. Hanke, 339 U.S. 470 (1950).
111. Hirabayshi v. United States, 320 U.S. 81 (1943); Yasui v. United States, 320 U.S. 115 (1943); Korematsu v. United States, 323 U.S. 214 (1944); and Ex Parte Endo, 323 U.S. 283 (1944).
112. 323 U.S. at 225.
113. Beauharnais v. Illinois, 343 U.S. 250, 261, 267 (1952); Dennis v. United States, 341 U.S. 494, 525 (1951); and Winters v. New York, 333 U.S. 507, 533 (1948).

3. *Justice Robert H. Jackson*

1. *Mr. Justice Jackson, Four Lectures in His Honor* (New York and London: Columbia University Press, 1969), p. 8.
2. Eugene C. Gerhart, *America's Advocate: Robert H. Jackson* (Indianapolis and New York: The Bobbs-Merrill Company, Inc., 1958), p. 29.
3. Leon Friedman and Fred L. Israel, *The Justices of the United States Supreme Court, 1789–1969: Their Lives and Major Opinions* (New York: Chelsea House, 1969); vol. IV, article by Philip B. Kurland, p. 2544.
4. Gerhart, note 2, p. 37.
5. *Mr. Justice Jackson,* note 1, pp. 16–17.
6. *Mr. Justice Jackson,* note 1, pp. 17–18.
7. Gerhart, note 2, pp. 58–59.
8. Friedman and Israel, note 3, p. 2545.
9. Gerhart, note 2, p. 60.
10. 301 U.S. 548 (1967).
11. Gerhart, note 2, p. 95.
12. NLRB v. Jones & Laughlin Steel Corp., 301 U.S. 1 (1937); Steward Machine Co. v. Davis, 301 U.S. 549 (1937).
13. Gerhart, note 2, p. 119.
14. Friedman and Israel, note 3, p. 2557.
15. Gerhart, note 2, p. 175.
16. Freidman and Israel, note 3, p. 2560.
17. Gerhart, note 2, p. 197.
18. Gerhart, note 2, pp. 214–21.
19. Friedman and Israel, note 3, p. 2562.
20. Gerhart, note 2, p. 308, and chapters 18–23.

21. Jones v. Opelika, 319 U.S. 103 (1943); Murdock v. Pennsylvania, 319 U.S. 105 (1943); Martin v. Struthers, 319 U.S. 141 (1943).

22. 319 U.S. at 114.

23. 319 U.S. at 143–44. Jackson's dissent is at p. 166.

24. Board of Education v. Barnette, 319 U.S. 624 (1943).

25. Kunz v. New York, 340 U.S. 290, 292 (1951).

26. 315 U.S. at 730.

27. Bakery Drivers Local v. Wohl, 315 U.S. 769 (1942).

28. See Appendix, *First Amendment—Picketing and Parading.*

29. Beauharnais v. Illinois, 343 U.S. 250, 252 (1952).

30. Terminiello v. Chicago, 337 U.S. 1, 16 (1949). See Jackson's dissent, pp. 17–22 for Terminiello's speech.

31. Dennis v. United States, 341 U.S. 494 (1951).

32. Saia v. New York, 334 U.S. 558, 559 (1948).

33. Kovacs v. Cooper, 336 U.S. 77, 78 (1949).

34. Thomas v. Collins, 323 U.S. 516 (1945).

35. Communications Assn. v. Douds, 339 U.S. 382, 422 (1950).

36. 341 U.S. 123 (1951).

37. Harisiades v. Shaughnessy, 342 U.S. 580 (1952).

38. Craig v. Harney, 331 U.S. 367, 369–70 (1947).

39. Edwards v. California, 314 U.S. 160, 170–71 (1941).

40. Cassell v. Texas, 339 U.S. 282, 298–99 (1950).

41. Oyama v. California, 332 U.S. 633, 641 (1948).

42. Johnson v. Eisentrager, 339 U.S. 763, 766 (1950).

43. Eisentrager v. Forrestal, 174 F. 2d. 961, 963 (1949).

44. 339 U.S. at 770–71.

45. Fay v. New York, 332 U.S. 261, 264 (1947).

46. Moore v. New York, 333 U.S. 565, 569 (1948).

47. Bd. of Education v. Barnette, 319 U.S. 624, 639 (1943).

48. Everson v. Board of Education, 330 U.S. 1, 26–7 (1947).

49. Beauharnais v. Illinois, 343 U.S. 250, 288 (1952).

50. 302 U.S. 319 (1937).

51. See Appendix, *The Bill of Rights and the States.*

52. Hirabayashi v. United States, 320 U.S. 81, 83 (1943).

53. Korematsu v. United States, 323 U.S. 214 (1944).

54. 319 U.S. at 180.

55. 321 U.S. 158, 177 (1944).

56. Schneider v. State, 308 U.S. 147, 163 (1939).

57. 334 U.S. at 571. See Appendix, *Freedom of Speech—Miscellaneous Speech Cases.*

58. 315 U.S. at 775.

59. See Appendix, *Freedom of Speech—Picketing and Parading.*

60. 342 U.S. at 592.

61. 333 U.S. at 508, note 1.

62. Breard v. Alexandria, 431 U.S. 622 (1951).

63. 339 U.S. 282 (1950).

64. Takahashi v. Fish Comm'n., 334 U.S. 410, 431 (1948).

65. Adamson v. California, 332 U.S. 46, 54 (1947).

4. Justice John Marshall Harlan

1. Tingsley E. Yarbrough, *John Marshall Harlan, Great Dissenter of the Warren Court* (New York: Oxford University Press, 1992), p. 62.

2. *The Supreme Court Justices, Illustrated Biographies 1789–1993* (Washington, D.C.: The Supreme Court Historical Society, *Congressional Quarterly*, 1993); article by Nathan Lewin, pp. 441–42.

3. Yarbrough, note 1, p. 15.

4. Yarbrough, note 1, p. 33.

5. *The Supreme Court Justices*, note 2, p. 443.

6. Yarbrough, note 1, p. 75.

7. *The Supreme Court Justices*, note 2, p. 443.

8. McGowan v. Maryland, 366 U.S. 420, 459 (1961).

9. Sherbert v. Verner, 374 U.S. 398, 399, note 1 (1963).

10. Welsh v. United States, 398 U.S. 333, 336–337 (1970).

11. United States v. Seeger, 380 U.S. 163 (1965).

12. 398 U.S. at 340.

13. Cohen v. California, 403 U.S. 15, 16–17 (1971).

14. United States v. O'Brien, 391 U.S. 367, 382 (1968).

15. Tinker v. Des Moines School Dist., 393 U.S. 503 (1969).
16. Fleming v. Nestor, 363 U.S. 603, 621–22 (1960).
17. 341 U.S. 494 (1951).
18. 367 U.S. 203 (1961).
19. Yates v. United States, 354 U.S. 298 (1957); Noto v. United States, 367 U.S. 290 (1961).
20. NAACP v. Alabama, 357 U.S. 449, 451 (1958).
21. Bates v. City of Little Rock, 361 U.S. 516 (1960); Louisiana v. NAACP, 366 U.S. 293 (1961).
22. 372 U.S. 539 (1963).
23. Konigsberg v. State Bar, 353 U.S. 252, 253 (1957).
24. Konigsberg v. State Bar, 366 U.S. 36, 44 (1961).
25. In re Anastaplo, 366 U.S. 82 (1961).
26. Baird v. State Bar of Arizona, 401 U.S. 1 (1971).
27. 401 U.S. at 35–36.
28. Shelton v. Tucker, 364 U.S. 479, 481 (1960).
29. NAACP v. Button, 371 U.S. 415, 420 (1963).
30. 377 U.S. 1 (1964).
31. United Mine Workers v. Illinois Bar, 389 U.S. 217, 218 (1967).
32. United Transportation Union v. Michigan Bar, 401 U.S. 576, 577 (1971).
33. Wood v. Georgia, 370 U.S. 375, 376 (1962).
34. 376 U.S. 254, 279–80 (1964).
35. 388 U.S. 130 (1967).
36. Rosenbloom v. Metromedia, 403 U. 29, 32–33 (1971).
37. Justices Byron White and Hugo Black also voted to affirm the dismissal of Rosenbloom's suit.
38. Chaplinsky v. New Hampshire, 315 U.S. 568, 571–72 (1942).
39. 354 U.S. 476 (1957).
40. Interstate Circuit v. Dallas, 390 U.S. 676 (1968).
41. Shapiro v. Thompson, 394 U.S. 618, 623 (1969).
42. 367 U.S. 497, 522—55 (1961).
43. 381 U.S. 479 (1965).
44. 347 U.S. 483 (1954).
45. Brown v. Board of Education, 349 U.S. 294 (1955).
46. See Appendix, *Equal Protection of the Law—Integration of Public Facilities.*
47. 373 U.S. 244 (1963).
48. Lombard v. Louisiana, 373 U.S. 267 (1963); Gober v. City of Birmingham, 373 U.S. 374 (1963); and Avent v. North Carolina, 373 U.S. 375 (1963).
49. 373 U.S. 267 (1963).
50. Evans v. Newton, 382 U.S. 296, 297 (1966).
51. Evans v. Abney, 396 U.S. 435, 436 (1970).
52. Reitman v. Mulkey, 387 U.S. 369, 372, note 1 (1967).
53. Hunter v. Erickson, 393 U.S. 385, 387 (1969).
54. Levy v. Louisiana, 391 U.S. 68, 70 (1968).
55. Glona v. American Guarantee, 391 U.S. 73 (1968).
56. 391 U.S. at 72.
57. 391 U.S. at 75–76.
58. Williams v. Rhodes, 393 U.S. 23 (1968).
59. Carrington v. Rash, 378 S. W. 2d 304, 305 (1964).
60. Carrington v. Rash, 380 U.S. 89 (1965).
61. 383 U.S. 663 (1966).
62. 351 U.S. 12 (1956).
63. Douglas v. California, 372 U.S. 353 (1963).
64. 372 U.S. 335 (1963).
65. Duncan v. Louisisa, 391 U.S. 145, 174 (1968).
66. Poe v. Ullman, 367 U.S. 497, 543 (1961).
67. Sherbert v. Verner, 374 U.S. 398, 423 (1963).
68. McGowan v. Maryland, 366 U.S. 420, 531 (1961).
69. James E. Leahy, *"Flamboyant Protest," The First Amendment and the Boston Tea Party,* 36 *Brooklyn Law Review* 185 (1970).
70. Fleming v. Nestor, 363 U.S. 603, 640 (1960).
71. Rosembloom v. Metromedia, 403 U.S. 29, 67 (1971).
72. Roth v. United States, 354 U.S. 476, 501 (1957).
73. Peterson v. Greenville, 373 U.S. 244, 250 (1963).
74. Lombard v. Louisiana, 373 U.S. 267 (1963); Gober v. City of Birmingham, 373 U.S. 374 (1963); Avent v. North Carolina, 373 U.S. 375 (1963).
75. Glona v. American Guarantee Co., 391 U.S. 73, 80 (1968).
76. McDonald v. Board of Elections, 394 U.S. 802 (1969); Kramer v. Union School Dist., 395 U.S. 621 (1969).
77. See Appendix, *Equal Protection of the Law—In Classification of Voters* (for other voting rights cases).

78. See Appendix, *Equal Protection of the Law—In the Criminal Justice System.*

79. Gardner v. California, 393 U.S. 367, 372 (1969).

80. 391 U.S. at 176.

81. Konigsberg v. State Bar, 366 U.S. 36, 49–56 (1961); Tinker v. Des Moines School District, 393 U.S. 503, 526 (1969); Cohen v. California, 403 U.S. 15, 26 (1971).

82. 383 U.S. at 686.

5. Justice Byron R. White

1. Leon Friedman and Fred L. Israel, *The Justices of the United States Supreme Court 1789–1969: Their Lives and Major Opinions* (New York: Chelsea House, 1969); vol. IV, article by Fred L. Israel, p. 2952.

2. Albert Wright, "A Modest All-American Who Sits on the Highest Bench," *Sports Illustrated*, December 10, 1962, p. 86.

3. Friedman and Israel, note ,1 p. 2953.

4. Wright, note 2, p. 91.

5. Friedman and Israel, note 1, p. 2953.

6. Wright, note 2, p. 96.

7. Friedman and Israel, note 1, p. 2954.

8. Wright, note 2, p.96.

9. Friedman and Israel, note 1, p. 2954.

10. *The Supreme Court Justices, Illustrated Biographies 1789–1993* (Washington, D.C.: The Supreme Court Historical Society, *Congressional Quarterly*, 1993), article by Dennis H. Hutchinson, p. 463.

11. Sherbert v. Verner, 374 U.S. 398, 418 (1963).

12. Thomas v. Review Board, 450 U.S. 707 (1981).

13. Hobbie v. Unempl. Appeals Comm'n., 480 U.S. 136 (1987).

14. Frazee v. Ill. Dept., 489 U.S. 829, 830 (1989).

15. Wisconsin v. Yoder, 406 U.S. 205, 238 (1972).

16. Goldman v. Weinberger, 475 U.S. 503 (1986).

17. Schaumberg v. Citizens for Better Environment, 444 U.S. 620, 633 (1980).

18. 452 U.S. 640 (1981).

19. Cox v. Louisiana, 379 U.S. 536, 538 (1965).

20. Cox v. Louisiana, 379 U.S. 559 (1965).

21. United States v. Grace, 461 U.S. 173, note 1 (1983).

22. Frisby v. Schultz, 487 U.S. 474, 477 (1988).

23. Street v. New York, 394 U.S. 576, 579 (1969).

24. Smith v. Goguen, 415 U.S. 566, 568 (1974).

25. Watts v. United States, 394 U.S. 705, 706 (1969).

26. Nat. Assn. of Letter Carriers v. United States Civil Service Com., 346 Fed. Supp. 578, 579–80 (1972).

27. CSC. v. Letter Carriers, 413 U.S. 548, 556 (1973).

28. Broadrick v. Oklahoma, 413 U.S. 601, 615–16 (1973).

29. Myers v. Connick, 507 Fed. Supp. 752, 753 (1981).

30. Connick v. Myers, 461 U.S. 138, 142 (1983).

31. Rankin v. McPherson, 483 U.S. 378, 381 (1987).

32. 316 U.S. 52 (1942).

33. Railway Express Agy. v. New York, 336 U.S. 106 (1949).

34. Pittsburgh Press Co. v. Human Relations Comm'n., 413 U.S. 376 (1973).

35. 421 U.S. 809 (1976).

36. Va. Pharmacy Bd. v. Va. Consumer Council, 425 U.S. 748, 762 (1976).

37. Metromedia, Inc. v. San Diego, 453 U.S. 490, 503 (1981).

38. 433 U.S. 350 (1977).

39. Peel v. Attorney Disc. Com., 496 U.S. 91, 96 (1990).

40. Amalgamated Food Employees Union v. Logan Valley Plaza, 391 U.S. 308, 309 (1968).

41. 326 U.S. 501 (1946).

42. 391 U.S. at 319.

43. 452 U.S. 61 (1981).

44. Community for Creative Non-Violence v. Watt, 703 F. 2d 586, 588, note 1 (1983).

45. Clark v. CCNV, 468 U.S. 288 (1984).

46. First Nat. Bank v. Bellotti, 435 U.S. 765, 769 (1978).

47. Barnes v. Glen Theatre, Inc., 501 U.S. 560 (1991).

48. 367 U.S. 203 (1960).

49. United States v. Robel, 389 U.S. 258 (1967).

50. Baggett v. Bullitt, 377 U.S. 360 (1964).

51. 384 U.S. 11 (1966).

52. 361 U.S. 516 (1960).

53. Gibson v. Fla. Legislative Comm., 372 U.S. 539 (1963).

54. Baird v. State Bar of Arizona, 401 U.S. 1, 4 (1971).

55. Williams v. Rhodes, 393 U.S. 23, 30 (1968).

56. Storer v. Brown, 415 U.S. 724 (1974).

57. Munro v. Social Wrkrs. Prty, 479 U.S. 189, 190 (1986).

58. Coates v. City of Cincinnati, 402 U.S. 611 (1971).

59. United Auto Wrkrs. v. Lyng, 648 F. Supp. 1234 (1986).

60. Lyng v. Auto. Workers, 485 U.S. 360, 365–66 (1988).

61. 468 U.S. 609 (1984); Bd. of Dir., Rotary Intl. v. Rotary Club, 481 U.S. 537 (1987); N.Y. State Club Assn. v. City of New York, 487 U.S. 1 (1988).

62. 376 U.S. 254 (1964).

63. Curtis Pub. Co. v. Butts, 388 U.S. 130, 164 (1967).

64. Gertz v. Robert Welch, Inc., 418 U.S. 322, 325 (1974).

65. Dun & Bradstreet, Inc. v. Greenmoss Builders, 472 U.S. 749 (1985).

66. New York Times Co. v. U.S., 403 U.S. 713 (1971).

67. Cox Broadcasting v. Cohn, 420 U.S. 469, 471–72 (1975).

68. 491 U.S. 524 (1989).

69. Zacchini v. Scripps-Howard Broadcasting Co., 433 U.S. 562, 563 (1977).

70. 383 U.S. 413, 418 (1966).

71. 413 U.S. 15 (1973).

72. Ward v. Illinois, 431 U.S. 767, 770 (1977).

73. Branzburg v. Hayes, 408 U.S. 665, 667 (1972).

74. 381 U.S. 479, 502 (1965).

75. 410 U.S. 113, 221–22 (1973).

76. Planned Parenthood v. Danforth, 428 U.S. 52 (1976).

77. H. L. v. Matheson, 450 U.S. 398 (1981).

78. Planned Parenthood v. Ashcroft, 462 U.S. 476 (1983).

79. Thornburgh v. Am. College of Obst. & Gyn., 476 U.S. 747, 788 (1986).

80. Michael H. v. Gerald D., 491 U.S. 110, 157 (1989).

81. Moore v. East Cleveland, 431 U.S. 494, 499 (1977).

82. Bowers v. Hardwick, 478 U.S. 186 (1986).

83. Swain v. Alabama, 380 U.S. 202, 204 (1965).

84. Batson v. Kentucky, 476 U.S. 79, 89 (1986).

85. Alexander v. Louisiana, 405 U.S. 625 (1972).

86. 443. U.S. 545 (1979).

87. 383 U.S. 683 (1963).

88. Palmer v. Thompson, 403 U.S. 217, 226 (1971).

89. Peterson v. Greenville, 373 U.S. 244, 246 (1963).

90. 373 U.S. 267 (1963).

91. 378 U.S. 130 (1964).

92. 387 U.S. 369 (1967).

93. 393 U.S. 385 (1969).

94. Mulkey v. Reitman, 413 P. 2d 825, 834 (1966).

95. Reitman v. Mulkey, 387 U.S. 369 (1967).

96. McLaughlin v. Florida, 379 U.S. 184 (1964).

97. Kahn v. Shevin, 416 U.S. 351, 361 (1974).

98. 441 U.S. 347 (1979).

99. See Appendix, *Equal Protection of the Law—For Aliens.*

100. Foley v. Connelie, 435 U.S. 291 (1978).

101. Ambach v. Norwick, 441 U.S. 68 (1979).

102. 435 U.S. at 296.

103. Cabell v. Chavez-Salido, 454 U.S. 432, 445 (1982).

104. Carrington v. Rash, 380 U.S. 89, 96 (1965).

105. Dunn v. Blumstein, 405 U.S. 330 (1972).

106. Phoenix v. Kolodziejski, 399 U.S. 204, 212 (1970).

107. Williams v. Rhodes, 393 U.S. 23, 34 (1968).

108. 372 U.S. 487 (1963).

109. See Appendix, *Equal Protection of the Law—For the Poor.*

110 San Antonio Sch. Dis. v. Rodriguez, 411 U.S. 1, 54–55 (1973).

111. Duncan v. Louisiana, 391 U.S. 145, 149 (1968).

112. Sherbert v. Verner, 374 U.S. 398, 407 (1963).

113. O'Lone v. Estate of Shabaz, 482 U.S. 342, 353 (1987).

114. Employ. Div., Oregon Dept. of Human Resources v. Smith, 494 U.S. 872, 874 (1990).

115. Brown v. Glines, 444 U.S. 348 (1980).

116. Spence v. Washington, 418 U.S. 405 (1974).

117. Central Hudson G. & E. v. Public Serv. Comm'n., 447 U.S. 557, 562–63 (1980).

118. See Appendix, *Freedom of Association—For Advancement of Legal Goals.*

119. Anderson v. Celebrezze, 460 U.S. 780 (1983).

120. Burdick v. Takushi, 504 U.S. 428 (1992).

121. Lyng v. Automobile Workers, 485 U.S. 360, 368 (1988).

122. 472 U.S. at 771.

123. Hazelwood School v. Kuhlmeier, 484 U.S. 260, 264, note 1 (1988).

124. Pittsburgh Press Co. v. Human Relations Comm'n., 413 U.S. 376, 378 (1973).
125. 431 U.S. at 503.
126. Cruzan v. Director, 497 U.S. 261 (1990).
127. Heart of Atlanta Motel v. U.S., 379 U.S. 241 (1964).
128. Katzenbach v. McClung, 379 U.S. 294 (1964).
129. Hamm v. Rock Hill, 379 U.S. 306 (1964).
130. Frontiero v. Richardson, 411 U.S. 677 (1973).
131. Plyler v. Doe, 457 U.S. 202 (1982).
132. Zablocki v. Redhail, 434 U.S. 374 (1978).
133. Washington v. Texas, 388 U.S. 14 (1967); Duncan v. Louisiana, 391 U.S. 145 (1968); Benton v. Maryland, 395 U.S. 784 (1969).

6. Chief Justice Warren E. Burger

1. *Minneapolis Star and Tribune*, June 18, 1986.
2. *Time*, May 30, 1969, p. 17.
3. Note 1.
4. Memorial to Chief Justice Warren E. Burger, October 16, 1995, Landmark Center, St. Paul, Minnesota.
5. *Overcoming Occupational Heredity at the Supreme Court*, by Everette E. Dennis, 56 ABAJ 41, 43 (Jan. 1980).
6. *The Supreme Court Justices, Illustrated Biographies 1789–1993* (Washington, D.C.: The Supreme Court Historical Society, *Congressional Quarterly*, 1993); article by Burnett Anderson, p. 482.
7. Note 2, p. 17.
8. Note 1.
9. Note 6, p. 482.
10. Note 2, p. 17.
11. *Ibid.*, p. 17.
12. Note 6, p. 483.
13. Leon Friedman and Fred L. Israel, *The Justices of the United States Supreme Court 1789–1969: Their Lives and Major Opinions*, (New York: Chelsea House, 1969), vol. IV; article by John P. Mackenzie, p. 3111.
14. Note 2, p. 16.
15. State v. Yoder, 182 N.W. 2d 539, 541 (1971).
16. Wisconsin v. Yoder, 406 U.S. 205 (1972).
17. Wolley v. Maynard, 430 U.S. 705 (1977).
18. Brown v. Roy, 476 U.S. 693, 695 (1986).

19. 450 U.S. 707 (1981).
20. 374 U.S. 398 (1963).
21. OBA v. Keefe, 402 U.S. 415, 416 (1971).
22. Glines v. Wade, 586 F. 2d 675, 677, note 1 (1978).
23. Brown v. Glines, 444 U.S. 348, 356 (1980).
24. Cohen v. California, 403 U.S. 15, 27 (1971).
25. Bethel Sch. Dist., v. Fraser, 478 U.S. 675 (1986).
26. Smith v. Goguen, 415 U.S. 566 (1974).
27. Spence v. Washington, 418 U.S. 405 (1974).
28. 421 U.S. 809 (1975).
29. Va. Pharmacy v. Va. Cit. Consumer Council, 425 U.S. 748, 774 (1976).
30. Bates v. State Bar of Arizona, 433 U.S. 350, 386–87 (1977).
31. Zauderer v. Of. of Disc. Counsel, 471 U.S. 626 (1985).
32. Schad v. Mount Ephraim, 452 U.S. 61, 87 (1981).
33. Clark v. CCNV, 468 U.S. 288, 301 (1984).
34. Elrod v. Burns, 427 U.S. 347 (1976).
35. Branti v. Finkel, 445 U.S. 507 (1980).
36. 424 U.S. 1 (1976).
37. 454 U.S. 290 (1981).
38. Greenbelt Pub. Assn. v. Bresler, 398 U.S. 6, 12 (1970).
39. Gertz v. Robert Welch, Inc., 418 U.S. 323, 355 (1974).
40. 472 U.S. 749 (1985).
41. Phila. Newspapers, Inc. v. Hepps, 475 U.S. 767 (1986).
42. New York Times Co. v. United States, 403 U.S. 713, 748 (1971).
43 Nebraska Press Assn. v. Stuart, 427 U.S. 539 (1976).
44. 443 U.S. 97 (1979).
45. Press-Enterprise Co. v. Superior Court of Cal., 478 U.S. 1, 8 (1986).
46. Globe News. Co. v. Superior Court, 457 U.S. 596 (1982).
47. Miller v. California, 413 U.S. 15, 22 (1973).
48. Paris Adult Theatre I v. Slaton, 413 U.S. 49 (1973); Kaplan v. Calif., 413 U.S. 115 (1973); U.S. v. 12-200 Ft. Reels of Super 8mm Film, 413 U.S. 123 (1973); U.S. v. Orito, 413 U.S. 139 (1973); and Heller v. New York, 413 U.S. 483 (1973).
49. Erznznik v. Jacksonville, 422 U.S. 205, 207 (1975).
50. H. L. v. Matheson, 450 U.S. 398, 399–400 (1981).

51. Thornburgh v. American College of Obst. & Gyn., 476 U.S. 747, 772 (1986).
52. Eisenstadt v. Baird, 405 U.S. 438 (1972).
53. Bowers v. Hardwick, 478 U.S. 186, 196 (1986).
54. Stanley v. Illinois, 405 U.S. 645, 646 (1972).
55. Batson v. Kentucky, 476 U.S. 79, 112 (1986).
56. 380 U.S. 202 (1985).
57. 476 U.S. at 129.
58. Swann v. Board of Education, 402 U.S. 1, 15 (1971).
59. Davis v. School Comm'rs. of Mobile County, 402 U.S. 33 (1971); McDaniel v. Barresi, 402 U.S. 39 (1971); Bd. of Education v. Swann, 402 U.S. 43 (1971).
60. 402 U.S. at 45–46.
61. Norwood v. Harrison, 413 U.S. 455, 467 (1973).
62. Palmer v. Thompson, 403 U.S. 217, 228 (1971).
63. 466 U.S. 429 (1984).
64. Reed v. Reed, 404 U.S. 71, 76 (1971).
65. Craig v. Boren, 429 U.S. 190, 201 (1976).
66. MUW v. Hogan, 458 U.S. 718, 744 (1982).
67. Labine v. Vincent, 401 U.S. 532 (1971).
68. 430 U.S. 762 (1977).
69. Lalli v. Lalli, 439 U.S. 259, 262 (1978).
70. Jimenez v. Weinberger, 417 U.S. 626, 630 (1974).
71. In re Griffiths, 413 U.S. 717, 719 (1973).
72. Nyquist v. Mauclet, 432 U.S. 1 (1977).
73. Foley v. Connelie, 435 U.S. 291, 297 (1978).
74. Hill v. Stone, 421 U.S. 289, 292 (1975).
75. O'Brien v. Skinner, 414 U.S. 524 (1974).
76. U.S. Dept. of Ag. v. Moreno, 413 U.S. 528, 532 (1973).
77. Lyng v. Castello, 477 U.S. 635, 636 (1986).
78. Williams v. Illinois, 399 U.S. 235, 236 (1970).
79. Mayer v. City of Chicago, 404 U.S. 189, 201 (1971).
80. Massachusetts Bd. of Retirement v. Murgia, 427 U.S. 307, 316–17 (1976).
81. 406 U.S. at 219.
82. See Appendix, *The Free Exercise of Religion.*
83. Welsh v. United States, 398 U.S. 333 (1970).
84. Johnson v. Robison, 415 U.S. 361, 385 (1974).
85. See Appendix, *Freedom of Speech—Pamphleteering and Soliciting.*

86. Gooding v. Wilson, 405 U.S. 518 (1972).
87. 418 U.S. at 416.
88. See Appendix, *Freedom of Speech—Public Employees.*
89. See Appendix, *Freedom of Speech—Places to Speak.*
90. Elrod v. Burns, 427 U.S. 347 (1976); Branti v. Finkel, 445 U.S. 507 (1980).
91. See Appendix, *Freedom of Association—Associational Privacy*
92. Cole v. Richardson, 405 U.S. 676 (1972).
93. First Nat. Bank of Boston v. Bellotti, 435 U.S. 765, 802 (1978).
94. Pell v. Procunier, 417 U.S. 817, 934 (1974).
95. See Appendix, *Freedom of the Press—Obscenity.*
96. Eisenstadt v. Baird, 405 U.S. 438, 467 (1972).
97. Moore v. East Cleveland, 431 U.S. 494 (1977); Cleveland Bd. of Ed. v. LaFleur, 414 U.S. 632 (1974); Santosky v. Kramer, 455 U.S. 745 (1982).
98. 404 U.S. at 77.
99. Schlesenger v. Ballard, 419 U.S. 498 (1975); Califano v. Goldfarb, 430 U.S. 199 (1977); Parham v. Hughes, 441 U.S. 347 (1979).
100. Fiallo v. Bell, 430 U.S. 878 (1977).
101. In re Griffiths, 413 U.S. 717 (1973); Foley v. Connelie, 435 U.S. 291 (1978); Ambach v. Norwick, 441 U.S. 68 (1979); Cabell v. Chavez-Salido, 454 U.S. 432 (1982); Bernal v. Fainter, 467 U.S. 216 (1984).
102. Evans v. Cornman, 398 U.S. 419 (1970).
103. See Appendix, *Equal Protection of the Law—For Voters.*
104. See Appendix, *Equal Protection of the Law—For the Poor.*
105. Little v. Streeter, 452 U.S. 1, 16–17 (1981).

7. Chief Justice William H. Rehnquist

1. John A. Jenkins, "The Partisan: A Talk with Justice Rehnquist," *New York Times Magazine*, March 3, 1985, p. 31.
2. *The Supreme Court Justice, Illustrated Biographies 1789–1993* (Washington, D. C.: The Supreme Court Historical Society, *Congressional Quarterly*, 1993); article by Craig M. Bradley, p. 496.

3. *Ibid.*, note 1, p. 32.

4. Leon Friedman, *The Justices of the United States Supreme Court, Their Lives and Major Opinions* (New York & London: Chelsea House, 1978); vol. V, article by David L. Shapiro, p. 109.

5. "William H. Rehnquist," *Current Biography*, 1972, p. 360.

6. *Ibid.*, p. 360.

7. The *New York Times*, October 24, Section 4.

8. The *New York Times*, October 28, 1971, p. 26.

9. For an account of Rehnquist's nomination hearings, see Donald E. Boles, *Mr. Justice Rehnquist, Judicial Activist: The Early Years* (Ames: Iowa State University Press, 1987).

10. *Ibid.*, 46.

11. The *New York Times*, October 22, 1971, p. 25.

12. Cruz v. Beto, 445 F. 2d 801, 802 (1971).

13. Cruz v. Beto, 405 U.S. 319 (1972).

14. Woolley v. Maynard, 430 U.S. 705, 720 (1977).

15. Goldman v. Sec. of Defense, 530 F. Supp. 12, 16 (1981).

16. Goldman v. Weinberger, 475 U.S. 503, 507 (1986).

17. Village of Schaumburg v. Citizens for a Better Environment, 444 U.S. 620, 622 (1980).

18. Forsyth County v. Nationalist Movement, 505 U.S. 123, 127 (1992).

19. 312 U.S. 569 (1941).

20. 505 U.S. at 136.

21. 512 U.S. 753 (1994).

22. See Appendix, *Freedom of Speech—Unpopular Speech.*

23. Smith v. Goguen, 415 U.S. 566 (1974).

24. Spence v. Washington, 418 U.S. 405, 407 (1974).

25. Texas v. Johnson, 491 U.S. 397 (1989).

26. Parker v. Levy, 417 U.S. 733, 736–37 (1974).

27. Mt. Healthy City. Bd. v. Doyle, 429 U.S. 274, 284 (1977).

28. Ayers v. Western Line Con. Sch. Dist., 555 F. 2d 1309, 1312 (1977).

29. Givhan v. Western Line Con. Sch. Dist., 439 U.S. 410, 415–16 (1979).

30. U.S. v. Nat. Treas. Emp. Union, 115 S. Ct. 1003 (1995).

31. Bates v. State Bar of Ariz., 433 U.S. 350, 404 (1977).

32. Va. Pharmacy Bd. v. Va. Consumer Council, 425 U.S. 748, 762 (1976).

33. Central Hudson Gas & Elec. v. Pub. Service Comm'n., 447 U.S. 557, 598 (1980).

34. Posadas De Puerto Rico Assoc. v. Tourism Co., 478 U.S. 328 (1986).

35. Flower v. United States, 407 U.S. 197, 198 (1972).

36. S. Promot. Ltd. v. Conrad, 420 U.S. 546, 548 (1975).

37. Council of Greenburgh v. U.S. Postal Service, 490 F. Supp. 157, 159 (1980).

38. U.S. Postal Service v. Greenburgh Civic Assn., 453 U.S. 114, 128 (1981).

39. Intl. Society for Krishna Consciousness, Inc. v. Lee, 505 U.S. 672, 679 (1992)

40. Board of Education v. Pico, 457 U.S. 853, 855–56 (1982).

41. FCC v. League of Women Voters of California, 468 U.S. 364, 366 (1984).

42. Anderson v. Celebrezze, 499 F. Supp. 121, 123 (1980).

43. Anderson v. Celebrezze, 460 U.S. 780 (9183).

44. Kusper v. Pontikes, 414 U.S. 51, 58 (1973).

45. North Carolina Prisoners' Labor Union, Inc. v. Jones, 409 F. Supp. 937, 940 (1976).

46. Jones v. N. C. Prisoners' Union, 433 U.S. 119 (1977).

47. Dawson v. Delaware, 503 U.S. 159, 161–62 (1992).

48. Gertz v. Robert Welch, Inc., 418 U.S. 323, 347 (1974).

49. Milkovich v. Lorain Journal Co., 497 U.S. 1, 3 (1990).

50. Smith v. Daily Mail Pub. Co., 443 U.S. 97, 98 (1979).

51. Richmond News., Inc. v. Virginia, 448 U.S. 555, 580 (1980).

52. Butterworth v. Smith, 494 U.S. 624, 626 (1990).

53. Hamling v. United States, 418 U.S. 87, 92 (1974).

54. 413 U.S. 15 (1973).

55. 418 U.S. at 105.

56. Jenkins v. Georgia, 418 U.S. 153, 161 (1974).

57. McKinney v. Alabama, 424 U.S. 669, 673–74 (1976).

58. Papish v. Univ. of Mo. Curators, 410 U.S. 667 (1973).

59. Cincinnati v. Disc. Net., Inc., 113 S. Ct. 1505 (1993).

60. Roe v. Wade, 410 U.S. 113 (1973).

61. Planned Parent. v. Casey, 505 U.S. 833, 966 (1992).

62. Santosky v. Kramer, 455 U.S. 745, 747 (1982).

63. 497 U.S. 261 (1990).

64. 424 U.S. 693 (1976).

65. 497 U.S. at 22.

66. 476 U.S. 79 (1986).
67. Irvis v. Scott, 318 F. Supp. 1246, 1247 (1970).
68. Moose Lodge v. Irvis, 407 U.S. 163, 172–73 (1972).
69. Craig v. Boren, 429 U.S. 190, 220 (1976).
70. Michael M. v. Superior Court, 450 U.S. 464, 469 (1981).
71. J.E.B. v. Ala., ex rel., T.B., 114 S. Ct. 1419 (1994).
72. Weber v. Aetna Cas. and Surety Co., 406 U.S. 164, 168 (1972).
73. 409 U.S. 535 (1973).
74. Mills v. Habluetzel, 456 U.S. 91 (1982).
75. Sugarman v. Dougall, 413 U.S. 634, 641 (1973).
76. In re Griffiths, 413 U.S. 717 (1973).
77. 413 U.S. at 649.
78. Bernal v. Fainter, 467 U.S. 216 (1984).
79. Ramirez v. Brown, 507 P. 2d 1345, 1346 (1973).
80. Richardson v. Ramirez, 418 U.S. 24, 55 (1974).
81. Holt Civic Club v. Tuscaloosa, 439 U.S. 60, 61–62 (1978).
82. Hunter v. Underwood, 471 U.S. 222, 223 (1985).
83. 444 U.S. at 644.
84. See Appendix, *Freedom of Speech—Picketing and Parading.*
85. See Appendix, *Freedom of Speech—Unpopular Speech.*
86. See Appendix, *Freedom of Speech—Public Employees' Right to Speak.*
87. 447 U.S. at 593–94. See Appendix, *Freedom of Speech—Commercial Speech.*
88. See Appendix, *Freedom of Speech—Places to Speak.*
89. Young v. American Mini Theaters, 427 U.S. 50 (1976), 90. 457 U.S. at 880.
91. 460 U.S. at 806.
92. Dawson v. Delaware, 503 U.S. 159 (1992).
93. Healy v. James, 408 U.S. 169, 203 (1972). Words in parentheses and italics added.
94. Bates v. Little Rock, 361 U.S. 516, 524 (1960).
95. 443 U.S. at 107.
96. See Appendix, *Freedom of the Press—Obscenity.*
97. Kelley v. Johnson, 425 U.S. 238, 248 (1976).
98. Griffith v. Kentucky, 479 U.S. 314, 329 (1987).
99. Powers v. Ohio, 499 U.S. 400 (1991).

100. Mississippi University for Women v. Hogan, 458 U.S. 718, 742 (1982).
101. See Appendix, *Equal Protection—Gender.*
102. Trimble v. Gordon, 430 U.S. 762, 786 (1977). See Appendix, *Equal Protection—Illegitimate Children.*
103. Sugarman v. Dougal, 413 U.S. 631, 651 (1977).
104. Holt Civic Club v. Tuscaloosa, 439 U.S. 60 (1978).
105. Jefferson v. Hackney, 406 U.S. 535 (1972).
106. U.S. Dept. of Ag. v. Moreno, 413 U.S. 528, 529 (1973).
107. Harris v. Rosario, 446 U.S. 651 (1980). See also Appendix, *Equal Protection—For the Poor.*
108. Weber v. Aetna Casualty and Surety Co., 406 U.S. 164, 185 (1972).

8. Justice Sandra Day O'Connor

1. *The Supreme Court Justices, Illustrated Biographies 1789–1993* (Washington, D.C.: The Supreme Court Historical Society, *Congressional Quarterly*, 1993); article by Peter William Huber, p. 506.
2. Judith Bentley, *Justice Sandra Day O'Connor* (New York: Julian Messner, 1983) pp. 13–14.
3. Harold and Geraldine Woods, *Equal Justice: A Biography of Sandra Day O'Connor,* (Minneapolis, Minn.: Dillon, 1985) p. 11.
4. Note 2, p. 17.
5. Note 2, p. 21.
6. Note 3, p. 17.
7. Note 3, pp. 17–18.
8. Note 2, p. 30.
9. Note 3, p. 25.
10. Note 1, p. 508.
11. Note 2, p. 67.
12. "The Brethren's First Sister," *Time,* July 20, 1981.
13. Note 2, p. 82.
14. *Ibid.,* note 15.
15. Goldman v. Weinberger, 475 U.S. 503, 528 (1986).
16. Bowen v. Roy, 476 U.S. 693 (1986).
17. Employment Div., Oregon Dept. of Human Res. v. Smith, 494 U.S. 872, 874 (1990).
18. Schultz v. Frisby, 619 F. Supp. 792, 793 (1985).

19. Frisby v. Schultz, 487 U.S. 474, 479 (1988).
20. U.S. v. Nat. Trea. Empl. Union, 115 U.S. 1003 (1995).
21. Rankin v. McPherson, 483 U.S. 378, 380–381 (1987).
22. Shapero v. Kent. Bar Assn., 486 U.S. 466, 469 (1988).
23. This is the case in which the Court held that lawyers' advertising was protected by the First Amendment.
24. Edenfield v. Fane, 113 S. Ct. 1792, 1804 (1993).
25. Fla. Bar v. Went For It, Inc., 115 S. Ct. 2371 (1995).
26. Airport Comm'rs. v. Jews for Jesus, Inc., 482 U.S. 569, 571 (1987).
27. 485 U.S. 312 (1988).
28. United States v. Kokinda, 497 U.S. 720 (1990).
29. Board of Education, v. Pico, 457 U.S. 853, 921 (1982).
30. Turner v. Safely, 482 U.S. 78, 81–82 (1987).
31. Phila. News., Inc. v. Hepps, 475 U.S. 767, 769 (1986).
32. Simon & Schuster, Inc. v. Members of N.Y. State Crime Victims Bd., 502 U.S. 105, 109 (1991).
33. Zobel v. Williams, 457 U.S. 55, 56 (1982).
34. 457 U.S. at 74.
35. Atty. General v. Soto-Lopez, 476 U.S. 898, 911 (1986).
36. Akron v. Akron Ctr. for Rep. Health, 462 U.S. 416, 453–54 (1983).
37. Planned Parenthood of S.E. Pennsylvania v. Casey, 505 U.S. 833, 846 (1992).
38. Turner v. Safley, 482 U.S. 78, 82 (1987).
39. Batson v. Kentucky, 476 U.S. 79, 111 (1986).
40. 500 U.S. 614 (1991).
41. Georgia v. McCollum, 505 U.S. 42, 44 (1992).
42. 347 U.S. 483 (1954).
43. United States v. Fordice, 505 U.S. 717 (1992).
44. MUW v. Hogan, 458 U.S. 718, 720 (1982).
45. J.E.B. v. Alabama, Ex. Rel. T.B., 114 S. Ct. 1419, 1420 (1994).
46. Clark v. Jeter, 486 U.S. 461 (1988).
47. 494 U.S. at 895.
48. See Appendix, *The Free Exercise of Religion*.
49. See Appendix, *Freedom of Speech—Picketing and Parading*.
50. See Appendix, *Freedom of Speech—Unpopular Speech*.
51. See Appendix, *Freedom of Speech—Public Employees' Right to Speak*.
52. See Appendix, *Freedom of Speech—Commercial Speech*.
53. Zauderer v. Office of Disciplinary Counsel, 471 U.S. 626, 647 (1985).
54. See Appendix, *Freedom of Speech—Places to Speak*.
55. United States v. Kokinda, 497 U.S. 720, 730 (1990).
56. See Appendix, *Freedom of the Press—Libel; Prior Restraint and Punishment for Publication;* and *Obscenity*.
57. Turner Broadcasting Systems, Inc. v. F.C.C., 114 S. Ct. 2445, 2475 (1994).
58. Pope v. Illinois, 481 U.S. 497 (1987).
59. See Planned Parenthood of S. E. Pennsylvania v. Casey, 505 U.S. 833, 845–46 (1992).
60. Lehr v. Robertson, 463 U.S. 248 (1983).
61. Bowers v. Hardwick, 478 U.S. 186, 190 (1986).
62. Cruzan v. Div., Missouri Dept. of Health, 497 U.S. 261, 287 (1990).
63. See Appendix, *Equal Protection of the Law—Blacks on Juries*.
64. See Appendix, *Equal Protection—Gender*.
65. See Appendix, *Equal Protection of the Law—For Aliens*.
66. See Appendix, *Equal Protection of the Law—In the Criminal Justice System*.

9. Justice Antonin Scalia

1. *New York Times*, June 18, 1986, p. A31.
2. *The Supreme Court Justices: Illustrated Biographies 1789–1993* (Washington, D.C.: The Supreme Court Historical Society, *Congressional Quarterly*, 1993), p. 511. Article by Sally Katzen.
3. Note 1 p. A31.
4. "Antonin Scalia," *Current Biography Yearbook* (New York: H. W. Wilson, 1986), p. 503.
5. Note 2, p. 512.
6. *Ibid.*, p. 512.
7. Note 4, p. 505.
8. *Ibid.*, p. 505.
9. Black v. Employ. Division, 707 P. 2d 1274, 1276 (1985).
10. Black v. Employment Division, 721 P. 2d 451 (1986).
11. Smith v. Employment Division, 721 P. 2d 445 (1986).

12. Employment Division v. Smith, 485 U.S. 660, 673 (1988).

13. Smith v. Employment Division, 763 P. 2d 146, 148 (1988).

14. Employment Division v. Smith, 494 U.S. 872 (1990).

15. Madsen v. Women's Health Center, Inc., 114 S. Ct. 2516 (1994).

16. McIntyre v. Ohio Elec. Comm., 115 S. Ct. 1511 (1995).

17. 505 U.S. 377 (1992).

18. Rankin v. McPherson, 483 U.S. 378, 381 (1987).

19. Central Hudson G. & E. Corp. v. Public Service Com'n., 447 U.S. 557, 566 (1980).

20. 841 F. 2d 1207 (2nd Cir. 1988).

21. Bd. of Trustees, SUNY v. Fox, 492 U.S. 469 (1989).

22. 496 U.S. 91, 119 (1990).

23. Burson v. Freeman, 504 U.S. 191, 193 (1992).

24. Bd. of County Com'rs., Wabaunsee County, Kansas v. Umbehr, 116 S. Ct. 2343, 2352 (1996).

25. O'Hare Truck Service, Inc. v. City of Northlake, 116 S. Ct. 2553 (1996).

26. Rutan v. Rep. Pty. of Ill., 497 U.S. 62, 66–67 (1990).

27. Tashjian v. Rep. Pty. of Conn., 479 U.S. 208, 214 (1986).

28. FW/PBS, Inc. v. Dallas, 493 U.S. 215, 220 (1990).

29. Arkansas Writer's Project, Inc. v. Ragland, 481 U.S. 221, 223 (1987).

30. Michael H. v. Gerald D., 491 U.S. 110, 113 (1989).

31. 410 U.S. 113 (1973).

32. Webster v. Reproductive Health Services, 492 U.S. 490, 537 (1989).

33. Ohio v. Akron Center for Reproductive Health, 497 U.S. 502, 521 (1990).

34. Planned Parenthood of S. E. Pa. v. Casey, 505 U.S. 833, 980 (1992).

35. 476 U.S. 79 (1986).

36. 499 U.S. 400 (1991).

37. Edmonson v. Leesville Conc. Co., 500 U.S. 614 (1991).

38. Georgia v. McCollum, 505 U.S. 42 (1992).

39. J.E.B. v. Ala., 114 S. Ct. 1419, 1422 (1994).

40. 116 S. Ct. 2264 (1996).

41. Note 40, p. 2287.

42. Romer v. Evans, 116 S. Ct. 1620, 1623 (1996).

43. 468 U.S. 186 (1986).

44. Note 42, p. 1631.

45. 494 U.S. at 882.

46. 115 S. Ct. at 1533.

47. 483 U.S. at 394.

48. 492 U.S. at 480.

49. 497 U.S. at 96.

50. Ill. St. Empl. Union, v. Lewis, 473 F. 2d 561 (1972).

51. 497 U.S. at 95, note 2.

52. 163 U.S. 537, 555–56 (1896).

53. Sweatt v. Painter, 339 U.S. 629 (1950) and McLaurin v. Oklahoma State Regents, 339 U.S. 637 (1950).

54. 504 U.S. at 221.

55. See Justice O'Connor at 116 S. Ct. 2342, 2350. See also 116 S. Ct. at 2357 for other cases relating to "traditions."

56. 413 U.S. 15 (1973).

57. Pope v. Illinois, 481 U.S. 497, 505 (1987).

58. See Appendix, *Pursuit of Liberty—The Right of Privacy.*

59. Turner v. Safley, 482 U.S. 78 (1987).

60. United States v. Virginia 116 S. Ct. 2264 (1996), J. E. B. v. Alabama, ex rel T. B., 114 S. Ct. 1419 (1994) and Romer v. Evans, 116 S. Ct. 1620 (1996).

Epilogue

1. Howard Simons and Joseph A. Califano, Jr., eds., *The Media and the Law,* pp. 36–37.

2. Edmond Cahn, *The Great Rights* (New York: Macmillan, 1963), p. 49.

INDEX